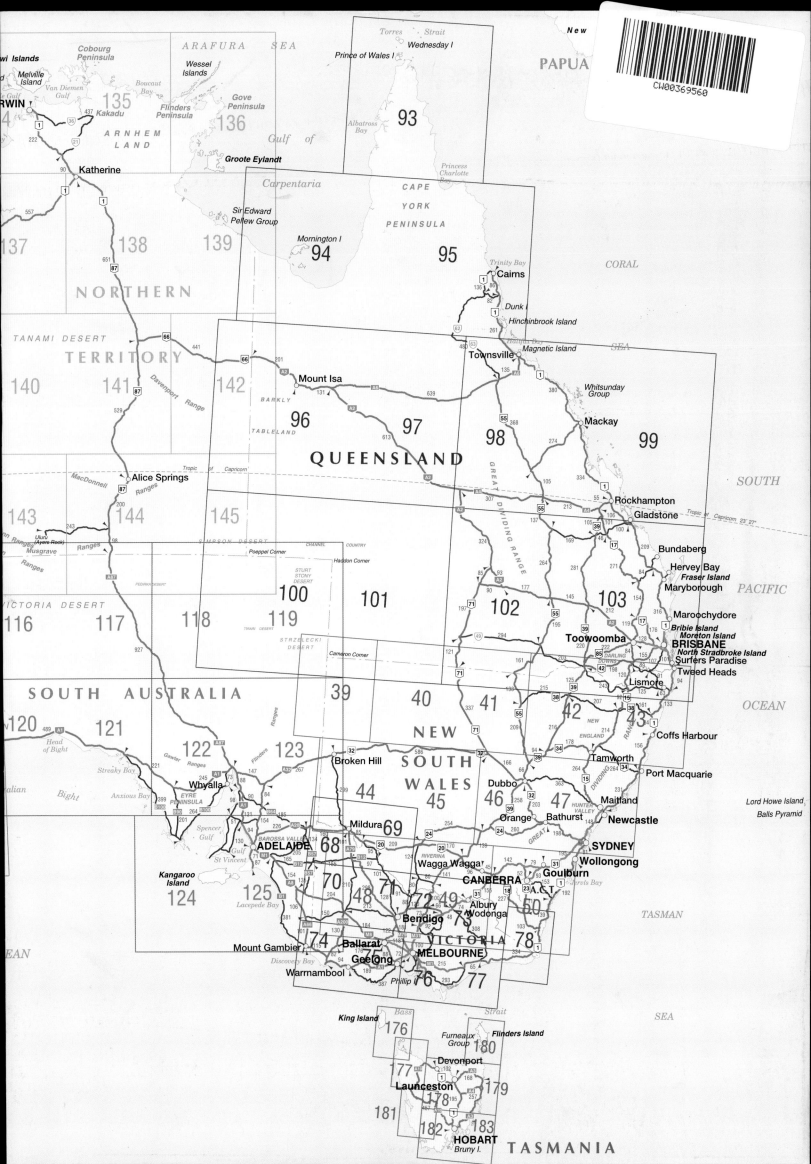

PRODUCED AND PUBLISHED
IN AUSTRALIA BY

A DIVISION OF UNIVERSAL PUBLISHERS PTY LTD
ABN 83 000 087 132

www.ubd.com.au

1 Waterloo Rd, Macquarie Park 2113
Postal Address: PO Box 1530, Macquarie Centre, NSW 2113
Ph: (02) 9857 3700 Fax: (02) 9888 9850

VICTORIA:
585 Burwood Rd, Hawthorn 3122 Ph: (03) 9818 4455 Fax: (03) 9818 6123

QUEENSLAND:
1 Manning St, South Brisbane 4101 Ph: (07) 3844 1051 Fax: (07) 3844 4637

SOUTH AUSTRALIA:
Ph: 1800 021 987

WESTERN AUSTRALIA
38A Walters Drive, Osborne Park 6017 Ph: (08) 9244 2488   Fax: (08) 9244 2554

Copyright © Universal Publishers Pty Ltd 2005

Publisher's Note
UBD welcomes contributions from users of this directory. Please contact the Cartographic Researcher in your State with any suggestions for improvements or information for corrections to future editions.

Universal Publishers is Australia's largest publisher and distributor of Street Directories, Maps, Travel and Guide Books, World Globes and Custom Mapping.

Digital Maps
UBD digital road maps are available for GIS, transportation, in-vehicle navigation and interactive mapping applications – phone Whereis Navigation on 1800 064 527.

CD ROM
UBD on CD ROM is now available for all capital cities and regional areas. It can be networked and customised to suit your needs, call (02) 9857 3700

Printed by Sing Cheong Printing Co Ltd

ISBN 0 7319 1421 X

5th Edition 2005

Photo Acknowledgements
Australian Capital Tourism: pp. 9 (B), 24 (T), 25, 26 (T, M, B)
Darran Leal Publishing & Photography Pty Ltd: p. 8
Geoff Higgins/Photography E-Biz: pp. 5 (T, M, B), 7 (T), 11, 13, 23, 24 (B), 109, 129 (T & B), 130 (T & B), 148, 149, 150 (T, M, B), 170, 171, 172 (T, M, B)
Northern Territory Tourist Commission: pp. 9 (T), 130 (M)
South Australian Tourism Commission: pp. 108, 110 (T, M, B)
Tourism New South Wales: pp. 9 (M), 30, 31, 32 (T, M, B), 38
Tourism Queensland: pp. 4(T), 6, 84, 85, 86 (T, M, B), 92
Tourism Victoria: pp. 4 (B), 60, 61, 62 (T, M, B)
Universal Publishers Pty Ltd: p. 187
Viewfinder Library: p. 7 (M & B)
Front Cover:
    Pinnacles at Sunrise, Nambung National Park, WA, Jeff Drewitz Photography
    Stuart Highway south of Elliott in the Top End, NT, Australian Scenics
    Waves rolling in at Chain of Lagoons Beach, Tas, Australian Scenics
Back Cover:
    Mt Sturgeon, Grampians National Park, Vic, Jeff Drewitz Photography
    Blue Lake, Kosciuszko National Park, NSW, Jeff Drewitz Photography
    Tree ferns, Tara Bulga National Park, Vic, Jeff Drewitz Photography
Back Cover Flap:
    Russell Falls in Mt Field National Park, Tas, Australian Scenics
    Thistle Cove at Cape Le Grand National Park, WA, Australian Scenics

Designer:
Designer Graphics International Pty Ltd

Disclaimer
The publisher disclaims any responsibility or duty of care towards any person for loss or damage suffered from any use of this directory for whatever purpose and in whatever manner. While considerable care has been taken by the publisher in researching and compiling the directory, the publisher accepts no responsibility for errors or omissions. No person should rely upon this directory for the purposes of making any business, investment or real estate decision.

COMPLETE MOTORING ATLAS
OF AUSTRALIA

FIFTH EDITION

STATE ROAD MAPS ■ CAPITAL CITY MAPS ■ NATIONAL PARK CHARTS ■ TOURING INFORMATION

CONTENTS

Top: Daydream Island, Whitsundays, Queensland
Bottom: The Twelve Apostles, Great Ocean Road, Victoria

Top left: Lake St Clair in winter, Tasmania
Top right: Boab tree in the Kimberleys, Western Australia
Bottom: Uluru (Ayers Rock), Uluru-Kata Tjuta National Park, Northern Territory

TOURING AUSTRALIA

The Land Down Under

 AREA: 7 692 300km²

 World's smallest continent and largest island

 World's lowest and flattest continent; average elevation is only 330m; Lake Eyre is 15m below sea level

 Sixth largest country in the world after the Russian Federation, Canada, China, USA and Brazil

 Fifth longest coastline in the world with the world's largest Exclusive Economic Marine Zone when offshore territories are included

 The Great Dividing Range is the fourth longest mountain range in the world

 World records: Uluru (largest monolith), Great Barrier Reef (longest coral reef), Nullarbor Plain (largest flat bedrock surface), Simpson Desert (largest sand ridge desert), Mount Augustus (largest exposed rocky outcrop)

GEOGRAPHY

The island of Australia is the world's sixth largest country and the only country to occupy an entire continent. Hidden away at the bottom of the South Seas, as far as possible from the centre of the known world, its very existence was doubted for centuries and its shape and size were not finally confirmed until Matthew Flinders made his circumnavigation in 1803. Flinders was the first person to use the name 'Australia' in his 3-volume work *Voyage to Terra Australis*, detailing his discoveries and surveys. Before discovery by Asians and Europeans, Australia was home to the Aborigines, who are thought to have lived on the continent for over 60 000 years. Many Aboriginal rock and cave paintings that can be seen today are thousands of years old.

The basic facts about Australia's size and geography are difficult for many visitors to grasp and even surprising to some Australians. The landmass stretches 4025km from west to east and 3300km north to south. Its surface area of almost 7 700 000km² is larger than Europe (excluding the former USSR) and similar in size to the USA mainland. 3 oceans — the Indian, Pacific and Southern — and 4 seas surround the Australian coastline.

This huge area forms the earth's driest and flattest continent. In the east, a narrow, fertile plain edges the Great Dividing Range, the remnant of a once-high mountain range that stretches almost the length of the continent from North Queensland to Victoria. Small by international standards, Mount Kosciuszko, in the south of the range, is the country's highest peak at 2228m. West of the range, grassy plains supporting sheep and cattle gradually give way to the hot dry Outback,

stretching almost all the way to the coastline of Western Australia. The map of Australia is testimony to the harsh and inhospitable nature of much of the land, showing very few main roads penetrating the vast semi-arid centre. Today, more sealed roads are available, but trips to the Outback still involve driving along dirt roads. Some of the world's great deserts are located here, broken by spectacular rocky ranges and outcrops that stand high in the surrounding flatness, and by huge, mainly dry lakes that are occasionally filled by intermittent rivers that flow inland to sink into the desert sands.

Modern transport and communications have opened up the Outback to visitors eager to see the unique Australian landscape and internationally-renowned landmarks. These include Uluru (Ayers Rock) and Kata-Tjuta (the Olgas), and the spectacularly beautiful gorges hidden in ancient mountain ranges such as the MacDonnell and Kimberleys. The desert landscape holds many surprises, such as hot springs, the overnight appearance of wildflowers after rain and the immediate arrival of birds at lakes that are only briefly full.

Wonderfully diverse and scenic coastal scenery has been created by the surrounding oceans. Undoubtedly a favourite destination of local and overseas visitors is the coral wonderland of the Great Barrier Reef and the numerous tropical islands lying just off the Queensland coast. Golden beaches and rocky headlands line New South Wales and the south-east. Along Victoria's southern coastline, the Great Ocean Road brings into view the spectacular cliffs and rocky outcrops carved by the wild Southern Ocean. Peninsulas and inlets provide a stunning mix of scenery in

Agincourt Reef pontoon in the Great Barrier Reef, Coral Sea, Queensland

South Australia. In the far west, the sandstone cliffs of the Nullarbor Plain drop into the Great Australian Bight. Western Australia's long beaches are lapped by the Indian Ocean, and in the tropical north, the warm waters of the Timor and Arafua seas wash the shore.

CLIMATE

The seasons in Australia are opposite to those in the Northern Hemisphere. It's hot in December and January. July and August are the midwinter months, but they are not necessarily cold. About 40% of the country lies north of the Tropic of Capricorn and experiences degrees of monsoonal conditions. Here there are just 2 seasons known as the wet and the dry. The wet (between November and April) is characterised by a lot of rain and the air is hot and humid. The dry season (between May and October) is hot but not wet. In the deserts around Alice Springs, night-time temperatures during the dry season can be cool to cold, while the days are warm.

South of the Tropic of Capricorn, the climate becomes gradually more temperate. On the mainland, it very rarely snows, except in the alpine regions and occasionally in the eastern highlands. The island of Tasmania, to the south, is on average the coldest and wettest state and the best times to visit are during spring and summer. Generally the seasons in Australia are not as defined as they are in the Northern Hemisphere, except in the highland regions. Here, European foliage trees flourish and are treasured for their seasonal variations.

AUSTRALIAN LANDSCAPES

Although much of Australia appears to be flat and dry, there is an amazing diversity of landscapes. In order to preserve the unique beauty and fragile nature of the environment, large areas surrounding many of the most spectacular features are protected as national parks and reserves. Most of Australia's well-known natural attractions, such as Uluru, Kakadu, the Great Barrier Reef, Fraser Island, the Blue Mountains, the Snowy Mountains, Wilsons Promontory, the Grampians, Tasmania's South-West, Cradle Mountain-Lake St Clair, the Flinders Ranges, Coorong, Stirling Ranges and Purnululu are protected by national parks.

National parks in each state and territory have similar general rules - always stick to designated roads and tracks, camp in approved areas, do not remove or damage any of the natural environment, and leave pets and firearms at home. Bushwalking is a very popular activity in Australia and most national parks have clearly signed and maintained walking trails. Fees are applicable in some parks where public access is encouraged; however there are also wilderness parks that have few facilities and public access is not actively encouraged.

NATIVE FAUNA

Australia's geographical isolation is believed to be the main reason for the existence of so many species of fauna not found elsewhere. Nearly half of the mammal species found here are marsupials. The most commonly found marsupials are kangaroos, wallabies, koalas, wombats and possums. There are a host of others that are less well-known, such as dunnarts, bandicoots, gliders and the carnivorous Tasmanian devil. These animals are rarely seen outside a zoo or animal park. Zoos in major cities, and animal parks, are excellent places to see native animals and they often specialize in their local and endangered creatures. As many of Australia's native animals are shy night-time creatures, the nocturnal houses at zoos and animal parks provide the best opportunity to see them.

Kookaburras and the noisy, colourful parrots and cockatoos are among the most common of the native birds. Many have adapted well to urban life and can frequently be seen in local parks. Australia's largest birds are the flightless emus and cassowaries. Shaggy brown emus, smaller in size than an ostrich, are often seen when driving on country roads. Cassowaries are more colourful and live in northern Queensland rainforests.

DANGEROUS CREATURES

Visitors sometimes express concern about Australia's poisonous and dangerous creatures. However, the number of people hurt or killed by native animals or insects is quite small and the risk is minimal if precautions are taken.

Many Australian snakes are venomous and some are deadly, but they are usually shy and will slither away if they hear a human approach. Long trousers and stout shoes are recommended when walking in the bush. Remember not to step over a snake and never deliberately prod at one with a stick.

Some Australian spiders are also venomous. One of the world's most poisonous is the Sydney funnel web (found only in the Sydney region) and the distinctive red-back is another to avoid. Both of these spiders are commonly found in backyards, but deaths are now rare since effective antivenenes are available. Other spiders such as the St Andrews Cross and white-tailed spider can give nasty bites.

The waters off Queensland and the northern coastline harbour the box jellyfish or sea wasp, a particularly dangerous creature that keeps

Top: Snow-laden tree near Mt Kosciuszko
Middle: Koala and joey
Bottom: King parrot

swimmers out of the ocean in the summer months. Its fine stinging tentacles drift some way from the creature itself and wrap themselves around a victim, causing severe pain and paralysis. Paddling in a few centimetres of water is also dangerous. Bites from the small blue-ringed octopus found in rock pools along the eastern coast, stone fish and certain cone shells can be fatal. Reef walkers should always wear shoes for protection against coral cuts and venomous creatures.

Saltwater crocodile, Northern Australia

There are 2 types of crocodile found in the northern parts of Australia — saltwater and freshwater. Saltwater crocodiles are particularly aggressive. They can grow up to 6m long and are the largest living reptiles. They are found in both saltwater and freshwater rivers, creeks and gorges. While considered less aggressive, freshwater crocodiles, which can grow to 3m, will also attack. Extreme caution must be taken when near the water in these parts.

NATIVE PLANTS

The arrival of Europeans over 200 years ago, bringing seeds, plants and domestic animals, altered and damaged Australia's botanical balance forever. Even so, most native plants growing at that time can still be found. These include some 15 000 species of flowering plants and about 500 species of ferns, conifers and cycads, as well as thousands of species of mosses, algae, lichens and fungus. The most prevalent tree is the eucalyptus or gum tree. It was first mentioned by Sir Joseph Banks at Botany Bay in 1770, when he wrote of a tree having gum exudations. More than 500 species of eucalyptus can be found in Australia. Some, such as ash, box, mahogany, stringybark, ironbark, peppermint, lemon-scented and mallee are named for their timber type.

The rainforests that once covered much of New South Wales and Queensland were logged by early settlers for timber and to clear land for pasture. What remains is mainly restricted to small protected pockets. Below the canopies, where staghorns, elkhorns, orchids and bird's-nest ferns grow in the tree-tops, rainforest floors are green worlds of dampness; dripping leaves, wet ground, and decaying logs covered with mosses, lichens and fungi.

Alpine regions provide a completely different floral environment. On the lower slopes, savannah woodlands dominate, with an understorey rich in herbaceous plants, including dandelions, buttercups and orchids. In the higher, colder woodlands are the manna gum and black sally, with stunted snow gums near the snowline.

Australia's wildflowers are distinctively beautiful. They include banksias, boronias, bottlebrushes, billy buttons, Christmas bushes, Sturt's desert peas, everlasting daisies, grevilleas, orchids, kangaroo paws, waratahs and wattles. Some parts of Australia have become well-known for their spring and summer wildflowers. Western Australia, the Flinders Ranges of South Australia, and the Grampians of Victoria are particularly famous for their spectacular displays.

HISTORY

Before European settlement, Australia was inhabited by various Aboriginal societies, and the histories of the continent were told by the Aboriginal people. The stories varied between different societies. None were written down, rather they were spoken, sung, painted on bark or rocks, inside caves or sculpted on the ground.

For many years, history books suggested that Captain James Cook discovered Australia in 1770. However, it is known that the northern shores were visited by Asian sailors long before, that the Dutchman Willem Jansz landed on Australian soil in 1601 and that Aboriginal people had lived across the continent for thousands of years before any European or Asian exploration had begun. The most notable voyage by the Dutch was that of Abel Tasman, who sailed around Tasmania and to New Zealand in 1642. The first Englishman to land was William Dampier, a buccaneer who went ashore in 1688, in the vicinity of the Western Australian town named after him. It is documented that he had nothing good to say about the land or its inhabitants.

The first European to navigate the eastern coastline, Captain James Cook wrote a more favourable report about the land he named New South Wales. This was remembered when the British parliament needed somewhere to establish a new penal colony, in order to relieve the overcrowded British prison system. In 1788, the 11 ships of the First Fleet, carrying a motley collection of sailors, soldiers and felons, under the command of Captain Arthur Phillip, sailed into Sydney Harbour. The first few years were very difficult for the little settlement, with starvation always threatening until farms could be established in the unfamiliar land. The Second Fleet arrived in 1790, and a year later the arrival of the Third Fleet increased the population to 4000. Prior to British settlement, no other European or Asian country had attempted to colonise the land.

For the first 20 years, the spread of settlement was slow. Sydney was established and there were small settlements at Norfolk Island and Hobart. Expansion inland was restricted until the formidable barrier of the Blue Mountains, west of Sydney, was crossed in 1813. This feat began a tide of exploration and movement of people across the land. Explorers whose names have gone into history and folklore, such as Charles Sturt, Ludwig Leichhardt, and Burke and Wills, made incredible journeys across this uncharted inhospitable country.

Initially, the whole landmass, except Western Australia (which was created as an independent colony in 1829), was known as New South Wales. This huge area was gradually reduced as the settlements established at Hobart, Brisbane, Adelaide and Melbourne became colonies in their own right. In 1851, gold was discovered near Orange in New South Wales. This was the first of many discoveries of gold and other sought-after metals in the colonies during the second half of the century. The resulting increase in population, as miners rushed to the diggings, did much to open up Australia. Wealth from the mines helped to build inland cities and, when the rush was over, many of the miners turned to farming and other pursuits.

GOVERNMENT

Australia is considered by some to be one of the most over-governed nations in the world. Its complex 3-tiered system of government — Federal, State and Local — evolved from when the country was a collection of 6 self-governing colonies. Although first discussed 50 years before, it was not until 1 January 1901 that the Commonwealth of Australia finally came into being. Rivalry between Sydney and Melbourne (which to some extent survives today), led to a new national capital being built in the specially created Australian Capital Territory. On insistence from Melbourne, this had to be established 'no less than 100 miles from Sydney'. Land was acquired by the Commonwealth Government in 1911 in the Brindabella Ranges, 290km south-west of Sydney, and a competition was launched for the design of a new capital to be known as Canberra. The first Parliament House building was completed in 1927. Although it was only intended as a temporary home for the

Parliament, it was used for 60 years until a permanent one was completed in 1988. As the nation's capital, it is the site of national monuments and institutions, many of them attractively placed around the shores of Lake Burley Griffin.

THE PEOPLE

It is thought that the Aborigines came from the northern landmass when New Guinea was still attached to the Australian mainland about 60 000 years ago. There are no accurate estimates of the Aboriginal population before European settlement. Estimates, ranging from 300 000 to over 1 million, were attempted after European settlement, but these figures are unreliable, as the population had been significantly reduced by introduced diseases and other factors such as cultural displacement. The decline of the Aboriginal population continued well into the 20th century. It is only in the past 20 years, more than 200 years after their ancestors lost ownership of the land they lived on, that the Aboriginal struggle for land rights has finally made some progress.

In the years before World War II, Australians were primarily of English-Scots-Irish descent, a mix of free settlers and descendants of the unfortunate convicts. There was also a minority of people from many lands who had made their way here as prospectors during the 19th century goldrushes and as refugees. The post-war immigration scheme, with the theme 'populate or perish', changed the ethnic mix, bringing in more British migrants and thousands of refugees from Italy, Greece, Yugoslavia, Germany and other parts of war-torn Europe. A new wave of refugees and migrants from Asia began after the Vietnam War in the 1960s and immigration continues to play an important role in this country. Australia is today a diverse, truly multicultural society.

ECONOMY

Mining and agriculture are important to the Australian economy, a situation that has changed little since the early days of colonisation, when wool and gold were the major exports. Although wool has declined since its heyday, it is still important, as are meat exports, grains, cotton, sugar, fruit, wine, dairy products and timber. The discovery of silver, lead and zinc at Broken Hill in the 1880s set off a chain of events that eventually established an iron and steel industry. Exploration in every corner of the country has revealed enormous mineral resources that ensure Australia leads the world in the supply of bauxite, brown coal and iron ore. Gold is still mined, and, in Western Australia's far north, the Argyle Diamond Mine is the largest in the country.

Top: Aboriginal women in Arnhem Land, Northern Territory
Middle: Australia's Parliament House, Canberra, ACT
Bottom: Wine is one of Australia's exports

AUSTRALIA'S NATIONAL PARKS

SYMBOLS

- ⛺ Camping Area/ Bush Camping
- Fireplace/ Barbeque
- Fishing
- Picnic Area
- Swimming
- Toilets
- Vehicle Entrance Fee
- Visitor Centre
- Walking Trails
- Wheelchair Access

These symbols are used for Australia's National Parks chart only

The Australian landscape offers great diversity: unspoilt coastline, vast deserts, tangled rainforests, pristine islands, majestic alpine areas and unique bushland. Fortunately, most of the continent's most outstanding areas of natural beauty have been preserved in national parks, state parks, nature reserves, sanctuaries, historic and Aboriginal sites, recreation and wilderness areas. In all, Australia possesses close to 6000 protected areas covering around 100 million hectares and including 15 World Heritage Areas — a source of delight for both Australians and overseas visitors seeking to experience the great outdoors.

Many national parks are not far from the beaten track and provide easy access and excellent public facilities with a great range of activities. However, it is also rewarding to explore some of Australia's more remote areas, which are less frequented. Walking is one of the most popular ways to appreciate the natural surroundings, and Australia offers an array of marvellous opportunities, from easy day walks to wilderness treks. State national park services run guided walks and activities (especially during school holidays), and many cities and regional centres have bushwalking clubs.

Other enjoyable pursuits include photography, canoeing, climbing, diving, skiing, fishing, mountain biking, camping and nature watching. The parks provide a refuge for Australia's unique native wildlife, encompassing many rare and endangered species. Native flora is also protected, with some parks hosting dazzling displays of wildflowers in spring and summer. Some of Australia's best assets — panoramic views, open spaces, abundant flora and fauna, and remarkable natural environments – are found in its protected areas. The following charts cover the most popular national parks.

NEW SOUTH WALES

www.nationalparks.nsw.gov.au
Information Ph: 1300 361 967

Park	map ref
Abercrombie River	46 E6
Bald Rock	43 B2
Barrington Tops	47 C2
Ben Boyd	50 D6
Biamanga	50 D5
Blue Mountains	47 A5
Bongil Bongil	43 C2
Booderee (Comm. Territory)	50 E2
Boonoo Boonoo	43 B2
Booti Booti	47 E3
Border Ranges	43 C1
Botany Bay	37 D4
Bouddi	47 C5
Bournda	50 D5
Brisbane Water	35 D1
Broadwater	43 D2
Budderoo	50 E1
Bundjalung	43 D3
Cathedral Rock	43 B5
Cattai	34 D1 & 47 B5
Chaelundi	43 B4
Clyde River	50 D3
Cocoparra	45 D6
Conimbla	46 C5
Conjola/Cudmirrah	50 E2
Coolah Tops	47 A2
Coorabakh	47 D2
Cottan-Bimbang	47 D1
Crowdy Bay	47 E2

Park	map ref
Culgoa	41 C2
Deua	50 D4
Dharug	47 B5
Dooragan	47 E2
Dorrigo	43 C5
Eurobodalla	50 D4
Gardens of Stone	47 A4
Garigal	35 D3
Georges River	36 E3
Gibraltar Range	43 B3
Goobang	46 D3
Goulburn River	47 A2
Gulaga	50 D4
Gundabooka	41 A5
Guy Fawkes River	43 B5
Hat Head	43 C6
Heathcote	36 E6
Jervis Bay	50 E2
Kanangra-Boyd	47 A5
Kinchega	44 C3
Kings Plains	43 A3
Koreelah	43 B1
Kosciuszko	50 B3
Ku-ring-gai Chase	35 C2
Kwiambal	42 E2
Lane Cove	35 C5
Macquarie Pass	(not on map)
Marramarra	35 B1
Mebbin	43 D1
Meroo	50 E3
Middle Brother	(not on map)
Mimosa Rocks	50 D5
Morton	50 E2

Thredbo River, Kosciuszko National Park

Park	map ref
Mount Imlay	50 D6
Mount Kaputar	42 D4
Mount Royal	47 C2
Mount Warning	43 D1
Mummel Gulf	43 A6
Mungo	44 E5
Murramarang	50 E3
Mutawintji	40 A6
Myall Lakes	47 D3
New England	43 B5
Nightcap	43 D1
Nymboi-Binderay	43 C4
Nymboida	43 B3
Oxley Wild Rivers	43 A5
Popran	47 C5
Richmond Range	43 C1
Royal	37 A6
Scheyville	34 C2
Seven Mile Beach	(not on map)
South East Forest	50 C6
Sturt	39 C2
Sydney Harbour	35 E6
Tapin Tops	47 D2
Thirlmere Lakes	50 E1
Tomaree	47 D4
Tooloom	43 B1
Toonumbar	43 C1
Towarri	47 B2
Turon	47 A4
Wadbilliga	50 C4
Wallingat	47 E3
Warrabah	42 E5
Warrumbungle	42 B6
Washpool	43 B3
Watagans	47 C4
Weddin Mountains	46 C6
Werrikimbe	43 B6
Willandra	45 B4
Woko	47 C2
Wollemi	47 B4
Wyrrabalong	47 C5
Yarriabini	(not on map)
Yengo	47 B4
Yuraygir	43 D4

AUSTRALIAN CAPITAL TERRITORY

www.environmentact.gov.au
Information Ph: (02) 6207 9777 or (02) 6207 2900

Park	map ref
Namadgi	29 B4

VICTORIA

www.parkweb.vic.gov.au
Information Ph: 13 1963

Park	map ref
Alfred	78 C4
Alpine	73 A6
Baw Baw	76 E2
Brisbane Ranges	75 E2
Burrowa-Pine Mountain	73 C2
Chiltern Box-Ironbark	73 A2
Churchill	65 C4
Coopracambra	78 C3
Croajingolong	78 C5
Dandenong Ranges	65 D2
Errinundra	78 B3
French Island	67 E4
Grampians	70 E6
Hattah-Kulkyne	68 E3
Kinglake	76 B1
Lake Eildon	72 D6
Lind	78 B4
Little Desert	70 B4
Lower Glenelg	74 C3
Mitchell River	77 B1
Mornington Peninsula	66 D5
Morwell	76 E4
Mount Buffalo	73 A4
Mount Eccles	74 D3
Mount Richmond	74 C4
Murray-Sunset	68 B4
Organ Pipes	(not on map)
Otway	75 C5
Port Campbell	75 A5
Snowy River	73 E6
Tarra-Bulga	76 E4
Terrick Terrick	71 D2
The Lakes	77 C2
Wilsons Promontory	76 E5
Wyperfeld	68 C6
Yarra Ranges	76 C1

QUEENSLAND

www.epa.qld.gov.au
Information Ph: (07) 3227 8186

Park	map ref
Auburn River	103 C2
Barron Gorge	(not on map)
Blackdown Tableland	99 A5
Bladensburg	97 B4
Blue Lake	(not on map)
Boodjamulla (Lawn Hill)	94 A5
Bowling Green Bay	98 D1
Brampton Island	99 A2
Bribie Island	89 D1
Bunya Mountains	103 C3
Burleigh Head	(not on map)
Burrum Coast	103 D1
Byfield	99 B4
Camooweal Caves	96 B1
Cania Gorge	99 C6

SYMBOLS

- 🏕 Camping Area/ Bush Camping
- 🔥 Fireplace/Barbeque
- 🎣 Fishing
- 🧺 Picnic Area
- 🏊 Swimming
- 🚻 Toilets
- $ Vehicle Entrance Fee
- ℹ Visitor Centre
- 🚶 Walking Trails
- ♿ Wheelchair Access

These symbols are used for Australia's National Parks chart only

Finch Hatton Gorge, Eungella National Park

Park	map ref
Cape Hillsborough	(not on map)
Cape Melville	93 E6
Cape Palmerston	99 A3
Cape Upstart	98 E1
Capricorn Coast	(not on map)
Capricornia Cays	99 C5
Carnarvon	102 D1
Cedar Bay (Mangkal-Mangkalba)	95 D2
Chillagoe-Mungana Caves	95 B3
Conway	98 E1
Crater Lakes	(not on map)
Crows Nest	103 D4
Currawinya	101 C6
Daintree	95 C2
Dalrymple	95 D6
Davies Creek	(not on map)
Deepwater	99 D6
Diamantina	96 E6
Dryander	98 E1
Edmund Kennedy	95 D4
Eungella	98 E2
Eurimbula	99 C6
Expedition	103 A2
Family Islands	(not on map)
Fitzroy Island	95 D3
Flinders Group	93 D6
Fort Lytton	(not on map)
Forty Mile Scrub	95 C4
Frankland Group	(not on map)
Girraween	103 C6
Girringun (Lumholtz)	95 D4
Glass House Mountains	(not on map)
Gloucester Islands	98 E1
Goold Island	95 D4
Great Sandy (Cooloola)	103 E3
Great Sandy (Fraser Island)	103 E2
Green Island	95 D3

Park	map ref
Hinchinbrook Island	95 E4
Hope Islands	(not on map)
Idalia	101 D1
Iron Range	93 C4
Isla Gorge	103 A1
Jardine River	93 B2
Keppel Bay Islands	99 C5
Kondalilla	(not on map)
Kroombit Tops	99 C6
Lakefield	95 B1
Lamington	103 E5
Lindeman Islands	99 A1
Lizard Island	93 E6
Lochern	97 B6
Magnetic Island	95 E5
Main Range	103 D5
Mapleton Falls	(not on map)
Millstream Falls	(not on map)
Minerva Hills	(not on map)
Molle Islands	(not on map)
Moogerah Peaks	(not on map)
Mooloolah River	(not on map)
Moorrinya	97 A3
Moreton Island	103 E4
Mount Archer	(not on map)
Mount Barney	103 D5
Mount Etna Caves	(not on map)
Mount Hypipamee	(not on map)
Mount Walsh	103 D2
Mungkan Kandju	93 B5
Newry Islands	(not on map)
Noosa	(not on map)
Orpheus Island	95 E5
Paluma Range	95 D5
Porcupine Gorge	98 A2
Ravensbourne	(not on map)
Repulse Islands	98 E2
Russell River	95 D3
St Helena Island	89 D6
Simpson Desert	100 B1
Smith Islands	(not on map)
South Cumberland Islands	99 A2
Springbrook	103 E5
Sundown	103 C6
Tamborine	103 E5
Undara Volcanic	95 C4
Venman Bushland	91 C5
Welford	101 B1
White Mountains	98 A2
Whitsunday Islands	99 A1
Wooroonooran	95 D3

SOUTH AUSTRALIA

www.environment.sa.gov.au

Information Ph: 13 2324

Park	map ref
Belair	114 E2
Canunda	125 C6
Coffin Bay	124 B1
Coorong	125 B3
Flinders Chase	124 D3
Flinders Ranges	123 A2
Gammon Ranges	123 B1
Gawler Ranges	122 B4
Innes	124 D2

	map ref												
Lake Eyre	118 D4									$			
Lincoln	124 C1						⛺	🚻		$		🚶	
Mount Remarkable	122 E5						⛺		🚻	$	ℹ	🚶	♿
Murray River	125 D1						⛺		🚻				
Naracoorte Caves	125 D5						⛺		🚻	$	ℹ		♿
Nullarbor	120 C3									$		🚶	
Onkaparinga River	114 C6						⛺					🚶	
Witjira	118 B1							🚻	🚻	$			

NORTHERN TERRITORY

www.nt.gov.au/ipe/pwcnt/
Information Ph: (08) 8951 8250 (Alice Springs), (08) 8999 4401 (Darwin),
(08) 8973 8888 (Katherine)

	map ref
Barranyi	139 D1
Charles Darwin	132 C4
Davenport Range	141 D3
Elsey	135 B6
Finke Gorge	144 C2
Garig Gunak Barlu	134 E1
Gregory	137 C2
Kakadu	135 A3
Keep River	137 A2
Litchfield	134 D4
Mary River	134 E2
Nitmiluk (Katherine Gorge)	135 A5
Uluru-Kata Tjuta	144 A4
Watarrka	144 E2
West MacDonnell	144 C2

WESTERN AUSTRALIA

www.naturebase.net
Information Ph: (08) 9334 0333

	map ref
Avon Valley	160 C5
Badgingarra	160 B3
Beedelup	162 C4
Cape Arid	165 B5
Cape Le Grand	163 E4
Cape Range	158 B1
D'Entrecasteaux	162 B5

	map ref
Eucla	165 E4
Fitzgerald River	163 B4
Francois Peron	158 B4
Geikie Gorge	157 C4
Gloucester	(not on map)
Goongarrie	161 E3
John Forrest	153 C1
Kalamunda	153 C3
Kalbarri	158 C6
Karijini	158 E2
Kennedy Range	158 G3
Leeuwin-Naturaliste	162 A3
Lesmurdie Falls	153 B4
Lesueur	160 B3
Millstream-Chichester	156 B6
Mirima (Hidden Valley)	164 E2
Moore River	160 B4
Mount Augustus	158 D3
Mount Frankland	162 D5
Nambung	160 A4
Peak Charles	163 D2
Porongurup	162 E5
Purnululu	157 E4
Scott	162 B4
Serpentine	155 B6
Shannon	162 C5
Stirling Range	162 E4
Stockyard Gully	(not on map)
Stokes	163 D3
Torndirrup	162 E5
Tuart Forest	(not on map)
Tunnel Creek	157 B4
Walpole-Nornalup	162 C5
Walyunga	(not on map)
Warren	162 C4
Watheroo	160 B3
Waychinicup	163 A5
Wellington	162 C3
West Cape Howe	162 E5
William Bay	162 D5
Windjana Gorge	157 B3
Yalgorup	162 B2
Yanchep	160 B5

TASMANIA

www.parks.tas.gov.au
Information Ph: 1300 135 513

	map ref
Ben Lomond	179 B4
Cradle Mountain-Lake St Clair	178 A5
Douglas-Apsley	179 D4
Franklin-Gordon Wild Rivers	181 D3
Freycinet	179 D6
Hartz Mountains	182 D5
Maria Island	183 D2
Mole Creek Karst	178 B4
Mount Field	182 D2
Mount William	179 D1
Narawntapu (Asbestos Range)	178 C2
Rocky Cape	177 D3
South Bruny	183 A6
Southwest	182 B5
Strzelecki	180 D3
Tasman	183 C4
Walls of Jerusalem	178 B5

Striped 'beehive' domes of the Bungle Bungles, Purnululu National Park, Western Australia

AUSTRALIAN INTERCITY DISTANCE CHART

Approximate Distance	Adelaide SA	Albany WA	Albury NSW	Alice Springs NT	Ayers Rock/Yulara NT	Bairnsdale VIC	Ballarat VIC	Bathurst NSW	Bega NSW	Bendigo VIC	Bordertown SA	Bourke NSW	Brisbane QLD	Broken Hill NSW	Broome WA	Bunbury WA	Cairns QLD	Canberra ACT	Carnarvon WA	Ceduna SA	Charleville QLD	Coober Pedy SA	Darwin NT	Dubbo NSW	Esperance WA	Eucla WA	Geraldton WA	Grafton NSW
Adelaide SA		2642	932	1526	1570	1006	611	1183	1329	770	267	1129	2054	514	4242	2855	2964	1153	3556	769	1583	837	3018	1175	2168	1256	3083	1815
Albany WA	2642		3424	3558	3602	3648	3253	3664	3810	3251	2909	3366	4291	2751	2582	361	5201	3634	1292	1873	3820	2869	4375	3503	474	1386	819	4079
Albury NSW	932	3424		2458	2502	310	372	443	426	297	665	847	1375	866	4905	3637	2650	346	4338	1551	918	1619	3662	531	2950	2038	3865	1162
Alice Springs NT	1526	3558	2458		442	2532	2137	2548	2694	2135	1793	2250	3004	1635	2735	3771	2293	2518	4128	1685	2332	689	1492	2387	3084	2172	3999	2963
Ayers Rock/Yulara NT	1570	3602	2502	442		2574	2181	2592	2738	2179	1837	2294	3219	1679	3177	3815	2735	2562	4516	1729	2748	733	1934	2431	3128	2216	4043	3007
Bairnsdale VIC	1006	3648	310	2532	2574		395	724	326	432	739	1157	1691	1120	5215	3861	2960	450	4562	1775	1611	1843	3972	841	3174	2262	4089	1334
Ballarat VIC	611	3253	372	2137	2181	395		815	721	121	344	995	1655	753	5436	3466	2830	718	4167	1380	1449	1448	3629	882	2779	1867	3694	1522
Bathurst NSW	1183	3664	443	2548	2592	724	815		468	740	1093	574	1004	958	5015	3877	2325	274	4578	1791	1028	1859	3772	206	3190	2278	4105	735
Bega NSW	1329	3810	426	2694	2738	326	721	468		758	1065	965	1373	1292	5406	4023	2723	222	4724	1937	1419	2005	4163	604	3336	2424	4251	1034
Bendigo VIC	770	3251	297	2135	2179	432	121	740	758		368	874	1534	697	4851	3464	2795	643	4165	1378	1328	1446	3627	761	2777	1865	3692	1401
Bordertown SA	267	2909	665	1793	1837	739	344	1093	1065	368		1242	1929	781	4509	3122	3160	1011	3823	1036	1779	1104	3285	1085	2435	1523	3350	1725
Bourke NSW	1129	3366	847	2250	2294	1157	995	574	965	874	1242		924	615	4441	3579	1835	743	4280	1493	454	1561	3198	368	2892	1980	3807	813
Brisbane QLD	2054	4291	1375	3004	3219	1691	1655	1004	1373	1534	1929	924		1540	4659	4504	1701	1223	5205	2418	754	2486	3416	844	3817	2905	4732	339
Broken Hill NSW	514	2751	866	1635	1679	1120	753	958	1292	697	781	615	1540		4351	2964	2450	1080	3665	878	1069	946	3127	752	2277	1365	3192	1328
Broome WA	4242	2582	4905	2735	3177	5215	5436	5015	5406	4851	4509	4441	4659	4351		2416	3948	5184	1461	3569	3987	3405	1861	4809	2948	3082	1934	4901
Bunbury WA	2855	361	3637	3771	3815	3861	3466	3877	4023	3464	3122	3579	4504	2964	2416		5414	3847	1069	2086	4033	3082	4183	3716	687	1599	596	4292
Cairns QLD	2964	5201	2650	2293	2735	2960	2830	2325	2723	2795	3160	1835	1701	2450	3948	5414		2435	5429	3328	1381	2982	2705	2119	4727	3815	5642	2048
Canberra ACT	1153	3634	346	2518	2562	450	718	274	222	643	1011	743	1223	1080	5184	3847	2435		4548	1761	1197	1829	3941	382	3160	2248	4075	884
Carnarvon WA	3556	1292	4338	4128	4516	4562	4167	4578	4724	4165	3823	4280	5205	3665	1461	1069	5429	4548		2787	4734	3783	3254	4417	1600	2300	473	4993
Ceduna SA	769	1873	1551	1685	1729	1775	1380	1791	1937	1378	1036	1493	2418	878	3569	2086	3328	1761	2787		1947	996	3177	1630	1399	487	2314	2206
Charleville QLD	1583	3820	918	2332	2748	1611	1449	1028	1419	1328	1779	454	754	1069	3987	4033	1381	1197	4734	1947		2015	2744	822	3346	2434	4261	997
Coober Pedy SA	837	2869	1619	689	733	1843	1448	1859	2005	1446	1104	1561	2486	946	3405	3082	2982	1829	3783	996	2015		2181	1698	2395	1483	3310	2274
Darwin NT	3018	4375	3662	1492	1934	3972	3629	3772	4163	3627	3285	3198	3416	3127	1861	4183	2705	3941	3254	3177	2744	2181		3566	4307	3664	3727	3658
Dubbo NSW	1175	3503	531	2387	2431	841	882	206	604	761	1085	368	844	752	4809	3716	2119	382	4417	1630	822	1698	3566		3029	2117	3944	640
Esperance WA	2168	474	2950	3084	3128	3174	2779	3190	3336	2777	2435	2892	3817	2277	2948	687	4727	3160	1600	1399	3346	2395	4307	3029		912	1319	3605
Eucla WA	1256	1386	2038	2172	2216	2262	1867	2278	2424	1865	1523	1980	2905	1365	3082	1599	3815	2248	2300	487	2434	1483	3664	2117	912		1827	2693
Geraldton WA	3083	819	3865	3999	4043	4089	3694	4105	4251	3692	3350	3807	4732	3192	1934	596	5642	4075	473	2314	4261	3310	3727	3944	1319	1827		4520
Grafton NSW	1815	4079	1162	2963	3007	1334	1522	735	1034	1401	1725	813	339	1328	4901	4292	2048	884	4993	2206	997	2274	3658	640	3605	2693	4520	
Horsham VIC	424	3066	508	1950	1994	582	187	951	908	211	157	1085	1745	609	4666	3279	3006	854	3980	1193	1539	1261	3442	972	2592	1680	3507	1612
Kalgoorlie/Boulder WA	2153	799	2935	3069	3113	3159	2764	3175	3321	2762	2420	2877	3802	2262	2185	764	4712	3145	1161	1384	3331	2380	3978	3014	389	897	988	3590
Katherine NT	2709	4066	3353	1183	1625	3663	3884	3463	3854	3318	2976	2889	3107	2818	1552	3874	2396	3632	2945	2868	2435	1872	309	3257	3998	3355	3418	3349
Kununurra WA	3202	3554	3865	1695	2137	4175	4396	3975	4366	3830	3488	3401	3619	3330	1040	3362	2908	4144	2433	3380	2947	2384	821	3769	3486	3867	2906	3861
Longreach QLD	2097	4334	1432	1818	2260	1671	1963	1542	1933	1842	2293	968	1186	1583	3473	4547	1053	1711	4954	2461	514	2507	2230	1336	3860	2948	4775	1428
Mackay QLD	2475	4712	2009	2396	2838	2319	2341	1684	2082	2220	2588	1346	980	1961	4051	4925	729	1860	5532	2839	892	2907	2808	1478	4238	3326	5153	1319
Meekatharra WA	2872	1116	3654	3788	3832	3837	3483	3894	4040	3481	3139	3596	4521	2981	1466	924	5344	3864	620	2103	4050	3099	3248	3733	1108	1616	540	4309
Melbourne VIC	723	3365	314	2249	2293	283	112	759	609	149	456	989	1658	837	4965	3578	2933	660	4279	1492	1443	1560	3741	814	2891	1979	3806	1476
Mildura VIC	372	2849	571	1733	1777	821	454	811	957	398	411	877	1647	299	4449	3062	2749	781	3763	976	1368	1044	3225	803	2375	1463	3290	1443
Moree NSW	1548	3812	904	2696	2740	1214	1255	579	977	1134	1458	445	479	1061	4616	4025	1790	755	4726	1939	629	2007	3373	373	3338	2426	4253	368
Mt Gambier SA	435	3077	677	1961	2005	695	305	1120	1026	426	183	1300	1960	870	4677	3290	3135	1023	3991	1204	1754	1272	3453	1187	2603	1691	3518	1827
Mount Isa QLD	2702	4734	2074	1176	1618	2313	2605	2184	2575	2484	2852	1610	1828	2225	2831	4947	1117	2353	4312	2861	1156	1865	1588	1978	4279	3348	4697	2070
Newcastle NSW	1509	3884	693	2768	2812	865	1065	326	570	990	1358	749	818	1133	5099	4097	2339	415	4798	2011	1121	2079	3856	381	3410	2498	4325	479
Perth WA	2689	406	3471	3605	3649	3695	3300	3711	3857	3298	2956	3413	4338	2798	2234	182	5248	3681	903	1920	3867	2916	4017	3550	714	1433	430	4126
Port Augusta SA	305	2337	1087	1221	1265	1311	916	1327	1473	914	572	1029	1954	414	3937	2550	2864	1297	3251	464	1483	532	2713	1166	1863	951	2778	1742
Port Hedland WA	3744	1988	4526	3349	3791	4750	4355	4766	4912	4353	4011	4468	5205	3853	614	1812	4543	4736	867	2975	4533	3971	2407	4605	1980	2488	1340	5447
Port Lincoln SA	642	2277	1424	1558	1602	1648	1253	1664	1810	1251	909	1366	2291	751	3973	2490	3201	1634	3191	404	1820	869	3050	1503	1803	891	2718	2079
Renmark SA	247	2724	696	1608	1652	940	573	1714	1082	517	279	1039	1772	424	4324	2937	2874	906	3638	857	1493	919	3100	928	2250	1388	3165	1568
Rockhampton QLD	2268	4505	1676	3389	3433	1986	2027	1351	1749	1906	2230	1139	647	1754	4154	4718	1062	1527	5419	2632	780	2700	2911	1145	4031	3119	4946	986
Sydney NSW	1384	3865	562	2749	2793	734	934	201	418	859	1227	775	957	1159	5216	4078	2400	284	4779	1992	1229	2060	3973	407	3391	2479	4306	618
Tamworth NSW	1510	3774	866	2658	2702	1129	1217	430	813	1096	1420	584	574	1023	4879	3987	2062	704	4688	1901	901	1969	3636	335	3300	2388	4215	305
Tennant Creek NT	2040	4072	2736	514	956	2975	2651	2846	3237	2649	2307	2272	2490	2149	2221	4285	1779	3015	3614	2199	1818	1203	978	2640	3598	2686	4087	2732
Toowoomba QLD	1894	4158	1250	3042	3086	1560	1601	925	1314	1480	1786	791	125	1407	4534	4371	1702	1205	5072	2285	629	2353	3291	719	3684	2772	4599	367
Townsville QLD	2617	4854	2303	2067	2509	2613	2483	1978	2420	2362	2813	1488	1376	2103	3722	5067	347	2088	5203	2981	1034	3049	2479	1772	4380	3468	5295	1701
Wagga Wagga NSW	936	3417	125	2301	2345	435	497	318	393	422	790	722	1250	863	5017	3630	2525	244	4331	1544	1176	1612	3793	406	2943	2031	3858	1046
Warrnambool VIC	617	3259	544	2143	2187	513	171	986	839	292	365	1162	1826	850	4859	3472	3001	889	4173	1386	1621	922	3635	1053	2785	1873	3700	1693
West Wyalong NSW	919	3400	278	2284	2328	588	626	264	501	505	829	572	1100	846	5000	3613	2375	271	4314	1527	1026	1595	3776	256	2926	2014	3841	896

Approximate Distance

	Horsham VIC	Kalgoorlie/Boulder WA	Katherine NT	Kununurra WA	Longreach QLD	Mackay QLD	Meekatharra WA	Melbourne VIC	Mildura VIC	Moree NSW	Mt Gambier SA	Mount Isa QLD	Newcastle NSW	Perth WA	Port Augusta SA	Port Hedland WA	Port Lincoln SA	Renmark SA	Rockhampton QLD	Sydney NSW	Tamworth NSW	Tennant Creek NT	Toowoomba QLD	Townsville QLD	Wagga Wagga NSW	Warrnambool VIC	West Wyalong NSW
Adelaide SA	424	2153	2709	3202	2097	2475	2872	723	372	1548	435	2702	1509	2689	305	3744	642	247	2268	1384	1510	2040	1894	2617	936	617	919
Albany WA	3066	799	4066	3554	4334	4712	1116	3365	2849	3812	3077	4734	3884	406	2337	1988	2277	2724	4505	3865	3774	4072	4158	4854	3417	3259	3400
Albury NSW	508	2935	3353	3865	1432	2009	3654	314	571	904	677	2074	693	3471	1087	4526	1424	696	1676	562	866	2736	1250	2303	125	544	278
Alice Springs NT	1950	3069	1183	1695	1818	2396	3788	2249	1733	2696	1961	1176	2768	3605	1221	3349	1558	1608	3389	2749	2658	514	3042	2067	2301	2143	2284
Ayers Rock/Yulara NT	1994	3113	1625	2137	2260	2838	3832	2293	1777	2740	2005	1618	2812	3649	1265	3791	1602	1652	3433	2793	2702	956	3086	2509	2345	2187	2328
Bairnsdale VIC	582	3159	3663	4175	1671	2319	3837	283	821	1214	695	2313	865	3695	1311	4750	1648	940	1986	734	1129	2975	1560	2613	435	513	588
Ballarat VIC	187	2764	3884	4396	1963	2341	3483	112	454	1255	305	2605	1065	3300	916	4355	1253	573	2027	934	1217	2651	1601	2483	497	171	626
Bathurst NSW	951	3175	3463	3975	1542	1684	3894	759	811	579	1120	2184	326	3711	1327	4766	1664	1714	1351	201	430	2846	925	1978	318	986	264
Bega NSW	908	3321	3854	4366	1933	2082	4040	609	957	977	1026	2575	570	3857	1473	4912	1810	1082	1749	418	813	3237	1314	2420	393	839	501
Bendigo VIC	211	2762	3318	3830	1842	2220	3481	149	398	1134	426	2484	990	3298	914	4353	1251	517	1906	859	1096	2649	1480	2362	422	292	505
Bordertown SA	157	2420	2976	3488	2293	2588	3139	456	411	1458	183	2852	1358	2956	572	4011	909	279	2230	1227	1420	2307	1786	2813	790	365	829
Bourke NSW	1085	2877	2889	3401	968	1346	3596	989	877	445	1300	1610	749	3413	1029	4468	1366	1039	1139	775	584	2272	791	1488	722	1162	572
Brisbane QLD	1745	3802	3107	3619	1186	980	4521	1658	1647	479	1960	1828	818	4338	1954	5205	2291	1772	647	957	574	2490	125	1376	1250	1826	1100
Broken Hill NSW	609	2262	2818	3330	1583	1961	2981	837	299	1061	870	2225	1133	2798	414	3853	751	424	1754	1159	1023	2149	1407	2103	863	850	846
Broome WA	4666	2185	1552	1040	3473	4051	1466	4965	4449	4616	4677	2831	5099	2234	3937	614	3973	4324	4154	5216	4879	2221	4534	3722	5017	4859	5000
Bunbury WA	3279	764	3874	3362	4547	4925	924	3578	3062	4025	3290	4947	4097	182	2550	1812	2490	2937	4718	4078	3987	4285	4371	5067	3630	3472	3613
Cairns QLD	3006	4712	2396	2908	1053	729	5344	2933	2749	1790	3135	1117	2339	5248	2864	4543	3201	2874	1062	2400	2062	1779	1702	347	2525	3001	2375
Canberra ACT	854	3145	3632	4144	1711	1860	3864	660	781	755	1023	2353	415	3681	1297	4736	1634	906	1527	284	704	3015	1205	2088	244	889	271
Carnarvon WA	3980	1161	2945	2433	4954	5532	620	4279	~3763	4726	3991	4312	4798	903	3251	867	3191	3638	5419	4779	4688	3614	5072	5203	4331	4173	4314
Ceduna SA	1193	1384	2868	3380	2461	2839	2103	1492	976	1939	1204	2861	2011	1920	464	2975	404	857	2632	1992	1901	2199	2285	2981	1544	1386	1527
Charleville QLD	1539	3331	2435	2947	514	892	4050	1443	1368	629	1754	1156	1121	3867	1483	4533	1820	1493	780	1229	901	1818	629	1034	1176	1621	1026
Coober Pedy SA	1261	2380	1872	2384	2507	2907	3099	1560	1044	2007	1272	1865	2079	2916	532	3971	869	919	2700	2060	1969	1203	2353	3049	1612	922	1595
Darwin NT	3442	3978	309	821	2230	2808	3248	3741	3225	3373	3453	1588	3856	4017	2713	2407	3050	3100	2911	3973	3636	978	3291	2479	3793	3635	3776
Dubbo NSW	972	3014	3257	3769	1336	1478	3733	814	803	373	1187	1978	381	3550	1166	4605	1503	928	1145	407	335	2640	719	1772	406	1053	256
Esperance WA	2592	389	3998	3486	3860	4238	1108	2891	2375	3338	2603	4279	3410	714	1863	1980	1803	2250	4031	3391	3300	3598	3684	4380	2943	2785	2926
Eucla WA	1680	897	3355	3867	2948	3326	1616	1979	1463	2426	1691	3348	2498	1433	951	2488	891	1388	3119	2479	2388	2686	2772	3468	2031	1873	2014
Geraldton WA	3507	988	3418	2906	4775	5153	540	3806	3290	4253	3518	4697	4325	430	2778	1340	2718	3165	4946	4306	4215	4087	4599	5295	3858	3700	3841
Grafton NSW	1612	3590	3349	3861	1428	1319	4309	1476	1443	368	1827	2070	479	4126	1742	5447	2079	1568	986	618	305	2732	367	1701	1046	1693	896
Horsham VIC		2577	3133	3645	2053	2431	3296	299	310	1345	261	2695	1201	3113	729	4168	1066	429	2117	1070	1307	2464	1691	2573	633	241	580
Kalgoorlie/Boulder WA	2577		3669	3157	3845	4223	719	2876	2360	3323	2588	4264	3395	594	1848	1591	1788	2235	4016	3376	3285	3583	3669	4365	2928	2770	2911
Katherine NT	3133	3669		512	1921	2499	2948	3432	2916	3064	3144	1279	3547	3708	2404	2098	2741	2791	2602	3664	3327	669	2982	2170	3484	3326	3467
Kununurra WA	3645	3157	512		2433	3011	2436	3944	3428	3576	3656	1791	4059	3196	2916	1586	3253	3303	3114	4176	3839	1181	3494	2682	3996	3838	3979
Longreach QLD	2053	3845	1921	2433		793	4564	1957	1845	1143	2268	642	1626	4381	1997	4068	2334	2007	681	1743	1406	1304	1061	706	1690	2134	1540
Mackay QLD	2431	4223	2499	3011	793		4942	2175	2223	1105	2624	1220	1764	4759	2375	4646	2712	2385	333	1715	1377	1882	973	382	1884	2512	1734
Meekatharra WA	3296	719	2948	2436	4564	4942		3595	3079	4042	3307	4227	4114	758	2567	872	2507	2954	4735	4095	4004	3617	4288	5094	3647	3489	3630
Melbourne VIC	299	2876	3432	3944	1957	2175	3595		538	1187	412	2599	1007	3412	1028	4467	1365	657	1959	876	1180	2763	1533	2477	439	230	558
Mildura VIC	310	2360	2916	3428	1845	2223	3079	538		1176	571	2524	1137	2896	512	3951	849	125	1948	1012	1138	2247	1522	2365	564	551	547
Moree NSW	1345	3323	3064	3576	1143	1105	4042	1187	1176		1560	1785	492	3859	1475	4914	1812	1301	772	610	272	2447	346	1443	779	1426	629
Mt Gambier SA	261	2588	3144	3656	2268	2624	3307	412	571	1560		2910	1370	3124	740	4179	1077	462	2332	1239	1522	2475	1906	2788	802	182	795
Mount Isa QLD	2695	4264	1279	1791	642	1220	4227	2599	2524	1785	2910		2268	4781	2397	3426	2734	2649	1323	2385	2048	662	1703	891	2332	2776	2182
Newcastle NSW	1201	3395	3547	4059	1626	1764	4114	1007	1137	492	1370	2268		3931	1547	4986	1884	1262	1264	152	277	2930	778	1992	591	1236	590
Perth WA	3113	594	3708	3196	4381	4759	758	3412	2896	3859	3124	4781	3931		2384	1630	2324	2771	4552	3912	3821	4119	4205	4901	3464	3306	3447
Port Augusta SA	729	1848	2404	2916	1997	2375	2567	1028	512	1475	740	2397	1547	2384		3439	337	387	2168	1528	1437	1735	1821	2517	1080	922	1063
Port Hedland WA	4168	1591	2098	1586	4068	4646	872	4467	3951	4914	4179	3426	4986	1630	3439		3776	3826	5607	4967	4876	2767	5080	4317	4519	4361	4502
Port Lincoln SA	1066	1788	2741	3253	2334	2712	2507	1365	849	1812	1077	2734	1884	2324	337	3776		724	2505	1865	1774	2072	2158	2854	1417	1259	1400
Renmark SA	429	2235	2791	3303	2007	2385	2954	657	125	1301	462	2649	1262	2771	387	3826	724		2073	1137	1263	2122	1647	2527	689	676	672
Rockhampton QLD	2117	4016	2602	3114	681	333	4735	1959	1948	772	2332	1323	1264	4552	2168	5607	2505	2073		1382	1044	1985	640	715	1554	2198	1401
Sydney NSW	1070	3376	3664	4176	1743	1715	4095	876	1012	610	1239	2385	152	3912	1528	4967	1865	1137	1382		395	3263	896	2053	470	1105	465
Tamworth NSW	1307	3285	3327	3839	1406	1377	4004	1180	1138	272	1522	2048	277	3821	1437	4876	1774	1263	1044	395		2710	501	1715	741	1388	591
Tennant Creek NT	2464	3583	669	1181	1304	1882	3617	2763	2247	2447	2475	662	2930	4119	1735	2767	2072	2122	1985	3263	2710		2365	1553	2815	2657	2798
Toowoomba QLD	1691	3669	2982	3494	1061	973	4288	1533	1522	346	1906	1703	778	4205	1821	5080	2158	1647	640	896	501	2365		1355	1125	1772	975
Townsville QLD	2573	4365	2170	2682	706	382	5094	2477	2365	1443	2788	891	1992	4901	2517	4317	2854	2527	715	2053	1715	1553	1355		2178	2654	2028
Wagga Wagga NSW	633	2928	3484	3996	1690	1884	3647	439	564	779	802	2332	591	3464	1080	4519	1417	689	1554	470	741	2815	1125	2178		668	153
Warrnambool VIC	241	2770	3326	3838	2134	2512	3489	230	551	1426	182	2776	1236	3306	922	4361	1259	676	2198	1105	1388	2657	1772	2654	668		661
West Wyalong NSW	580	2911	3467	3979	1540	1734	3630	558	547	629	795	2182	590	3447	1063	4502	1400	672	1401	465	591	2798	975	2028	153	661	

TOURING ROUTE MAPS
see pages 18 to 21

SYDNEY to MELBOURNE
via HUME HWY / FWY `31` `M31`

SYDNEY to ADELAIDE
via HUME HWY `31` STURT HWY `20` `A20`

BRISBANE to SYDNEY
via PACIFIC HWY / MWY `1` `M1`

BRISBANE to SYDNEY
via NEW ENGLAND HWY `15`

SYDNEY to MELBOURNE
via PRINCES HWY `1` `A1` `M1`

BRISBANE to MELBOURNE
via NEWELL HWY `A2` `85` `39` `A39` `M31`

MELBOURNE to ADELAIDE
via PRINCES HWY `M1` `A1` RIDDOCH HWY `A66`
WESTERN HWY `A8`

MELBOURNE to ADELAIDE
via WESTERN HWY `M8` `A8` `M1`

CAIRNS to BRISBANE
via BRUCE HWY `1`

DARWIN to BRISBANE
via STUART HWY `1` `87` BARKLY HWY `66` `A2`
LANDSBOROUGH HWY `A2` WARREGO HWY `A2`

DARWIN to ADELAIDE
via STUART HWY `1` `87` `A87` `A1`

SYDNEY to ADELAIDE
via GREAT WESTERN HWY `32` MITCHELL HWY `32`
BARRIER HWY `32` `A32`

ADELAIDE to PERTH
via EYRE HWY `A1` `1` COOLGARDIE-ESPERANCE
HWY `94` GREAT EASTERN HWY `94`

ADELAIDE to PERTH
via EYRE HWY `A1` `1` COOLGARDIE-ESPERANCE HWY `1`
SOUTH COAST HWY `1` SOUTH EASTERN HWY `1`

DARWIN to PERTH
via STUART HWY `1` VICTORIA HWY `1` GREAT NORTHERN
HWY `1` NORTH WEST COASTAL HWY `1` BRAND HWY `1`

**DEVONPORT to LAUNCESTON
to HOBART**
via BASS HWY `1` MIDLAND HWY `1`

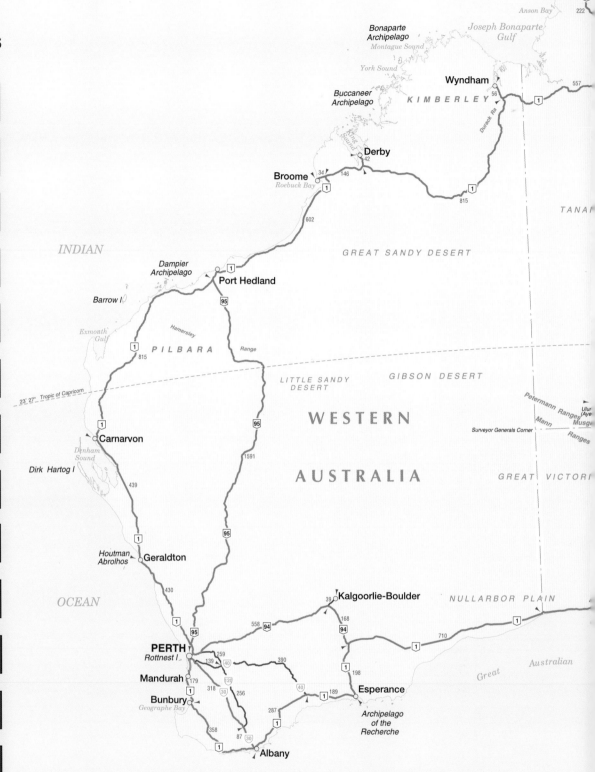

Australia's Major Highways

SCALE 1:12 700 000

0 100 200 300 400 500 600 700 800
Kilometres
Lamberts Conformal Conic Projection with two standard parallels 18°S and 36°S
© UNIVERSAL PUBLISHERS PTY LTD 2005

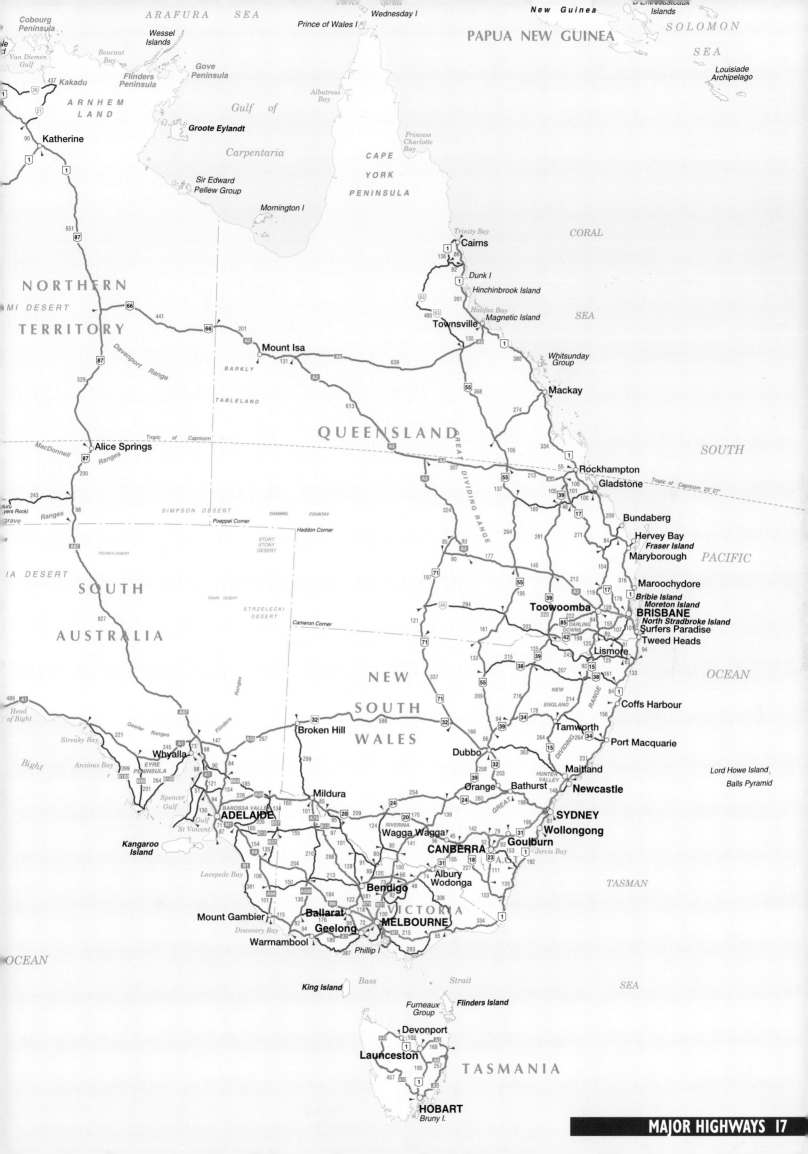

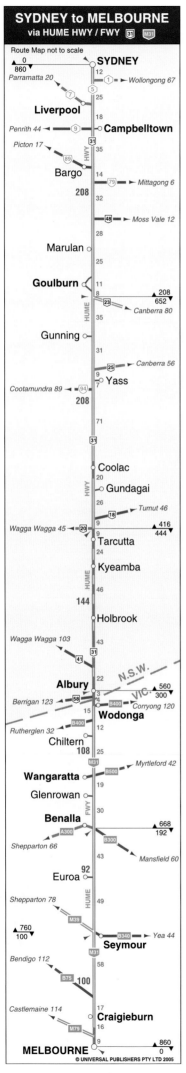

SYDNEY to MELBOURNE
via HUME HWY / FWY 31 M31

Route Map not to scale

0 / 860	SYDNEY	
	12	
Parramatta 20	1 → Wollongong 67	
	5	
	25	
Liverpool	7	
	18	
Penrith 44	9 **Campbelltown**	
	31	
Picton 17	89	35
Bargo	14	
208	79 → Mittagong 6	
	32	
	48 → Moss Vale 12	
	28	
Marulan	25	
Goulburn	11	
	23 → 208 / 652	8
	35 → Canberra 80	
Gunning	31	
	25 → Canberra 56	
Yass	7	
Cootamundra 89 → 94	**208**	
	71	
	31	
Coolac	20	
Gundagai	26	
	18 → Tumut 46	9
Wagga Wagga 45 → 20	9 → 416 / 444	
Tarcutta	24	
Kyeamba	46	
144		
Holbrook	43	
Wagga Wagga 103	41	
	22	N.S.W. / VIC.
Albury	3 → 560 / 300	
Berrigan 123 → 58	15 → Corryong 120	
	B400 **Wodonga**	
Rutherglen 32 → B400	12	
Chiltern	108	25
	M31 B500 → Myrtleford 42	
Wangaratta	19	
Glenrowan		
Benalla	A300 → 668 / 192	
Shepparton 66 → B300	43 → Mansfield 60	
Euroa	92	
Shepparton 78 →	49	
760 / 100 → M39	B340 → Yea 44	
	58 **Seymour**	
Bendigo 112 → B75	100	
Castlemaine 114 →	17	
	M79 **Craigieburn**	16
	9 → 860	
MELBOURNE		

© UNIVERSAL PUBLISHERS PTY LTD 2005

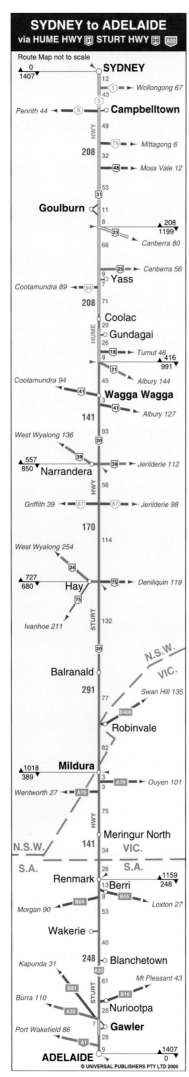

SYDNEY to ADELAIDE
via HUME HWY 31 STURT HWY 20 A20

Route Map not to scale

0 / 1407	SYDNEY	
	12	
	43 → Wollongong 67	
	5	
Penrith 44 → 9	**Campbelltown**	
	49	
208	79 → Mittagong 6	
	32	
	48 → Moss Vale 12	
	53	
	31	
Goulburn	11	
	23 → 208 / 1199	8
	66 → Canberra 80	
	25 → Canberra 56	
	9 **Yass**	
Cootamundra 89 → 94	7	
	208	71
Coolac	20	
Gundagai	26	
	18 → Tumut 46	9
	31 → 416 / 991	
Cootamundra 94 →	45 → Albury 144	
	41 **Wagga Wagga**	3
	41 → Albury 127	
	141	93
	20	
West Wyalong 136 →	39	
557 / 850 →	39 → Jerilderie 112	
Narrandera	56	
Griffith 39 → 87	87 → Jerilderie 98	
	170	
West Wyalong 254 →	114	
	24	
727 / 680 →	75 → Deniliquin 119	
Hay	75	
Ivanhoe 211 →	132	
	20	N.S.W. / VIC.
Balranald	**291**	Swan Hill 135
	77	
	B400	
Robinvale	82	
1018 / 389 →	**Mildura**	3
Wentworth 27 → A79	A79 → Ouyen 101	
	75	
	141	Meringur North
N.S.W. / VIC.	34	
S.A.	**Renmark**	26 → 1159 / 248
Morgan 90 → B64	13 **Berri**	
	9 B55 → Loxton 27	
Wakerie	53	
	40	
	248 → **Blanchetown**	
Kapunda 31 →	61 → Mt Pleasant 43	
	A20	
Burra 110 → B81	28 **Nuriootpa**	
	A32	
Port Wakefield 86 → A1	7 **Gawler**	
	28	
	9 → 1407	
ADELAIDE		

© UNIVERSAL PUBLISHERS PTY LTD 2005

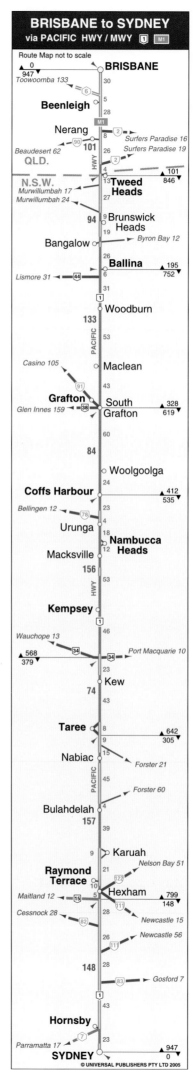

BRISBANE to SYDNEY
via PACIFIC HWY / MWY 1 M1

Route Map not to scale

0 / 947	BRISBANE	
Toowoomba 133 →	30	
	6	
Beenleigh	28	
	M1	
Nerang	8	
Beaudesert 62 → 90	**101** → Surfers Paradise 16	26 → Surfers Paradise 19
QLD.	2	
	4 → 101 / 846	
N.S.W.	13 **Tweed Heads**	
Murwillumbah 17 →	27	
Murwillumbah 24 →	9 **Brunswick Heads**	
	94	19 → Byron Bay 12
Bangalow	26	
	Ballina → 195 / 752	
	6	
Lismore 31 → 44	31	
	1 **Woodburn**	
	133	53
	Maclean	
Casino 105 →	43	
Grafton	91	
Glen Innes 159 → 38	**South Grafton** → 328 / 619	
	60	
	84	
	Woolgoolga	
	23	
Coffs Harbour → 412 / 535		
Bellingen 12 → 78	23	
Urunga	18	
	Nambucca Heads →	12
Macksville	53	
	156	
	1	
Kempsey	46	
Wauchope 13 →	34	
568 / 379 →	34 → Port Macquarie 10	
	23	
	Kew	
	74	43
	8	
Taree → 642 / 305	9	
Nabiac	15 → Forster 21	
	45 → Forster 60	
	4	
Bulahdelah	**157**	
	39	
	9 **Karuah**	
	21 → Nelson Bay 51	
Raymond Terrace	122	
Maitland 12 → 15	10 / 5 **Hexham** → 799 / 148	
Cessnock 28 →	28 → Newcastle 15	
	82	26 → Newcastle 56
	11	
	28	
	148	28
	83 → Gosford 7	
	1	
	43	
Hornsby	7	
Parramatta 17 →	23 → 947	
SYDNEY → 0		

© UNIVERSAL PUBLISHERS PTY LTD 2005

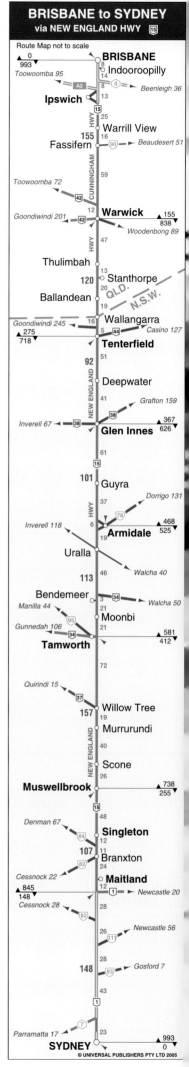

BRISBANE to SYDNEY
via NEW ENGLAND HWY 15

Route Map not to scale

0 / 993	BRISBANE	
Toowoomba 95 → A2	14 **Indooroopilly**	
	4 → Beenleigh 36	
Ipswich	13	
	15	
	Warrill View	
	155	16 → Beaudesert 51
Fassifern	90	
	59	
Toowoomba 72 →	42	
Goondiwindi 201 → 42	12 **Warwick** → 155 / 838	
	42 → Woodenbong 89	
Thulimbah	47	
	13 → Stanthorpe	
Ballandean	**120**	
	19	QLD. / N.S.W.
Goondiwindi 245 →	16 → Wallangarra	
275 / 718 →	5 44 → Casino 127	
	Tenterfield	
	92	51
	Deepwater	
Inverell 67 → 38	41 → Grafton 159	
	38 → 367 / 626	
	Glen Innes	
	61	
	15	
	101	
	Guyra	
Inverell 118 →	37 78 → Dorrigo 131	
	6 → 468 / 525	
	19 **Armidale**	
	Uralla	
	113	46 → Walcha 40
	3 34 → Walcha 50	
Manilla 44 →	**Bendemeer**	21
Gunnedah 106 → 34	**Moonbi**	
	95	21 → 581 / 412
	Tamworth	
	72	
Quirindi 15 →	37	
	157	**Willow Tree**
	19	
	Murrurundi	
	40	
	Scone	
	26 → 738 / 255	
Muswellbrook	15	
Denman 67 → 84	48	
	12 **Singleton**	
	11 82	
	107 → **Branxton**	
Cessnock 22 →	12	
845 / 148 →	1 → Newcastle 20	
Maitland		
Cessnock 28 →	82	26 → Newcastle 56
	11	
	148	28
	83 → Gosford 7	
	43	
	1	
Parramatta 17 →	7	
SYDNEY → 0 / 993	23	

© UNIVERSAL PUBLISHERS PTY LTD 2005

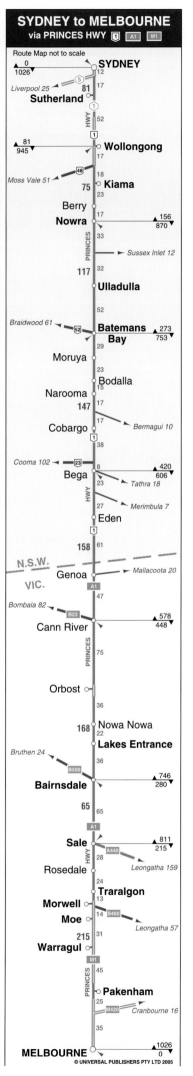

SYDNEY to MELBOURNE via PRINCES HWY

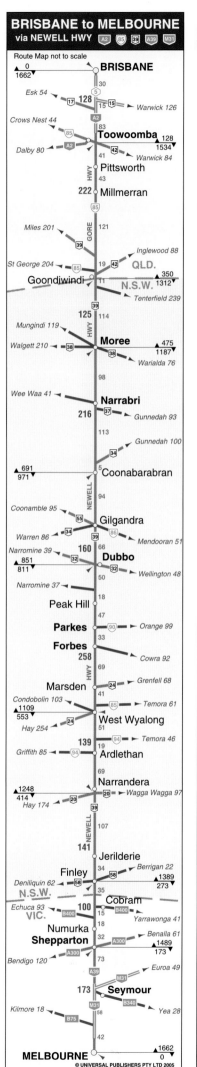

BRISBANE to MELBOURNE via NEWELL HWY

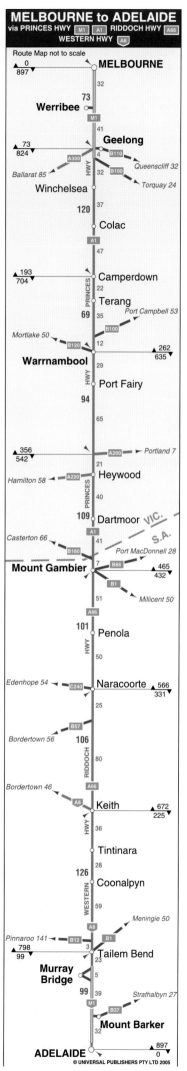

MELBOURNE to ADELAIDE via PRINCES HWY — RIDDOCH HWY — WESTERN HWY

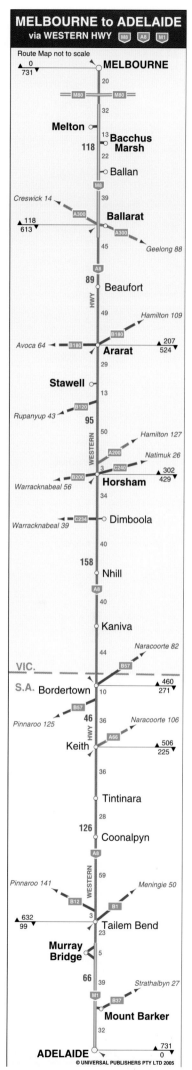

MELBOURNE to ADELAIDE via WESTERN HWY

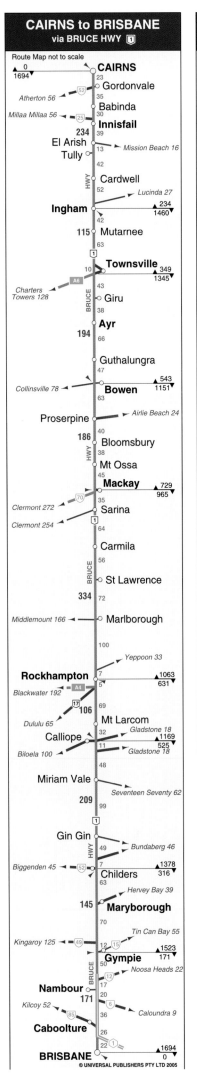

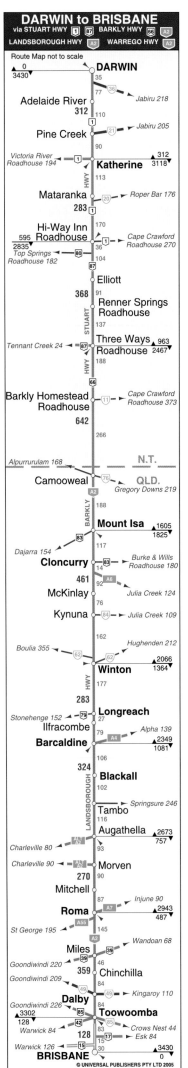

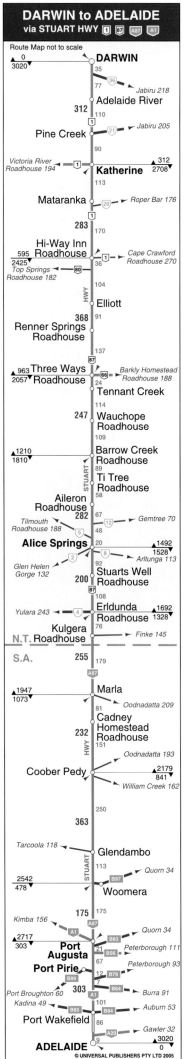

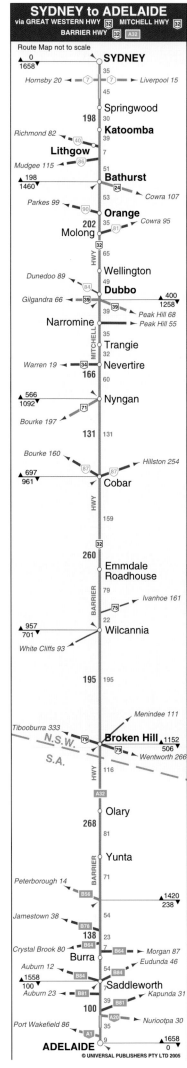

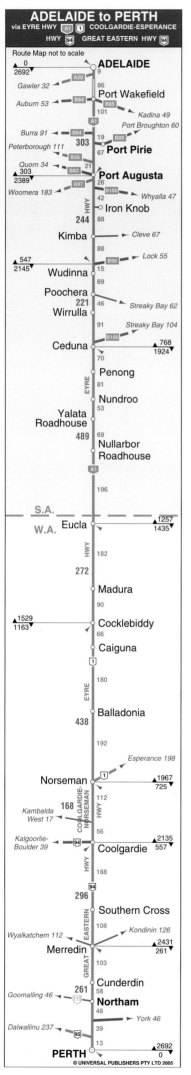
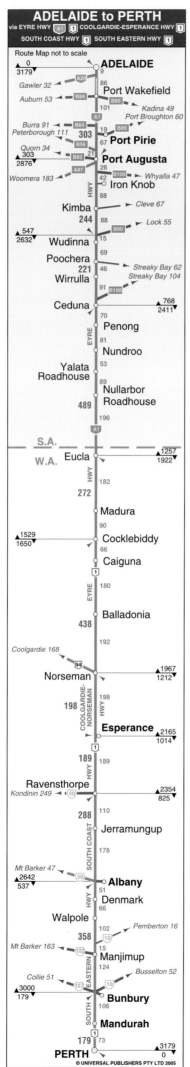
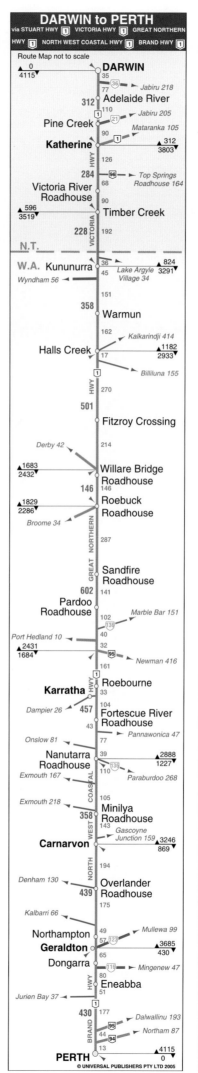
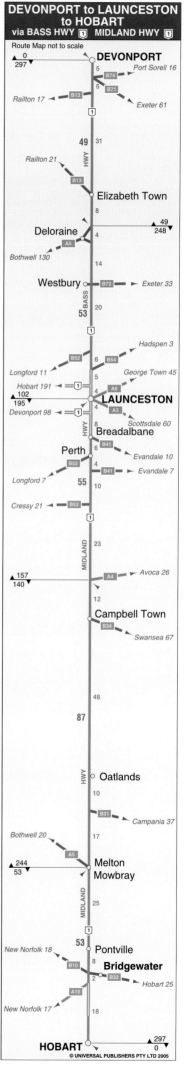

MAP SYMBOLS

Explanation of Map Symbols

MOTORWAY	HUME HIGHWAY	Dual Carriageway
HIGHWAY	PACIFIC HIGHWAY	Metroad, City Link
HIGHWAY	NEPEAN HIGHWAY	Through Route (Sealed Unsealed)
MORT ST	VULTURE ST	Major Road (Sealed Unsealed)
LAWSON RD	HONEYPOT RD	Minor Road (Sealed Unsealed)
LEURA ST		Street (Sealed Unsealed)
		Railway line, station
🚲 🚶	🚲 🚶	🚲 🚶 Cycle, Walking Track
		Ferry Route

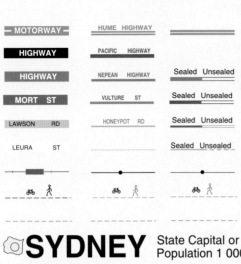

◎ **SYDNEY**	State Capital or Population 1 000 000 plus
○ **Geelong**	City - Population 100 000 - 1 000 000
○ **Bendigo**	City - Population 50 000 - 99 999
○ **Albany**	Town - Population 20 000 - 50 000
○ **Ulverstone**	Town - Population 5 000 - 20 000
○ Childers	Town - Population 1 000 - 5 000
○ Elliott	Town - Population 200 - 1000
○ Loch Sport	Locality - Population under 200
▢ *Birrimba*	Homestead
♠ Arawerr	Aboriginal Community
SYDNEY	Major Centre
Frankston	Main Centre
Toowong	Suburb
	Aboriginal Land
	Coral Reef
	Educational Institution
	Mall (City Map)
	Marine Park
	National Park
	Other Areas
	Prohibited Area
	Reserve, State Park, Conservation Park
	Sand
	State Forest

✈	Aerodrome
✈	Airport
✚	Ambulance
✗	BBQ
⋯	Beach
⛵	Boat Ramp
Wiso Bore	Bore
▬ ▪	Building
▲	Camping Ground
⌂	Caravan Park
Coolong Caves	Cave
12	Cumulative distance
↖	Cumulative distance marker
⚓	Forest Recreation Area
⛳ ⛳	Golf Course
✚ ✚	Hospital
⚙ Cluny	Hydro-Electric Power Station
ℹ ℹ	Information Centres
5	Intermediate distance
⛯	Lighthouse
✳ ✳	Lookout 360° and 180°
①	Metroad Route Marker
The ✕ Granites	Mine, Fossicking Area
Burke & Wills ▲ Memorial	Monument
+ *Glebe Hill* 135	Mountain, height in metres
23 A1 A1	National Route Marker
⬤ Della Gas Field	Oil/Gas Field
→	One Way Street
Ⓟ	Parking Area
⛩ ⛩	Picnic Area
★ ▪	Point of Interest
○	Roundabout
The ⠶ Granites	Ruins
⛲ Rocket, 1880	Shipwreck
🛒	Shopping Centre
20 C3	State Route Marker
🚻	Toilets
○ *Alice Well*	Well
⚘	Winery

Sleepy Bay, Freycinet National Park, Tasmania

AUSTRALIAN CAPITAL TERRITORY

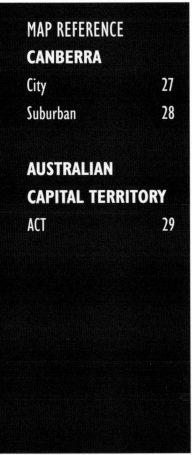

Main Information Centre
Canberra & Region
Visitors Centre
330 Northbourne Ave
Dickson, ACT 2602
Ph: (02) 6205 0044
or 1300 554 114
www.visitcanberra.com.au

Hot-air balloon in flight near Telstra Tower

The Australian Capital Territory has more to offer than just an insight into the political workings of the country, although it does this well. It's a place where Australia's history comes face-to-face with architectural modernity. You can discover the scientific workings of the universe, pay your respects to the soldiers who fought and died in the wars, venture back in time to the dinosaurs, create your own dollar coin or catch a close-up view of the fittest bodies on the continent. You can see artworks from all over the world, cycle around or sail on a large man-made lake, rise above it all in a hot-air balloon, visit Australia's only zooquarium, or stroll through the Australian National Botanic Gardens. The Australian Capital Territory has a diverse range of attractions and sights to suit every taste.

Located on perhaps some of the best sheep and cattle grazing land in Australia, the national capital is bordered by farmland, bushland, national parks and the Boboyan, Tidbinbilla and Booth ranges. It is completely surrounded by New South Wales and was selected as the site of the national capital in 1909, 8 years after Federation. Located inland, the creation of the Australian Capital Territory was a compromise to appease bitter interstate rivalry between New South Wales and Victoria.

The Australian Capital Territory encompasses only 0.03% of the entire continent, yet it is the political centre of the nation — rich with history and fine examples of modern architecture, art and culture. The capital city, Canberra, occupies around 15% of the Australian Capital Territory — a large percentage relative to the other capital cities of Australia. In addition to being Australia's only planned modern capital city, Canberra also has the distinction of being the only Australian capital city located inland.

Gilbraltar Rocks, Tidbinbilla Nature Reserve

MAIN PLACES OF INTEREST

Place	Map ref	Place	Map ref
Australian Institute of Sport	28 B2	Mt Ainslie Lookout	28 C3
Australian National Botanic Gardens	27 A1	Mugga Mugga	28 C4
Australian Reptile Centre/Bird Walk	28 B1	Namadgi National Park	29 B4
Australian War Memorial	27 E2	National Dinosaur Museum	28 B1
Calthorpes House	28 C4	National Gallery of Australia	27 D4
Canberra Deep Space		National Library of Australia	27 C4
Communication Complex	29 B3	National Museum of Australia	27 C3
Canberra Space Dome & Observatory	28 C2	National Zoo & Aquarium	28 B3
Cockington Green Gardens	28 B1	Old Parliament House	27 C4
Corin Forest	29 B3	Parliament House	27 C5
Cotter Dam	29 B2	Questacon — the National Science	
CSIRO Discovery	27 B1	& Technology Centre	27 D4
Gold Creek Village/Ginnindera Village	28 B1	Royal Australian Mint	28 B3
High Court of Australia	27 D4	ScreenSound Australia — the National	
Lake Burley Griffin	27 A3/D3	Film & Sound Archive	27 C2
Lanyon Historic Homestead	28 B6	Telstra Tower	28 B3
Molonglo Gorge	28 E4	Tidbinbilla Nature Reserve	29 B3

Parliament House at night

CANBERRA CITY

The area that is now known as Canberra was called the Limestone Plains in 1820 by the first European settlers. In 1824, Joshua Moore was the first European settler on a property of 2500ha beside the Murrumbidgee River. He named his property 'Canberry', an Aboriginal word meaning 'meeting place', and it is thought that the name Canberra derives from this. In 1825, wealthy Sydney merchant Robert Campbell took up 10 000ha of land, forming the first part of the Duntroon estate. In 1911, the Commonwealth Government acquired the surrounding land for the new capital city of Canberra. Construction began on the first public buildings in 1913, and the railway between Sydney and Canberra was built in 1914.

Canberra is known as one of the world's best planned cities. American architect Walter Burley Griffin was responsible for designing the city, which now occupies about 15% of the Australian Capital Territory. The Molonglo River, a tributary of the Murrumbidgee, was dammed in 1964 to create Lake Burley Griffin, Canberra's shimmering centrepiece. Many of Canberra's most important public buildings are situated close to its 35km shoreline. Ferries offer day and dinner cruises and the lake is popular for water activities such as swimming, sailing, sailboarding, rowing and fishing. A special time to visit Canberra is during Floriade, the annual spring flower festival. This is celebrated in September/October each year in Commonwealth Park on the banks of Lake Burley Griffin.

CANBERRA CITY PLACES OF INTEREST

	ref		ref
Anzac Parade	E2	Lake Burley Griffin	A3./D3
Australian National Botanic Gardens	A1	National Capital Exhibition	D3
Australian National University	B2	National Carillon	E4
Australian War Memorial	E2	National Gallery of Australia	D4
Blundell's Cottage	E3	National Library of Australia	C4
Canberra Museum & Gallery	D2	National Museum of Australia	C3
Canberra Theatre Centre	D2	National Rose Garden	D4
Captain Cook Memorial Water Jet	C3	Old Parliament House/	
Casino Canberra	D2	National Portrait Gallery	C4
City Hill Lookout	C2	Parliament House	C5
Commonwealth Park	D3	Questacon — the National Science	
CSIRO Discovery	B1	& Technology Centre	D4
Gorman House Arts Centre	D1	ScreenSound Australia — the National Film	
High Court of Australia	D4	& Sound Archive	C2

Top: Questacon — the National Science & Technology Centre; Middle: Australian War Memorial at dusk; Bottom: Floriade, spring flower festival

Scale 1:24 160

0   500   Metres

CONTINUES PAGE 28

Canberra Nature Park

Black Mountain
Nature Reserve

Australian National
Botanic Gardens

Australian National
Botanic Gardens

TURNER

BRADDON

Merici
College

Black
Mountain
Peninsula

West

Lake

Springbank
Island

Spinnaker
Island

Australian
National
University

Australian
National
University

Screensound
Australia

ACTON

City Hill
Lookout

Canberra Theatre Cntr

Casino

National
Convention
Centre

Canberra
Institute of
Technology

REID

Gorman House
Arts Centre

Australian
War
Memorial

Anzac
Parade

Yarralumla
Bay

Ferry Terminal
& Boat Hire

National Museum
of Australia

Captain Cook
Memorial Water Jet

Central
Basin

Commonwealth
Park

National Capital
Exhibition

Burley

West
Basin

Griffin

Blundell's
Cottage

Kings
Park

RUSSELL

National Library
of Australia

Questacon

High Court
of Australia

National
Carillon

National Gallery
of Australia

National
Rose Garden

National
Rose Garden

PARKES

East
Basin

Old Parliament
House / National
Portrait Gall.

Charles Sturt
University
Canberra Campus

Prime Minister's
Lodge

CAPITAL
HILL

Parliament
House

BARTON

Police
College

Forrest
Tennis
Club

FORREST

Manuka
Oval

KINGSTON

DEAKIN

Collins
Park

Canberra
Nature Park

Red Hill 720m

© UNIVERSAL PUBLISHERS PTY LTD 2005

CONTINUES PAGE 28

CONTINUES PAGE 28

CONTINUES PAGE 28

Scale 1:146 200

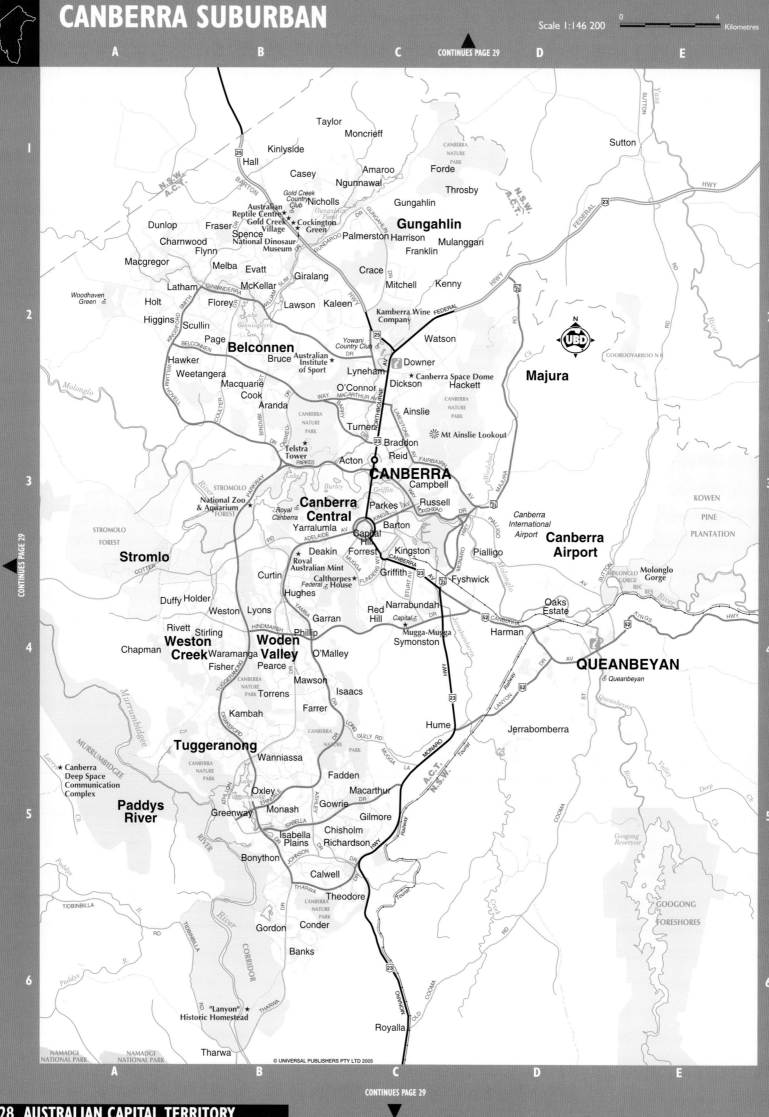

CONTINUES PAGE 29

CONTINUES PAGE 29

© UNIVERSAL PUBLISHERS PTY LTD 2005

Scale 1:384 600

0   10
Kilometres

CONTINUES PAGE 50

TO YASS
TO GUNNING
TO GOULBURN

A **B** **C** **D** **E**

Lake Burrinjuck

WEE JASPER N.R.

Wee Jasper

Lake George

Wombat

Oakey Ck

Sutton

Hillbrook
Purrorumba 886

BRINDABELLA NATIONAL PARK

Murrumbidgee

Wandana

Surveyor's Hill

Pankhurst

Brindabella Hills

Ginninderra Falls ★

Hall

Gungahlin

CANBERRA NATURE PARK

Affleck

Gidgee

Bywong

BRINDABELLA STATE CONS. AREA

Uriarra

WOODSTOCK N.R.

Uriara Crossing

Belconnen

Australian Institute of Sport ★

CANBERRA NATURE PARK

Mt Majura 888

Majura Field

Lambert

MiLiMANi

Lark Hill

Wamboin

Bungendore

Devils Peak

Coree Mtn 1421

Molonglo

Coppins Crossing

Black Mountain 813m

Mt Ainslie 843

CANBERRA

Fairbairn RAAF Base

KOWEN

BONDO STATE FOREST

Cotter Dam

National Zoo & Aquarium

Capital Hill

Lake Burley Griffin

Canberra International

PINE FOREST

HWY

Brindabella

Murrays Corner

BULLEN

Weston Creek

Red Hill

Woden Valley

KINGS

Queanbeyan

Burbong

Balcombe Hill 953

Molonglo

Hoskinstown

BIMBERI N.R.

Flints Crossing

Canberra Deep Space Communication Complex ★

Kambah Pool

RANGE NATURE

CANBERRA NATURE PARK

Mt Jerrabomberra 781

CUUMBUN I.N.R.

GOOGONG FORESHORES

Mt Aggie 1496

Mt Franklin 1644

★ Franklin Chalet

TIDBINBILLA

RESERVE

Bendora Dam

NATURE

Murrumbidgee River

Tuggeranong

Michelago Tourist Railway Steam Train Excursions ★

Googong Reservoir

Mt Molonglo 1120

Googong Hill 1019

Mt Ginni 1775

Gibraltar

Murrumbidgee River

Corridor

ROB ROY N.R.

YANUNUNBEYAN NATIONAL PARK

BIMBERI

Corin Dam

RESERVE

Woods Reserve

Booroomba

Lanyon

Tharwa

Craft Centre ★

Royalla

YANUNUNBEYAN STATE CONSERVATION AREA

KOSCIUSZKO

Corin Forest Mountain Retreat ★

Namadgi Visitor Centre

NATURE RESERVE

NATIONAL

Booroomba Rocks + Track

Mt Tennent 1383

GIGERLIN N.R.

Burra

Captains Flat

Mt Gingera 1857

NAMADGI

Canberra Deep Space Tracking Station (Honeysuckle Campground) ★

Honeysuckle

Williamsdale

KOSCIUSZKO

PARK

Walking

Naas

TINDERRY

Ballinafad

NATIONAL

Mt Bimben 1911

King Rock 1495

NATIONAL

Orroral Former Space Tracking Station ★

Rocky Crossing

TINDERRY NATURE

Mt Murray 1845

Orroral Crossing Campground

Glendale Crossing

RESERVE

Tinderry 1613

PARK

Middle

Mt Kelly

Rendezvous

Naas River

Clear

Tantangara reservoir

Morgan Peak 1875

SCABBY RANGE NATURE RESERVE

Gudgenby Hill 1740

Booth

Roberts

GOUROCK NATIONAL PARK

Mt Tamanang 1476

Yaouk

Sams

Michelago

BURNT SCHOOL N.R.

Jingera

YAOUK N.R.

Shanahans Mtn

MONARO HWY

STRIKE-A-LIGHT N.R.

Wallaby Hill 1310

Anembo

SNOWY MOUNTAINS HWY

Mt Clear Campground

Mt Clear 1603

Jerangle

Bredbo

TO COOMA

CONTINUES PAGE 50

NEW SOUTH WALES

Main Information Centre
Sydney Visitor Centre
106 George St
The Rocks, NSW 2000
Ph: (02) 9240 8788 or 132 077
www.visitnsw.com.au

Skiing in the Snowy Mountains

From the Snowy Mountains to the beaches of the east coast, New South Wales certainly has something for everyone. Spend a few days skiing; explore the magnificent gorges and waterfalls of the Blue Mountains by foot; take a tour of the Hunter Valley, home to some of the best wineries in Australia; discover hidden rainforests; fish in some of the country's most secluded spots; sail or cruise the bays of Sydney Harbour; watch whales and dolphins off the coast, visit the country's oldest townships; or perhaps just let a saltwater wave wash you ashore on one of the state's golden beaches.

The oldest state in Australia, New South Wales is a prime example of the diversity of the continent's landscape and climate. Located in the south-east of the country, New South Wales is 7 times the size of Great Britain and the same size as California. It boasts the largest population of any state or territory in Australia with around 6.5 million people. The climate varies from subtropical temperatures in the north and along parts of the coast, to the dry, desert-like conditions of the far west, and to the snowfalls of the Southern Alps.

Throughout New South Wales, there are many reminders of a rich historical and cultural heritage. Aboriginal middens, rock art and 60 000 year-old artefacts at Lake Mungo are amongst the lasting legacy of the first Australians.

European settlement, despite its relatively shorter history, has had a profound impact on the land. The relics of gold-mining towns, heritage-listed buildings and the present-day built environment are testament to the tremendous changes that have taken place since Captain Arthur Phillip raised the British flag at Sydney Cove in 1788.

Sydney, the state capital, also has the largest population of any city in the country and is the business and financial capital of Australia. Since the 2000 Olympic Games, Sydney has cemented its reputation as a city with a uniquely welcoming and cosmopolitan atmosphere.

MAIN PLACES OF INTEREST

Place	Map ref	Place	Map ref
Abercrombie Caves	46 E6	Moree Hot Mineral Baths	42 C3
Age of Fishes Museum, Canowindra	46 D5	Mount Warning National Park	43 D1
Australian Reptile Park, Gosford	47 C5	Mungo National Park	44 E5
Bald Rock National Park	43 B2	Murramarang National Park	50 E3
Barrington Tops National Park	47 C2	Myall Lakes National Park	47 D3
Blue Mountains National Park	47 A5	Port Stephens	47 D3
Bondi Beach, Sydney	37 E2	Royal National Park	37 A6
Bradman Museum, Bowral	52	Shear Outback, Hay	45 B6
Cape Byron	43 D1	Siding Spring Observatory, Coonabarabran	46 D1
Central Tilba	50 D4	Sydney Harbour Bridge	33 C1
Cowra Japanese Garden	46 D5	Sydney Opera House	33 D1
CSIRO Radio Telescope, Parkes	46 C4	Sydney Tower	33 C3
Darling Harbour, Sydney	33 B4	Taronga Zoo, Sydney	35 D6
Dorrigo National Park	43 C5	The Great Lakes, Foster	47 E3
Hill End & Sofala	46 E4	The Rocks, Sydney	33 C1
Hunter Valley Wineries	47 B3	The Three Sisters, Katoomba	47 A5
Jenolan Caves	47 A5	Timbertown, Wauchope	47 E1
Kiama Blowhole	50 E1	Trial Bay Gaol, South West Rocks	43 C6
Killer Whale Museum, Eden	50 D6	Warrumbungle National Park	46 D1
Kosciuszko National Park	50 B4/5	Wellington Caves	46 D3
Lake Macquarie	47 C4	Western Plains Zoo, Dubbo	46 D2
Maitland & Morpeth	47 C3	Wombeyan Caves	50 D1
Menindee Lakes	44 C3	Zig Zag Railway, Lithgow	47 A5

NEW SOUTH WALES KEY MAP

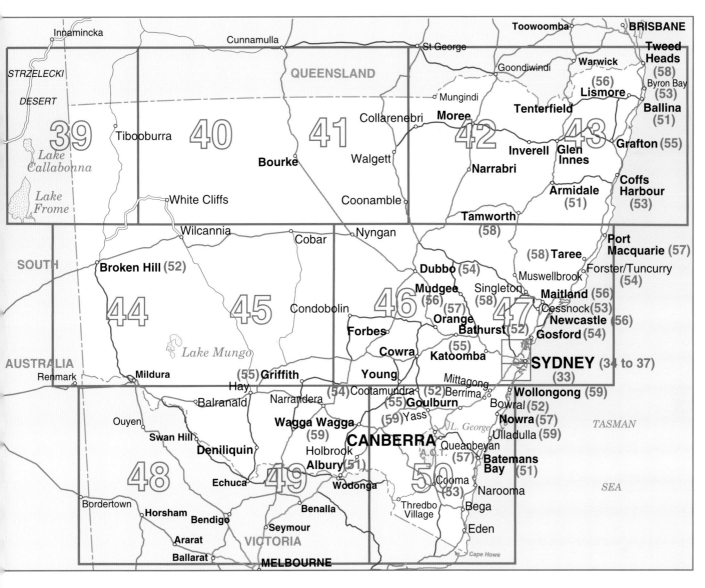

Tomaree Head Lookout, Tomaree National Park, Port Stephens

SYDNEY CITY

Sydney Cove, now known as Circular Quay, was where Captain Arthur Phillip proclaimed the colony of New South Wales on 26 January 1788. First Fleet convicts laboured to clear the site around Sydney Cove that was later to become the City of Sydney. The Rocks is an integral part of Sydney's history and the sandstone buildings and winding lanes built by the convicts in this area are still in use today.

Sydney, Australia's largest city, is a cosmopolitan city that offers a huge variety of attractions for visitors. The magnificent natural harbour defines the city. Along its shores are Sydney's major icons, the Sydney Harbour Bridge and Sydney Opera House. Circular Quay, the Rocks, Darling Harbour, Cockle Bay and the Royal Botanic Gardens are also around the harbour's shoreline and are main attractions for visitors and locals. Sightseeing and getting around Sydney's CBD is fairly easy as it is quite compact.

Sydney's surburbia reaches out to the Hawkesbury River to the north, the Blue Mountains to the west and the Royal National Park to the south. Historic suburbs that reflect early colonial times include Richmond, Windsor and Parramatta. A string of easily accessible family and surf beaches runs all the way from Palm Beach to Manly north of the harbour, and from world-famous Bondi to Cronulla in the south.

SYDNEY CITY PLACES OF INTEREST

	ref		ref
Anzac War Memorial	C4	National Maritime Museum	B3
Archibald Fountain	C4	National Trust Centre	B2
Art Gallery of New South Wales	D3	Powerhouse Museum	B5
Australian Museum	C4	Queen Victoria Building	C4
Cadman's Cottage	C2	Royal Botanic Gardens	D2
Chinatown	B5	St Marys Cathedral	C4
Chinese Garden of Friendship	B4	Star City Casino	A3
Circular Quay	C2	State Library of New South Wales	C3
Customs House	C2	Sydney Aquarium	B3
Darling Harbour	B4	Sydney Entertainment Centre	B5
Fort Denison	E1	Sydney Harbour Bridge	C1
Hyde Park	C4	Sydney Observatory	B2
Justice & Police Museum	C2	Sydney Opera House	D1
Martin Place	C3	Sydney Tower	C3
Museum of Contemporary Art	C2	Sydney Town Hall	B4
Museum of Sydney	C2	The Rocks	C1

Top: Sydney Harbour Bridge; Middle: Sydney Opera House; Bottom: Darling Harbour at night

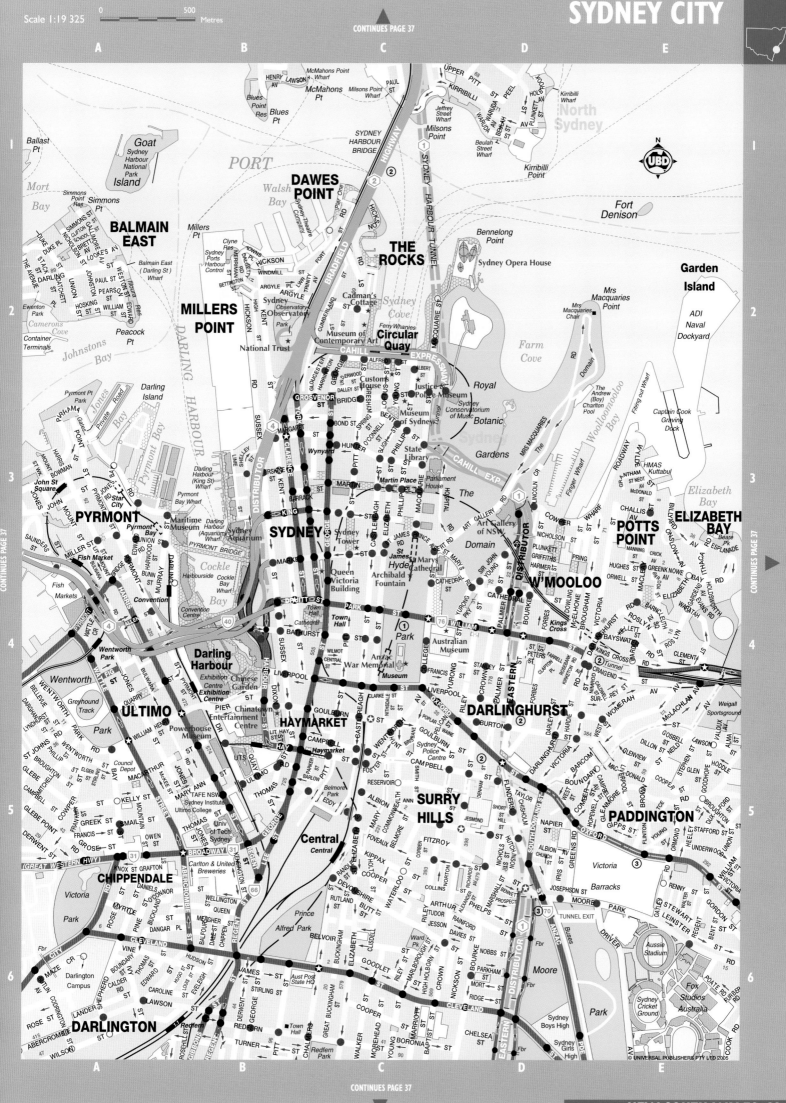

0 5 Kilometres

CONTINUES PAGE 47

A   B   C   D   E

East Kurrajong
Stanley Park
The Slopes
Tennyson
Glossodia
Pacific Park Water Ski Gardens
Maroota South
Ebenezer
Hawkesbury Waters Leisure Park
Kallawatta Park
Riverside Oaks
Carawah Campsite
Wheeny Lagoon
70
Kurmond
Freemans Reach
Wilberforce
Historic Church
Hope Farm
CATTAI NATIONAL PARK
Cattai
Arondunter Swamp
Forest Glen
50
North Richmond
Lowlands
Park Entrance
Cattai National Park (Mitchell Park)
65
45
Windsor Riverside
Cornwallis
Windsor Riverside Tourist Park
Gronos Point
Canning
Riverside
Pitt Town
Pitt Town
60
Maraylya
Hillside
Glenorie
Richmond Bridge
Richmond Ex-servicemens Club Sporting Complex
Windsor Bridge
Fitzroy Bridge
Pitt Town Bottoms
Pitt Town Lagoon
SCHEYVILLE NATIONAL PARK
Richmond
Clarks Island
RICHMOND RAAF BASE
Scheyville
Middle Dural
Agnes Banks
Yarramundi Bridge
Clarendon
Windsor
Mcgraths Hill
55
Oakville
Box Hill
65
Yarramundi Lagoon
Western Sydney Institute TAFE Richmond Campus
University of Western Sydney (Hawkesbury) Richmond Campus
Windsor Country Club
Mulgrave
A-Vina
Nelson
Kenthurst
AGNES BANKS NAT. RES.
South Windsor
Nepean Raceway
Bligh Park
Vineyard
Annangrove
Londonderry
WINDSOR DOWNS NATURE RESERVE
50
Round Corner
John Morony Correctional Centre
Windsor Downs
Glenhaven
Berkshire Park
Waste Services Depot
45
Rouse Hill Estate
Rouse Hill
Riverstone
Vinegar Hill Woolshed & Kellyville
CASTLEREAGH NATURE RESERVE
Guard Dog Training Centre
Schofields
Ok Caravan Corral
Kellyville Ridge
Kellyville
Glenhaven
Cranebrook
Shanes Park
Marsden Park
Waste Services Depot
Stanhope Gardens
Parklea Gardens
Parklea
Castle Hill
Llandilo
Airservices Australia International Radio Transmitter Station
50
Western Sydney Institute of TAFE
Quakers Hill
Acacia Gardens
Norwest Business Park
Penrith Whitewater Stadium
Sydney International Regatta Centre
Willmot
Shalvey
Colebee
Uni of Western Syd (Hawkesbury)
Kings Park
Glenwood
Bella Vista
Cambridge Gardens
Werrington Downs
Bidwill
Hassall Grove
Dean Park
40
Kings Langley
Baulkham Hills
Penrith
Cambridge Park
Werrington County
Dunheved
Lethbridge Park
Blackett
Oakhurst
Hebersham
Glendenning
Marayong
Lalor Park
Kingswood
Werrington
North St Marys
Tregear
Emerton
Dharruk
Plumpton
Woodcroft
Woodstock
Doonside
Featherdale Wildlife Park
Seven Hills
Winston Hills
University of Western Sydney (Nepean)
St Marys
Whalan
Mount Druitt
Rooty Hill
Mount Druitt
Blacktown
Old Toongabbie
Northmead North Parramatta
South Penrith
Western Sydney Institute of TAFE
Oxley Park
Colyton
Minchinbury
Arndell Park
Huntingwood
Seven Hills
Toongabbie
James Ruse
Claremont Meadows
45
Eastern Creek
Girraween
Pendle Hill
Westmead
Chatsworth
St Clair
Hewitt
40
MOTORWAY
WESTERN
Prospect
Wentworthville
Parramatta
Orchard Hills
Erskine Park
Eastern Creek Raceway
35
Prospect Reservoir
Greystanes
South Wentworthville
Mays Hill
Harris Park
RAAF DEFENCE AREA
Western Sydney International Dragway
Sydney Water Supply
Holroyd
Merrylands West
Merrylands
Granville
Horsley Park
Supply
Pipeline
Woodpark
Guildford West
South Granville
Sydney International Equestrian Centre
Wetherill Park
Smithfield
Guildford
Mt Vernon
CSIRO Research Station
Mills Cross (Radio Telescope)
Bossley Park
Fairfield
Prairiewood
Fairfield Heights
Yennora
Old Guildford
© UNIVERSAL PUBLISHERS PTY LTD 2005

CONTINUES PAGE 47

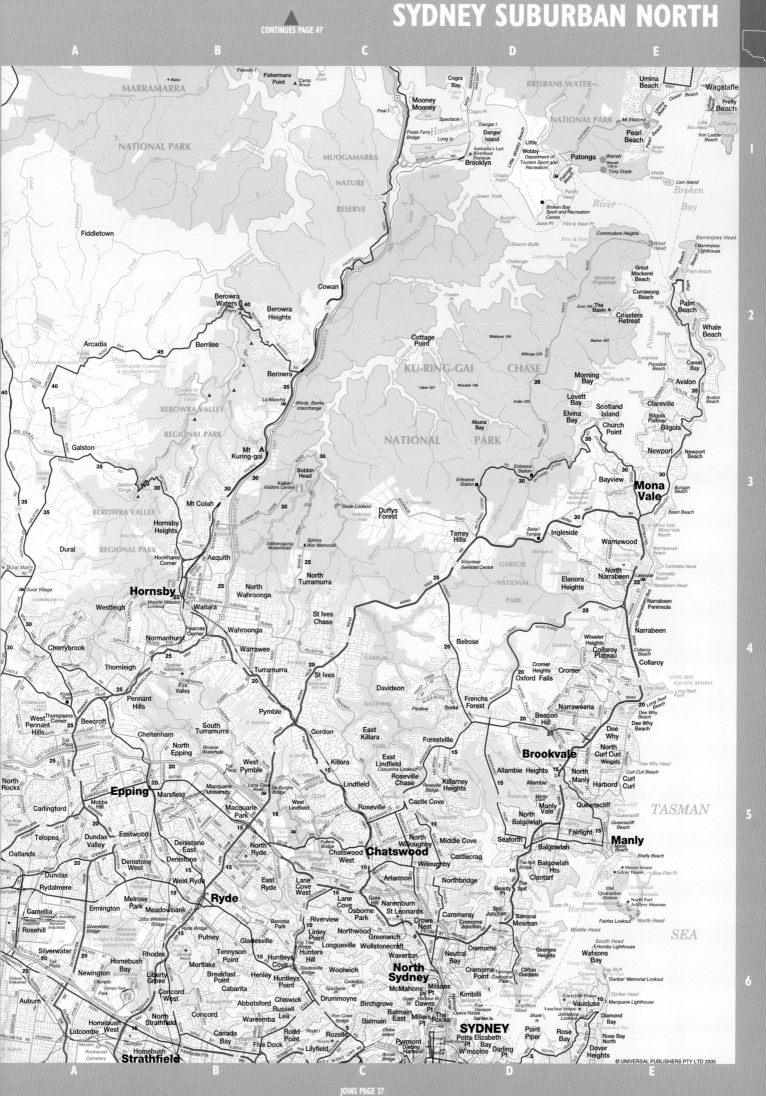

CONTINUES PAGE 47

© UNIVERSAL PUBLISHERS PTY LTD 2005

0 5 Kilometres

JOINS PAGE 34

A   B   C   D   E

Parramatta

RAAF
DEFENCE AREA

Erskine
Park

Prospect

South
Wentworthville
Mays
Hill
Greystanes
Holroyd
Merrylands
West   Merrylands
Woodpark
Guildford
West

Horsley Park

Mt Vernon

Wetherill Park
Smithfield
Yennora   Old Guildford
Guildford
Chester
Hill

Luddenham

Mills Cross
(Radio Telescope)
University of Sydney
McGarvie Smith
Veterinary Farm
Kemps
Creek

Bossley
Park
Prairiewood
Fairfield
West
Fairfield
Heights
Fairfield
Fairfield
East
Villawood
Sefton

CSIRO
Research
Station

Badgerys
Creek

Sydney International
Shooting Centre

Abbotsbury
Greenfield
Park
St Johns
Park
Wakeley
Edensor
Park
Canley
Heights
Canley
Vale
Carraman

Cecil
Hills

Bonnyrigg
Heights
Bonnyrigg
Cabramatta
West
Cabramatta
Bass Hill

Vicarys

Cecil
Park

Green
Valley
Heckenberg
Mt
Pritchard
Lansvale
Chipping
Norton
Georges
Hall

Rossmore

Austral

West
Hoxton
Hoxton
Park
Carnes
Hill

Hinchinbrook
Busby
Sadleir
Ashcroft

Warwick
Farm
Bankstown
Airport
Condell
Park

Bringelly

Miller
Cartwright
Liverpool
Moorebank
Milperra

University
of
Sydney

Prestons
Lumea
Casula
Moorebank
Village
Anzac
Village
Hammondville
Wattle
Grove

Horningsea
Park
Chatham
Village
Engineer
Barracks
Panania
East
Hills
Picnic
Point

Cobbitty

Leppington

Edmondson
Park
The Cross Roads
Glenfield
Holsworthy
Barracks
Voyager
Point
Pleasure
Point
Sandy
Point

Denham
Court
Ingleburn
Military Camp
Macquarie
Links

Oran
Park
Catherine
Field

Varroville
Macquarie
Fields
Holsworthy

Gledswood Homestead
& Winery

St Andrews
Home for Boys
"Emerald Hill"

Ingleburn
Long
Point

Harrington
Park

Kearns
Raby
St
Andrews
Bow
Bowing
Barden
Ridge

Ellis
Lane
Eschol Park
Odyssey
House
Eagle
Vale
Minto
Lucas Heights

HOLSWORTHY

Kirkham
Smeaton
Grange
Currans
Hill
Claymore
Minto
Heights

MILITARY RESERVE

RESTRICTED ACCESS

Narellan
Narellan
Vale
Blairmount
Woodbine
Leumeah
Kentlyn

Elderslie
Camden
Mount
Annan
Blair
Athol
Campbelltown
Ruse

Spring
Farm
Macarthur
Bridge
Glen
Alpine
Ambarvale
Airds

Camden
South
Menangle
Park
Rosemeadow
St
Helens
Park

Cawdor
Sugarloaf
213m
Wedderburn
Heathcote
Scout Camp

HEATHCOTE
NATIONAL
PARK

Menangle
Macarthur
Bridge
Gilead
Lake
Woronora
Waterfall   Waterfall

© UNIVERSAL PUBLISHERS PTY LTD 2005

A   B   C   D   E

CONTINUES PAGE 47

JOINS PAGE 35

CONTINUES PAGE 47

Cascades, Katoomba Falls, Blue Mountains National Park

Scale 1:1 547 400

0   40   Kilometres

CONTINUES PAGE 101

A   B   C   D   E

Gidgealpa Gas Field
Moomba Oil & Gas Field
Burke-Dullingan Oil & Gas Field
Moomba (Private)
157
Della Gas Field
INNAMINCKA REGIONAL RESERVE
Toolachee Gas Field
Orientos
Bransby
Bransby Ck.
Epsilon
Santos
Tickalara Oil Field
Munro Oil Field
Naryilco
Ticklara
Merty Merty
STRZELECKI DESERT
Gas Pipeline
TRACK
Gas Pipeline
QUEENSLAND / SOUTH AUSTRALIA
Omicron
Bulloo Lake
Warry Ck.
QUEENSLAND
Bollards Lagoon
Strzelecki Crossing
120 Bollards Lagoon
Cameron Corner
Corner Store
Tooma Gate
Warri Gate
Wompah Gate
Adelaide Gate
Onepah
NEW SOUTH WALES
Lindon
Fort Grey
Olive Downs
96
STURT NATIONAL PARK
123 STRZELECKI REGIONAL RESERVE
Lake Blanche
Montecollina Bore
Waka
Lake Stewart
133
Mount Wood Gorge
Narriearra
Tibooburra
Gum Vale
Mount Wood
Pindera Downs
PINDERA DOWNS
Hewart Downs
Mt Poole 250
Mt Sturt
Clifton Downs
UBD (compass)
Theldarpa
Depot Glen
Yandama
Pooles Grave
Milparinka
LAKE CALLABONNA FOSSIL RESERVE
Lake Callabonna
Mt Brown 274
Peak Hill
Mount Browne
Brindiwilpa
Salisbury Downs
Hawker Gate
Hawker Gate House
Mt Shannon 332
Mount Shannon
Coally
111
One Tree
Salt L.
North Mulga
Smithville House
Boolka Gate
Lake Wallace
Boullia
Mount Arrowsmith
Callindary
Lake Cootabarlow
Old Quinyambie
Pincally
Bullea L.
Cobham
Pulgamurtie
94
Allandy
Border Downs
Pimpara Lake
47
SILVER CITY HWY
Milpa
Morden
Lake Pundalpa
Sanpah
Packsaddle
Yelka
Packsaddle Roadhouse
Wonnaminta
Kayrunnera
Lake Elder
Pine Ridge
Pine View
The Veldt
Nundora
Nuntherungie
Westwood Downs
Balcannia L.
The Selection
Broughams Gate
Avenel
Tielta
Mount Westwood
Nundoolka
Noonthorangie
Marrapina
Koonawarra
COTURAUNDEE N.R.
New Quinyambie
Floods Creek
121
MUTAWINTJI NATIONAL PARK
LAKE FROME REGIONAL RESERVE
Fowlers Gap
155
Mt Wright 349
McDougalls Well
Mutawintji Historic Site
Tirlta
Mutawintji
Lake Frome
Mount Woowoolahra
Frome Downs
Vermin Proof Fence
Kantappa
Corona
Sturts Meadows
Acacia Downs
Grassmere
Benagerie
Bijerkerno
Langawirra
Boorungie
Mulga Valley
Wilangee
Mawarra
Waterbag
Woolshed
Paringa
Mount Gipps
Langidoon
Glenora
Mulyungarie

20 © UNIVERSAL PUBLISHERS PTY LTD 2005

CONTINUES PAGE 123

JOINS PAGE 40

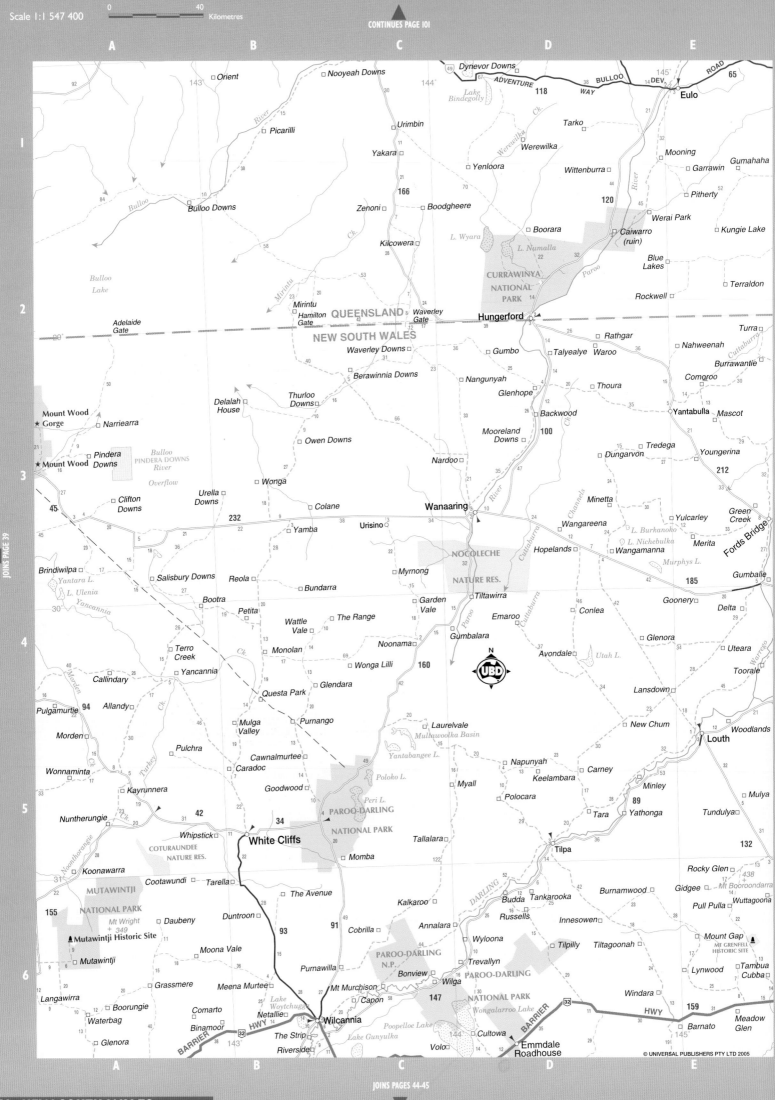

CONTINUES PAGE 101

JOINS PAGE 39

JOINS PAGES 44-45

CONTINUES PAGE 102

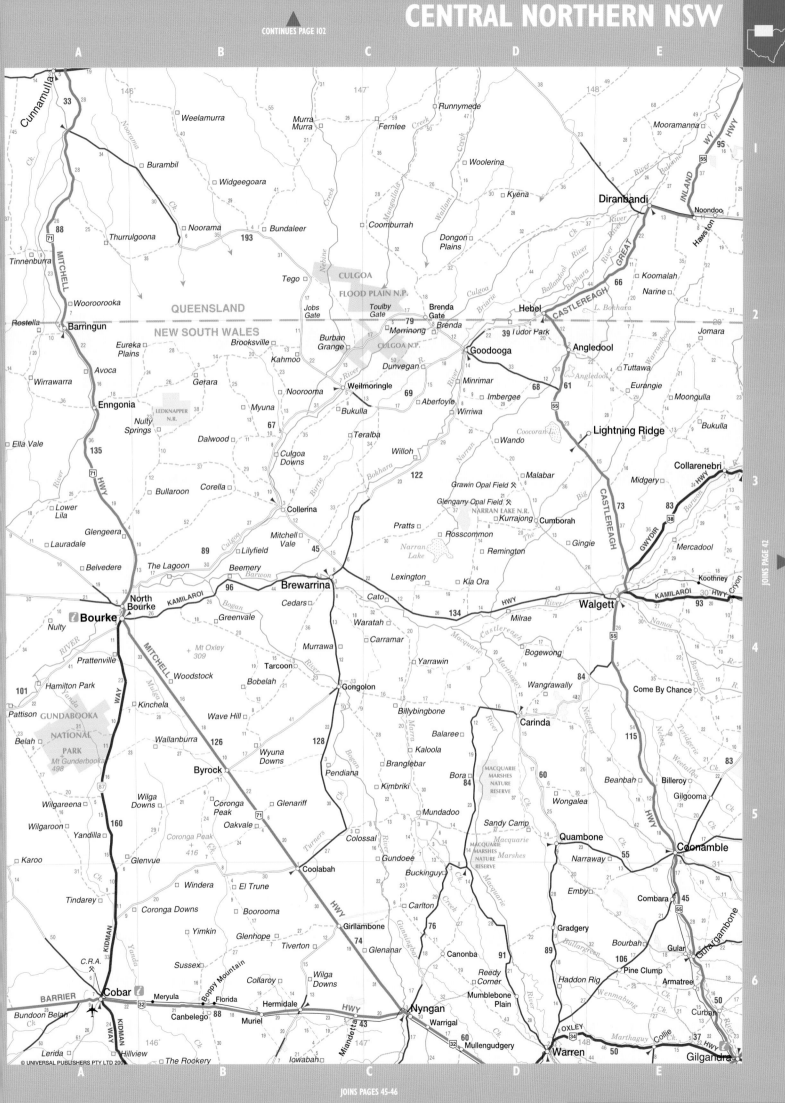

JOINS PAGE 42

Scale 1:1 547 400

0 ___ 40 Kilometres

CONTINUES PAGE 103

A   B   C   D   E

QUEENSLAND
NEW SOUTH WALES

Mooramanna
Dirranbandi
Noondoo
Hawston
Dumminnie
Koomalah
Narine
Nindigully
Thallon
Daymar
Gradule
Weengallon
Nariel
Talwood
Bungunya
Toobeah
Booberoi
Goondiwindi
Boggabilla
Kurumbul
Yelarbon
Wyaga
Whetstone
Inglewood
Cobba-da-mana
Koorongara
Magee
Beebo
Texas
Boomi
Wearne
North Star
Yetman
Bonshaw
Mungindi
Neeworra
Weemelah
Bengerang
Garah
Moppin
Ashley
Croppa Creek
Yallaroi
Crooble
Coolatai
Wallangra
Ashford
Bukkulla
Oakwood
Nullamanna
Collarenebri
Midgery
Pokataroo
Bullarah
Moree
Wongabinda
Pallamallawa
Biniguy
Gravesend
Warialda
Graman
Inverell
Elsmore
Gilgai
Stannifer
Tingha
Merrywinebone
Rowena
Millie
Tycannah
Gurley
Terry Hie Hie
Bingara
Gum Flat
Mount Russell
Delungra
Sapphire City
Mercadool
Koothney
Cryon
Bugilbone
Old Burren
Yarranbah
Bunna Bunna
Bellata
Caroda
Upper Horton
Burren Junction
Cubbaroo
Merah North
Wee Waa
Edgeroi
Trevallyn
Cobbadah
Barraba
Torryburn
Abington
Come By Chance
Pilliga
Culgoora
CSIRO Australia Telescope
Kiandool
Narrabri
MOUNT KAPUTAR
Mt Kaputar 1508
NATIONAL PARK
Turrawan
Maules Creek
Bundarra
Yarrowyck
Kingstown
Brushgrove
Rocky River
Gwabegar
Baan Baa
Wean
Upper Manilla
Retreat
Watsons Creek
Billeroy
Gilgooma
Kenebri
Boggabri
Kelvin
Manilla
Mundowney
Coonamble
Teridgerie
Emerald Hill
Somerton
Attunga
Moore
Woolbrook
Baradine
Goorianawa
Gunnedah
Carroll
Winton
Westdale
Moonbi
Limbri
Kootingal
Combara
Bugaldie
Yearinan
Rocky Glen
Mullaley
Curlewis
Piallaway
Nea
Tamworth
Nemingha
Piallamore
Weabonga
Bourbah
Gular
Gulargambone
Warrumbungle
Siding Spring Observatory
WARRUMBUNGLE N.P.
Coonabarabran
Warkton
Purlewaugh
Tambar Springs
Spring Ridge
Breeza
Currabubula
Duri
Dungowan
Loombrah
Woolomin
Niangala
Armatree
Tooraweenah
Curban
Biddon
New Mollyan
Binnaway
Murrawal
Deringulla
Premer
Yanergee
Tamarang
Caroona
Werris Creek
Nundle
Collie
Gilgandra
Mooren
Piambra
Weetaliba
Bomera
Connemarra
Bundella
Yarraman
Blackville
Pine Ridge
Quirindi
Old Warrah
Willow Tree
Wallabadah
Barry

HWY — NEWELL HWY — CARNARVON HWY — CASTLEREAGH HWY — GWYDIR HWY — KAMILAROI HWY — OXLEY HWY — KAMILAROI HWY — FOSSICKERS WAY — NEW ENGLAND HWY — BRUXNER HWY — CUNNINGHAM HWY — LEICHHARDT HWY — GORE HWY

© UNIVERSAL PUBLISHERS PTY LTD 2005

JOINS PAGE 41
JOINS PAGES 46-47

42 NEW SOUTH WALES

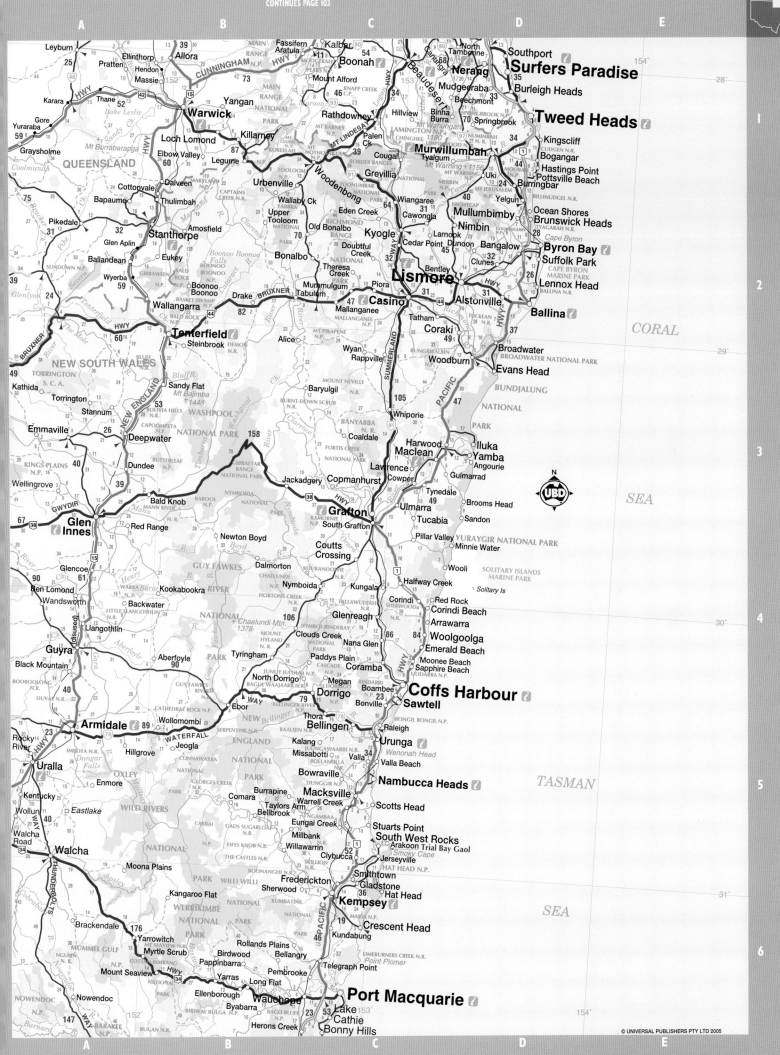

CONTINUES PAGE 103

0   40   Kilometres

JOINS PAGES 39-40

A   B   C   D   E

New Quinyambie
Avenel   Tielta   Tielta
Mount Westwood
Floods Creek 121
Fowlers Gap
Selection
Marrapina   Koonawarra   COTURAUNDEE NATURE RES.
Cootawundi   Tarella   The Avenue
McDougalls Well
Mount Woowoolahra
Corona
Sturts Meadows
155
MUTAWINTJI NATIONAL PARK
Mt Wright + 349
Daubeny   Duntroon
93   91   Cobrilla
Kantappa
Mulga Valley
Wilangee
Bijerkerno
Acacia Downs
Tirlta
Mutawintji Historic Site
Mutawintji
Moona Vale
Purnawilla
Mulyungarie
Paringa
Mawarra
Langawirra
Grassmere   Meena Murtee   Mt Murchison   Capon
Mooleulooloo   Yarramba
Eldee
Purnamoota
Mount Gipps
Langidoon
Boorungie
Waterbag
Glenora
Comarto
Binamoor   Netallie   Wilcannia
Kalkaroo
54   Yanco Glen
Stephens Creek
Daydream
Glen Idol
Metford
Hazel Vale   BARRIER 195
Churinga
The Strip
Cawkers Well   Riverside
Goonalga
Boolcoomata
Mundi Mundi   Silverton   Living Desert Sculptures   Mount Gipps   K Tank
Glen Gipps
Topar   Little Topar Roadhouse
Bilpa
Culpaullin   Billilla   Goonoolchrach   Wave Hill
Broken Hill
Inkerman
Byrnedale   153   Carmala
Allambie
Wompinie   HWY 32   Cockburn
Fruit Fly Exclusion
Quarry Hill
Nelia Gaan   Barraroo   Teryawynnia   Cowary
Mingary   A32   150   Cultana   Tepco   Pine Creek
Eureka   Kinalung
Horse Lake
Wirryilka
Four Mile Lake
Balaka   Viewmont   Blantyre   Nyngynderry
Glen Albyn
Aroona   Corella
Pinnacles   Huonville   Mulculca
Quondong 111
Kars
Balaka Lake   Windalla   Denian   Moseys Lake   Terrawynya Lake
Ballara   Ascot Vale   Redan
Sunset Strip   KINCHEGA   Haythorpe   Pamamaroo L.   Glen Ora
Maldorkey   Enmore   Pine Point   Eaglehawk
L. Surprise   Menindee   Larloona   Ashmont
Boola Boolka   Surveyors Lake
Burta   Wonga   Langwell
Eurobilli Lake   Menindee Lake   Menindee
Wanda   North Lake   Boola Boolka Lake   Brummeys Lake   Burtundy
Mutooroo   125   Netley   Blackwell
Cawndilla Lake   Kinchenga   Waterloo Lake
Kaleentha Loop   Ratcatchers Lake
Duffield   Buckalow   Middle Camp   Kudgee
NATIONAL PARK   Nettlegoe Lake   Tandou Lake
Nelia Outstation   Gum Lake   Manara Mine
Mazar   South Ita
Tandau   Bindarra   Blackfellows   Sayers Lake   Manara   201   Darnick
Kimberley   Budgeree   Harriedale
Willaba   Dalmorino   Karpa Kora   Overnewton
Terrananya   Nagaela   Woolcunda   Double Yards   Harcourt   123   Mooloolerie
Tor Downs   Karoola
Oakvale   Loch Lilly   Coombah Roadhouse   Popio   Cuthero   Whurlie   Wilkurra   C Lake
Oakbank   Twin Wells   Popiltah L.   Popio Lake   Chalky Well   Bulgamurra   Mururulu Lake
Nanya   Popiltah   Travellers Lake   Eulo   Panban
Morgan Vale   DANGGALI   Aston   Mullingar   Pooncarie   Balmoral   Mandelman
CONSERVATION PARK   TARAWI NATURE RESERVE   Nialia Lake   Yelta L.   Manilla   Garnpung Lake   Gol Gol   Binda
Windamingle   Nearie Lake   Reaka
Canopus   Warrawenia Lake   NEARIE LAKE N.R.   Milkengay L.   Trelega   Top Hut   Lake Leaghur   Round Plain
Hypurna   141   Bunneringee   Twelve Mile   Cavan   Mungo   MUNGO NATIONAL PARK   Boree Plains
CHOWILLA REGIONAL RESERVE   118   Arumpo   Marona
Pine Camp   Nulla   Lamplough   Burtundy   The Walls of China   Iona
Hazeldel   Ashvale   Petro   Chibnalwood Lakes   Langleydale
CHOWILLA GAME RESERVE   NEW SOUTH WALES   Warranangra   Avoca   Wamberra   Turlee   68
Chaffey   Cal Lal   Rufus River   Moorna   Dareton   34 HWY   Belinar   Bidura
Renmark   Paringa   Wentworth   Mildura   Gol Gol
Renmark North   COOLTONG CON. PARK   Yamba   STURT 73   Meringur North   81   Merbein   Merbein South   Monak   Upson Downs   Prungle
Berri   Taldra   Morkalla   Meringur   Cullulleraine   Irymple   Red Cliffs   Monak   85   Gulthul   Bramah
Loxton   Noora   Werrimull   Benetook   Yatpool   Koorakee   Penarie
Nangari   Wunkar   VICTORIA   Carwarp   Nangiloc   Benanee   Euston   Robinvale   Balranald

JOINS PAGE 48

© UNIVERSAL PUBLISHERS PTY LTD 2005

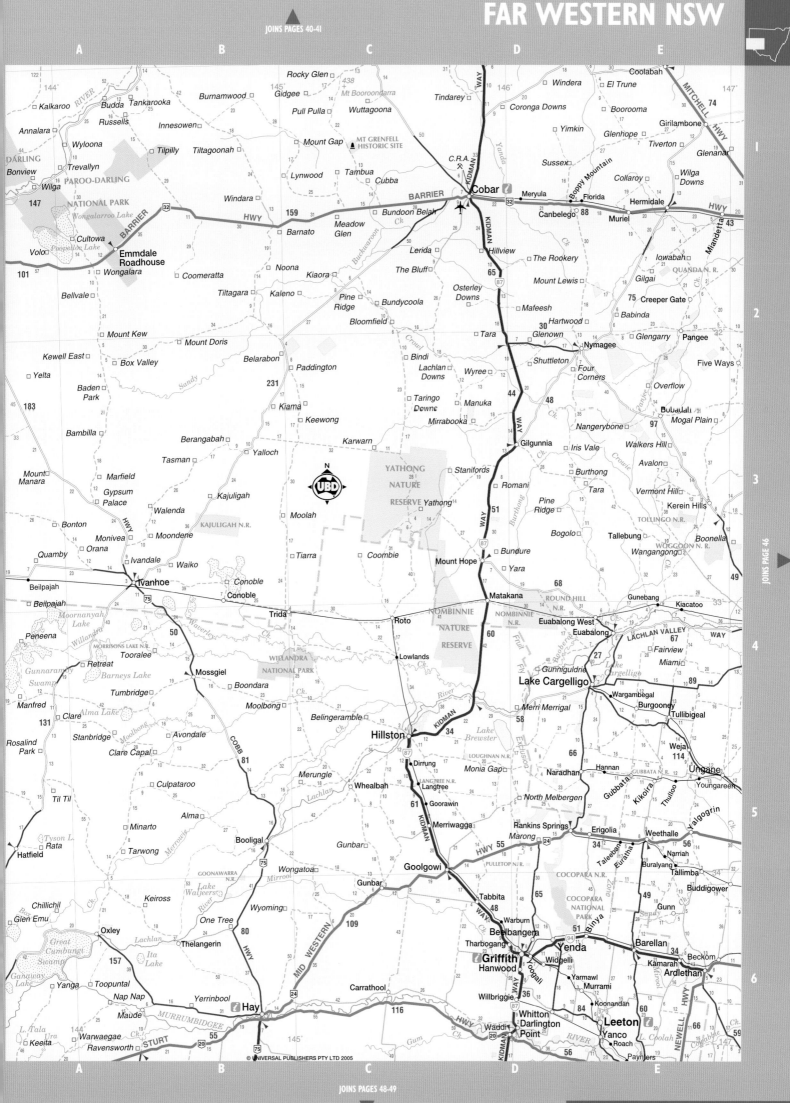

JOINS PAGE 46

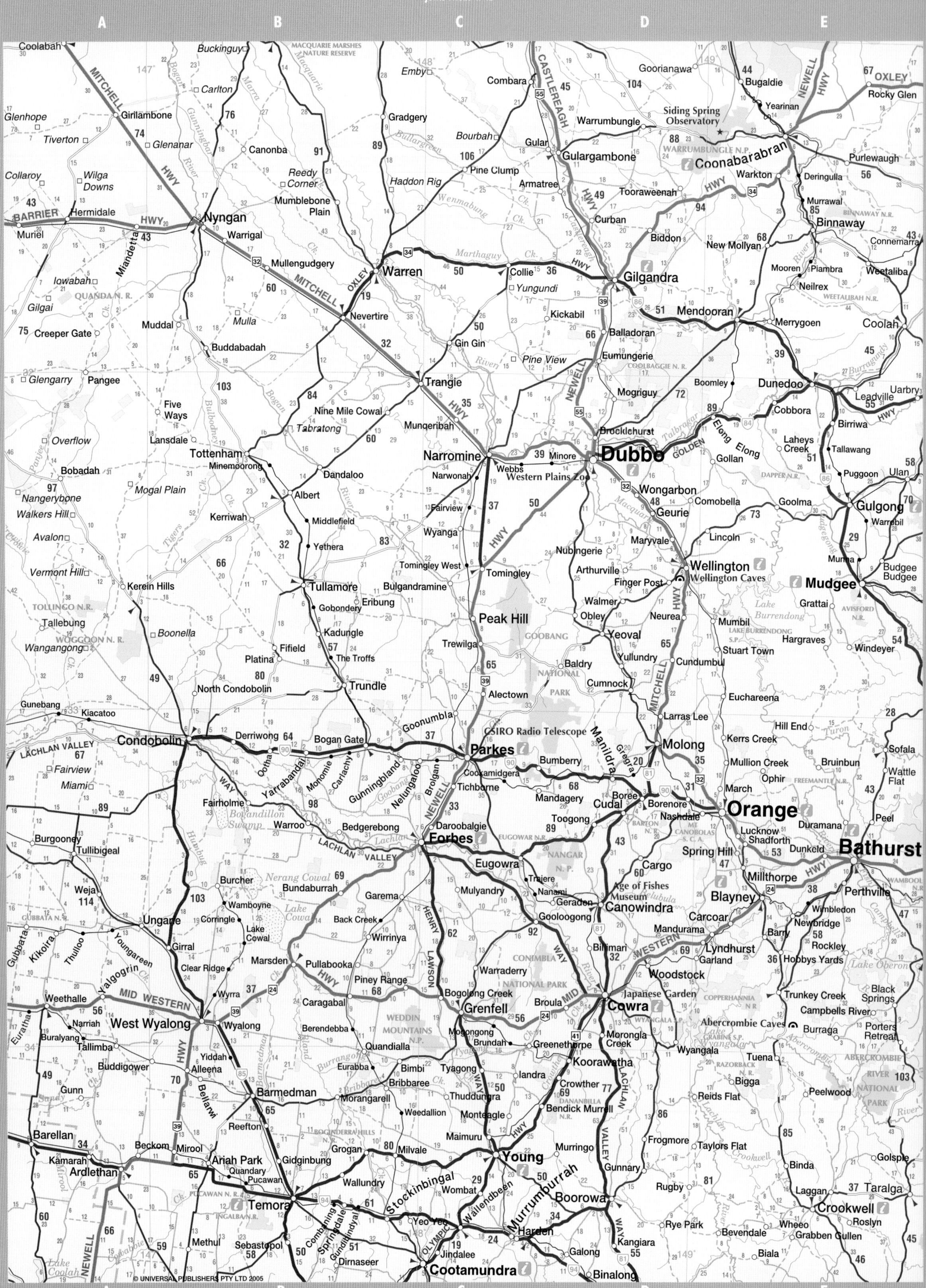

Scale 1:1 547 400

0   40   Kilometres

JOINS PAGE 45

Road map of central New South Wales showing major centres including Nyngan, Warren, Trangie, Narromine, Dubbo, Gilgandra, Coonabarabran, Mudgee, Gulgong, Dunedoo, Wellington, Orange, Bathurst, Parkes, Forbes, Condobolin, Cowra, Canowindra, Grenfell, Young, Boorowa, Crookwell, West Wyalong, Temora, Cootamundra, Barellan, and Ardlethan.

© UNIVERSAL PUBLISHERS PTY LTD 2005

JOINS PAGES 42-43

A | B | C | D | E

Gunnedah · Mullaley · Carroll · Curlewis · Nea · Moore · Moonbi · Woolbrook · Walcha · Willawarrin · Clybucca · Smithton · Frederickton · Sherwood · Kempsey · Gladstone

Tamworth · Piallaway · Winton · Westdale · Kootingal · Limbri · Moona Plains · Kangaroo Flat · Crescent Head

Werris Creek · Warral · Duri · Nemingha · Piallamore · Dungowan · Loomberah · Woolomin · Weabonga · Brackendale · Niangala · Yarrowitch · Myrtle Scrub · Rollands Plains · Birdwood · Bellangry · Pappinbarra · Port Macquarie · Pembrooke · Telegraph Point · Kundabung

Quirindi · Pine Ridge · Caroona · Currabubula · Wallabadah · Barry · Nowendoc · Ellenborough · Wauchope · Byabarra · Timbertown · Lake Cathie

Spring Ridge · Yanergee · Blackville · Old Warrah · Willow Tree · Herons Creek · Kendall · Bonny Hills · North Haven · Laurieton

Tamarang · Premer · Bundella · Yarraman · Ardglen · Murrurundi · Timor · Ellerston · Upper Lansdowne · Lorne · Kew · Diamond Head

Cassilis · Borambil · Merriwa · Blandford · Wingen · Parkville · Moonan Flat · Belltrees · Gundy · Woolooma · Gloucester · Barrington · Burrell Creek · Wingham · Purfleet · Harrington · Manning Point · Taree · Old Bar

Turill · Scone · Aberdeen · Bunnan · Stratford · Craven · Forbesdale · Gangat · Krambach · Nabiac · Hallidays Point

Merriwa · Gungal · Roxburgh · Castle Rock · Muswellbrook · McCullys Gap · Salisbury · Eccleston · Wards River · Coolongolook · Failford · Tuncurry · Forster · Coomba

Wollar · Bylong · Sandy Hollow · Denman · Baerami · Kerrabee · Baerami Creek · Jerrys Plains · Glen Gallic · Ravensworth · Camberwell · St Clair · Mirannie · Dungog · Alison · Stroud Road · Booral · Girvan · Stroud · Bulahdelah · Bungwahl · Seal Rocks · Elizabeth Beach · Wootton

Lue · Rylstone · Olinda · Kandos · Clandulla · Bogee · Holbrook · Singleton · Eldredie · Warkworth · Bulga · Paterson · East Gresford · Wirragulla · Waterobba · Vacy · Clarence Town · Karuah · Nerong · Bombah Pt · Broughton Island · Tea Gardens · Hawks Nest

Ilford · Running Stream · Glen Alice · Glen Davis · Newnes · Putty · Bedford · Broke · Pokolbin · Greta · Branxton · Lochinvar · Maitland · Karuah · Nelson Bay · Lemon Tree Passage · Anna Bay

Capertee · Ben Bullen · Howes Valley · Hunter Valley Wineries · Cessnock · Bellbird · Kurri Kurri · Raymond Terrace · Williamtown

Cullen Bullen · Portland · Wallerawang · Bucketty · Millfield · Mulbring · Freemans Waterhole · Hexham · Newcastle

Lithgow · Bell · Hartley · Bilpin · Kurmond · Cooranbong · Wollombi · Laguna · Toronto · Belmont

Tarana · Mt Victoria · Blackheath · Richmond · Berowra · Morisset · Swansea

Hampton · Lawson · Springwood · Windsor · Wyee · Yarramalong · Kulnura · Central Mangrove · Budgewoi · Toukley

Oberon · Katoomba · The Three Sisters · Hazelbrook · Blaxland · Penrith · Hornsby · Wyong · The Entrance · Gosford · Woy Woy · Australian Reptile Park

Edith · Jenolan Caves · Glenbrook · Wallacia · Parramatta · Mona Vale · Long Reef · Manly

Kanangra · Yerranderie · Oakdale · Liverpool · Sydney · La Perouse

Colong Caves · The Oaks · Heathcote · Camden · Cronulla · Sutherland · Campbelltown

Wombeyan Caves · Picton · Thirlmere · Appin · Stanwell Park · Buxton · Bargo · Bulli · Berrima · Mittagong · Bowral · Dapto · Port Kembla · Wollongong

Moss Vale · Sutton Forest · Yerrinbool · Robertson · Shellharbour · Exeter · Brayton

TASMAN SEA

WOLLEMI NATIONAL PARK · YENGO NATIONAL PARK · MYALL LAKES NATIONAL PARK · BARRINGTON TOPS NATIONAL PARK

UBD

Scale 1:1 547 400

0   40   Kilometres

MURRAY - SUNSET NATIONAL PARK

WYPERFELD NATIONAL PARK

BIG DESERT WILDERNESS PARK

BIG DESERT

LITTLE DESERT NATIONAL PARK

GRAMPIANS (GARIWERD) NATIONAL PARK

NEW SOUTH WALES

VICTORIA

SOUTH AUSTRALIA

Mildura   Wentworth   Merbein   Merbein South   Irymple   Red Cliffs   Gol Gol   Monak

Cal Lal   Rufus River   Meringur North   Cullulleraine   Morkalla   Meringur   Werrimull   Benetook   Yatpool   Carwarp

Nangari   Taplan   Nadda   Meribah   Peebinga

Pinnaroo   Panitya   Cowangie   Carina   Murrayville   Underbool   Linga   Boinka   Torrita   Walpeup   Patchewollock

Ouyen   Galah   Kiamal   Kulwin   Winnambool   Speed   Turriff   Tempy

Robinvale   Euston   Balranald   Manangatang   Tooleybuc   Moulamein   Swan Hill   Nyah   Nyah W.   Woorinen

Bannerton   Wemen   Annuello   Hattah   Kulkyne   Koorakee   Benanee   Nangiloc   Kemendok   Kooloonong   Haysdale   Natya   Kyalite   Piambie   Wood Wood

Boundary Bend   Yangalake   Penarie   Yanga   Nap Nap   Perekerten   Windourah   Warwaegae   Keeita   Toopuntal

Belinar   Prungle   Upson Downs   Gulthul   Bramah   Bidura   Glen Emu   Chillichil   Oxley

Sea Lake   Lascelles   Hopetoun   Woomelang   Watchupga   Curyo   Yaapeet   Green Lake   Banyan   Berriwillock   Culgoa   Nullawil   Whirily   Narraport

Lake Boga   Mystic Park   Lake Charm   Ultima   Goschen   Lalbert   Quambatook   Cannie   Leaghur   Gredgwin   Dumosa   Wycheproof   Thalia

Kerang   Kerang Sth   Ballbank   Gonn Crossing   Murrabit   Myall   Westby   Barham   Tragowel   Loddon Vale   Minmindie   Pyramid Hill   Durham Ox   Boort   Mysia   Borung   Jarklin

Rainbow   Kenmare   Pella   Ellam   Beulah   Galaquil   Wilkur   Birchip   Willenabrina   Brim   Watchem   Corack East

Jeparit   Netherby   Lorquon   Glenlee   Tarranyurk   Aubrey   Antwerp   Warracknabeal   Litchfield   Charlton   Buckrabanyule   Korong Vale

Telopea Downs   Yanac   Broughton   Boyeo   Nhill   Kiata   Salisbury   Wail   Dimboola   Pimpinio   Jung   Murtoa   Minyip   Rupanyup North   Rupanyup   Banyena   Rich Avon   Marnoo   Donald   Cope Cope   Laen East

Bordertown   Dinyarrack   Lillimur   Kaniva   Miram   Mt Elgin   Walseley   Serviceton   Frances   Western Flat

St Arnaud   Logan   Slaty Creek   Stuart Mill   Wedderburn   Wedderburn Junction   Kingower   Rheola   Arnold   Inglewood   Bridgewater   Llanelly   Marong   Lockwood   Bears Lagoon   Serpentine

Horsham   Natimuk   Murra Warra   Dooen   Lubeck   Wallaloo   Rostron   Callawadda   Navarre   Redbank   Stawell   Great Western   Deep Lead   Joel   Landsborough   Navarre

Goroke   Mitre   Gorke   Neuarpur   Binnum   Kybybolite   Hynam   Apsley   Wombelano   Edenhope   Langkoop   Poolaigelo   Coonawarra   Chetwynd   Dergholm   Penola

Naracoorte   Manimay   Noradjuha   Wonwondah North   Toolondo   Douglas   Harrow   Balmoral   Coojar   Brit Brit   Gatum   Cavendish   Wando Vale

Hall's Gap   Pomonal   Glenisla   Glenorchy   Dadswells Bridge   Moyston   Willaura   Buangor   Ararat   Maroona   Rossbridge   Mininera

Maryborough   Avoca   Moolort   Talbot   Natte Yallock   Havelock   Moliagul   Bealiba   Dunolly   Maldon   Carisbrook   Newstead   Elmhurst   Lexton   Clunes   Smeaton   Creswick   Daylesford   Hepburn Springs   Waterloo   Learmonth   Miners Rest   Evansford   Cardigan Village   Beaufort   Ballarat

Scorpion Springs C.P.   Ngarkat Con. Pk.   Mount Shaugh Con. Park   Mt Crozier   Mt Cowra   Mt Jess   Mt Observatory   Mt Jenkins   Mt Arapiles-Tooan S.P.   Mt William   Mt Buangor S.P.   Langi Ghiran S.P.

Lake Victoria   Lake Wallawalla   Rocket Lake   Pink Lake   L. Agnes   Lake Albacutya   Lake Hindmarsh   L Wyn Wyn   Mitre L.   Lake Tyrrell   Lake Lalbert   Lake Bael Bael   Lake Buloke   Lake Lonsdale   Lake Wartook   Lake Fyans   Lake Bellfield   Rocklands Reservoir   Toolondo Reservoir   Lake Burrumbeet   Lake Goldsmith   L. Tala   L. Benanee   Tin Tin Lake   Pitarpunga Lake   L. Caringay   Yanga Lake   Yerren

MALLEE CLIFFS NATIONAL PARK (no public access)

HATTAH-KULKYNE PARK   MURRAY-KULKYNE PARK

THE GRAMPIANS   BLACK RANGE S.P.   DERGHOLM

WIMMERA   SUNRAYSIA   CALDER HWY   STURT HWY   WESTERN HWY   HENTY HWY   MALLEE HWY   MURRUMBIDGEE   MURRAY RIVER

N   UBD

CONTINUES PAGE 125

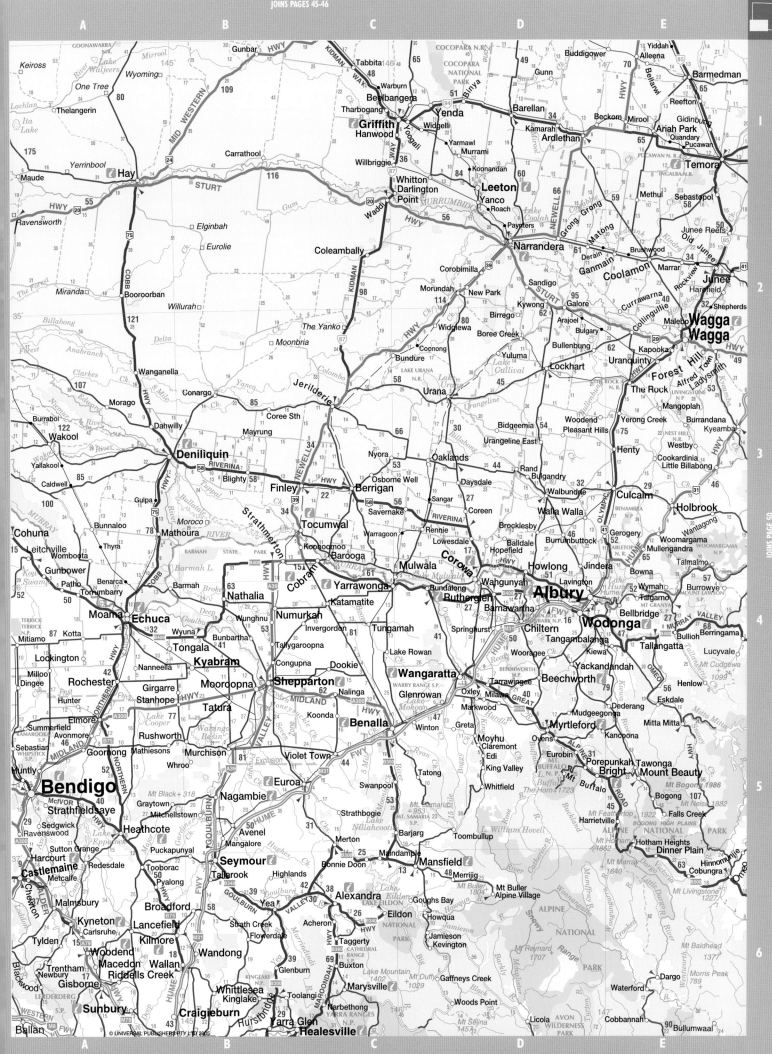

A   B   C   D   E

1

Quandialla Eurabba Bimbi Tyagong Iandra Crowther 77
Morangarell Bribbaree Thuddungra Monteagle Bendick Murrell 86 Tuena
Weedallion Maimuru Murringo Frogmore Bigga Peelwood
Grogan Milvale **Young** Reids Flat Taylors Flat Crookwell 103 Kanangra Walls
Wallundry Wombat Wallendbeen Gunnary Rugby Binda Wombeyan Caves Golsple The Oaks Oakdale **Camden**
Stockinbingal 29 50 **Boorowa** 81 Laggan Taralga Colong Caves Yerranderie Picton **Campbelltown**
Springdale 61 34 Harden Kangiara Rye Park Wheeo Grabben Gullen Roslyn 45 High Range Thirlmere Appin
Combaning 51 Jindalee 19 24 Galong Biala Bevendale Buxton Bargo Yerrinbool
Dirnaseer Frampton **Cootamundra** Binalong 62 Bowning Dalton **Goulburn** 47 Marulan Berrima 34 **Wollongong**
Junee Reefs Brawlin 38 Muttama 87 Jugiong Bookham Gunning Kingsdale Brayton 59 Wingello **Moss Vale** **Bowral** **Mittagong**
Bethungra Illabo **Junee** Coolac Burrinjuck **Yass** Bookham Collector Bungonia Caves Sutton Forest Exeter Kangaroo Valley Dapto Shellharbour

2

Eurongilly 20 Nangus Burrinjuck N.R. **Murrumbateman** Gundaroo Inveralochy Lake Bathurst Bungonia Robertson Jamberoo **Kiama**
Gundagai Wee Jasper N.R. 52 Tarago Nerriga 115 Bundanoon Berry Gerringong 58
Tumblong 33 Careys Caves Wee Jasper Sutton 86 99 Mt Fairy 56 Sassafras **Bomaderry** **Nowra** Greenwell Pt
9 Mt Horeb Gocup Tumorrama Hall BRINDABELLA Lower Boro Tomerong Yalwal Culburra Beach
Tarcutta **Tumut** Brindabella **CANBERRA** Gooroo Yarroo Mt Fairy Charleyong Jervis Bay Currarong Huskisson

3

Adelong Gilmore Molonglo **Bungendore** Braidwood Brooman Lake Conjola **Milton**
Kyeamba Wondalga **Batlow** Tharwa **Queanbeyan** 54 27 **Ulladulla** Burrill Lake
Humula Carabost Laurel Hill 7 92 Williamsdale Captains Flat Majors Creek 61 52 Termeil Bawley Point Lake Tabourie
Rosewood 69 Araluen North Araluen Nelligen Kioloa
Coppabella Yarrongobilly Caves Michelago Wyanbene Caves **Batemans Bay** Durras
Mannus **Tumbarumba** 98 Jerangle Bendethera Caves Mogo Batehaven **Moruya**

4

Jingellic Munderoo Kiandra 38 Shannons Flat Bredbo 29 Mossy Point Broulee
Walwa Tooma Mt Selwyn Bredbo Nerrigundah Moruya Head
Gudgewa 35 Welaregang **Adaminaby** Peakview Turlinjah Bergallia Tuross Head
Lucyvale 19 Tintaldra Eucumbene 52 Bunyan Numeralla Countegany Eurobodalla Potato Point Bodalla
Cabramurra Buckenderra Numeralla **Dalmeny** **Narooma**
Nariel Creek Towong **Corryong** Khancoban **Cooma** Kybeyan Montague I. **TASMAN**

5

Guthega Blue Cow Mtn 33 Rock Flat Tilba Tilba Central Tilba
Perisher Valley Smiggin Holes **Berridale** 51 45 **Cobargo** 72 **Bermagui**
Charlotte Pass **Jindabyne** Dalgety Kybeyan Bermagui South
Mt Kosciuszko Bullocks Flat 31 Nimmitabel Brown Mountain Brogo Quaama
2228m **Thredbo** Beloka Maffra 57 **Bega** Tanja **SEA**
54 145 Ingebyra 68 41 Kameruka **Tathra**
116 Ando Candelo Wolumia

6

Benambra Suggan Buggan 36 Cathcart 76 **Merimbula**
Hinnomunjie Delegate River **Bombala** Wyndham Pambula
Omeo Wulgulmerang **Delegate** Mila 28 Burragate **Eden** Killer Whale Museum
Tubbut Bendoc Craigie Davidson Whaling Station Historic Site
Swifts Creek Gelantipy Cabanandra 55 Bonang Wonboyn Green Cape
Tongio West Butchers Ridge 90 Erinundra COOLUMBOOKA Gipsy Point
Ensay Malinns Combienbar 54 Mt Kaye Genoa Cape Howe
Murrindal Buchan Club Terrace Noorinbee 47 **Mallacoota** Gabo I.
Canh River Mt Cann

JOINS PAGE 49

Albury page 49 D4

Information Centre
Lincoln Causeway,
Wodonga
Ph: 1300 796 222

Armidale page 43 A5

Information Centre
82 Marsh St
Ph: (02) 6772 4655

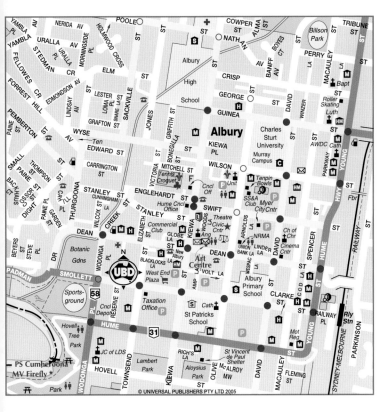

Ballina page 43 D2

Information Centre
River St/La Balsa Plaza
Ph: (02) 6686 3484

Batemans Bay page 50 D3

Information Centre
Princes Hwy/Beach Rd
Ph: (02) 4472 6900

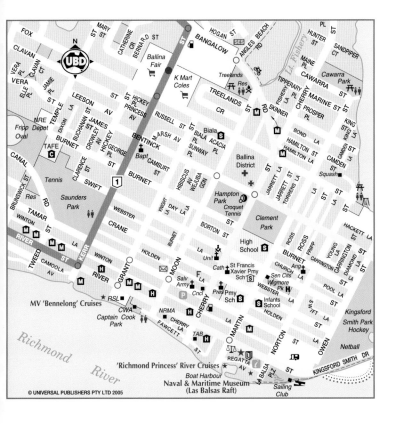

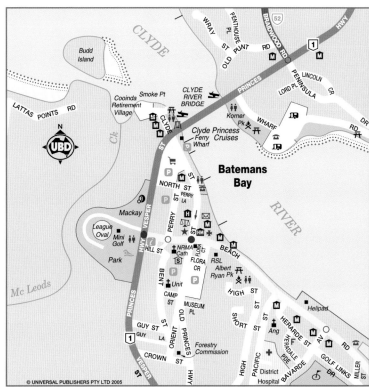

Bathurst page 46 E5

Information Centre
Kendall Ave
Ph: (02) 6332 1444

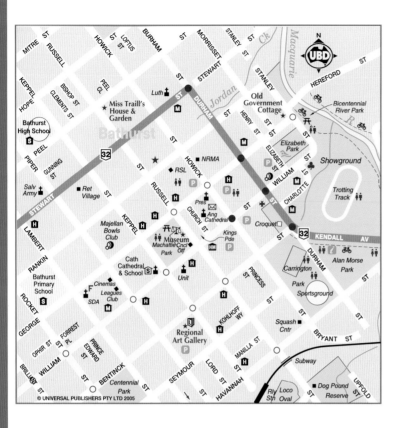

Berrima page 50 EI

Information Centre
62-70 Main St,
Mittagong
Ph: (02) 4871 2888

Bowral page 50 EI

Information Centre
62-70 Main St,
Mittagong
Ph: (02) 4871 2888

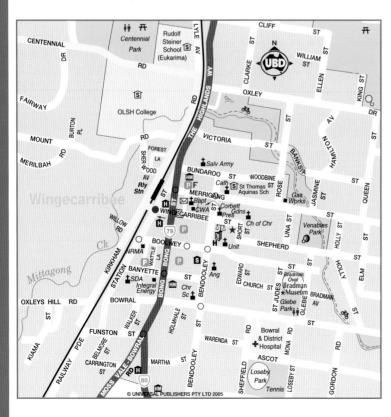

Broken Hill page 44 B2

Information Centre
Blende St/Bromide St
Ph: (02) 8087 6077

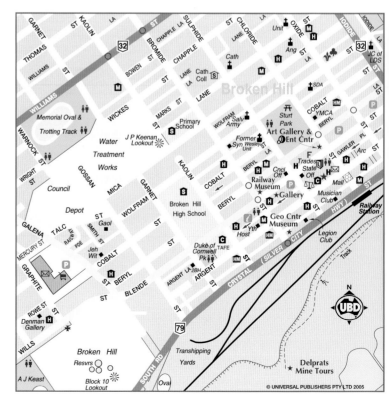

Byron Bay page 43 DI

Information Centre
80 Jonson St
Ph: (02) 6680 8558

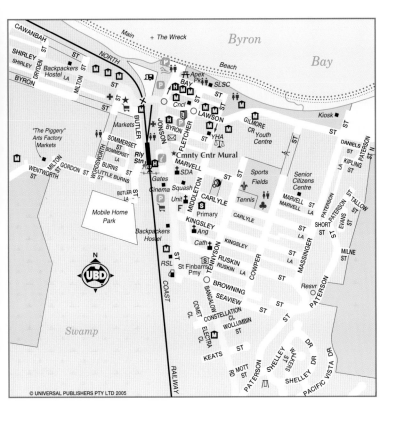

Cessnock page 47 C4

Information Centre
455 Wine Country Dr,
Pokolbin
Ph: (02) 4990 4477

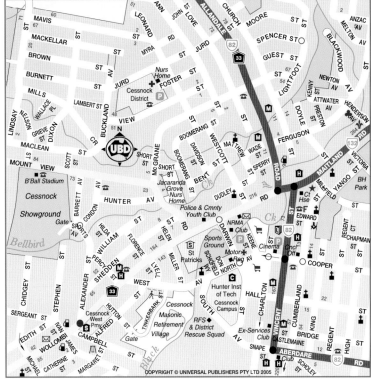

Coffs Harbour page 43 C5

Information Centre
Pacific Hwy/McLean St
Ph: (02) 6652 1522

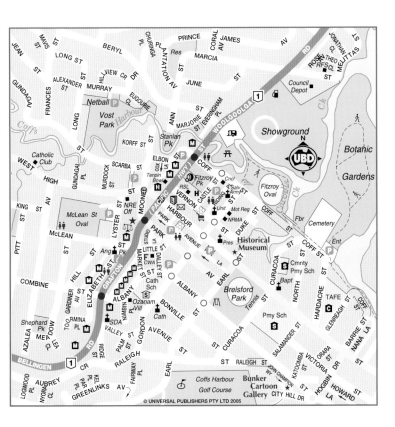

Cooma page 50 C4

Information Centre
119 Sharp St
Ph: (02) 6450 1742

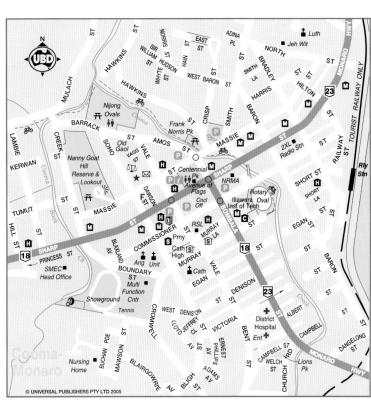

Cootamundra page 50 AI

Information Centre
Railway Station,
Hovell St
Ph: (02) 6942 4212

Dubbo page 46 D2

Information Centre
Macquarie St/Erskine St
Ph: (02) 6884 1422

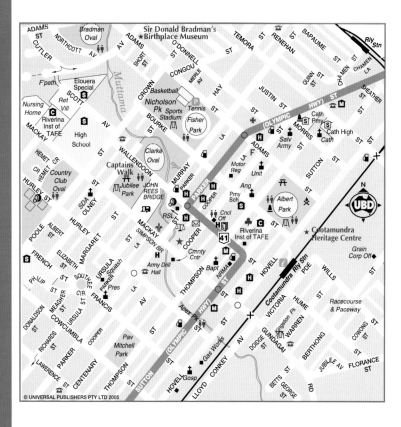

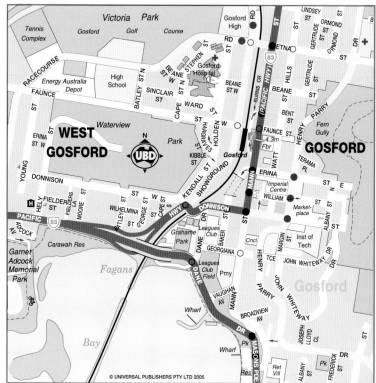

Forster/Tuncurry page 47 E2

Information Centre
Little St
Ph: (02) 6554 8799

Gosford page 47 C5

Information Centre
200 Mann St
Ph: 1300 130 708

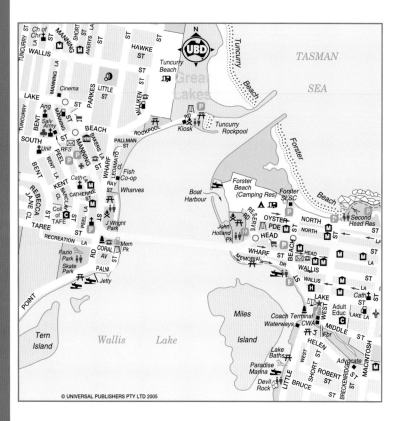

Goulburn page 50 DI

Information Centre
201 Sloane St
Ph: (02) 4823 4492

Grafton page 43 C3

Information Centre
Pacific Hwy/Spring St,
Sth Grafton
Ph: (02) 6642 4677

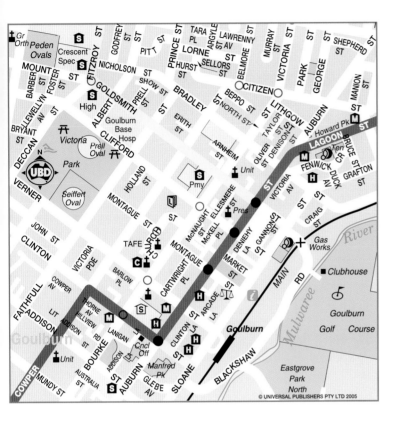

Griffith page 45 D6

Information Centre
Banna Ave/Jondaryan Ave
Ph: (02) 6962 4145

Katoomba page 47 A5

Information Centre
Echo Point
Ph: 1300 653 408

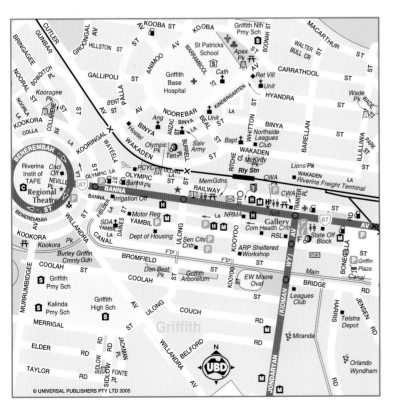

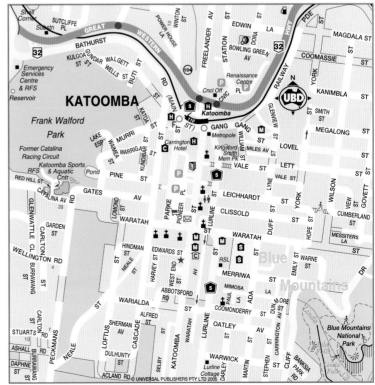

Lismore page 43 D2

Information Centre
Ballina St/Molesworth St
Ph: (02) 6622 0122

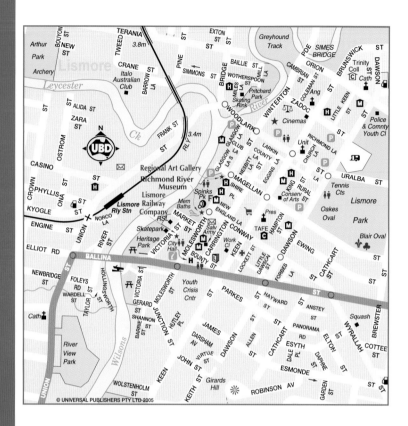

Maitland page 47 C3

Information Centre
High St/New England Hwy
Ph: (02) 4931 2800

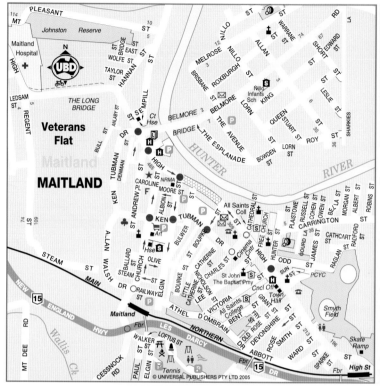

Mudgee page 46 E3

Information Centre
84 Market St
Ph: (02) 6372 1020

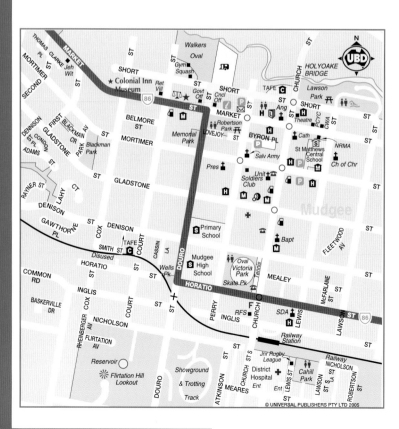

Newcastle page 47 C4

Information Centre
361 Hunter St
Ph: (02) 4974 2999

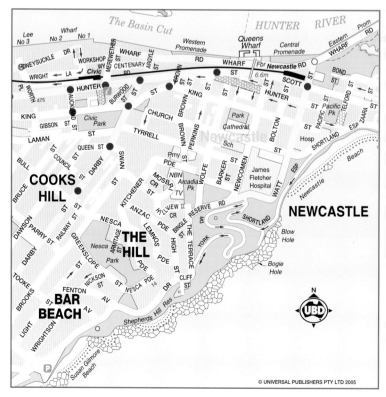

Information Centre
Princes Hwy/Pleasant Way
Ph: (02) 4421 0778

Information Centre
Byng St
Ph: (02) 6393 8226

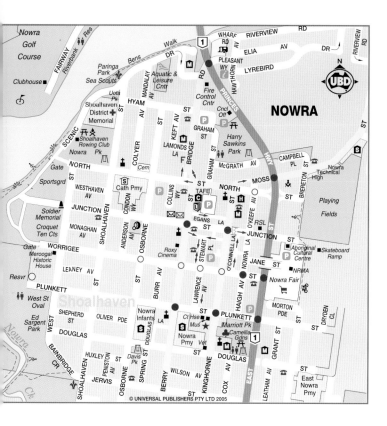

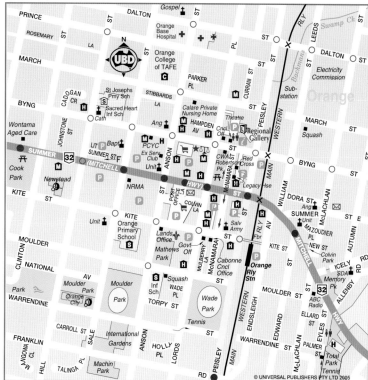

Information Centre
Clarence St/Hay St
Ph: (02) 6581 8000

Information Centre
I Farrer Pl
Ph: (02) 6298 0241

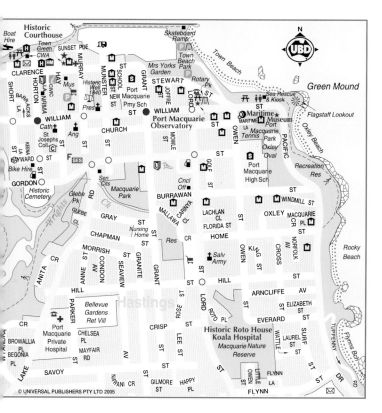

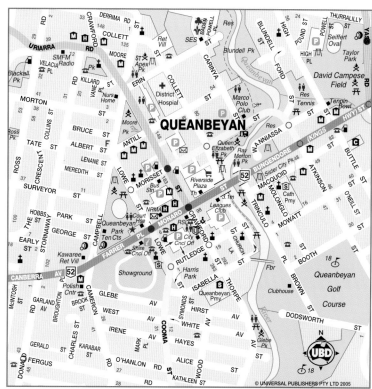

Singleton page 47 C3

Information Centre
39 George St
Ph: (02) 6571 5888

Tamworth page 42 E6

Information Centre
Peel St/Murray St
Ph: (02) 6755 4300

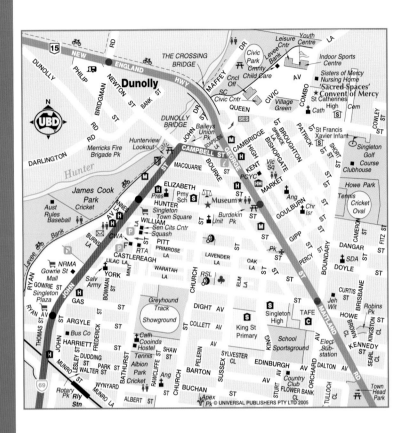

Taree page 47 E2

Information Centre
21 Manning River Dr,
Taree Nth
Ph: (02) 6592 5444

Tweed Heads page 43 D1

Information Centre
Centro Tweed, Wharf St
Ph: (07) 5536 4244

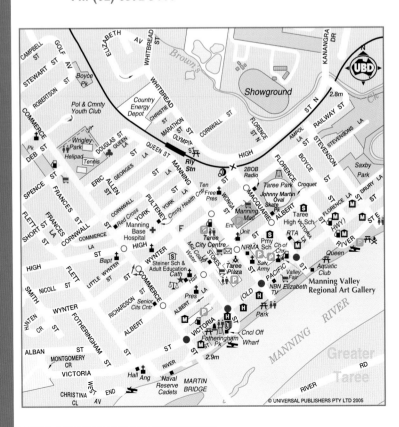

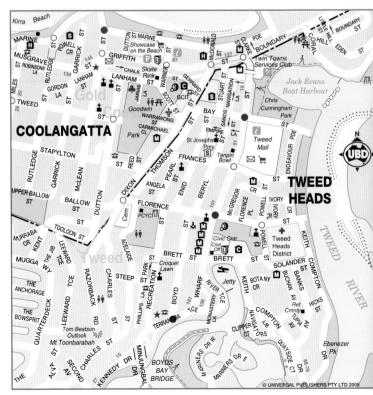

Ulladulla page 50 E3

Information Centre
Civic Centre, Princes Hwy
Ph: (02) 4455 1269

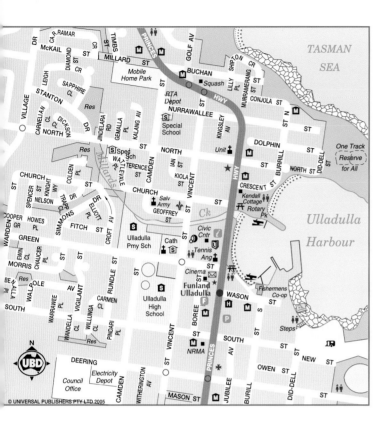

Wagga Wagga page 49 E2

Information Centre
Tarcutta St
Ph: (02) 6926 9621

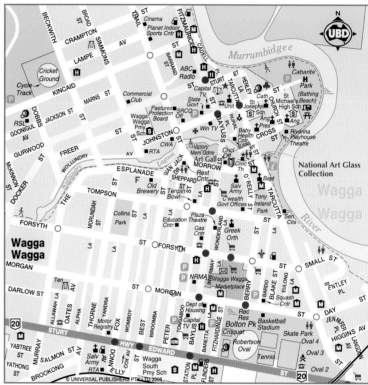

Wollongong page 50 E1

Information Centre
93 Crown St
Ph: (02) 4227 5545

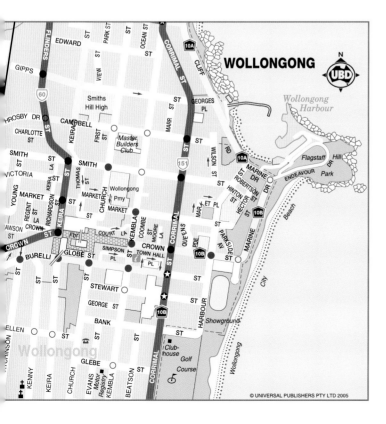

Yass page 50 B2

Information Centre
Comur St
Ph: (02) 6226 2557

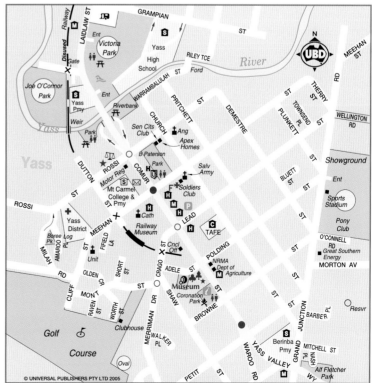

VICTORIA

Main Information Centre
Melbourne Visitor Centre
Federation Square, Vic 3000
Ph: (03) 9658 9658
or 132 842
www.visitvictoria.com.au

Phillip Island Penguin Parade

Covering 227 600km² of the south-eastern corner of Australia, Victoria is a relatively compact state, the second smallest after Tasmania. The state's mostly temperate climate has 4 distinct seasons, each with its own attractions. As a result of its manageable size and efficient road system, travelling the state is easy and comfortable. Transport options are excellent: coaches, trains and planes carry visitors into and around the state, and for those who want to explore independently, touring by car is convenient. Most places can be reached within a day's drive of the capital city, Melbourne, and there is a huge array of natural, cultural and historic areas just waiting to be discovered.

Victoria packs a lot within its boundaries. The Murray River stretches along the border with New South Wales and is a delightful destination in itself. The southern coastline is spectacular and varied, taking in the Great Ocean Road to the west, Wilsons Promontory and the beautiful Gippsland Lakes area to the east. Victoria's magnificent Alpine region has much to explore and the goldfields districts reveal an exciting episode in the state's history. Tranquil lakes, an exciting selection of national parks, cool forests and fertile countryside await the visitor, with accessible cities, towns and villages offering their hospitality.

Victoria caters well for the discerning traveller. Fresh produce is a specialty all over the state, with specific gourmet focal points like the Milawa Gourmet Region near Wangaratta and the Gourmet Deli Trail in West Gippsland. Wine-lovers can select from 14 winery regions and over 350 wineries, ranging from the Grampians in the south-west to Rutherglen in the north-east. Victorian vineyards are renowned for producing excellent vintages for the Australian and international market.

MAIN PLACES OF INTEREST

	Map ref		Map ref
Alexandra Timber Tramway	72 C6	Melbourne Zoo	64 C
Alpine National Park	73 C4	Mornington Peninsula	66,67
Beechworth	73 A3	Mount Buffalo National Park	73 A4
Buchan Caves	77 D1	Murray River	68,69,71,72,73
Central Deborah Goldmine, Bendigo	71 D4	Otway Fly Tree Top Walk	75 C5
Coal Creek Heritage Village, Korumburra	76 D4	Phillip Island Penguin Parade	76 B4
Croajingolong National Park	78 C5	Pioneer Settlement Museum, Swan Hill	69 C5
Crown Entertainment Complex	63 C4	Port Campbell National Park	75 A4
Dandenong Ranges National Park	65 D2	Port of Echuca	72 A2
Federation Square, Melbourne	63 D3	Portland Maritime Discovery Centre	82
Flagstaff Hill, Warrnambool	83	PowerWorks, Morwell	76 E3
Gippsland Heritage Park, Moe	76 E3	Puffing Billy Steam Railway	65 D2
Gippsland Lakes	77 C3	Rutherglen Wineries	72 E2
Glenrowan	72 E3	Sovereign Hill, Ballarat	75 C1
Golden Dragon Museum, Bendigo	79	Stawell Gift Club Hall of Fame Museum	82
Grampians National Park	70 E6	Surfworld Surfing Museum, Torquay	75 E4
Gum San Chinese Heritage Centre, Ararat	71 A6	Tarra-Bulga National Park	76 E4
Hanging Rock	71 E6	Tower Hill State Game Reserve	74 E4
Healesville Sanctuary	76 C1	Victoria's Open Range Zoo, Werribee	76 A2
Lake Eildon	72 D5	Victorian Goldfields Railway	71 D5
Melbourne Aquarium	63 B4	William Ricketts Sanctuary, Mt Dandenong	65 D2
Melbourne Cricket Ground	63 E3	Wilsons Promontory	76 E5
Melbourne Museum	63 D1	Wonthaggi State Coal Mine	76 C4

VICTORIA KEY MAP

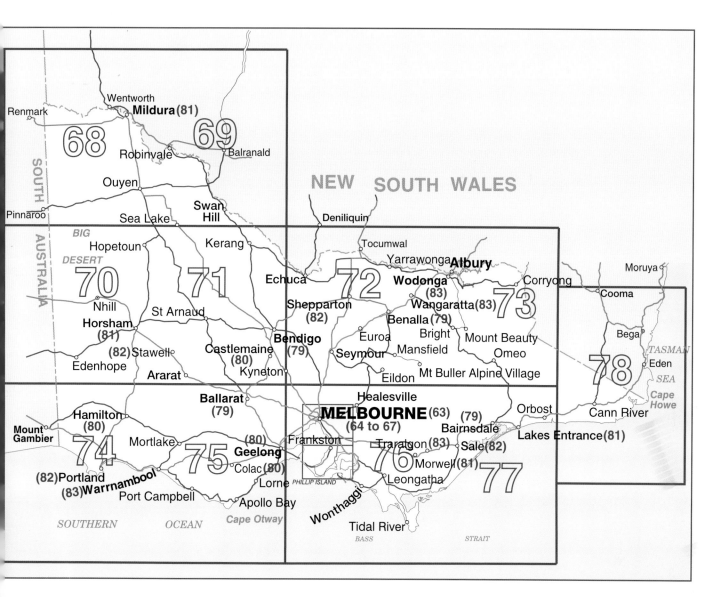

Viewing platform, The Twelve Apostles, Port Campbell National Park

MELBOURNE CITY

Melbourne, the capital of Victoria, is a culturally sophisticated city, with grand buildings in a somewhat traditional European style. It is Australia's second largest city and offers many attractions for visitors. In 1835, the first settlers arrived, mooring their boats on the Yarra River. Melbourne became a wealthy city after gold was discovered to the north-west in 1851. The impressive buildings, wide streets and boulevards, and large and beautiful public gardens, all reflect the wealth of the time.

Melbourne is a city renowned for its fine cuisine. Lygon St in Carlton is perhaps one of the better known streets, lined with pubs, cafes, bistros and restaurants that offer menus to suit all tastes. Melbourne hosts major events, including the Australian Tennis Open, Australian Grand Prix, Melbourne Cup and Melbourne Moomba Festival

The city is also known for its excellent shopping, with the majority of the city's major stores to be found on the streets running west of Swanston St. Brunswick St is also known for its vibrant shops as well as many fine restaurants. The Crown Entertainment Complex and Southgate also feature cafes, lively bars and boutiques on the southern edge of the Yarra River. Many of Melbourne's attractions can be linked by travelling on its famous trams, one of the most unique public transport systems in Australia.

MELBOURNE CITY PLACES OF INTEREST

	ref		ref
Albert Park	C6	Melbourne Museum	D
Australian Centre for Contemporary Art	D4	Melbourne Observation Deck	B3
Australian Centre for the Moving Image	D3	Melbourne Park	E4
Carlton Gardens	D1	Museum of Chinese Australian History	D2
Champions - Australian Racing Museum	D3	National Gallery of Victoria	D4
Chinatown	C2	Old Melbourne Gaol	C2
Crown Casino	B4	Parliament House	D2
Crown Entertainment Complex	C4	Polly Woodside Maritime Museum	B4
Federation Square	D3	Queen Victoria Market	B2
Fitzroy Gardens	E2	Royal Botanic Gardens Melbourne	E5
Flagstaff Gardens	B2	Royal Exhibition Building	D
Gold Treasury Museum	D2	Sidney Myer Music Bowl	D4
Immigration Museum	C3	Southgate Arts & Leisure Centre	C4
Melbourne Aquarium	C4	State Library of Victoria	C2
Melbourne Cricket Ground	E3	The Arts Centre	D4

Top: Little Bourke Street, Chinatown; Middle: Conservatory, Fitzroy Gardens; Bottom: Parklands along the Yarra River and city skyline

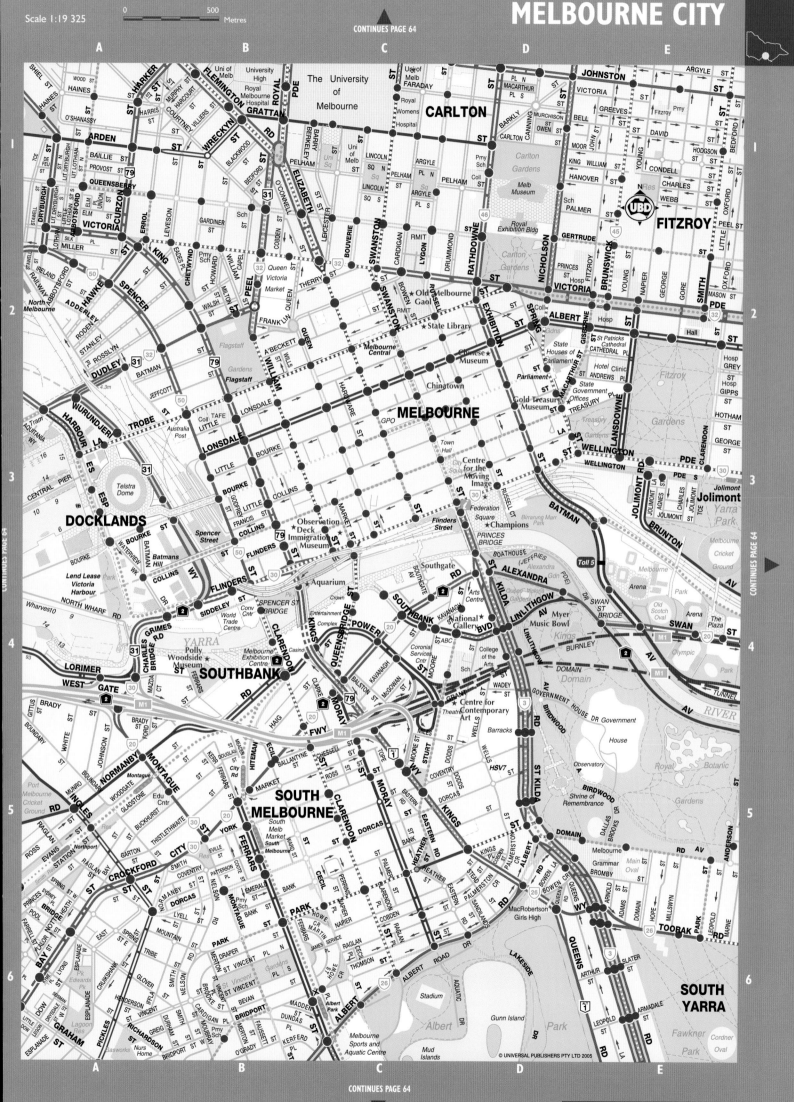

Scale 1:165 650

0 — 5 Kilometres

CONTINUES PAGE 76

CONTINUES PAGE 76

A   B   C   D   E

1

Caroline Springs   Kings Park   Taylors   St Albans East   Kealba   Keilor East   Niddrie   Essendon Nth   Strathmore   Essendon Airport   Pascoe Vale Sth   Coburg   Coburg North   Preston   Heidelberg West   View Bank

Burnside   Albanvale   St Albans   Essendon West   Aberfeldie   Essendon   Brunswick West   Coburg East   Thornbury   Bellfield   Heidelberg Hts   Heidelberg

Ravenhall   Avondale Heights   Moonee Ponds   Ascot Vale   Brunswick East   Brunswick   Northcote   Fairfield   Ivanhoe   Eaglemont   Bulleen

Ardeer   Albion   Maribyrnong   Flemington   Travancore   Parkville   Princes Hill   Carlton Nth   Fitzroy Nth   Clifton Hill   Alphington   Ivanhoe East   Balwyn North

Deer Park   **Sunshine**   Braybrook   Maidstone   Kensington   North Melbourne   Carlton   Fitzroy   Abbotsford   Kew East   Kew   Deepdene   Mont Albert

Sunshine North   Footscray West   Footscray   West Melbourne   **MELBOURNE**   Richmond   Hawthorn   Auburn   Canterbury   Balwyn

2

Laverton North   Sunshine West   Tottenham   Seddon   Kingsville   West Melbourne   Docklands   Southbank   Burnley   Hawthorn East   Camberwell   Surrey Hills   Riversdale

Truganina   Brooklyn   Sth Kingsville   Yarraville   Fishermans Bend   South Melbourne   Cremorne   Toorak   Kooyong   Hawthorn East

Derrimut   Spotswood   Newport   Port Melbourne   Albert Park   Prahran   Armadale   Glen Iris

Altona North   Middle Pk   Windsor   Malvern

3

Laverton   Altona   Seaholme   **Williamstown**   St Kilda West   St Kilda   Balaclava   Caulfield Nth   Malvern East   Ashburton   Ashwood

Altona Meadows   Elwood   Ripponlea   Caulfield East   Caulfield   Glen Huntly   Carnegie   Murrumbeena   Hughesdale   Chadstone

Seabrook   Elsternwick   Gardenvale   Caulfield Sth   Ormond   Oakleigh

Point Cook   Brighton   Brighton East   McKinnon   Bentleigh East   Oakleigh South

4

Sandringham   Hampton   Moorabbin   Bentleigh   Heatherton

Highett   Cheltenham   Moorabbin Air Museum   Moorabbin Airport

Black Rock   Mentone

Beaumaris   Parkdale   Mordialloc

5

Port   *Phillip*   Aspendale

N   UBD

6

A   B   C   D   E

© UNIVERSAL PUBLISHERS PTY LTD 2005

JOINS PAGE 66

CONTINUES PAGE 76

A B C D E

Lower Plenty
Templestowe
Templestowe Lower
Doncaster
Doncaster East
Warrandyte
Warrandyte South
Warranwood
Park Orchards
Donvale
Chirnside Park
Croydon Hills
Croydon North
Lilydale
Mount Evelyn
Wandin North
Seville
Crystal Brook TAFE
Schramms Cottage
Blackburn North
Nunawading
Ringwood North
Croydon
Mooroolbark
Museum of Lilydale
Swinburne Uni of Tech
Swinburne Uni Eastern Campus
Mont De Lancey Home & Museum
Five Oaks
Elmswood Estate
Mont Albert North
Box Hill North
Blackburn
Mitcham
Ringwood
Ringwood East
Croydon Sth
Bayswater North
Kilsyth
Montrose
Kalorama
Silvan
Wandin East
Box Hill
Box Hill South
Blackburn South
Forest Hill
Heathmont
Kilsyth South
Mt Dandenong Arboretum
Mt Dandenong 633
GTV9 Tower
Mount Dandenong
Tesselaar Silvan Tulip Farm
Seville Estate
Burwood
Vermont
Bayswater
Boronia
The Basin
Burkes 630
ATV10 Tower
Olinda
Edward Henty Cottage
Sassafras
Monbulk
Burwood East
Vermont South
Wantirna
Wantirna South
R.J. Hamer Forest Arboretum
Mount Waverley
Glen Waverley
Knoxfield
Knox City
Ferntree Gully
Tremont
Ferny Creek
Sherbrooke
The Patch
Oakleigh East
Notting Hill
Scoresby
Wheelers Hill
Upper Ferntree Gully
Upwey
Tecoma
Kallista
Huntingdale
Clayton
Rowville
Belgrave
Menzies Creek
Avonsleigh
Clarinda
Mulgrave
Lysterfield
Belgrave Heights
Selby
Clematis
Emerald
Springvale
Clayton South
Lysterfield South
Lysterfield Lake Park
Belgrave South
Emerald Lake Pk
Dingley Village
Noble Park
Dandenong North
Springvale South
Churchill National Park
Narre Warren East
Harkaway
Dewhurst
Braside
Keysborough
Dandenong
Doveton
Endeavour Hills
Narre Warren North
Beaconsfield Upper
Aspendale Gardens
Dandenong South
Hallam
Narre Warren
Guys Hill
Berwick
Beaconsfield
Chelsea Heights
Bangholme
Hampton Park
Monash University
Chisholm Institute
Chelsea
Lyndhurst
Narre Warren South
Officer
Bonbeach
Carrum
Patterson Lakes
Carrum Downs
Skye
Cranbourne North
Clyde North
Officer South
Pakenham
Seaford
Seaford Beach
Carrum Downs
Cranbourne West
Cranbourne
Cranbourne East
Clyde

CONTINUES PAGE 76

© UNIVERSAL PUBLISHERS PTY LTD 2005

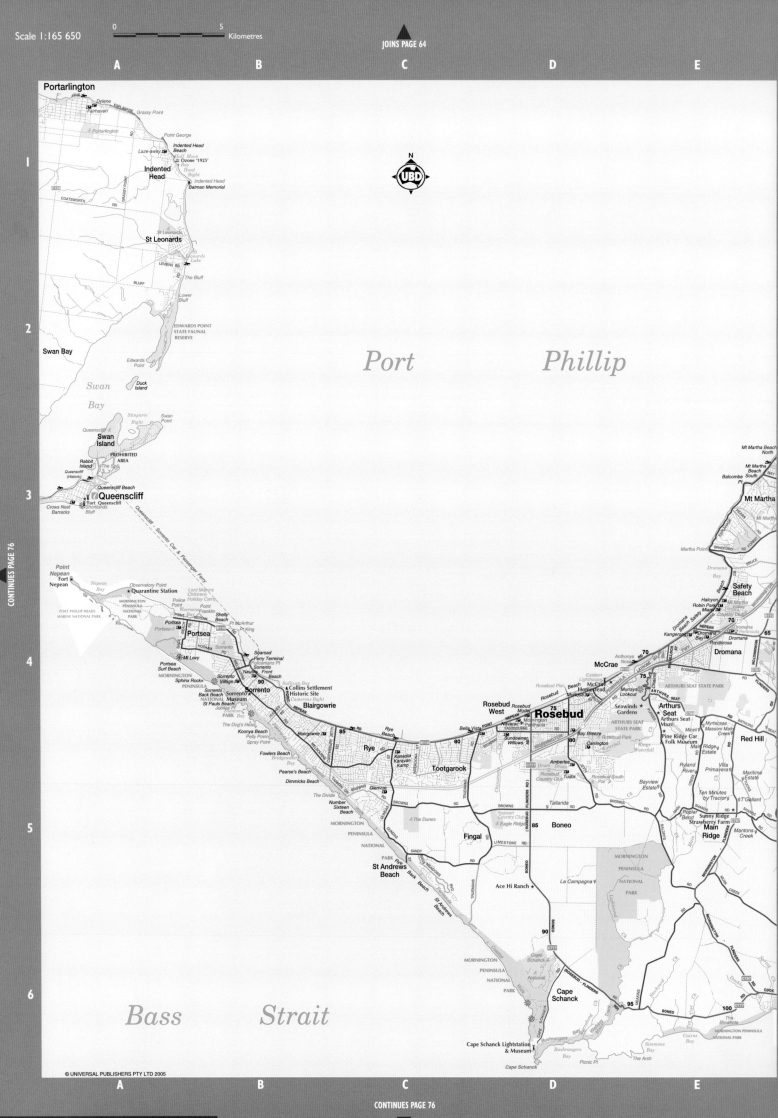

CONTINUES PAGE 76

CONTINUES PAGE 76

Portarlington

Indented Head

St Leonards

Swan Bay

Swan Bay

Swan Island

Queenscliff

Point Nepean
Fort Nepean

Portsea

Sorrento

Blairgowrie

Rye

Tootgarook

St Andrews Beach

Fingal

Boneo

Ace Hi Ranch

Cape Schanck

Cape Schanck Lightstation & Museum

Port   Phillip

Bass   Strait

Mt Martha

Safety Beach

Dromana

McCrae

Rosebud West

Rosebud

Arthurs Seat

Red Hill

Main Ridge

JOINS PAGE 65

A B C D E

1 2 3 4 5 6

Frankston
Frankston North
Cranbourne
Cranbourne South
Junction Village
Clyde
Royal Botanic Gardens Wylans
Mt Eliza
Mount Eliza
Langwarrin
Devon Meadows
Five Ways
Olivers Hill
Ballam Pk Homestead
McClelland Art Gallery
Log Cabin
Ranelagh Beach
Morning Star
Frankston South
Mulberry Hill (National Trust)
Frankston Holiday Village
Langwarrin South
Pearcedale
Cannons Creek
Blind Bight
Tooradin
Moondah Beach
North Sunnyside Beach
Sunnyside Beach
Baxter
Tooradin
Warneet
Mornington
Vintira
TV World
Somerville
Quail Island
QUAIL ISLAND WILDLIFE RESERVE
YARINGA MARINE NATIONAL PARK
Watsons Inlet
Schnapper Point
Royal Beach
Mornington Gardens
Mornington Racecourse
Mornington Peninsula Regional Art Gallery
Moorooduc
Bembridge
Treehaven Equestrian Centre
Western Port Harbour
Chinaman Island
Western Port
Fossil Beach
Dava Beach
Bird Rock Beach
Craigie Beach
Barrymore Tuerong
Ermes Estate
Devil Bend
Garden
Stumpy Gully
Tyabb
Tyabb Spout Park Camp Fairhills
Western Port Airfield
The Briars
The Pines
Nedlands Lavender Farm
Melbourne Water Dam
Denham
BHP Steel Western Port Works
Scrub Point
North Arm
FRENCH ISLAND MARINE NATIONAL PARK
Mt Martha
Devilbend Reservoir
Reservoir
Tyabb Old Township
Hastings
Loading Jetty
Long Island Point
River Point
Red Bill
FRENCH ISLAND NATIONAL PARK
Osborns Harwood Box Stallion
Tuerong
Hodgins
The Bays
Hastings
Western Port Marina
Hastings Bight
Mt Wellington +98
Turramurra Estate
Tanglewood Estate
Hickinbotham of Dromana
Bittern Reservoir
Marina View
Sandstone Island
Palmhaven
The Pinnacles + 66
FRENCH ISLAND
Dromana Karina
Elgee Park
Bittern
Northway Downs Estate
Jacks Beach
Woolleys Beach Crib Point
Bayview Chicory Kiln
Park Office
Craig Avon
Willow Creek
Kings Creek
Balnarring Racecourse
Crib Point Terminal Shell · Mobil
Passenger Ferry
Tea Tree Point
Charlottes Vineyard
Port Phillip Estate
Wildcroft Estate
Elan
Merricks North
Balnarring
Hurley
Balnarring
HMAS CERBERUS
Crib Point
Stony Point
Tankerton
Tankerton
Red Hill Gallery
Merricks Creek
Merricks Estate
Coolart Historic Homestead
Somers
HMAS Cerberus
Stony Point
Tortoise Head
Red Hill South
Stonier
Merricks
Somers
HMAS CERBERUS
Paringa Estate
The Duke
Red Hill Estate
Tuck's Ridge
Merricks Beach
Balnarring Beach
Somers Beach
South Beach
Sandy Point
Elizabeth Island
Merricks
Merricks Beach
Montalto
Ashcombe Maze
Point Leo
Peck Point
Long Point
Pier 10's
Point Leo
Pt Leo (Bobbanaring Pt)
Point Leo Beach
Shoreham
Shoreham Beach
Western Port
Flinders
RAN West Head Gunnery Range
West Head
Mushroom Reef Marine Sanctuary
Cowes
Mussel Rocks
Red Rocks
Erehwon Point
Anchor Belle
Cowes
Bayside
Kaloha
Silverleaves
Observation Point
Cowes Heritage Centre
Bushy Pk
Beach Pk
Amaroo
Boomerang
Islander
Rhyll Inlet State Wildlife Reserve
Lady Nelson Pt
Seaview
Rhylston Park Historic Homestead
Cowes - Rhyll
Swan Bay
Fishermans Pt
McHaffie Point
Rhyll
Reid Bight
Elizabeth Cove
Rhyll Swamp
Wimbledon Heights
Oswin Roberts Koala Reserve
Phillip Island Nature Park
Woolshed Bight
McHaffie Lagoon
Swan Lake
A Maze 'N Things
Koala Conservation Centre
Long Point
Denne Bight
Farm Beach
Flynn Lagoon
Ventnor
PHILLIP ISLAND
Sunset Strip
Pleasant Point
Chambers Point
North Point
Churchill Island Historic Homestead
Grants Monument
Flynns Beach
Back Beach
Smiths Beach
Churchill Island Marine National Park
Swan Corner
Summerlands
Phillip Island
Sunderland
Shelly Beach
Cat Bay
Phillip Island Racing Circuit
Newhaven
Cowrie Beach

CONTINUES PAGE 76

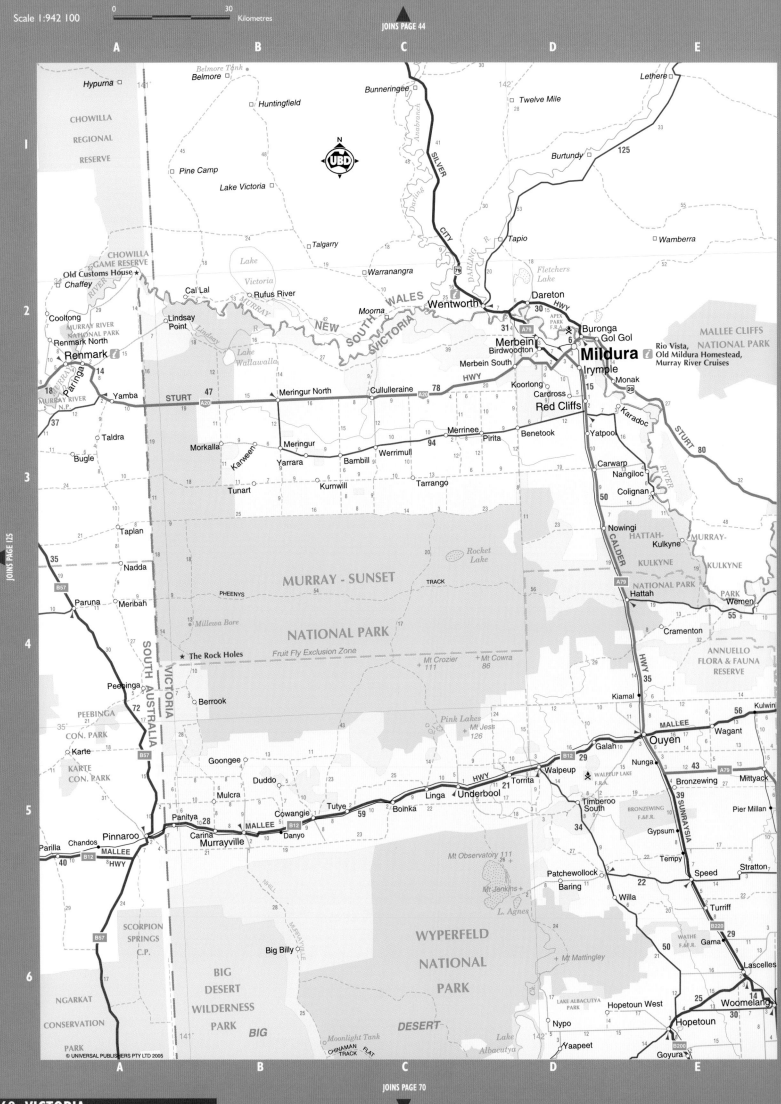

Scale 1:942 100

0   30   Kilometres

JOINS PAGE 125

JOINS PAGE 70

68 VICTORIA

© UNIVERSAL PUBLISHERS PTY LTD 2005

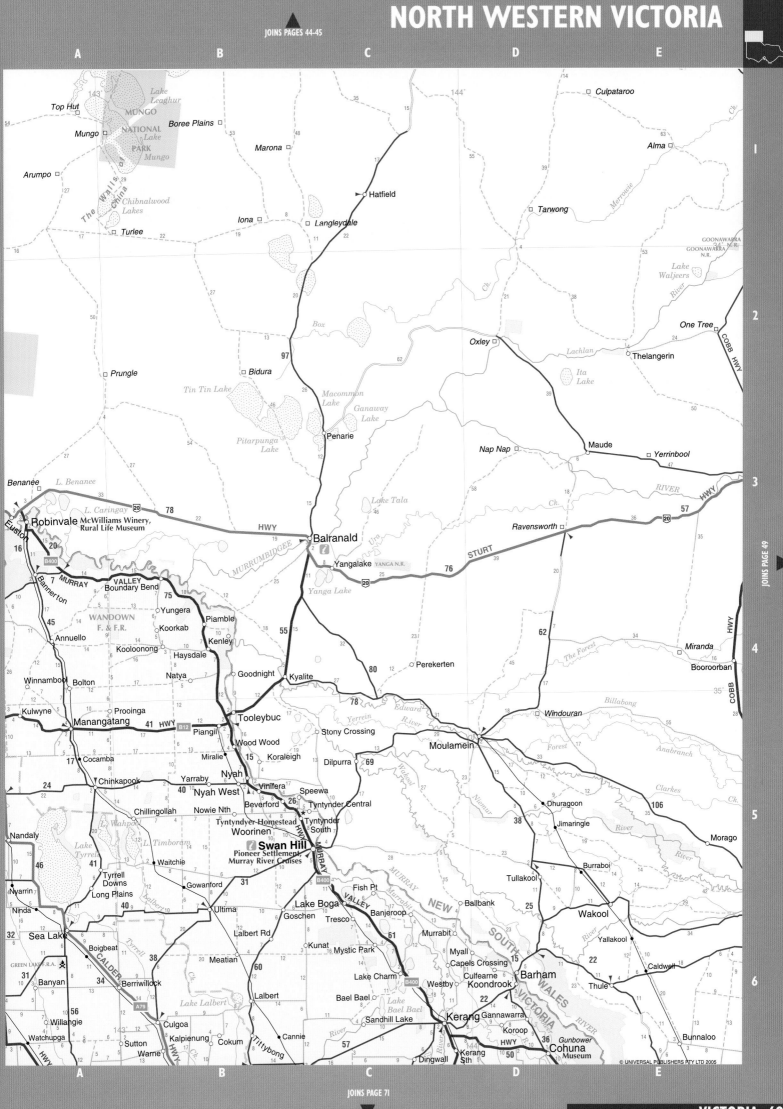

Scale 1:942 100

0   30   Kilometres

N UBD

A   B   C   D   E

SCORPION SPRINGS C.P.

BIG DESERT WILDERNESS PARK

BIG DESERT

WYPERFELD NATIONAL PARK

NGARKAT CONSERVATION PARK

MURRAYVILLE

NHILL

Big Billy

Mt Observatory 111+
Mt Jenkins +
Mt Mattingley +
L. Agnes

Baring   Willa   Speed   Stratton
Patchewollock   Turriff
Gama
Lascelles

MT SHAUGH C.P.
RED BLUFF F. & F.R.

SOUTH AUSTRALIA   VICTORIA

Moonlight Tank
CHINAMAN FLAT
Chinaman Flat
Wagon Flat
Pella

Lake Albacutya Park
Hopetoun West
Nypo
Yaapeet
Albacutya
Lake Albacutya

Hopetoun
Goyura
Hopevale   Rosebery   Roseberry East

Woomelang

BIRDCAGE F. & F.R.
Lake Hindmarsh
Perenna
Netherby
Rainbow   Kenmare   Beulah West   Beulah East
Brentwood   Galaquil   Reedy E.
Pullut   Galaquil East

Telopea Downs
Yanac
Broughton
Lorquon
Ellam
Willenabrina
Angip   Brim
Batchica   Lah

Jeparit   Peppers Plains
Tarranyurk
Warracknabeal
Historical Centre, Agricultural Machinery Museum
Challambra
Areegra

Wirrega
Cannawigara
DUKES HWY
Bordertown

Dinyarrak
Sandsmere
Yearinga
Boyeo
Tarranginnie
Woorak   Glenlee
Salisbury   Antwerp   Katyil   Ailsa
Gerang Gerung   Arkona   Wallup
Kellalac
Sheep Hills
Nullan

Mundulla   Wolseley   Lillimur   Kaniva   Miram   Diapur   Nhill Museum   Kiata   Minyip
Serviceton   WESTERN HWY   Mt Elgin   Winiam
Lillimur South   Lawloit   Kinimakatka   Winiam East   Murra Warra   Kewell
Miram South   Dimboola   Byrneville
Kalkee   Jung   Murtoa
Wail   Rupanyup North   Coromby

Western Flat   Pimpinio
Bangham   LITTLE DESERT NATIONAL PARK   Dooen   Rupanyup
BANGHAM C.P.   L Wyn Wyn   Longerenong   Ashens
Mitre L   Rupanyup South   Lubeck

Frances   Minimay   Morea   Goroke   Mitre   Quantong   Horsham
Keppoch   Neuarpurr   Gymbowen   MT ARAPILES-TOOAN S.P.   Marma
Binnum   Booroopki   Natimuk   Drung Sth   Wal Wal
Lower Norton   McKenzie Ck   St Helens Plains
Kangawall   Noradjuha   Drung
Bringalbert   Ozenkadnook   Karnak   Jallumba   Wonwondah North   Wonwondah East   Dadswells Bridge
Kybybolite   Benayeo   Clear Lake   Nurrabiel   Laharum
Hynam   Miga Lake   Mockinyah   Wartook   Fyans Ck

Naracoorte   Apsley   WIMMERA HWY   Charam   Brooksby   Toolondo   Brimpaen
Struan   Joanna   Langkoop   Wombelano   Douglas   Telangatuk   Zumstein   Cherrypool   Halls Gap
Edenhope   St Evins   The Grampians
Kadnook   Kanagulk   Glenisla
Wrattonbully   Harrow   GRAMPIANS (GARIWERD) NATIONAL PARK
Glenroy   Poolaigelo   Coonewirrecoo   Kanagulk   Woohlpooer   Pomonal
Comaum   Powers Creek   Balmoral
Coonawarra   DERGHOLM STATE PARK   Pigeon Ponds   Englefield   Mt William 1167
Chetwynd   Tarrayoukyan   Gatum   Moralla
Penola   Dorodong   Coojar   Nareen   Gringegalgona   Victoria Valley
Red Cap Creek   Brit Brit
Krongart   Dergholm   Wando Bridge   Melville Forest   Cavendish
Lake Mundi   Dunrobin   Carapook

Murtoa   Minyip

THE GRAMPIANS
L Muirhead

© UNIVERSAL PUBLISHERS PTY LTD 2005

CONTINUES PAGE 125

JOINS PAGE 72

© UNIVERSAL PUBLISHERS PTY LTD 2005

Scale 1:942 100

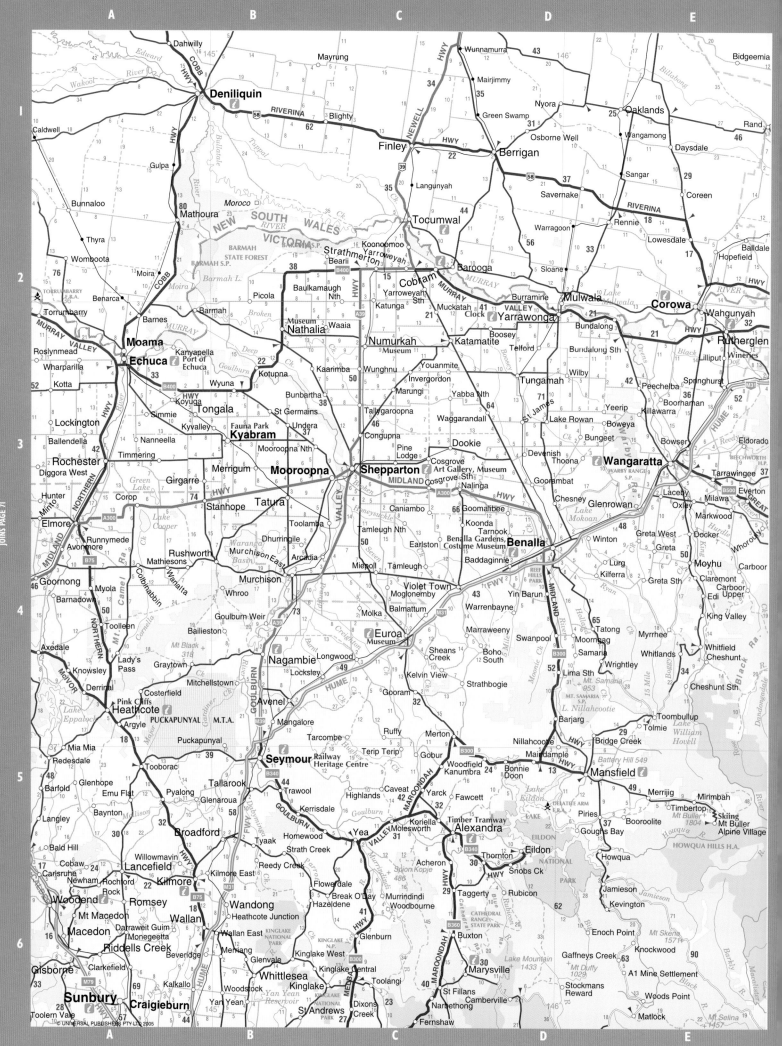

A B C D E

Woodend
Pleasant Hills
Urangeline East
Henty
Burrandana
Kyeamba
Westby
Humula
Wondalga
Cookardinia
Batlow
KOSCIUSZKO
Bulgandry
Little Billabong
Carabost
Talbingo
Laurel Hill
32
Walbundrie
Culcairn
Rosewood
Snowy
90
Walla Walla
Holbrook
Tumbarumba
Brocklesby
Mannus
Burrumbuttock
Gerogery
Woomargama
Lankeys Creek
Munderoo
Kiandra
Howlong
Mullengandra
Bowna
Dora Dora
Talmalmo
Jingellic
Maragle
Cabramurra
Mt Selwyn
Jindera
Table Top
Walwa
Tooma
HWY 38
Albury
Wymah
Tologolong
Burrowye
Guys Forest
Tintaldra
Welaregang
Anglers Reach
Wodonga
Bellbridge
Talgarno
Granya
Cudgewa Nth
Eucumbene
Barnawartha South
Bonegilla
Bethanga
Bungil
Cudgewa Falls
Towong
Leneva
Ebden
Old Tallangatta
Koetong
Cudgewa
Thowgla
Khancoban
Indigo Upper
Baranduda
Bullioh
Shelley
Colac Colac
Corryong
Murray 2
Murray 1
NATIONAL
Staghorn Flat
Huon
Tallangatta
Berringama
Biggara
Wooragee
Red Bluff
Sandy Ck
Tallangatta Valley
Lucyvale
Thowgla Upper
Yackandandah
Kiewa
Wyeebo
Nariel Creek
Guthega Skiing
Sawpit Creek
Beechworth
Kergunyah
Glen Creek
Tallandoon
Noorongong
WABBA
Geehi
Blue Cow Mountain
East Jindabyne
Stanley
Kergunyah Sth
Gundowring
Bullhead Ck
WILDERNESS
Nariel
Perisher Valley
Smiggin Holes
Murmungee
Eskdale
Cravensville
PARK
Charlotte Pass
Skitube
Jindabyne
Mt Stanley
Dederang
Bucheen Ck
Nariel
Bullocks Flat
Gapstead
Mudgeegonga
Gundowring Upper
Mt Kosciuszko
Thredbo
Moonbah
Myrtleford
Running Creek
Mitta Mitta
Dartmouth
Tom Groggin
Ovens
Rosewhite
Kancoona
Granite Flat
Dartmouth Dam
Ingebyra
Buffalo River
Havilah
Eurobin
ALPINE
Lake Dartmouth
Porepunkah
Tawonga
Sassafras Gap
Bright
Mount Beauty
NATIONAL
Mt Buffalo Skiing
Germantown
Freeburgh
Bogong
Sunnyside
Uplands
Suggan Buggan
Dandongadale
Wandiligong
Buckland
Smoko
Glen Valley
Benambra
Abbeyard
Buckland Junction
Harrietville
Falls Creek Skiing
Anglers Rest
Suggan Buggan
Hotham Heights
Dinner Plain Skiing
Horsehair Plain
Hinnomunjie
Mackillop Bridge
Cobungra
Omeo
Bindi
Wulgulmerang
Tubbut
Cabanandra
Cassillis
Tongio
Gelantipy
Bonang
Dargo
Tongio West
Swifts Creek
Butchers Ridge
Waterford
Doctors Flat
Timbarra
Goongerah
Castleburn
Tabberabbera
Ensay
Murrindal
Buchan Caves
Malinns
Tambo Crossing
Buchan
Buchan Sth

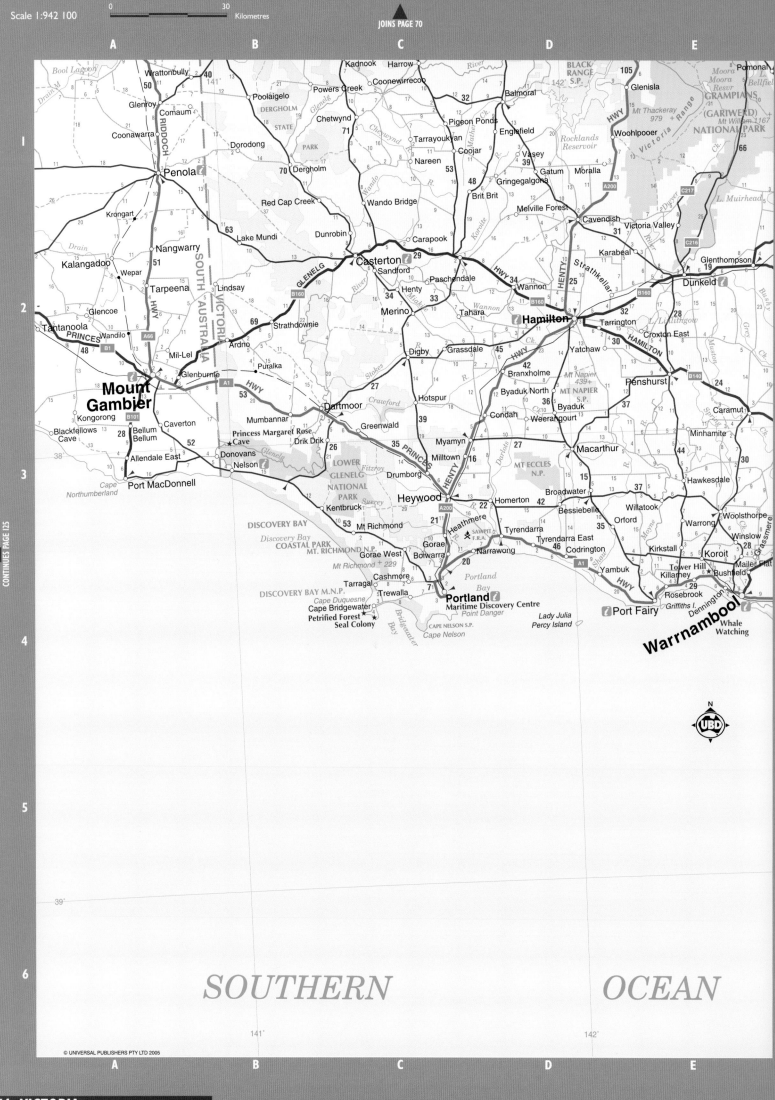

Scale 1:942 100

0   30 Kilometres

SOUTHERN   **OCEAN**

CONTINUES PAGE 125

© UNIVERSAL PUBLISHERS PTY LTD 2005

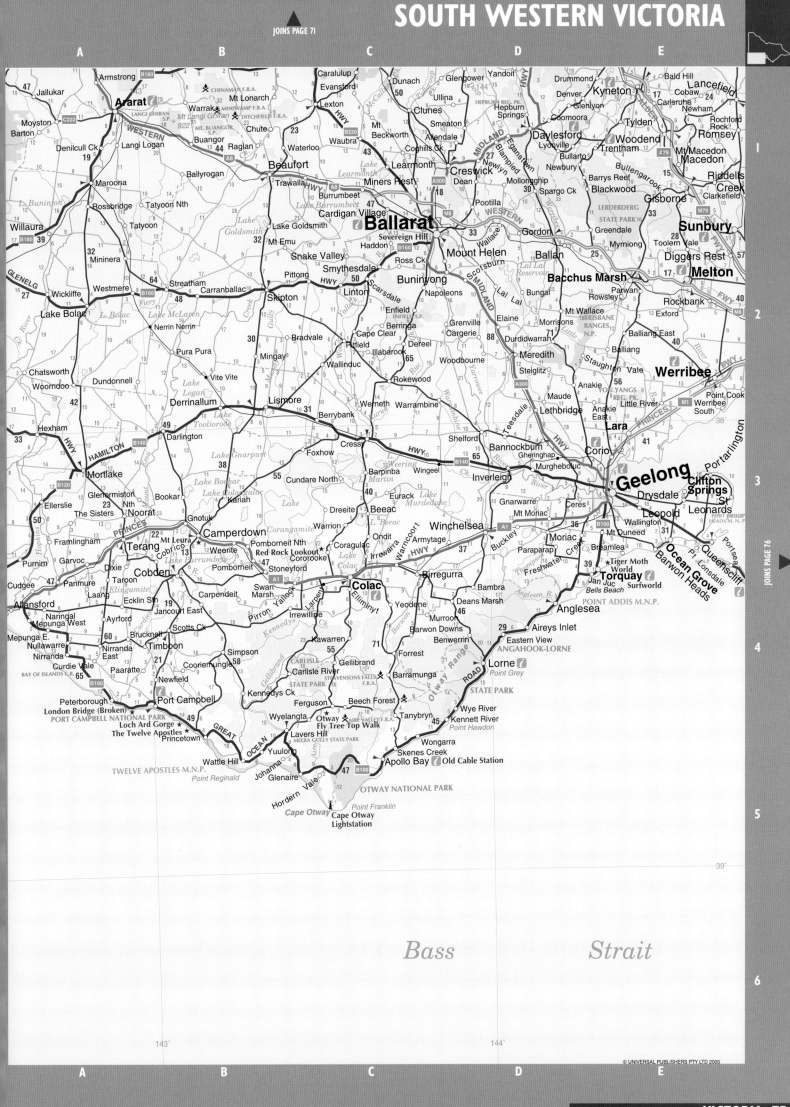

JOINS PAGE 76

Bass Strait

Scale 1:942 100

0   30   Kilometres

JOINS PAGE 72

JOINS PAGE 75

A   B   C   D   E

MELBOURNE

Sunbury • Craigieburn • Melton • Werribee • Frankston • Dandenong • Pakenham • Cranbourne • Warragul • Moe • Morwell • Traralgon • Healesville

Bald Hill • Cobaw • Carlsruhe • Newham • Rochford • Rock • Woodend • Mt Macedon • Macedon • Riddells Creek • Gisborne • Clarkefield • Lancefield • Romsey • Kilmore • Kilmore East • Wallan • Wallan East • Beveridge • Kalkallo • Monegeetta • Darraweit Guim • Bullengarook • Toolern Vale • Diggers Rest • Rockbank • Exford • Sydenham • Sunshine • Laverton • Little River • Werribee Sth

Willowmavin • Tyaak • Strath Creek • Reedy Creek • Heathcote Junction • Wandong • Mernda • Hurstbridge • Epping • Panton Hill • Whittlesea • Kinglake West • Kinglake • Kinglake Central • St Andrews • Woodstock • Yan Yean • Glenvale • Mernda • Heidelberg • Coburg • Ringwood • Knox • Belgrave • Emerald • Cockatoo • Gembrook

Flowerdale • Break O Day • Hazeldene • Glenburn • Toolangi • Dixons Creek • Yarra Glen • Coldstream • Lilydale • Seville • Woori Yallock • Yarra Junction • Gladysdale • Launching Place • Warburton • Millgrove • Powelltown • Noojee • Neerim • Neerim South • Neerim Junct. • Rokeby • Jindivick • Drouin • Nilma

Acheron • Murrindindi • Woodbourne • Buxton • Taggerty • Rubicon • Marysville • St Fillans • Narbethong • Fernshaw • Cambarville • McMahons Ck • Upper Yarra Dam • Loch Valley • Tanjil Bren • Vesper • Icy Ck • Fumina Sth • Willow Grove • Brandy Ck • Ellinbank • Darnum • Yarragon • Trafalgar • Allambee • Thorpdale • Driffield • Yinnar

Eildon • Thornton • Snobs Ck • Howqua • Jamieson • Kevington • Enoch Point • Knockwood • Gaffneys Creek • A1 Mine Settlement • Stockmans Reward • Woods Point • Matlock • Aberfeldy • Mt Useful • Beardmore • Walhalla • Rawson • Erica • Moondarra • Tanjil Sth • Yallourn North • Tyers • Glengarry • Moe • Morwell • Traralgon • Churchill • Boolarra • Mirboo North • Jumbuk • Balook

Portarlington • Clifton Springs • Drysdale • Wallington • Ocean Grove • Barwon Heads • Queenscliff • Pt Lonsdale • Portsea • Sorrento • St Leonards • Mt Eliza • Mornington • Mt Martha • Dromana • Rosebud • Rye • Boneo • Flinders • Shoreham • Somers • Merricks • Balnarring • Crib Pt • Hastings • Tyabb • Somerville • Pearcedale • Tooradin • Koo-Wee-Rup • Cardinia • Tynong • Garfield • Lang Lang • Yannathan • Grantville • Corinella • Coronet Bay • Cowes • Rhyll • Woolamai • Bass • Anderson • San Remo • Newhaven • Kilcunda • Dalyston • Wonthaggi • Inverloch • Cape Paterson • Venus Bay • Tarwin Lower • Walkerville • Waratah Nth • Waratah Bay • Sandy Point • Yanakie • Tidal River • South Point • South East Point

Nyora • Poowong • Loch • Bena • Korumburra • Coal Creek • Krowera • Kongwak • Archies Ck • Leongatha • Leongatha Sth • Koonwarra • Tarwin • Meeniyan • Dumbalk Nth • Dumbalk • Mirboo • Nerrena • Mardan • Berrys Ck • Boolarra South • Delburn • Allambee Sth • Ranceby • Hallston • Strzelecki • Foster • Toora • Welshpool • Port Welshpool • Port Franklin • Fish Creek • Hedley • Alberton West • Binginwarri • Woorarra • Ryton • Wonyip • Dollar

Port Phillip • Western Port • French Island • Bass Strait • Waratah Bay • Corner Inlet • Wilsons Promontory

© UNIVERSAL PUBLISHERS PTY LTD 2005

A | B | C | D | E

ALPINE
NATIONAL
Snowy Range
Mt Reynard 1707
Arbuckle Junction
PARK
147°
Wonnangarry River
Crooked R
GRANT H.A.
Dargo
73
Wellington R
AVON
WILDERNESS
PARK
Ben Cruachan 839+
Licola
53
Lake Glenmaggie
Glenmaggie
Seaton
Newry
Heyfield
Cowwarr
Winnindoo
Toongabbie
19
Kilmany
Fulham
Flynn
Rosedale
24
HOLEY PLAINS S.P.
Flynns Ck Upper
Willung
Gormandale
56
Carrajung
73
Darriman
Won Wron
Calrossie
Greenmount
Yarram
Alberton
Port Albert
Manns Beach
Clonmel I.
Kate Kearney Entrance
Port Albert Entrance

Waterford
Castleburn
Cobbannah
Tabberabbera
DIVIDING
Den of Nargun
Glenaladale
Culloden
Valencia Creek
Briagolong
Boisdale
Upper Maffra West
Tinamba
Maffra
Denison
Bundalagauh
Nambrok
16
Kilmany Sth
Wurruk
28
Sale
Longford
Dutson
A440
33
Stradbroke
Woodside
Woodside Beach
McLoughlins Beach

73
Mt Baldhead 1377
Morris Peak + 789
Mt Sugarloaf 890
MITCHELL RIVER N.P.
Bullumwaal
Mt Taylor
Wuk Wuk
Calulu
Lindenow
Lindenow Sth
90
Fernbank
Munro
50
Montgomery
Clydebank
Cobains
Perry Bridge
59
Meerlieu
Bengworden
Stratford
PRINCES HWY
A1
Sugar Beet Museum
St Mary's Church
Bairnsdale
Eagle Pt
Paynesville
Goon Nure
Hollands Landing
Seacombe
The Heart
Sale Common
Golden Beach
Letts Beach (Paradise Beach)
61
Lake Reeve
Seaspray
Giffard
NINETY MILE BEACH MARINE N.P.
Jack Smith Lake

Cassilis
Tongio West
Tongio
Swifts Creek
Doctors Flat
B500
Ensay
97
Mt Nugong 1482
148
Timbarra
RANGE
ALPINE
Tambo Crossing
GREAT
Ash Ra
B500
Mt Little Dick 320+
FAIRY DELL F.R.A.
Wiseleigh
Sarsfield
Nicholson
Johnsonville
Bruthen
22
Tambo Upper
COLQUHOUN F.R.A.
Swan Reach
Metung
Nyerimilang Park
Lake King
Raymond I.
Victoria
THE LAKES N.P.
Steam Whale Head
Lake Wellington
GIPPSLAND LAKES
COASTAL PARK

Gelantipy
SNOWY
Bonang
Butchers Ridge
57
RIVER
Rodger R.
Murrindal
NATIONAL
Goongerah
Malinns
89
Buchan Caves
Buchan
14
Mt Murrungowar + 728
Buchan Sth
28
Mt Buck + 507
Murrungowar
MURRUNGOWAR F.R.A.
Wairewa
7
Nowa Nowa
PRINCES
Orbost
A1
Newmerella
Brodribb River
34
Cabbage Tree Creek
HWY
Lake Tyers
36
Marlo
51
Lake Corringle
Lakes Entrance
Fishermen's Cooperative
Cape Conran
38°

Tuna Gas & Oil Field

Snapper Gas & Oil Field

Marlin Gas & Oil Field

Barracouta Gas & Oil Field

Flounder Oil Field

Fortescue Oil Field

Halibut Oil Field

Bream Gas & Oil Field

Mackerel Oil Field

Cobia Oil Field

Kingfish West Oil Field

Kingfish B Oil Field

Kingfish A Oil Field

JOINS PAGE 78

39°

N
UBD

Bass Strait

Hogan I.

Scale 1:942 100

0   30
Kilometres

CONTINUES PAGE 50

	A	B	C	D	E

JOINS PAGES 73 & 77

Snowy Mtns Hwy

Sawpit Creek
Blue Cow Mountain
Smiggin Holes
Skitube ALPINE WAY
Jindabyne
Bullocks Flat
Moonbah
Beloka
Dalgety
East Jindabyne
Berridale
Cooma
Rock Flat
Kybeyan
KYBEYAN N.R.
WADBILLIGA
WADBILLIGA NATIONAL PARK
KOORABAN N.P.
Mt Dromedary 797m
Narooma
Montague I.
EUROBODALLA N.P.
Central Tilba
GULAGA N.P.
Tilba Tilba
Wallaga Lake
Cobargo
BIAMANGA
BERMAGUI N.R.
Bermagui
Quaama
Brogo
BIAMANGA NATIONAL PARK
PRINCES HWY

KOSCIUSZKO NATIONAL PARK
Ingebyra
BARRY
Maffra
Nimmitabel
SNOWY
Bemboka
SOUTH EAST FOREST NATIONAL PARK
Kameruka
Candelo
Bega
Tanja
MIMOSA ROCKS NATIONAL PARK
Jellat Jellat
Tathra
Wapengo Lake

GREAT DIVIDING RANGE
Corrowong
MERRIANGAAH N.R.
Ando
Bukalong
QUIDONG N.R.
Bibbenluke
Cathcart
SOUTH EAST FOREST
Wyndham
Lochiel
Wolumla
BOURNDA NATURE RESERVE
Wallagoot Lake
BOURNDA NATIONAL PARK
Merimbula
TASMAN

MONARO HWY
Mila
Craigie
BONDI GULF N.R.
Rockton
Delegate
Delegate River
Tubbut
Cabanandra
Bonang
Bendoc
Burragate
Towamba
MT IMLAY N.P.
Eden
Boydtown
Twofold Bay
Kiah
BEN BOYD NATIONAL PARK
Mackillop Bridge
Deddick
ALPINE N.P.
Pambula
Pambula Beach
Pambula Lake
BEN BOYD NATIONAL PARK

SNOWY RIVER NATIONAL PARK
Rodger R.
ERRINUNDRA N.P.
Goongerah
Errinundra
Malinns
COOPRACAMBRA N.P.
Chandlers Creek
Weeragua
Combienbar
Noorinbee Nth
Wangarabell
Maramingo Hill 386
Mt Kaye 984
NEW SOUTH WALES
VICTORIA
Wonboyn
Green Cape
Disaster Bay
SEA
NADGEE N.R.

Club Terrace
CROAJINGOLONG N.P. (LIND N.P.)
Noorinbee
Cann River
ALFRED N.P.
Genoa
Genoa Peak 489
Gipsy Point
Mt Cann 530
Mallacoota
Mallacoota Inlet
Cape Howe
CAPE HOWE M.N.P.
Gabo I.

Mt Buck 507
Orbost
Murrungowar
MURRUNGOWAR F.R.A.
PRINCES HWY
Brodribb River
Cabbage Tree Creek
Bemm River
CAPE CONRAN C.P.
Tamboon
CROAJINGOLONG NATIONAL PARK
PT HICKS M.N.P.
Cape Everard
Pt Hicks
Wingan Inlet
Rame Head
Little Rame Head
Sandpatch Point

Marlo
Lake Corringle
Cape Conran
BEWARE REEF MARINE SANCTUARY
Tamboon Inlet
Sydenham Inlet
Marlo Inlet

Bass Strait

🛢 Tuna Gas & Oil Field

🛢 Flounder Oil Field

© UNIVERSAL PUBLISHERS PTY LTD 2005

Bairnsdale page 77 C2

Information Centre
240 Main St
Ph: (03) 5152 3444

Ballarat page 75 C1

Information Centre
39 Sturt St
Ph: (03) 5320 5741

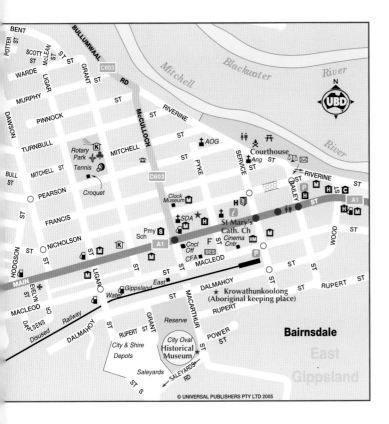

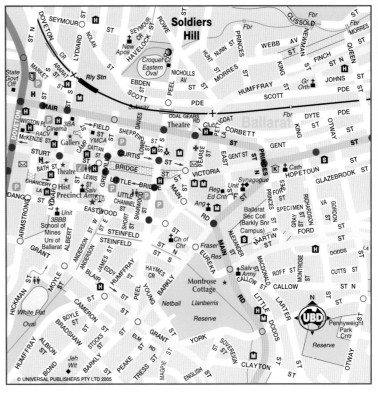

Benalla page 72 D4

Information Centre
Costume Museum,
14 Mair St
Ph: (03) 5762 1749

Bendigo page 71 D4

Information Centre
Pall Mall
Ph: (03) 5444 4445

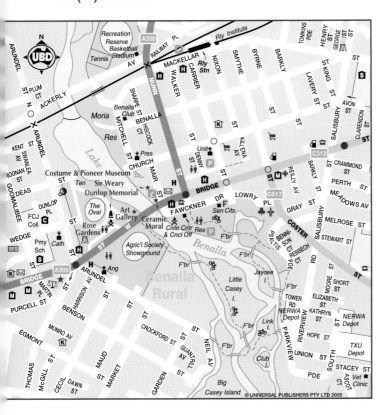

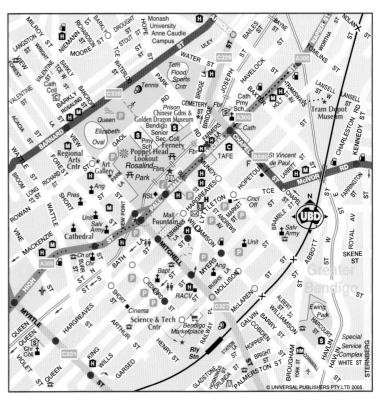

Castlemaine page 71 D5

Information Centre
Market Building,
Mostyn St
Ph: (03) 5470 6200

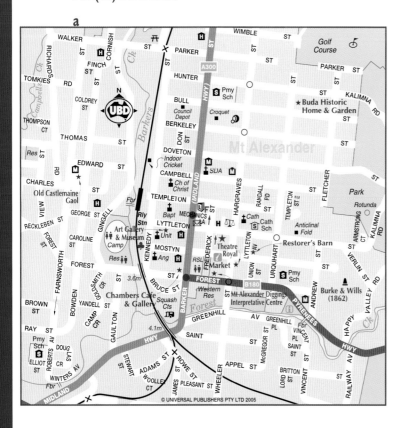

Colac page 75 C4

Information Centre
Queen St/Murray St
Ph: (03) 5231 3730

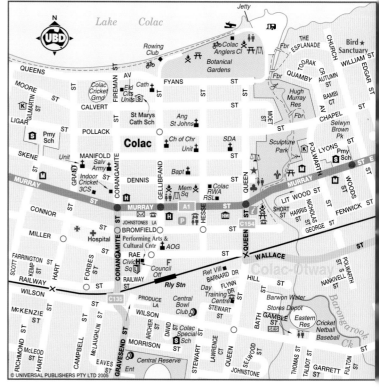

Geelong page 75 E3

Information Centre
Wool Museum,
Moorabool St/Brougham St
Ph: 1800 620 888

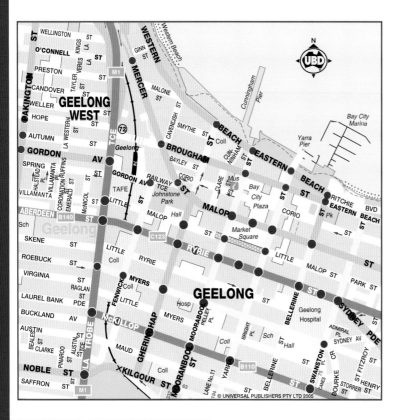

Hamilton page 74 D2

Information Centre
Lonsdale St
Ph: (03) 5572 3746

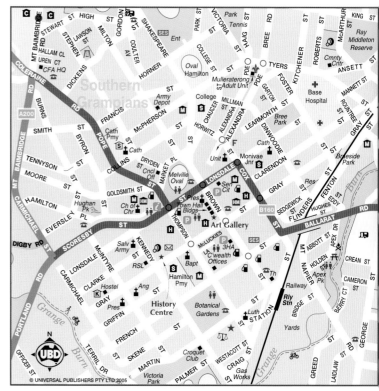

Horsham page 70 E4

Information Centre
20 O'Callaghans Pde
Ph: (03) 5382 1832

Lakes Entrance page 77 D2

Information Centre
Marine Pde/Esplanade
Ph: (03) 5155 1966

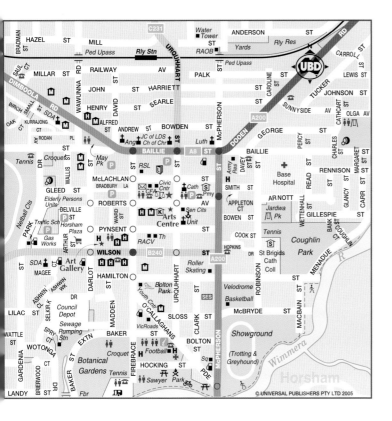

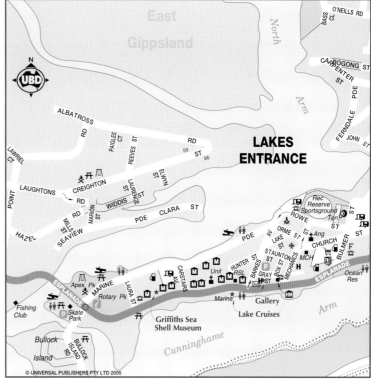

Mildura page 68 D2

Information Centre
Alfred Deakin Centre,
180 Deakin Ave
Ph: (03) 5018 8380

Morwell page 76 E3

Information Centre
Princes Hwy, Traralgon
Ph: 1800 621 409

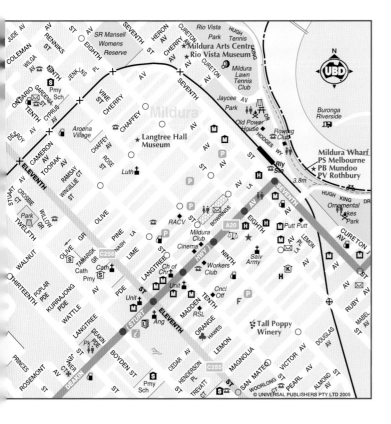

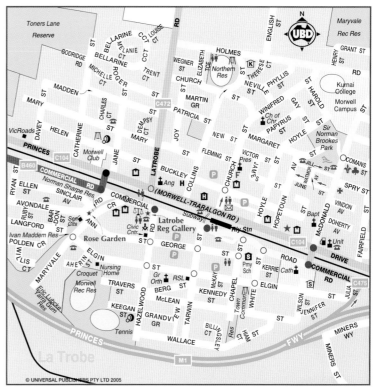

Portland page 74 C4

Information Centre
Maritime Discovery Centre,
Lee Breakwater Rd
Ph: (03) 5523 2671

Sale page 77 B3

Information Centre
8 Foster St
Ph: (03) 5144 1108

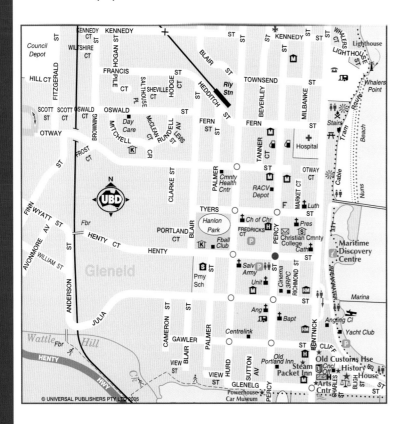

Shepparton page 72 C3

Information Centre
534 Wyndham St
Ph: (03) 5831 4400

Stawell page 71 A5

Information Centre
50-52 Western Hwy
Ph: (03) 5358 2314

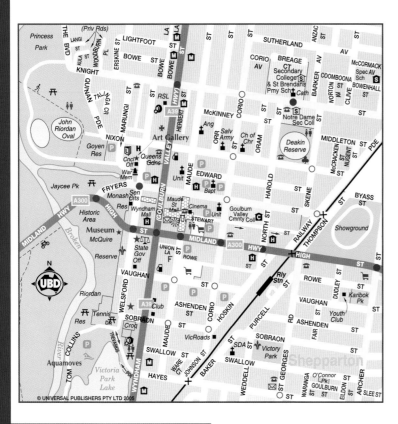

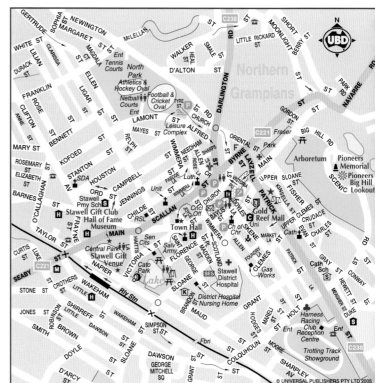

Traralgon page 76 E3

Information Centre
'The Old Church',
Princes St
Ph: 1800 621 409

Wangaratta page 72 E3

Information Centre
100-104 Murphy St
Ph: (03) 5721 5711

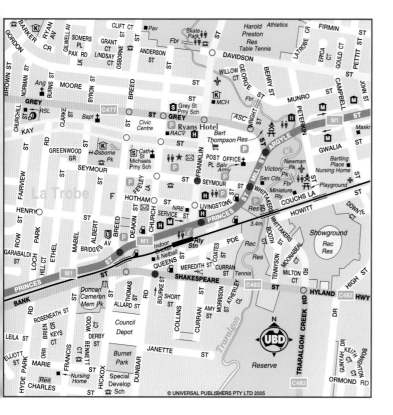

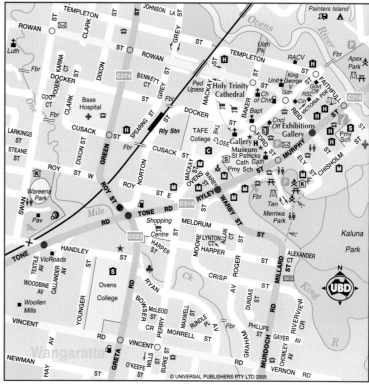

Warrnambool page 74 E4

Information Centre
Flagstaff Hill, Merri St
Ph: (03) 5564 7837

Wodonga page 73 A2

Information Centre
Gateway Complex,
Lincoln Causeway
Ph: 1300 796 222

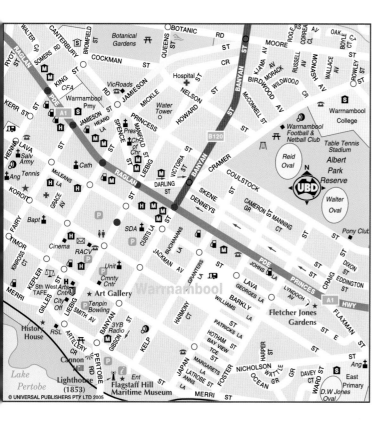

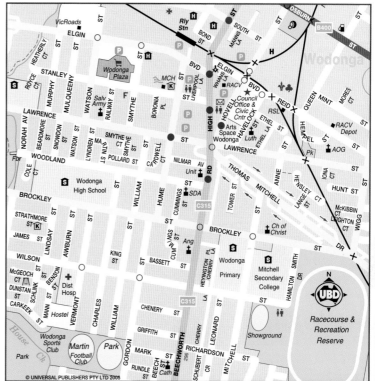

QUEENSLAND

Main Information Centre

Queensland Travel Centre
30 Makerston St,
Brisbane, Qld 4000
Ph: 138 833
www.queenslandholidays.com.au

Whale breaching, Hervey Bay

The second largest state in Australia, Queensland is big, covering some 1 727 200km², and incredibly varied, stretching as it does from the tropics to the temperate zone. From north to south its greatest distance is 2092km and from east to west 1448km.

Shadowing the coastline for about 2000km, the stunning Great Barrier Reef is one of the natural wonders of the world and perhaps the state's greatest asset. Even so, the Reef is only one of the fabulous natural assets found throughout the state. Visitors to Queensland will also discover some of the world's most beautiful beaches, luxuriant tropical rainforests, paradisiacal islands, vast deserts, national parks and fascinating towns.

Evidence that Aboriginal people have lived in Queensland for many thousands of years can be seen in the traditional rock art found in such places as Carnarvon Gorge in the Central Highlands and Quinkan Galleries, located in the Laura River valley on Cape York. There are opportunities for visitors to inspect significant sites with Aboriginal guides, learn about indigenous lifestyles at cultural centres such as the Dreamtime Centre near Rockhampton or be entertained by the world-renowned Tjapukai Dance Theatre near Cairns.

Touring Queensland by car is easy, although a 4WD is required to reach some of the more remote Outback regions. The Bruce Hwy links Brisbane with Cairns and gives access to all coastal areas in between. A sealed road continues to Mossman, but dirt roads take over further north into the pristine wilderness of Cape York. A network of roads covers the vast Outback areas, with convenient links to many points on the Bruce Hwy. The enormous distances can also be covered by rail or air. Brisbane, Cairns and Coolangatta have international airports and there are regional airports at many of the larger towns and cities.

MAIN PLACES OF INTEREST

	Map ref		Map ref
Atherton Tableland	95 D3	Lone Pine Koala Sanctuary, Brisbane	90 D3
Australia Zoo	103 E4	Mount Coot-tha, Brisbane	90 D2
Australian Stockmans Hall of Fame	97 C5	Museum of Tropical Queensland	107
Birdsville	100 C2	Noosa National Park	103 E3
Bundaberg Rum Distillery	99 D6	Outback at Isa, Mount Isa	106
Cape York	93	Queensland Art Gallery, Brisbane	87 B4
Carnarvon Gorge	98 E6	Queensland Museum & Sciencentre	87 B4
Cobb & Co Museum, Toowoomba	103 C4	Queen Street Mall, Brisbane	87 C4
Currumbin Wildlife Sanctuary	103 E5	Rainbow Beach	103 E2
Daintree National Park	95 C2	Reef HQ, Townsville	107
Dreamtime Cultural Centre	99 B5	Richmond Fossil Centre	97 B2
Dreamworld	103 E5	Roma Street Parkland, Brisbane	87 B3
Fraser Island	103 E2	Sea World	103 E5
Glass House Mountains	103 D4	Skyrail Rainforest Cableway, Cairns	95 D3
Granite Belt Wineries	103 C6	South Bank Parklands, Brisbane	87 C5
Great Barrier Reef	93,95,99	Surfers Paradise	103 E5
Hervey Bay	103 D2	Tamborine Mountain	103 E5
Hughenden Dinosaur Display Centre	97 C2	Tjapukai Aboriginal Culture Park, Cairns	95 D3
Johnstone River Crocodile Farm	95 D4	The Big Pineapple, Nambour	103 D3
Jupiters Casino	103 E5	Undara Volcanic Tubes	95 C4
Kuranda Scenic Railway	95 D3	UnderWater World, Mooloolaba	103 E3
Lamington National Park	103 D5	Warner Bros Movie World	103 E5
Lawn Hill Gorge	94 A5	Whitsunday Passage	98 E1

QUEENSLAND KEY MAP

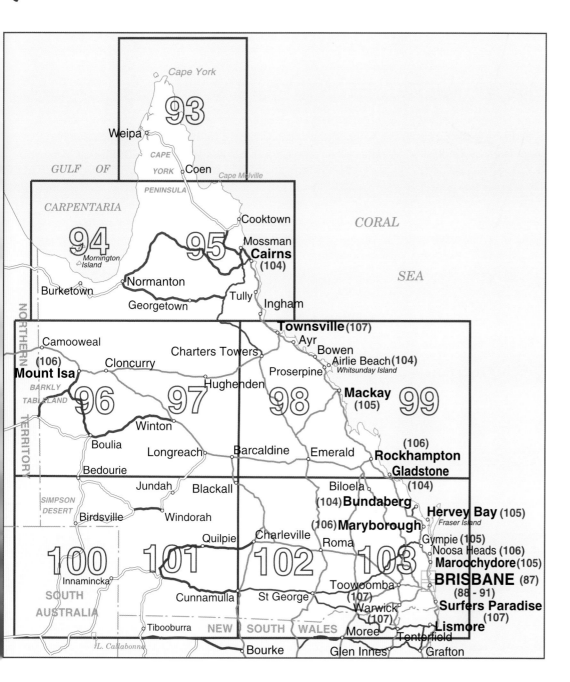

Cape York

93

Weipa

CAPE

GULF OF

YORK

Coen

Cape Melville

PENINSULA

CARPENTARIA

Cooktown

CORAL

94

Mossman

95

Mornington
Island

Cairns
(104)

Normanton

SEA

Burketown

Georgetown

Tully

Ingham

NORTHERN

Townsville (107)

Camooweal

Ayr

Bowen

(106)

Charters Towers

Airlie Beach (104)

Mount Isa

Cloncurry

Proserpine

Whitsunday Island

BARKLY

Hughenden

Mackay

TABLELAND

96

97

98

(105)

99

TERRITORY

Winton

Boulia

Longreach

Barcaldine

Emerald

(106)

Bedourie

Rockhampton

Gladstone

SIMPSON

Jundah

Blackall

Biloela

(104)

DESERT

Birdsville

Windorah

(104)**Bundaberg**

Hervey Bay (105)

Fraser Island

(106)**Maryborough**

100

101

Quilpie

Charleville

Roma

102

103

Gympie (105)

Noosa Heads (106)

Innamincka

Maroochydore(105)

SOUTH

Cunnamulla

St George

Toowoomba

BRISBANE (87)

AUSTRALIA

(107)

(88 - 91)

Warwick

Surfers Paradise

Tibooburra

NEW SOUTH WALES

(107)

(107)

L. Callabonna

Bourke

Moree

Lismore

Tenterfield

Glen Innes

Grafton

Lawn Hill Gorge, Boodjamulla (Lawn Hill) National Park

BRISBANE CITY

Brisbane is the northernmost capital on Australia's east coast, a subtropical city on the banks of the Brisbane River. The city lies 14km inland and the river has always been an integral part of Brisbane life. Paddlesteamers, yachts, floating restaurants, ferries and cruise boats can be seen along the river, and there are restaurants and cafes with beautiful water views.

John Oxley, Surveyor-General, sailed up this river in 1823 and named it the Brisbane River after Sir Thomas Brisbane, then Governor of New South Wales. From 1825-1839, Brisbane was a penal settlement. The old windmill on Wickham Tce is the city's oldest building, constructed by convicts in 1828. It became known as the 'Tower of Torture' because, when the wind dropped, the convicts had to crush the grain on a treadmill.

Brisbane today is a busy, modern city with an extensive transport system, a variety of restaurants, entertainment and nightlife. The city has many parks and gardens, with the largest, the City Botanic Gardens, situated on a bend of the Brisbane River. Roma Street Parkland is the world's largest subtropical garden in a city centre. Mount Coot-tha Botanic Gardens, at Toowong, feature a scented garden, tropical plant dome and the Sir Thomas Brisbane Planetarium.

BRISBANE CITY PLACES OF INTEREST

	ref		ref
ANZAC Square	D3	Queen Street Mall	C4
Brisbane City Hall & Tower	C4	Queensland Art Gallery	B4
Brisbane Convention & Exhibition Centre	B5	Queensland Maritime Museum	C5
Brisbane Cricket Ground (the Gabba)	E6	Queensland Museum & Sciencentre	B4
City Botanic Gardens	D4	Queensland Performing Arts Centre	C5
Commissariat Store	C4	Riverside Centre & Markets	D3
Conrad Treasury Brisbane (Casino)	C4	Roma Street Parkland	B3
Customs House	D3	St Johns Anglican Cathedral	D3
Fortitude Valley	E2	South Bank Parklands	C5
Kangaroo Point	E3	State Library of Queensland	B4
King George Square	C4	Story Bridge	E3
Old Government House	D5	Suncorp Metway Stadium	A3
Old Windmill Observatory	C3	Victoria Barracks	B3
Parliament House	D5	Victoria Park	C1

Top: Brunswick Street Markets, Fortitude Valley; Middle: South Bank Parklands; Bottom: Story Bridge

KELVIN GROVE

Queensland University of Technology (Kelvin Grove Campus)

Kelvin Grove High

Victoria Park

Royal Brisbane Hospital

RNA Exhibition Grounds

FORTITUDE VALLEY

SPRING HILL

Roma Street Parkland

Petrie Terrace

Suncorp Metway Stadium

Victoria Barracks

Castlemaine Perkins Brewery

MILTON

St. Johns Cathedral

Kangaroo Pt

Story Bridge

Customs House

Riverside Centre

Eagle St Pier & Riverside Markets

King George Square

Brisbane City Hall

Queen St Mall

CITY

ANZAC Square

Casino

BRISBANE RIVER

Milton Reach

State Library

Queensland Art Gallery & Museum

Old Commissariat Store

WILLIAM JOLLY BRIDGE

MERIVALE BRIDGE

VICTORIA BRIDGE

South Brisbane

Performing Arts Centre

Brisbane Convention & Exhibition Centre

South Bank

SOUTH BRISBANE

THE GOODWILL BRIDGE

Queensland Maritime Museum

Queensland University of Technology Gardens Point Campus

Old Government House

Parliament House & Annexe

Botanic Gardens

Gardens Pt

CAPTAIN COOK BRIDGE

KANGAROO POINT

Town Reach

WEST END

HIGHGATE HILL

Musgrave Park

St Laurences College

Mater Hospital

Brisbane Cricket Ground

© UNIVERSAL PUBLISHERS PTY LTD 2005

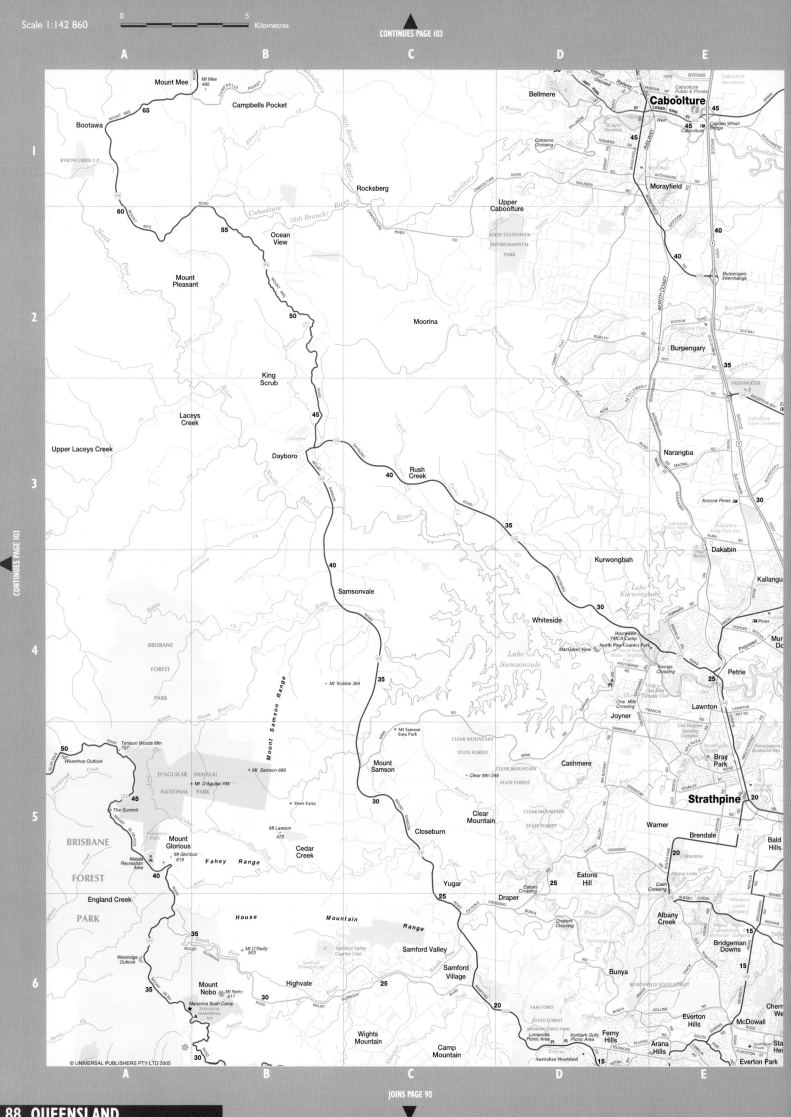

0   5   Kilometres

CONTINUES PAGE 103

Mount Mee
Mt Mee 495
Campbells Pocket
Bootawa
65
BYRON CREEK C.P.
60
55
Rocksberg
Ocean View
Mount Pleasant
50
Moorina
King Scrub
45
Laceys Creek
Dayboro
Upper Laceys Creek
40
Rush Creek
35
40
Samsonvale
30
Mt Kobble 384
35
Mount Samson Range
BRISBANE FOREST PARK
Mt Samson Emu Park
Mount Samson
50
Tenison Woods Mtn 757
Wivenhoe Outlook
Mt Samson 689
CLEAR MOUNTAIN STATE FOREST
45
D'AGUILAR (MAIALA) NATIONAL PARK
Mt D'Aguilar 745
Deer Farm
30
Clear Mtn 246
40
Greene's Falls
Mount Glorious
Mt Glorious 619
Mt Lawson 473
Cedar Creek
Closeburn
Clear Mountain
CLEAR MOUNTAIN STATE FOREST
BRISBANE
Maiala Recreation Area
FOREST
England Creek
Fahey Range
Yugar
Eatons Hill
PARK
35
Westridge Outlook
HOUSE
Mountain
Range
25
Draper
25
Mt O'Reilly 503
Samford Valley
35
Mount Nebo
Mt Nebo 617
Highvale
30
Samford Village
25
Samford Valley Country Club
20
Wights Mountain
Camp Mountain
30

© UNIVERSAL PUBLISHERS PTY LTD 2005

Bellmere
Caboolture
Morayfield
45
45
Upper Caboolture
SHEEP STATION CK ENVIRONMENTAL PARK
40
40
Burpengary Interchange
Burpengary
35
Narangba
30
Arizona Pines
Dakabin
Kurwongbah
Kallangur
30
Whiteside
Lake Kurwongbah
Lake Samsonvale
Warrawee YMCA Camp
North Pine Country Park
MacGavin View
Youngs Crossing
25
Petrie
Lawnton
Joyner
Cashmere
Bray Park
Strathpine
20
Warner
Brendale
Bald Hills
Eatons Hill
25
Eatons Crossing
Drapers Crossing
Albany Creek
15
Bunya
Bridgeman Downs
BUNYAVILLE STATE FOREST
15
Everton Hills
McDowall
Ferny Hills
Arana Hills
Everton Park
BRISBANE FOREST PARK
Lomandra Picnic Area
Ironbark Gully Picnic Area
Australian Woolshed
15

CONTINUES PAGE 103

CONTINUES PAGE 103

A B C D E

Abbey Museum
Restricted Vehicle Access
State Forest
50
55
Ningi
Ningi Island
ROAD
60
BRIBIE ISLAND
Silver Shores
Bellara
65
Bellara
Bribie Bridge
BRIBIE ISLAND N.P.
Woorim
Bribie Island
AVENUE
Sandstone Point
Welsby Bridge
Bongaree
Bribie Pines
Bribie Island
FIRST
Godwin Beach
Sandstone Point
Bribie Island
Buckleys Hole
South Pt
BUCKLEYS HOLE C.P.
Woody Bay
Bald Pt
Skirmish Pt
Red Beach

1

BEACHMERE ENVIRONMENTAL PARK

River
ROAD
Beachmere

Deception

Bay

N
UBD

Vehicular Ferry

Moreton

2

Creek
Four Star
35
Deception Bay
Rothwell
Redcliffe Aerodrome
NEWPORT MARINA
NATHAN ROAD WETLANDS RESERVE
Scarborough Boat Harbour
Oyster Pt
North Reef
Castlereagh (or Reefi) Pt
Scarborough Boat Harbour
35
Scarborough
Scarborough Pt
Scarborough Beach
Drury Pt
Queens Beach Nth
Osbourne Pt

3

Rothwell Memorial
30
Kippa - Ring
30
HAYS INLET C.P. NO.2
Redcliffe
REDCLIFFE
Margate
30
Queens Beach
Queens Beach South
Redcliffe Jetty
Settlement Cove Lagoon
Margate Redcliffe Pt
Mango Hill
Railway
Clontarf
KING
Bramble Bay
Bells Beach
Woody Point
Scotts Pt

4

Mango Hill
25
HAYS INLET C.P. NO.1
Griffin
Redcliffe
Clontarf Beach
Clontarf Pt
Woody Point Beach
Picnic Pt
Woody Pt
25
River
Bramble
Bay
Bay

5

HWY
20
BRUCE
TINCHI TAMBA WETLANDS RESERVE
Brighton
NORTH
Brighton
20
Nashville
20
Sandgate Foreshores
Bracken Ridge
TAFE
Bald Hills
Sandgate
Grays
Deagon
Shorncliffe
Cabbage Tree
DEAGON WETLANDS
Sandgate Head

Mud Island

Telegraph
Fitzgibbon
North Boondall
Brisbane Int. Centre
Boondall Wetlands Visitor Centre
Nudgee Beach
Nudgee Beach
18
15
Carseldine
QUT Carseldine Campus
Colonial Village
15
Boondall
BOONDALL WETLANDS PARK
Caravan Village
Taigum
15
Zillmere
Aspley Acres
Nudgee
Nudgee

Juno Point
Port of Brisbane
25
BISHOP DR

6

Chermside
10
Geebung
Banyo
15
Virginia
Bingha
Nudgee
Proposed Western Parallel Runway
Myrtletown
Luggage Point Waste Water Treatment Plant
Port of Brisbane HQ
Brisbane Express Park
Fisherman Islands
St Helena Island
St Helena Island National Park

Wavell Hts
10
Northgate
Brisbane Airport
10
RAIL LINK
15
Domestic Terminal
Prince Charles

A B C D E

© UNIVERSAL PUBLISHERS PTY LTD 2005

0 ___ 5 Kilometres

A   B   C   D   E

1

Mount Nebo Mt Nebo 617
Manorina Bush Camp
D'AGUILAR (MANORINA) N.P.
D'AGUILAR (BOOMBANA) N.P.
D'AGUILAR (JOLLYS LOOKOUT) N.P.
Samford Showground
Samford Village
Highvale
Bunya
BUNYAVILLE STATE FOREST
Aspley
Chermside West   Chermside
McDowall
Everton Hills
SAM FORD STATE FOREST
BRISBANE FOREST PARK
Lomandra Picnic Area
Ironbark Gully Picnic Area
Australian Woolshed
Ferny Hills
Arana Hills
Stafford Heights
Wights Mountain
Camp Mountain
Ferny Grove
Brisbane Tramway Museum
Oxford Park
Grovely
Everton Park
Stafford
Kedron
Keperra Country Club
Mitchelton
Gordon Park
Jollys Lookout
Camp Mountain Lookout
Peewee Bend
Bellbird Grove
Upper Kedron
Keperra
Gaythorne
Enoggera
Alderley
Grange
Lutwyche

2

McAfees Lookout
Enoggera Reservoir
The Gap
Enoggera Hill
ENOGGERA MILITARY CAMP
St Johns Wood
Newmarket
Windsor
Wilston
BRISBANE   FOREST   PARK
Brisbane Forest Park HQ & Info Centre
Ashgrove
Dorrington
Herston
Royal Brisbane
Q.U.T.
Gold Creek Reservoir
The Summit 287+
Mount Coot-tha
Bardon
Rainworth
Jubilee
Ithaca
Red Hill
Kelvin Grove
INNER CITY
BRISBANE
Spring Hill
GPO
Paddington
Petrie Terrace
Story Bridge

3

Upper Brookfield
Mount Coot-tha
The Pinnacle
Constitution Hill 258+
Mt Coot-tha 244+
Milton
BRISBANE
South Brisbane
South Bank
Kholo
Lake Manchester
Kenmore Hills
Sir Thomas Gaffney Lookout
Toowong
Auchenflower
West End
Highgate Hill
Brookfield
Mt Elphinstone
Chapel Hill
Taringa
St Lucia
Dutton Park
Indooroopilly
University of Queensland St Lucia Campus
Fairfield
Pullenvale
Chelmer
Jay Park
Yeronga
MOGGILL STATE FOREST
Mt Seimon 130
Mount Crosby
Mt Crosby 182
Kenmore
Graceville
Long Pocket
Tennyson
Yeerongpilly
Karana Downs
Anstead
Jindalee
Fig Tree Pocket
Sherwood
Corinda
Mooroka

4

Lloyd Bird Environ. Park
Colleges Crossing
Karalee
Johnsons Rocks
Pinjarra Hills
Westlake
Mount Ommaney
Seventeen Mile Rocks
Sinnamon Park
Oxley
Rocklea
Salisbury
Chuwar
Kholo Bridge
Bellbowrie
Middle Park
Jamboree Hts
Riverhills
Sumner
Darra
Archerfield
Archerfield Airport
Barellan Point
Moggill
Department of Primary Industries
Moreton Correctional Centre
North Tivoli
Bremer Junction

5

Raymonds Hill
Tivoli Hill
Tivoli
North Ipswich
Bundamba
Dinmore
Riverview
Redbank
Wacol
ARMY BARRACKS
Richlands
Inala
Durack
Acacia Ridge
Willawong
Doolandella
Algester
Ipswich
West Ipswich
Newtown
Booval
East Ipswich
North Booval
Ebbw Vale
New Chum
Priors Pocket
Gailes
Goodna
Ellen Grove
Forest Lake
Pallara
Parkinson
Silkstone
Bergins Hill
Collingwood Park
Carole Park
Heathwood
Eastern Heights
Churchill
Blackstone
Raceview
Redbank Plains
Bellbird Park
Camira
Larapinta

6

Flinders View
Swanbank
Springfield
GREENBANK MILITARY CAMP
Forestdale
Hillcrest
Yamanto
Ripley
White Rock
Boronia Heights
Deebing Heights
South Ripley
WHITE ROCK CONSERVATION PARK

CONTINUES PAGE 103

A   B   C   D   E

JOINS PAGE 89

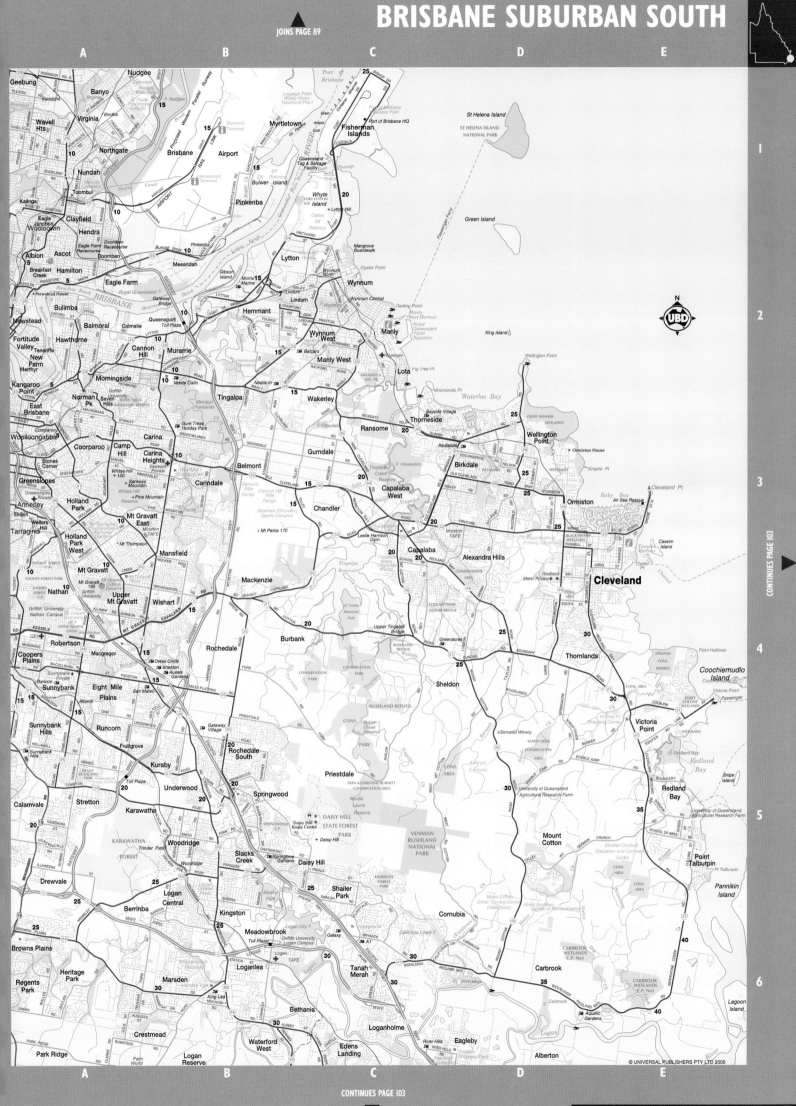

CONTINUES PAGE 103

Snorkelling off Cid Island, Whitsundays

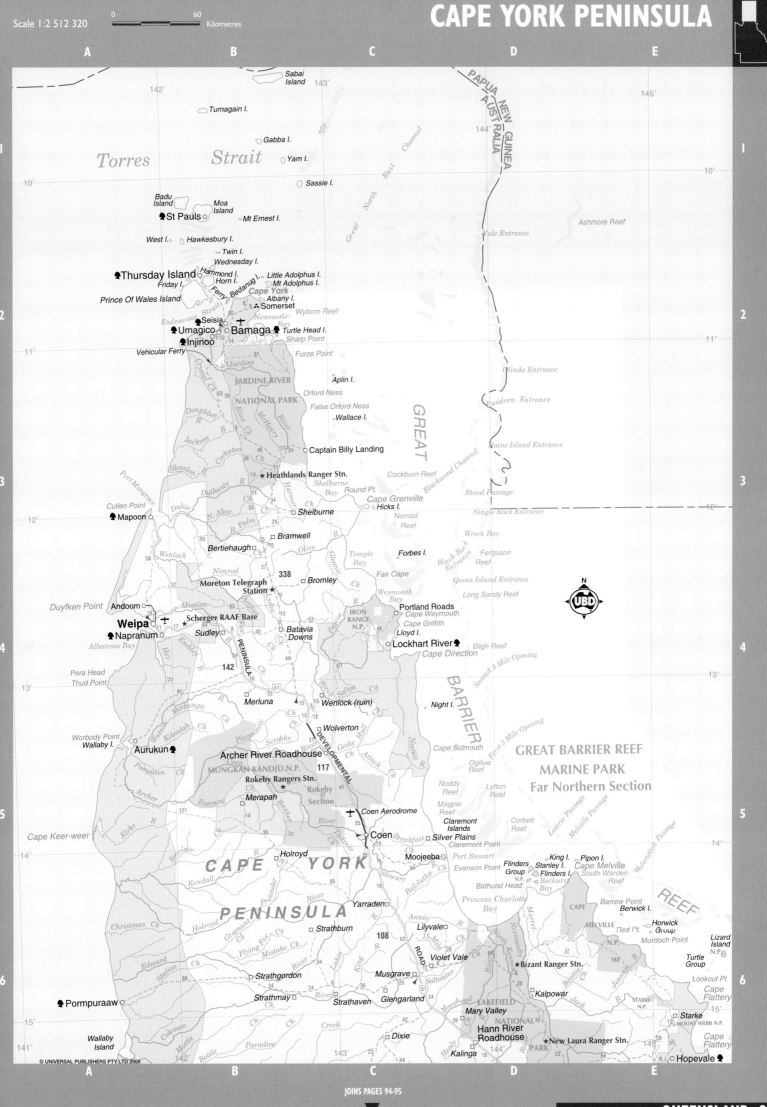

Scale 1:2 512 320

0   60   Kilometres

A B C D E

Torres   Strait

Sabai Island
Turnagain I.
Gabba I.
Yam I.
Sassie I.

PAPUA NEW GUINEA
AUSTRALIA

Ashmore Reef

Yule Entrance

Badu Island
Moa Island
♠St Pauls
Mt Ernest I.
West I.
Hawkesbury I.
Twin I.
Wednesday I.
♠Thursday Island
Hammond I.
Horn I.
Friday I.
Little Adolphus I.
Mt Adolphus I.
Prince Of Wales Island
Cape York
Albany I.
♣Somerset
Wyborn Reef
Endeavour Strait
Newcastle Bay
♠Seisia
Bamaga
♠Turtle Head I.
♠Umagico
♠Injinoo
Sharp Point
Vehicular Ferry
Furze Point

Olinda Entrance

JARDINE RIVER NATIONAL PARK
Aplin I.
Orford Ness
False Orford Ness
Wallace I.

Pandora Entrance

GREAT

Raine Island Entrance

Captain Billy Landing

★Heathlands Ranger Stn.
Shelburne Bay
Round Pt.
Cape Grenville
Hicks I.
Cockburn Reef
Stead Passage

♠Mapoon
Cullen Point
Shelburne
Nomad Reef
Single Rock Entrance

Bramwell
Bertiehaugh
Wreck Bay
Forbes I.
Temple Bay
Black Rock Entrance
Ferguson Reef

Nimrod
338
Moreton Telegraph Station ★
Bromley
Fair Cape
Quoin Island Entrance
Long Sandy Reef

Duyfken Point
Andoom
Weymouth Bay
IRON RANGE N.P.
Portland Roads
Cape Weymouth
Cape Griffith
N ⊕ UBD

Weipa
Scherger RAAF Base
Sudley
Batavia Downs
Lloyd I.
♠Napranum
Albatross Bay
Lockhart River ♠
Bligh Reef
Cape Direction

BARRIER

Pera Head
Thud Point
142
PENINSULA
16
Second 3 Mile Opening

Merluna
Wenlock (ruin)
Night I.

First 3 Mile Opening

Worbody Point
Wallaby I.
♠Aurukun
Wolverton
DEVELOPMENTAL
Cape Sidmouth

GREAT BARRIER REEF MARINE PARK Far Northern Section

Archer River Roadhouse
MUNGKAN-KANDJU N.P.
117
Rokeby Rangers Stn. ★
Rokeby Section
Ogilvie Reef
Noddy Reef
Lytton Reef
Merapah
Magpie Reef
Coen Aerodrome
Claremont Islands
Corbett Reef
Lowrie Passage
Melville Passage
Watson Passage

Cape Keer-weer
Coen
Breakfast
Silver Plains
Claremont Point

Holroyd
Moojeeba
Port Stewart
King I.
Pipon I.
CAPE YORK
Evanson Point
Flinders Group
Stanley I.
Flinders I.
Cape Melville
South Warden Reef

Yarraden
Balclutha
Bathurst Head
Bathurst Bay
CAPE MELVILLE N.P.
Barrow Point
Berwick I.
Horwick Group
REEF
PENINSULA
Strathburn
Princess Charlotte Bay
Lilyvale
108
Violet Vale
Murdoch Point
Lizard Island N.P.
Turtle Group

♠Pormpuraaw
Strathgordon
Musgrave
★Bizant Ranger Stn.
163
Lookout Pt
Cape Flattery

Strathmay
Strathaven
Glengarland
LAKEFIELD
Kalpowar
STARKE N.P.
♠Starke
MOUNT WEBB N.P.
Wallaby Island
Dixie
NATIONAL PARK
Mary Valley
Hann River Roadhouse
★New Laura Ranger Stn.
Cape Flattery

Kalinga
Hopevale ♠

© UNIVERSAL PUBLISHERS PTY LTD 2005

Scale 1:2 512 320

0   60   Kilometres

A   B   C   D   E

138°   139°   140°   141°   142°

15°
16°

GULF   OF   CARPENTARIA

Pormpuraaw

Wallaby Island

Christmas Ck

Greenant Ck

Flying

Edward

Station

Coleman

Mitchell

Bottle

Paradise

Kowanyama

MITCHELL & ALICE RIVERS N.P.

Rutland Plains

Scrutton

Alice

Hoddo

Koolatah

Nassau

River

Station

Dunbar

ROAD

Surprise

Ck

82

19

48

Inkerman

Galbraith

Staaten

22

61

Dorunda

Wydaba

33

Vanrook

Middle

225

40

DEVELOPMENTAL

Pelican

Sandy

Rocky I.
Thabugan Point
Halls Point
Lingnoonganee I.

Mornington Island
Cape Van Diemen

WELLESLEY ISLANDS

Gee Wee Point
Gunana   Sydney I.   Bountiful I.

Denham I.

Forsyth I.

Pains I.   FORSYTH ISLANDS
Bayley I.
Horseshoe I.   Oaktree Point

Allen I.   Bentinck I.

Sweers I.

SOUTH WELLESLEY ISLANDS

Point Burrowes
Point Austin

Delta Downs

Lotus Vale

Stirling

Miranda Downs

36   27

Glencoe

Fourteen Mile

Fitzmaurice Point

Karumba   KARUMBA   BURKE   RD

Alligator Point   DEV   41
30

Maggieville

Fish Hole

Mutton Hole

Oakland Park

102

Normanton

Clarina

Glenore

Timora

Blackbull

153

Tabletop

1

GULF

SAVANNAH

Magowra

Burke & Wills Cairn

Haydon

61

13

Inverleigh
153

Wernadinga
WAY

McAllister

Milgarra

Gum Creek

Belmore

Coralie

Croydon

12

Floraville

Neumayer Valley

196

Warren Vale

Wondoola

Mittagong

Augustus Downs

69

Talawanta

Bang Bang

Vena Park

Claraville

Gregory Downs

Donors Hills

Iffley

Prospect

Nardoo

Cowan Downs

68   84

Lorraine

DEVELOPMENTAL   WAY

Myally

77   49

Burke & Wills Roadhouse

Mellish Park

Canobie

Myola

Taldora

Savannah Downs

Kamileroi

Chidna
Waggabundi

Gleeson

Boomarra

Arizona

Pelham

Mt Oxide

Thorntonia

Gunpowder

Lady Annie   Resort

Mt Gordon
Mammoth

BURKE

MATILDA

Alcala

Monstraven

Brinard

234

Millungera

Coolullah

180

Granada

Spoonbill

Sedan Dip

Dalgonally

Lara

Rocklands

56

Camooweal

70

Gereta   Kajabbi

Calton Hills

Clonagh

Gypsy Downs

Bunda Bunda

BARKLY

CAMOOWEAL CAVES N.P.

66

OVERLANDERS   WAY   HWY

Quamby

Bauhinia Downs

Kilberry

Don

Yelvertoft   118

GULF WILDERNESS

Wollogorang
Gulf Wilderness Lodge
Redbank

Westmoreland

NORTHERN   TERRITORY

Hells Gate Roadhouse
228

Kingfisher Camp

Corinda (ruin)
Doomadgee

Bowthorn   4WD

Escott Resort   Burketown

Tirranna Roadhouse

Armraynald
73

Punjaub   117

Almora

QUEENSLAND

CONTINUES PAGES 139 & 142

BOODJAMULLA (LAWN HILL) NATIONAL PARK

Highland Plains

Lawn Hill

Gregory Downs

Adels Grove
Century Zinc Mine

Lawn Hill Gorge

Riversleigh Fossils

Old Herbert Vale

Riversleigh   128

Gallipoli

Norfolk

Morstone Downs

Undilla

Split Rock

91

© UNIVERSAL PUBLISHERS PTY LTD 2005

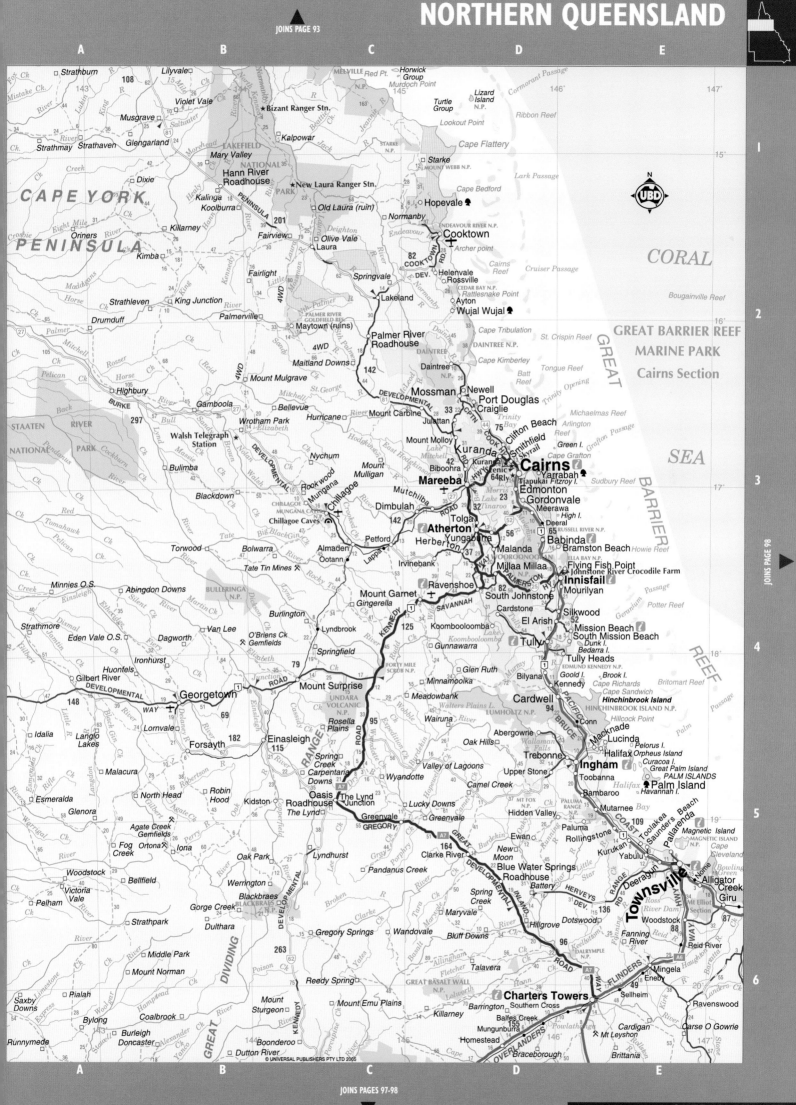

JOINS PAGE 93

JOINS PAGE 98

Scale 1:2 512 320

0   60 Kilometres

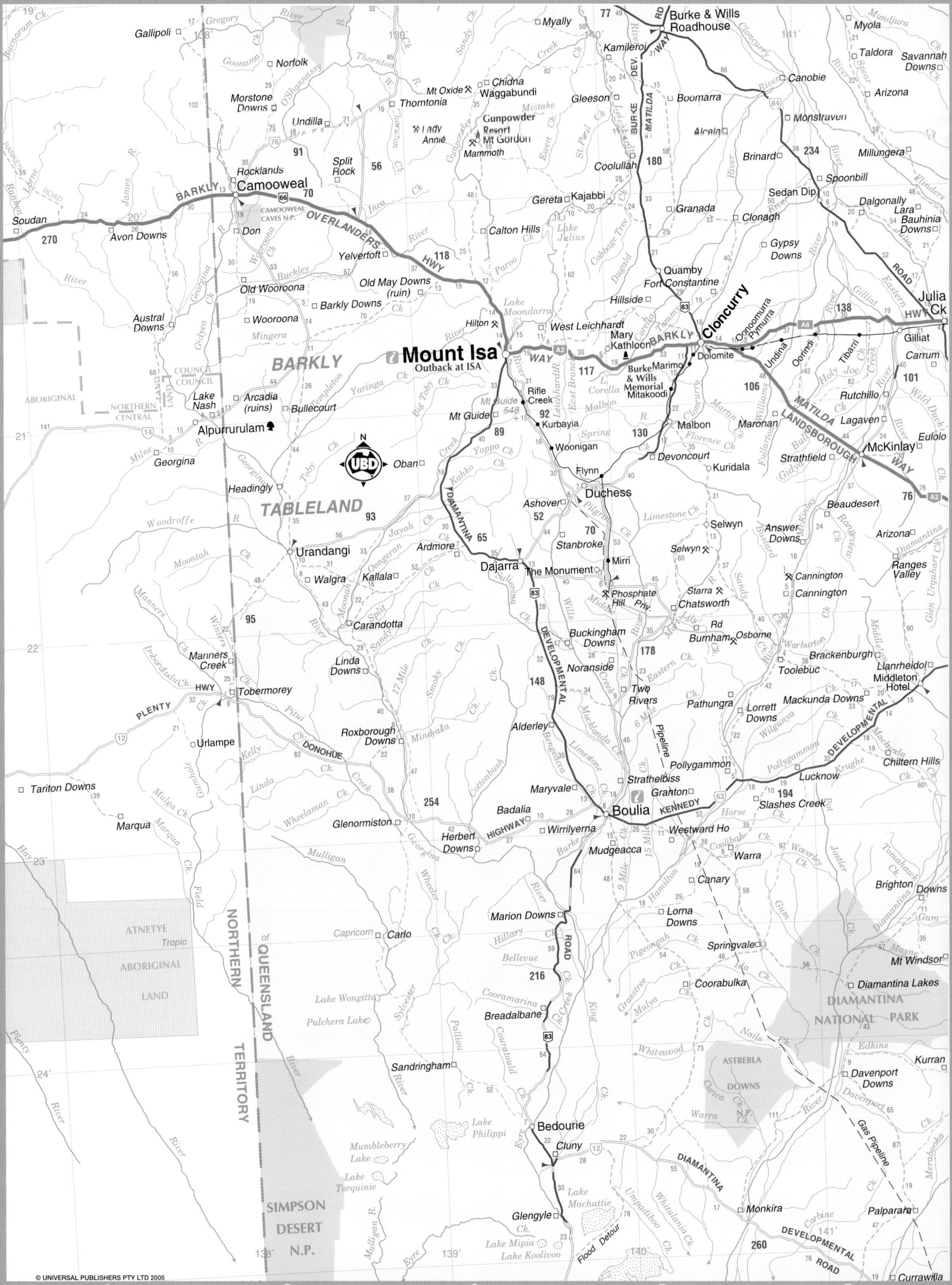

CONTINUES PAGES 142 & 145

BARKLY TABLELAND

Mount Isa
Outback at ISA

Camooweal

Cloncurry

Burke & Wills Roadhouse

Julia Ck

McKinlay

Duchess

Dajarra

Boulia

Bedourie

NORTHERN TERRITORY

SIMPSON DESERT N.P.

DIAMANTINA NATIONAL PARK

ASTREBLA DOWNS N.P.

OVERLANDERS HWY

BARKLY WAY

DIAMANTINA DEVELOPMENTAL ROAD

LANDSBOROUGH HWY

MATILDA HWY

KENNEDY DEVELOPMENTAL ROAD

PLENTY HWY

DONOHUE HWY

© UNIVERSAL PUBLISHERS PTY LTD 2005

JOINS PAGES 94-95

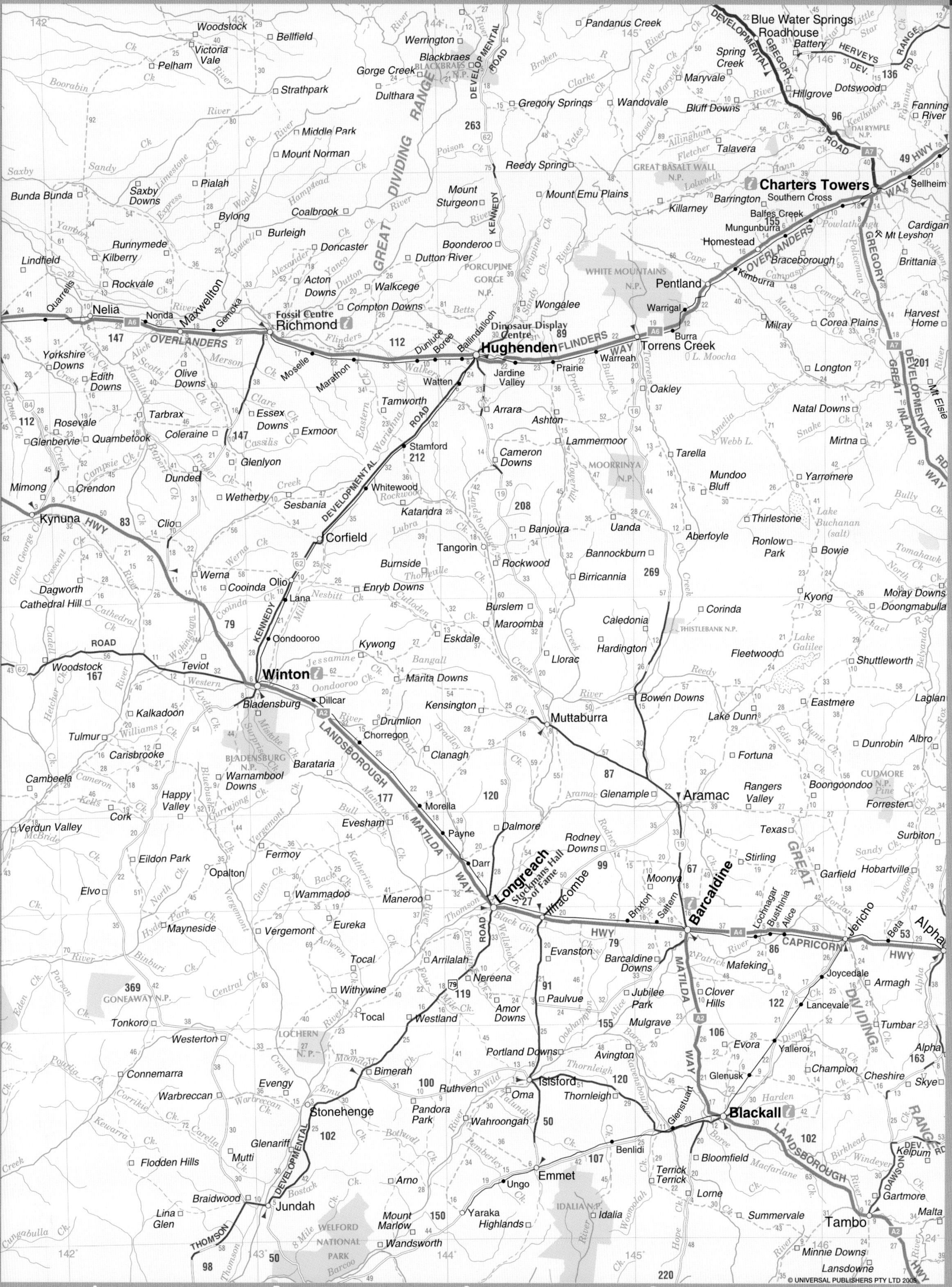

JOINS PAGE 98

JOINS PAGE 101

Scale 1:2 512 320

0   60   Kilometres

JOINS PAGE 97

Oak Park
Werrington
Pandanus Creek
Blackbraes N.P.
Clarke River
Blue Water Springs Roadhouse
Battery
Spring Creek
Maryvale
Hillgrove
Dotswood
Yabulu
Deeragun
Townsville
Nome
Aligator Creek
Institute of Marine Science
Cape Bowling Green
Darley Reef
Old Reef

Gregory Springs
Wandovale
Bluff Downs
Fanning River
Reid River
Woodstock
Giru
Barrana
Pioneer
Alva
Ayr
Rita Island
Cape Upstart
CAPE UPSTART N.P.

Reedy Spring
Talavera
Mount Sturgeon
Mount Emu Plains
GREAT BASALT WALL N.P.
Charters Towers
Mingela
Eneby
Sellheim
Brandon
Home Hill
Clare
Bobawaba
Guthalungra
Gumlu
Bowen
Gloucester I.
Hideaway Bay
Dingo Beach
George Pt

Boonderoo
PORCUPINE GORGE N.P.
WHITE MOUNTAINS N.P.
Barrington
Southern Cross
Balfes Creek
Killarney
Mungunburra
Homestead
Braceborough
Kimburra
Cardigan
Mt Leyshon
Brittania
Carse O Gowrie
Dalbeg
Millaroo
Wilmington
Wathana
Armuna
Merinda
Jaraga
Debella
Binbee
Briaba
Airlie Beach
Shute Harbour
CONWAY

Ballindalloch
Hughenden
FLINDERS
Pentland
Warrigal
Burra
Torrens Creek
Milray
Corea Plains
Harvest Home
Mount Cooper
Weir
Strathmore
Almoola
Collinsville
Birralee
Proserpine
Conway
Mount Hector
Bloomsbury
Midge Pt
Yalboroo
Calen
Mount Ossa

Jardine Valley
Prairie
Warreah
Oakley
Longton
Lornesleigh
Mt McConnell
Dandenong Park
Sphinx
Scartwater
Bungobine
Havillah
Newlands Mine
Eungella
EUNGELLA N.P.
Kuttabul

Arrara
Ashton
Lammermoor
Tarella
Natal Downs
Mt Elsie
Mt Coolon
Glenden
Finch Hatton
Elphinstone
Epsom
Gargett
Mirani

Cameron Downs
MOORRINYA N.P.
Mundoo Bluff
Yarromere
Mirtna
Belyando Crossing
Gunjulla
Pasha
Nth Goonyella Mine
Riverside Mine
Nebo
Waitara

Banjoura
Uanda
Aberfoyle
Thirlestone
Ronlow Park
Bowie
Lake Buchanan (salt)
Willandspey
Disney
Avon Downs
Goonyella Mine
Wotonga
Mindi
Braeside

Rockwood
Bannockburn
Birricannia
Corinda
Kyong
Doongmabulla
Moray Downs
Moranbah
Coppabella
Ingsdon
Red Mountain
Morpeth

Burslem
Maroomba
Caledonia
Hardington
THISTLEBANK N.P.
Fleetwood
Lake Galilee
Shuttleworth
EPPING FOREST N.P.
Frankfield
Villafranca
Iffley
Peak Downs Mine

Llorac
Kensington
Bowen Downs
Eastmere
Laglan
Beresford
Mt McLaren
Saraji Mine

Muttaburra
Lake Dunn
Dunrobin
Albro
Springvale
Blair Athol Mine
Clermont
Norwich Park Mine
Dysart
Cosmos
May Downs
Middle

Fortuna
CUDMORE N.P.
Boongoondoo Pine
Forresten
Redrock
NARRIEN RANGE N.P.
Langton
Nanva
Retro
Capella
Tieri
Oaky Ck Mine
Gregory Mine
Fairhill

Glenample
Aramac
Rangers Valley
Texas
Surbiton
Craven
Peak Vale
Anakie Gemfields
Bullery
Kabelbarra
German Creek Mine

Payne
Dalmore
Rodney Downs
Stirling
Moonya
Garfield
Hobartville
Islay Plains
Mt Tabletop
Withersfield
Rubyvale
Sapphire
Emerald
Blackwater

Darr
Longreach
Ilfracombe
Brixton
Saltern
Barcaldine
Jericho
Beta
Alpha
Pine Hill
Willows
Anakie
Yamala
Comet
Burngrove Mine
Kinrola Mine
Koorilgah Mine
South Blackwater Mine

CAPRICORN
Evanston
Barcaldine Downs
Mafeking
Joycedale
Armagh
Sedgeford
Drummond
Bogantungan
Mt Portwine
Willows Gemfields
Taroborah
Gindie
Fernlees

Nereena
Jubilee Park
Clover Hills
Lancevale
Tumbar
Durabrook
Avoca
Vandyke
Springsure
Somerby

Amor Downs
Paulvue
Mulgrave
Evora
Yalleroi
Alpha
Glen Avon
Echo Hills
Riverside
Kareela
Springwood
Consuelo

Portland Downs
Avington
Glenusk
Champion
Cheshire
Skye
Mantuan Downs
Castlevale
Rolleston
Basalt Creek

Ruthven
Oma
Isisford
Thornleigh
Glenstuart
Blackall
Harden
Kelpum
Tanderra
Deepdale Extension
Purbrook

Wahroongah
Benlidi
Bloomfield
Lorne
Cungelella
Ka Ka Mundi Section
Carnarvon
Wyseby

Emmet
Ungo
Terrick Terrick
Summervale
Gartmore
Carwell
CARNARVON NATIONAL PARK
Salvator Rosa Section
Mt Moffatt Section
Carnarvon Gorge Section
Ranger Stn
Oasis Lodge

Yaraka
Idalia
IDALIA N.P.
Tambo
Malta
Caldervale
Mt King
Babbiloora
Minnie Downs
Lansdowne

© UNIVERSAL PUBLISHERS PTY LTD 2005

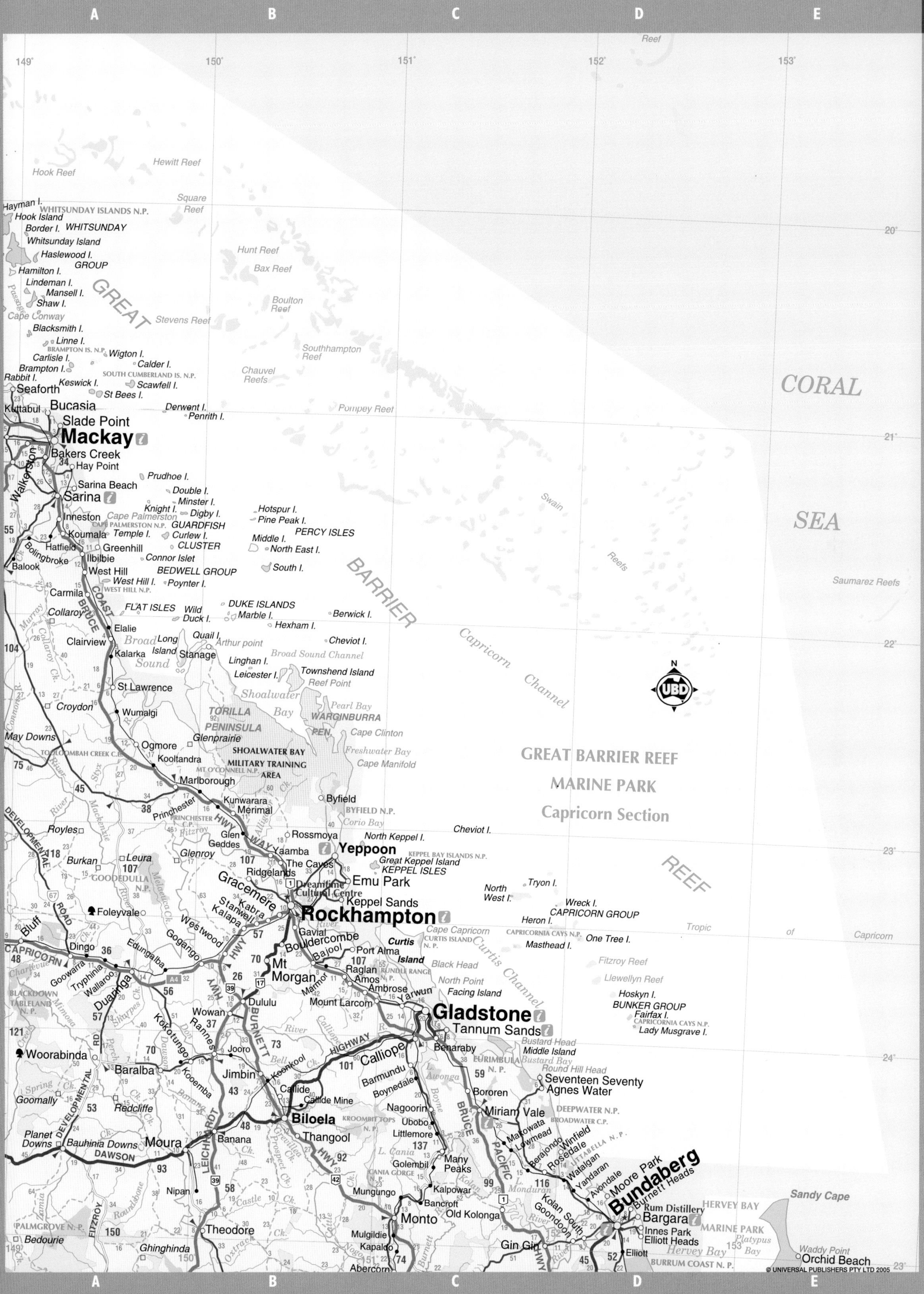

CORAL

SEA

GREAT BARRIER REEF

MARINE PARK

Capricorn Section

Mackay
Sarina
Rockhampton
Yeppoon
Emu Park
Gladstone
Calliope
Biloela
Moura
Bundaberg
Bargara
Monto
Gin Gin
Orchid Beach

WHITSUNDAY ISLANDS N.P.
PERCY ISLES
DUKE ISLANDS
CAPRICORN GROUP
BUNKER GROUP

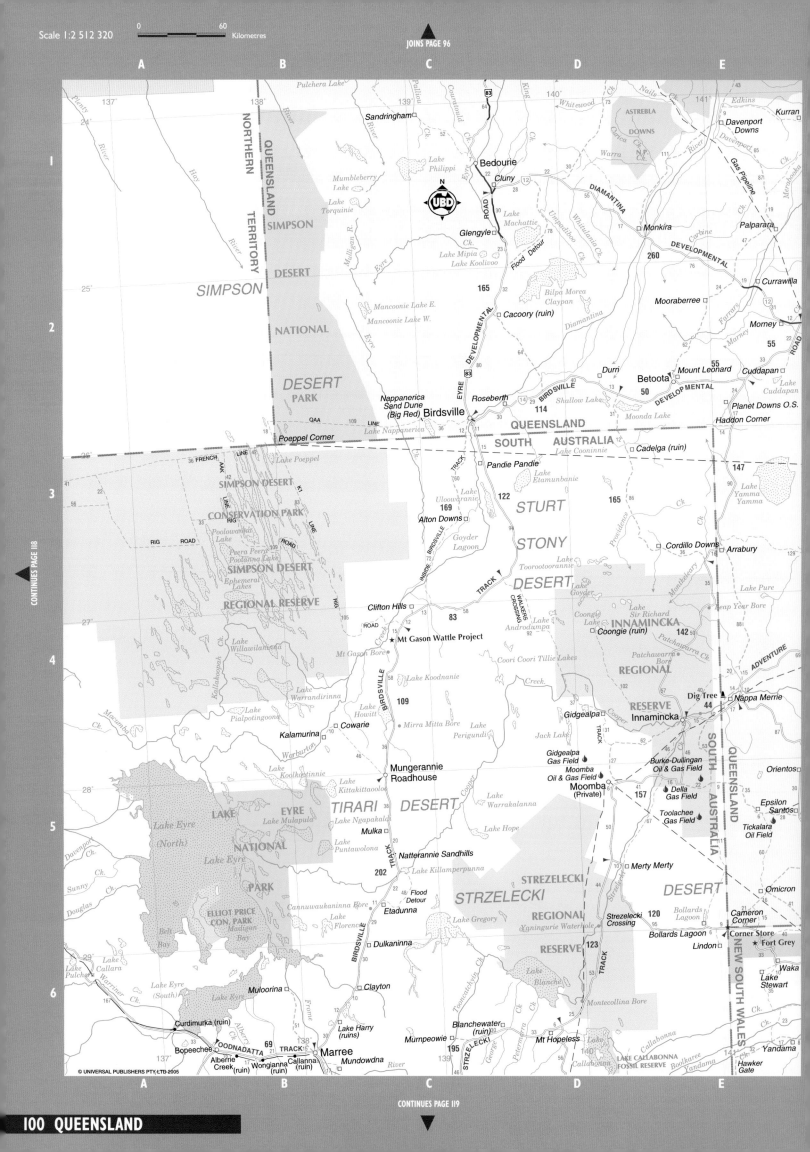

JOINS PAGE 97

A B C D E

1 2 3 4 5 6

Tonkoro · Westerton · Connemara · Warbreccan · Corrikite · Kewarra Ck · Poolia Ck · Ck 142

LOCHERN N.P. · Bimerah · Evengy · Stonehenge · Pandora Park · Ruthven · Oma · Isisford · Portland Downs · Avington · Mulgrave · Evora · Yalleroi · Champion · Cheshire · Skye · Alpha · Tumbar

Thornleigh · Wahroongah · Thornleigh · Glenusk · Blackall · Kelpum · Gartmore · Malta

Glenariff · Mutti · Flodden Hills · Braidwood · Lina Glen · Jundah · Arno · Mount Marlow · Wandsworth · Yaraka Highlands · Ungo · Emmet · Benlidi · Bloomfield · Terrick Terrick · Lorne · Summervale · Tambo · Minnie Downs · Lansdowne

Waverney (abandoned) · Carranya · Galway Downs · Hammond Downs · Oakham · Budgerygar · Retreat · WELFORD NATIONAL PARK · Gilmore · Listowel Downs · Lumeah · Chatham · Coolabri

Windorah · South Galway · Tanbar · Clifton · Tenham · Lynwood · Trinidad · Bulgroo · HELL HOLE GORGE N.P. (no public access) · Milo · Wakes Lagoon · Wellclose · Baykool · Noella · Barford · Wansey Downs · Augathella

Keeroongooloo · Thylungra · Ray · Canaway Downs · Adavale · Sherwood Park · Mona Vale · Grenfield · Gumbardo · MARIALA N.P. · Lake Dartmouth · Mt Morris · Oakleigh · Cairns · Combanning · Yarrawonga · Sommaria

Malagarga · Mount Howitt · Kyabra · Pinkilla · Nickavilla · Pingine · Boothulla · Charleville · Arabella · Westgate · Wallal

Plevna Downs · Eromanga · Yambutta · Quilpie · Comongin · Winbin · Coolbinga · Winbin · Cheepie · Cooladdi · Tiranna · Myendell · Wanko · Coothalia · Lyston

Durham Downs · Bellalie · Mount Margaret · Congie · Boolbanna · Moble · Gas · Pipeline · Napoleon · Yalamurra · Yarronvale · Allambie · Doobibla · Dillalah · Yanna · Mangalore · Fortland · Fortland

Ballera Gas Centre · Karmona · Bundeena · Kihee · Jackson Oil Field · Tobermory · Wombin · Tinderry · Ardoch · Prairie · Toompine Hotel · Wareo · Big Creek · Duck Ck Opal Field · Aldville · Humeburn · Boobera · Wyandra · Claverton · Mirrabooka · Offham · Elmina · Murweh · Quilberry · Coongoola

Naccowlah Oil Field · Nockatunga · Karwalke · Dundoo · Koroit Opal Field · Tilbooroo · Glendilla · Kubill · Nardoo · Cobbrum

Nuccundra Hotel · Wiralia · Alroy · Bundoona · Cunnamulla · Phillpott · Blairmore

Thargomindah · Orient · Nooyeah Downs · LAKE BINDEGOLLY N.P. · Yowah · Yowah Oil Opal Field · Eulo · Burambil · Widgeegoara · Noorama

Thyangra · Picarilli · Dynevor Downs · Lake Bindegolly · Garrawin · Pitherty · Kungie Lake · Tinnenburra · Thurrulgoona · Bundaleer

Naryilco · Bransby · Yakara · Yenloora · Wittenburra · Boodgheere · Zenoni · Kilcowera · Boorara · Caiwarro (ruin) · Blue Lakes · Wombah · Wooroorooka

Ticklara · Bulloo Downs · L. Wyara · L. Numalla · CURRAWINYA N.P. · Rostella · Barringun · Avoca

Tooma Gate · Warri Gate · Wompah Gate · Adelaide Gate · QUEENSLAND · Hamilton Gate · Waverley Gate · Hungerford · Gumbo · Warroo · Burrawinna · Gerara · Myuna

Olive Downs · Onepah · NEW SOUTH WALES · Waverley Downs · Glenhope · Yantabulla · Ella Vale · Enngonia · Collerina

STURT NATIONAL PARK · Thurloo Downs · Owen Downs · Dungarvon · Youngerina · Bullaroon

Tibooburra · Mount Wood · PINDERA DOWNS · Urella Downs · Wonga · Colane · Nardoo · Minetta · Yulcarley · Fords Bridge · Lauradale

Gum Vale · Mt Poole · Mt Sturt · Milparinka · Peak Hill · Brindiwilpa · Salisbury Downs · Reola · Yamba · Urisino · Wanaaring · Hopelands · NOCOLECHE N.R. · Murphys L.

CONTINUES PAGE 40

Scale 1:2 512 320

0   60   Kilometres

JOINS PAGE 101

JOINS PAGE 98

A B C D E

Portland Downs · Avington · Mulgrave · Evora · Yalleroi · Alpha · Avoca · Echo Hills · Vandyke · Springsure · Somerby
Ruthven · Isisford · Glenusk · Champion · Cheshire · Skye · Glen Avon · Riverside · Kareela · Springwood · Basalt Creek · Purbrook · 76
Oma · Thornleigh · Blackall · Castlevale · Mantuan Downs · Tanderra · Consuelo · 71
Wahroongah · 50 · Benlidi · Bloomfield · DEVELOPMENTAL · Cungelella · Ka Ka Mundi Section · Deepdale Extension
Emmet · Terrick Terrick · Lorne · Gartmore · Kelpum · Salvator Rosa Section · Carnarvon · CARNARVON NATIONAL PARK · Wyseby
Yaraka Highlands · Idalia · Summervale · Tambo · Malta · Caldervale · Mt Moffatt Section · Ranger Stn · Oasis Lodge · Moolayember Section · Arcadia
IDALIA N.P. · Minnie Downs · Lansdowne · Babbiloora · Mt Tabor · Warrong · 173
Listowel Downs · Chatham · Coolabri · Crystalbrook · Merivale · 102 · Westgrove · Ridgelands
HELL HOLE GORGE N.P. (no public access) · Lumeah · Barford · Waverley · Lorne · Hillside · Oak Vale · Hutton
Gilmore · Wellclose · Wakes Lagoon · Baykool · Noella · Moorak · Redford · Tooloombilla · Injune · Gunnewin
Milo · Bronte · Mt Morris · Wansey Downs · Augathella · Angellala · Forest Vale · Cornwall · Stirling
Adavale · Sherwood Park · Oakleigh · Barradeen · Combanning · Yarrawonga · Chesterton Range N.P. · 171 · Landwreath · 90 · Roma
MARIALA N.P. · Gumbardo · Grenfield · Cairns · Charleville · Morven · WARREGO · Mitchell · Bindango · Hodgson · 87
Nickavilla · Comongin · Pingine · Boothulla · Tiranna · Arabella · Sommariva · Tregole N.P. · Amboola · Womalilla · Amby · Muckadilla · Brucedale
Quilpie · DEVELOPMENTAL · 209 · Cooladdi · Westgate · Angellala · Authoringa · Dulbydilla · Bonus Downs · Springfield · Megine · 33
Boolbanna · Coolbinga · Winbin · Cheepie · Kalamurra · Logton · Wallal · Mangalore · Dillalah · Ularunda · Dunkeld
Napoleon · Allambie · Yarronvale · Yanna · 98 · Quilberry · Murweh · Fortland · Tomoo · 208 · Woodlands · 209
Wombin · Wareo · Aldville · Doobibla · Wyandra · Gunnawarra · Boatman · Tongy · Abbieglassie · Begonia
Toompine Hotel · Big Creek · Humeburn · Claverton · Mirrabooka · Elmina · 212 · Homeboin · Landridge · 116
Ardoch · Prairie · Dundoo · Boobera · Offham · Coongoola · Corfu · Cashmere West
Karwalke · Koroit Opal Field · Glendilla · Kubill · Nardoo · Cobbrum · Binda · THRUSHTON N.P. · Boolba
Wiralia · Alroy · Tilbooroo · Phillpott · Blairmore · BALONNE · Yunnerman · ADVENTURE WAY · St George
Yowah · Bundoona · Cunnamulla · 134 · Bollon · 113 · Nindigully
LAKE BINDEGOLLY N.P. · Bulloo · Eulo · Weelamurra · Runnymede · Honeymah · Mooramanna · 95
Dynevor Downs · Yenloora · Garrawin · Burambil · Widgeegoara · Woolerina · Kyena · Diranbandi · Noondoo · Thallon · 74
Boodgheere · Wittenburra · Pitherty · Noorama · Bundaleer · Coomburrah · Hawkston · Dunwinnie · Mungindi
Boorara · Caiwarro (ruin) · Kungie Lake · Tinnenburra · Thurrulgoona · 226 · Dongon Plains · Brenda Gate · Hebel · QUEENSLAND
Kilcowera · CURRAWINYA · Blue Lakes · Wombah · Wooroorooka · Tego · CULGOA FLOOD PLAIN N.P. · Goodooga · Angledool · Tuttawa
Waverley Gate · Hungerford · Barringun · Rostella · Avoca · Gerara · Kahmoo · Dunvegan · NEW SOUTH WALES
Gumbo · Warroo · Burrawantie · Myuna · Weilmoringle · Aberfoyle · Lightning Ridge · Mercadool
Glenhope · Yantabulla · Ella Vale · Enngonia · 136 · Bullaroo · Grawin Opal Field · Collarenebri · Pokataroo
Nardoo · Dungarvon · Youngerina · Fords Bridge · Glengarry Opal Field · Collerina · Cumborah · Rosscommon · 73 · 83
Wanaaring · Minetta · Yulcarley · Lauradale · Murphys L. · NARRAN LAKE · Rowena
Hopelands · L. Burkanoko · L. Nichebulka · 89 · 47 · Narran Lake · 149
NOCOLECHE · 215

© UNIVERSAL PUBLISHERS PTY LTD 2005

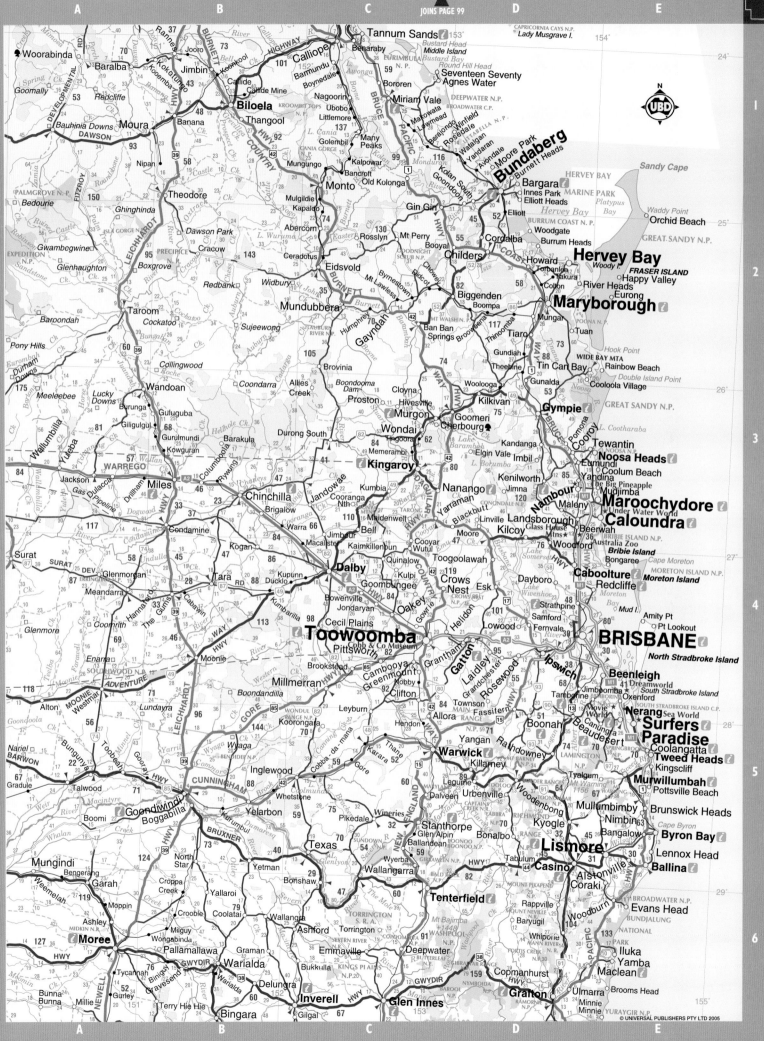

© UNIVERSAL PUBLISHERS PTY LTD 2005

CITY AND TOWN CENTRES

Airlie Beach page 98 E1

Information Centre
Bruce Hwy, Proserpine
Ph: (07) 4945 3711

Bundaberg page 103 D1

Information Centre
186 & 271 Bourbong St
Ph: (07) 4153 8888

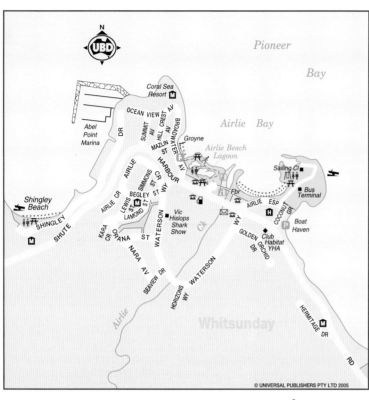

Cairns page 95 D3

Information Centre
51 The Esplanade
Ph: (07) 4051 3588

Gladstone page 99 C6

Information Centre
Ferry Terminal,
Bryan Jordan Dr
Ph: (07) 4972 4000

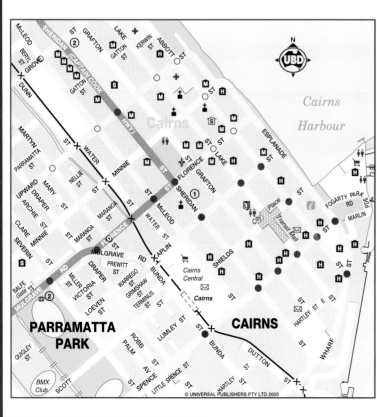

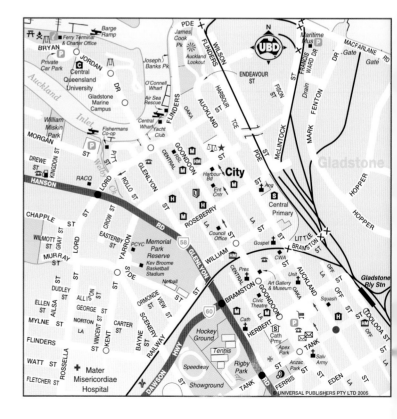

Gympie page 103 D3

Information Centre
Bruce Hwy, Kybong
Ph: (07) 5483 5554

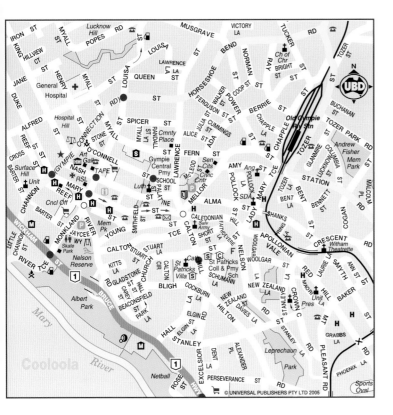

Hervey Bay page 103 D2

Information Centre
Urraween Rd/
Maryborough-Hervey Bay Rd
Ph: (07) 4125 9855

Mackay page 99 A2

Information Centre
The Mill, 320 Nebo Rd
Ph: (07) 4944 5888

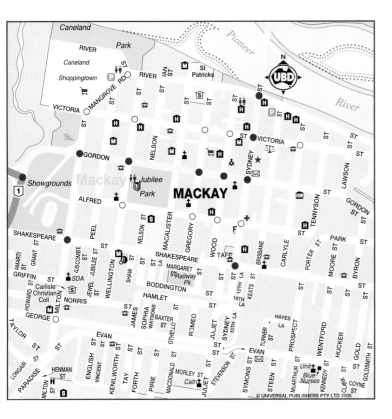

Maroochydore page 103 E3

Information Centre
Sixth Ave/Aerodrome Rd
Ph: (07) 5479 1566

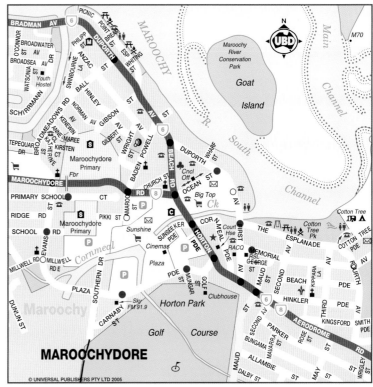

Maryborough page 103 D2

Information Centre
Maryborough Sth Travel Stop,
Bruce Hwy
Ph: (07) 4121 4111

Mount Isa page 96 C2

Information Centre
Outback at Isa,
19 Marian St
Ph: (07) 4749 1555

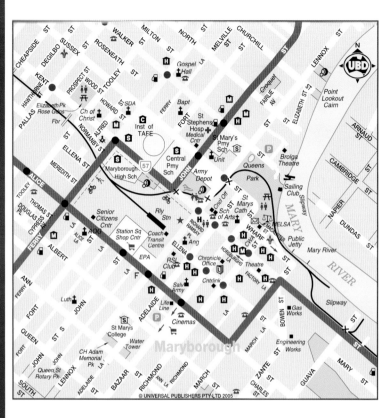

Noosa Heads page 103 E3

Information Centre
Hastings St
Ph: (07) 5447 4988

Rockhampton page 99 B5

Information Centre
'The Spire', Gladstone Rd
Ph: (07) 4927 2055

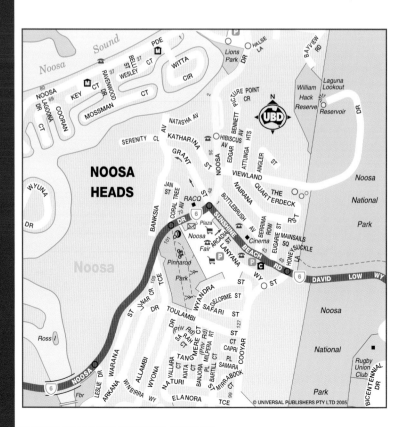

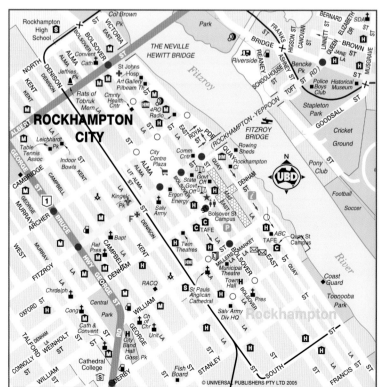

Surfers Paradise page 103 E5

Information Centre
Cavill Ave
Ph: (07) 5538 4419

Toowoomba page 103 C4

Information Centre
86 James St
Ph: (07) 4639 3797

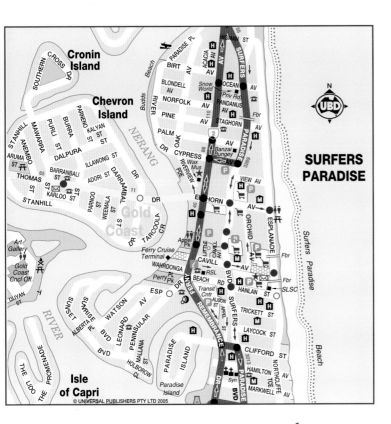

Townsville page 95 E6

Information Centre
Flinders Mall, Flinders St
Ph: (07) 4721 3660

Warwick page 103 D5

Information Centre
49 Albion St
Ph: (07) 4661 3122

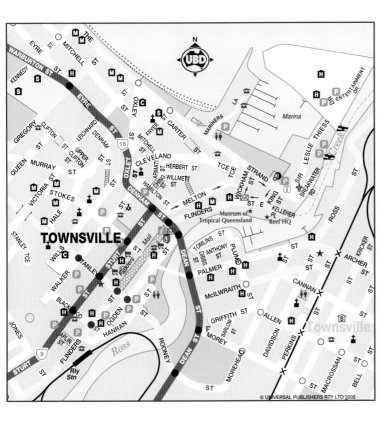

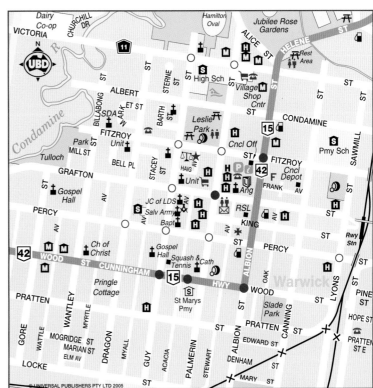

SOUTH AUSTRALIA

Main Information Centre
**South Australian Visitor
& Travel Centre**
18 King William St,
Adelaide 5000
Ph: 1300 655 276
www.southaustralia.com

Eden Valley, Barossa Valley

The fourth largest state (including the Northern Territory) and the driest in Australia, South Australia is a place of contrasts. In the unique position of bordering all the other mainland states, two-thirds of South Australia is dominated by a near-desert environment. Although conditions here are harsh and unrelenting, the varied landscapes of immense deserts, rugged mountains and dry lakes entice many visitors. The beautiful Flinders Ranges are among the state's top attractions.

In contrast to the arid lands of the north and west are the gulf lands, which include the Eyre, Yorke and Fleurieu peninsulas, fringed by quiet beaches and fishing towns; the rolling hills of the Mount Lofty Ranges; and the dry south-east plains watered by the mighty Murray, Australia's longest river, as it flows to the sea. The extensive 3700km South Australian coastline offers scenic driving and walking routes along its many indentations as well as offshore islands to explore, the largest being Kangaroo Island.

Touring South Australia by car is generally easy. From the state's sophisticated capital, Adelaide, there are links to the Barrier, Sturt, Ouyen, Dukes and Princes highways to the eastern states; the Stuart Hwy, which crosses the continent to Darwin; and the Eyre Hwy, which traverses the virtually treeless Nullarbor Plain to Western Australia.

There are many reasons to visit South Australia, including the spectacular scenery, fishing, flora, fauna and the national, conservation and recreation parks that make up over 20% of the state. However, wine is usually top of the list. South Australia's wineries are legendary — the names Barossa Valley, McLaren Vale and Coonawarra are recognised by most Australians and overseas visitors. 4 out of every 10 glasses of Australian wine are produced from vineyards in the south-east corner of South Australia.

MAIN PLACES OF INTEREST

	Map ref		Map ref
Adelaide Festival Centre	111 C3	Lincoln National Park	124 C1
Australian Arid Lands Botanic Garden	122 E4	Loxton Historical Village	125 D1
Axel Stenross Maritime Museum	124 C1	McLaren Vale Wineries	114 C6
Banking & Currency Museum, Kadina	122 E6	Mount Lofty Summit & Botanic Garden	114 E2
Barossa Valley Wineries	125 B1	Murphy's Haystacks	121 D5
Belair National Park	114 E2	Naracoorte Caves	125 D5
Birdsville Track	119 A6/C2	National Motor Museum, Birdwood	113 D5
Blue Lake, Mount Gambier	125 C6	National Wine Centre of Australia	111 E3
Clare Valley Wineries	123 A6	Nullarbor Cliffs	120 C3
Cleland Wildlife Park	114 E2	Penneshaw Maritime & Folk Museum	124 E3
Cockle Train, Victor Harbor	125 A3	Pichi Richi Railway, Quorn	122 E4
Coober Pedy Opal Mines	117 D5	Remarkable Rocks, Kangaroo Island	124 D3
Coonawarra Wineries	125 C5	River Murray	125 B2/D1
Coorong National Park	125 B3	SA Whale Centre, Vicotr Harbor	127
Flinders Ranges National Park	123 A3	South Australian Maritime Museum	112 B6
Glenelg	114 B2	South Australian Museum	111 D3
Granite Island	125 A3	The Barossa Goldfields	113 B2
Hahndorf	115 B3	The Big Orange, Berri	125 C1
Hallett Cove Conservation Park	114 B4	Wadlata Outback Centre, Port Augusta	126
Innamincka	119 D4	Wallaroo Mines Historic Area	122 E6
Kangaroo Island	124 D3	Whalers Way	124 B1
Koppio Smithy Museum	124 B1	Whyalla Maritime Museum	122 E5
Lake Eyre	118 E4	Wilpena Pound	123 A3

SOUTH AUSTRALIA KEY MAP

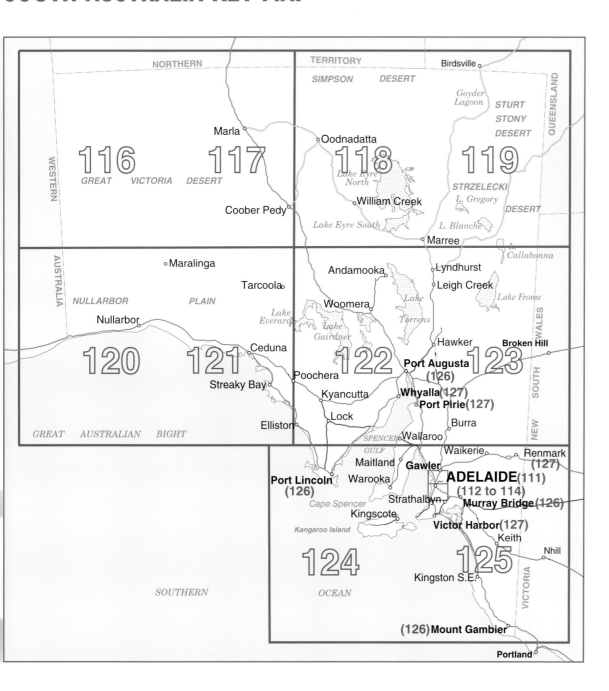

NORTHERN   TERRITORY   Birdsville

SIMPSON   DESERT

WESTERN

116   117   118   119

GREAT   VICTORIA   DESERT

Marla

Oodnadatta

Goyder Lagoon   STURT STONY DESERT

QUEENSLAND

Lake Eyre North

William Creek

Coober Pedy

Lake Eyre South

L. Gregory

STRZELECKI

L. Blanche

Marree

DESERT

L. Callabonna

AUSTRALIA

NULLARBOR   PLAIN

Maralinga

Tarcoola

Andamooka

Lyndhurst

Leigh Creek

Lake Frome

Nullarbor

Woomera

Lake Everard

Lake Gairdner

Lake Torrens

NEW   SOUTH   WALES

120   121   122   123

Ceduna

Hawker

Broken Hill

Streaky Bay

Poochera

Port Augusta (126)

GREAT   AUSTRALIAN   BIGHT

Kyancutta

Whyalla (127)

Port Pirie (127)

Lock

Burra

Elliston

Wallaroo

SPENCER GULF

Waikerie   Renmark (127)

Maitland   Gawler

Port Lincoln (126)

Warooka

ADELAIDE (111) (112 to 114)

Strathalbyn

Murray Bridge (126)

Cape Spencer

Kingscote

Victor Harbor (127)

Keith

Kangaroo Island

Nhill

124   125

SOUTHERN

OCEAN

Kingston S.E.

VICTORIA

(126) Mount Gambier

Portland

Nullarbor Cliffs, Great Australian Bight Marine Park, Nullarbor National Park

ADELAIDE CITY

South Australia's capital city, Adelaide, was named after King William IV's queen. This well-planned city of gardens, historic buildings and churches lies on a narrow coastal plain between the Mount Lofty Ranges and the waters of Gulf St Vincent. As envisioned by Colonel William Light, Surveyor-General for the new colony from 1836, the city centre is surrounded by open parklands, which separate the CBD from the suburbs. The tree-lined boulevard of North Terrace contains so many fine colonial buildings and places of interest that it is not uncommon to see groups of people on organised history walks. At the western end of the street is Holy Trinity Church, the oldest church in the state. Nearby are the 2 oldest buildings remaining in Adelaide: the Regency-style Government House, started in 1838 and not completed until 1878; and Adelaide Gaol, last used in 1988.

Adelaide is known for its café culture, restaurants and wines. The city has a multicultural population and this is reflected in the city's markets and restaurants. Adelaide is well-known for its festivals, including the legendary Adelaide Festival, held biannually in even-numbered years; the parallel Adelaide Fringe Festival; and the Adelaide International Film festival, held in odd-numbered years.

ADELAIDE CITY PLACES OF INTEREST

	ref		ref
Adelaide Botanic Gardens	D3	Lion Arts Centre	C4
Adelaide Convention Centre	C3	Migration Museum	D3
Adelaide Festival Centre	C3	National Wine Centre of Australia	E3
Adelaide Himeji Garden	D5	Old Adelaide Gaol	B3
Adelaide Town Hall	D4	Palm House	D3
Adelaide Zoo	D3	Parliament House	C3
Art Gallery of South Australia	D3	Rundle Mall	D4
Ayers House	D3	Skycity Adelaide	C3
Central Market & Chinatown	C4	South Australian Museum	D3
Elder Park & Rotunda	C3	State Library of South Australia	D3
Exhibition Centre	C3	Tandanya Aboriginal Culture Institute	D4
Glenelg Tram Terminal	D4	Torrens Lake	C3
Government House	D3	University of South Australia	D3
International Rose Garden	E3	Victoria Park Racecourse	E4
Light's Vision	C3	Victoria Square	D4

Top: Adelaide Botanic Gardens; Middle: Rotunda, Elder Park; Bottom: City skyline at sunset

Scale 1:28 980

0   750   Metres

CONTINUES PAGE 114

CONTINUES PAGE 110

© UNIVERSAL PRESS PTY LTD 2002

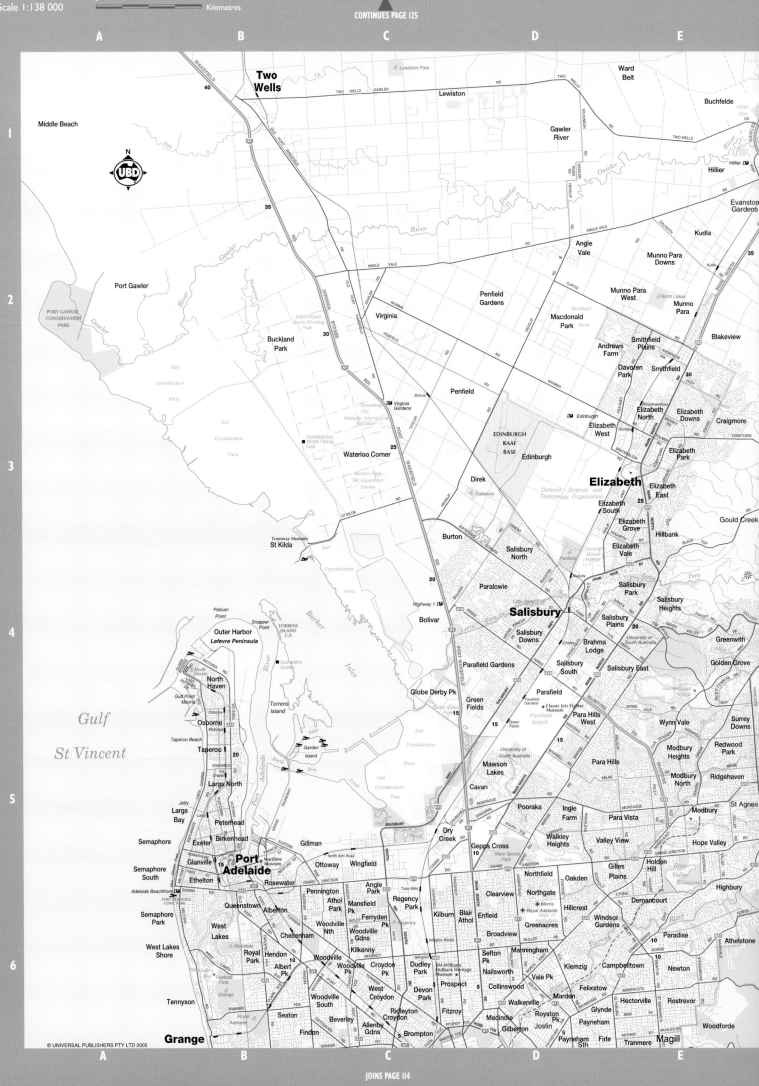

Scale 1:138 000

0   4
Kilometres

A   B   C   D   E

N
UBD

Middle Beach

Two Wells

Lewiston Park

Lewiston

Ward Belt

Buchfelde

Gawler River

Hillier

Evanston Gardens

Port Gawler

Kudla

Angle Vale

Munno Para Downs

PORT GAWLER CONSERVATION PARK

Penfield Gardens

Munno Para West

Munno Para

Virginia

Macdonald Park

Blakeview

Buckland Park

Andrews Farm

Smithfield Plains

International Sports Shooting Park

Davoren Park

Smithfield

Penfield

Elizabeth North

Elizabeth Downs

Craigmore

Virginia Gardens

Bolivar

Elizabeth West

Speedway City Adelaide International Raceway

Constellation Model Flying Club

EDINBURGH RAAF BASE

Edinburgh

Elizabeth South

Elizabeth East

Waterloo Corner

Winston Park SA Equestrian Centre

Direk

Salisbury

Elizabeth

Elizabeth Grove

Gould Creek

Defence Science and Technology Organisation

Hillbank

St Kilda

Tramway Museum St Kilda

Burton

Salisbury North

Elizabeth Vale

Little Para

Salisbury Park

Salisbury Heights

Highway 1

Paralowie

Salisbury

Greenwith

Bolivar

Salisbury Plains

Golden Grove

Pelican Point

Salisbury Downs

Brahma Lodge

Outer Harbor

Snapper Point

TORRENS ISLAND C.P.

University of South Australia

Salisbury South

Salisbury East

Lefevre Peninsula

North Haven

Parafield Gardens

Parafield

Wynn Vale

Surrey Downs

Gulf Point Marina

Quarantine Station

Globe Derby Pk

Green Fields

Parafield Gardens Classic Jets Fighter Museum

Para Hills West

Modbury Heights

Redwood Park

Osborne

Torrens Island

Parafield Airport

Para Hills

Ridgehaven

Gulf
St Vincent

Taperoo Beach

Garden Island

University of South Australia

Mawson Lakes

Modbury North

Taperoo

Cavan

Pooraka

Ingle Farm

Para Vista

Modbury

St Agnes

Largs North

Salisbury

Walkley Heights

Valley View

Hope Valley

Jetty

Largs Bay

Peterhead

Dry Creek

Northfield

Gilles Plains

Holden Hill

Semaphore

Exeter

Birkenhead

Gillman

Gepps Cross

State Sports Park

Yatala Prison

Oakden

Highbury

Semaphore South

Glanville

Port Adelaide

Maritime Museum

Ottoway

Wingfield

Clearview

Northgate

Dernancourt

Hillcrest

Windsor Gardens

Paradise

Adelaide Beachfront

Etholton

Rosewater

North Arm Road

Royal Adelaide

Greenacres

Athelstone

Semaphore Park

Queenstown

Albert on

Pennington

Athol Park

Mansfield Pk

Angle Park

Regency Park

Kilburn

Blair Athol

Enfield

Broadview

Morris

Manningham

Klemzig

Campbelltown

Newton

West Lakes

Cheltenham

Woodville Gdns

Ferryden Pk

Sefton Pk

Nailsworth

Vale Pk

Marden

Felixstow

Hectorville

West Lakes Shore

Royal Park

Hendon

Albert Pk

Woodville

Woodville Pk

Kilkenny

Croydon Pk

Dudley Park

Devon Park

Prospect

Collinswood

Walkerville

Klemzig

Glynde

Rostrevor

Tennyson

Woodville South

West Croydon

JM Williams Outback Heritage Museum

Royston Pk Joslin

Woodforde

Grange

Seaton

Beverley

Ridleyton Croydon

Allenby Gdns

Brompton

Fitzroy

Medindie

Gilberton

Payneham

Paynham Sth

Findon

Magill

Firle

Tranmere

© UNIVERSAL PUBLISHERS PTY LTD 2005

A   B   C   D   E

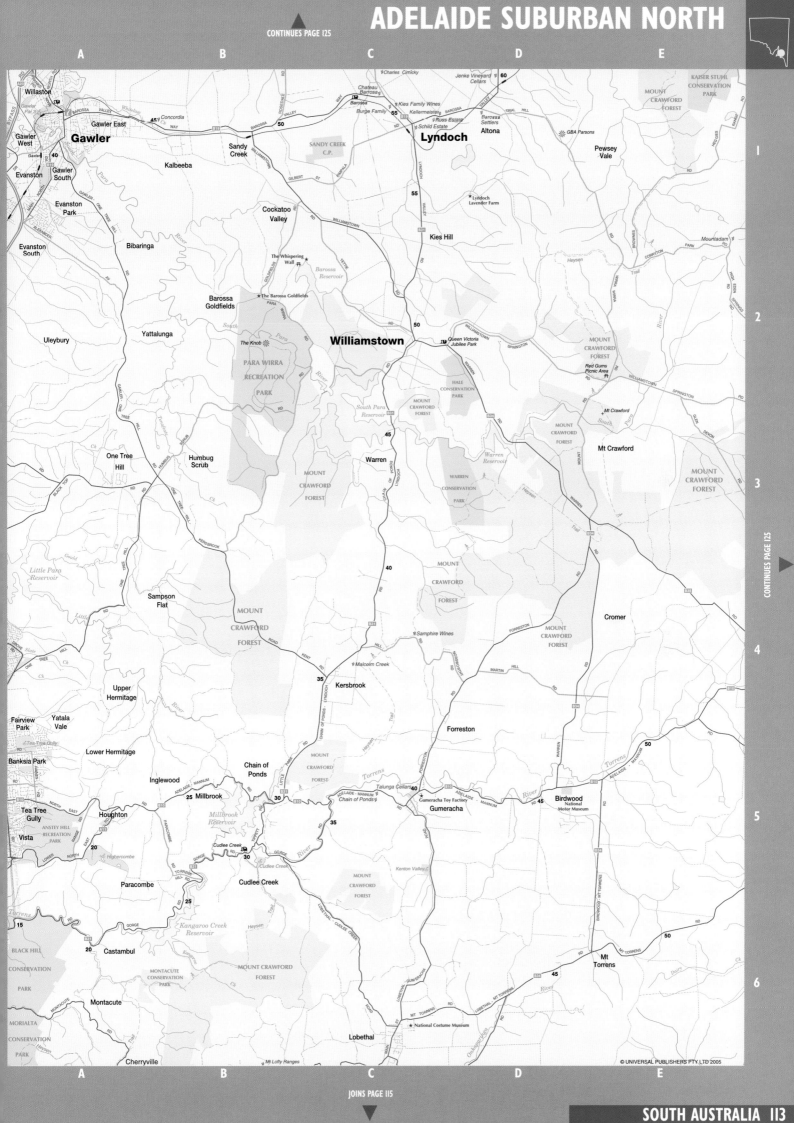

CONTINUES PAGE 125

CONTINUES PAGE 125

JOINS PAGE 115

© UNIVERSAL PUBLISHERS PTY. LTD 2005

Scale 1:138 000

0   4   Kilometres

A   B   C   D   E

N
UBD

Grange

Henley Beach
Henley Beach South
West Beach
Fulham Gardens
Kidman Park
Fulham
Findon
Flinders Park
Allenby Gdns
Hindmarsh
Brompton
Gilberton
Joslin
Payneham Sth
Firle
Tranmere
Woodforde
Magill
Teringie
Auldana
Summit

Lockleys
Underdale
Torrensville
Thebarton
North Adelaide
St Peters
Hackney
Stepney
Evandale
Trinity
St Morris
Kensington Gdns
Rosslyn Pk
Skye

Brooklyn Park
Cowandilla
Mile End
ADELAIDE
Kent Town
The Norwood
Beulah Pk
Kensington Park
Kensington
Leabrook
Erindale
Wattle Pk

Hilton
Mile End Sth
Keswick Term
Rose Pk
Toorak Gdns
Dulwich
Heathpool
Tusmore
Stonyfell
Hornsdale

West Richmond
Richmond
Marleston
Keswick
Wayville
Eastwood
Unley
Parkside
Glenside
Hazelwood Park
Linden Pk
Burnside
Greenhill
Hornsell Park

Adelaide Airport
Netley
Galway
Ashford
Goodwood
Malvern
Highgate
Fullarton
St Georges
Beaumont
Glen Osmond
Mt Osmond
Waterfall Gully
CLELAND CONSERVATION PARK
Mt Lofty 727

North Plympton
Kurralta Park
Everard Pk
Black Forest
Millswood
Hyde Pk
Unley Pk
Myrtle Bank
Glenunga
Urrbrae
Leawood Gardens
Eagle on the Hill
Cleland

Novar Gardens
Camden Park
Plympton
Glandore
Clarence Pk
Clarence Gdns
Hawthorn
Kingswood
Netherby
Springfield
Brown Hill Creek
Crafers West
Crafers

Glenelg
Glenelg North
Glenelg East
Plympton Park
South Plympton
Cumberland Park
Westbourne Park
Colonel Light Gdns
Lwr Mitcham
Clapham
Mitcham
Torrens Park

Glenelg South
Glengowrie
Park Holme
Ascot Park
Melrose Park
Daw Park
Panorama
Lynton
Belair
Upper Sturt

Somerton Park
Morphettville
Edwardstown
St Marys
Pasadena
BELAIR NATIONAL PARK
Mt Lofty

North Brighton
Warradale
Marion
Mitchell Park
Clovelly Park
Glenalta
Hawthorndene

Hove
Oaklands Park
Sturt
Bedford Park
Eden Hills
Blackwood

Brighton
South Brighton
Dover Gardens
Seacombe Gdns
Flinders University
Bellevue Heights

Seacliff
Seacliff Park
Darlington
Seacombe Hts
Coromandel East
Ironbank

Gulf
Seaview Downs
Craigburn Farm
Coromandel Valley
Scott Creek

St Vincent
Kingston Park
Marino
O'HALLORAN HILL RECREATION PARK

HALLETT COVE CONSERVATION PARK
O'Halloran Hill
Flagstaff Hill
Cherry Gardens
SCOTT CREEK CONSERVATION PARK

Hallett Cove
Trott Park
CSIRO Research Station
Aberfoyle Park
Chandlers Hill
Dorset Vale

Sheidow Park
Reynella East
Happy Valley
Horndale
Clarendon
Mt Bold Reservoir

Reynella
Old Reynella
Mount Hurtle Winery
Geoff Merrill Wines

Lonsdale
Woodcroft
Baker Gully
Mt Bold
Clarendon Weir

O'Sullivan Beach
Woodcroft Park
Kangarilla

Christies Beach
Morphett Vale
Onkaparinga Hills

Noarlunga Centre
Hackham West
Huntfield Heights
Hackham
Mt Panorama

Port Noarlunga
Noarlunga Downs
ONKAPARINGA RIVER NATIONAL PARK
Blewitt Springs

Port Noarlunga South
Seaford Meadows
Chapel Hill
KUITPO FOREST

Moana
Seaford
Seaford Heights
Seaford Rise
Old Noarlunga
McLaren Vale Wineries
McLaren Vale
McLaren Flat

© UNIVERSAL PUBLISHERS PTY LTD 2005

114 SOUTH AUSTRALIA

JOINS PAGE 113

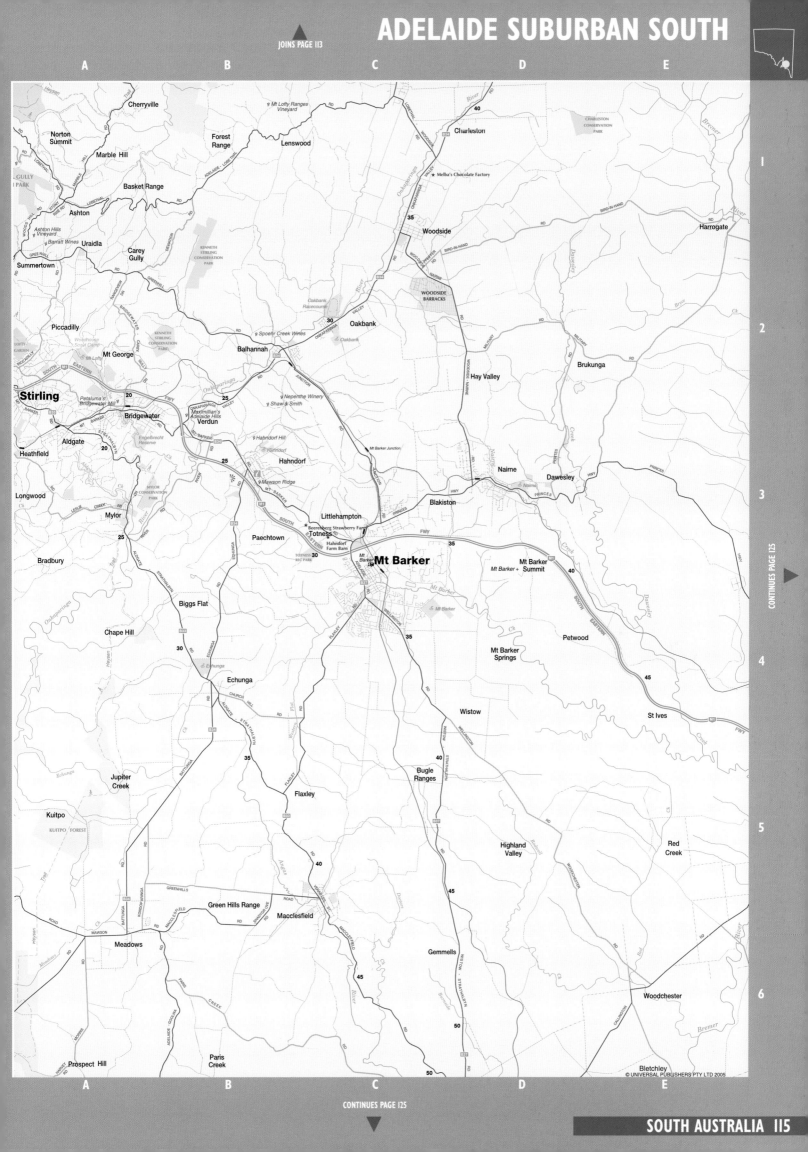

A B C D E

Cherryville
Mt Lofty Ranges Vineyard
Norton Summit
Forest Range
Lenswood
Marble Hill
Charleston
CHARLESTON CONSERVATION PARK
40
Basket Range
Melba's Chocolate Factory

Ashton
35
Woodside
Harrogate
Ashton Hills Vineyard
Barratt Wines
Uraidla
BIRD-IN-HAND
Summertown
Carey Gully
KENNETH STIRLING CONSERVATION PARK
WOODSIDE BARRACKS

Piccadilly
Brukunga
Spoehr Creek Wines
30
Oakbank
Mt George
KENNETH STIRLING CONSERVATION PARK
Balhannah
Oakbank
Hay Valley

Stirling
20
Nepenthe Winery
Shaw & Smith
Verdun
Maximillian's Adelaide Hills
Bridgewater
Dawesley
Nairne
Aldgate
20
Hahndorf Hill
Hahndorf
25
Mt Barker Junction
Heathfield
Mawson Ridge

Longwood
Blakiston
Mylor
MYLOR CONSERVATION PARK
Littlehampton
35
Bradbury
25
Paechtown
Totness
Beerenberg Strawberry Farm
Hahndorf Farm Barn
Mt Barker
Mt Barker Summit
40

Biggs Flat
30
Totness Rec Park
Mt Barker +
Petwood

Chape Hill
30
Mt Barker Springs
45
St Ives

Echunga
Wistow
Jupiter Creek
35
40
Kuitpo
Bugle Ranges
KUITPO FOREST
Flaxley
40
Highland Valley
Red Creek

Green Hills Range
45
Macclesfield
Meadows
Gemmells
Woodchester
Prospect Hill
Paris Creek
45
50
Bletchley
50
© UNIVERSAL PUBLISHERS PTY LTD 2005

A B C D E

CONTINUES PAGE 125
CONTINUES PAGE 125

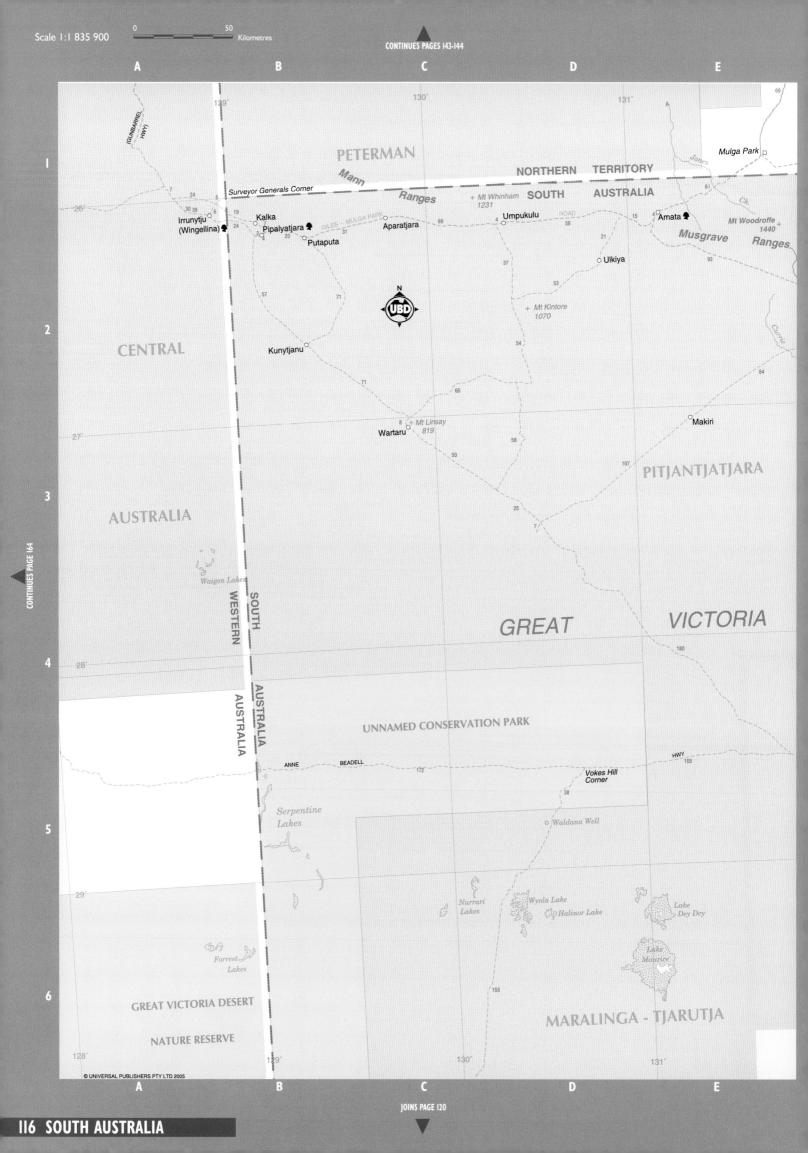

0   50
Kilometres

A   B   C   D   E

129°   130°   131°   69

PETERMAN   NORTHERN   TERRITORY   *Mulga Park* □

1

Mann   *Jones*   61

Surveyor Generals Corner   Ck   Ranges
26°   7   24   5   + Mt Whinham   SOUTH   AUSTRALIA
30 39   6   19   1231   Umpukulu   ROAD   15   Amata   Mt Woodroffe
Irrunytju   24   Kalka   4   58   1440 +
(Wingellina)   7   GILES - MULGA PARK   69   Musgrave   Ranges
Pipalyatjara   31   Aparatjara   21   Ulkiya   93
2   20
Putaputa   37

CENTRAL   57   71   N   54   Mt Kintore   Currie
UBD   1070

2

Kunytjanu   84

27°   71   65   107   Makiri
8 + Mt Linsay   58   PITJANTJATJARA
AUSTRALIA   Wartaru   819   25

3   50   7

Waigen Lakes

180

28°   UNNAMED   GREAT   VICTORIA

4   CONSERVATION PARK

ANNE   BEADELL   HWY   105
172   38   Vokes Hill
Serpentine   Corner
Lakes   Waldana Well

5   Nurrari   Wyola Lake   Lake
Lakes   Halinor Lake   Dey Dey

Forrest   Lake
Lakes   Maurice

155

6   GREAT VICTORIA DESERT   MARALINGA - TJARUTJA
NATURE RESERVE

128°   129°   130°   131°

A   B   C   D   E

CONTINUES PAGE 164

JOINS PAGE 120

CONTINUES PAGES 144-145

A B C D E

132° 133° 134° 135°

Umbeara
Bloodwood Bore
Mt Beddome
New Crown

Kulgera Roadhouse
Kulgera Siding
Beddome Range

Johnstone Geodetic
Mount Cavenagh
NORTHERN
TERRITORY
Charlotte
Waters
McDills
Bore

Victory Downs
SOUTH
AUSTRALIA
Goyder Ck
Mt Darling 541
Mt Anderson 358
Abminga (ruin)
Mount Dare

Boorndoolyanna
Marryat
Tieyon
Eringa (ruin)
WITJIRA

Pukatja (Ernabella)
Hamilton Ck
Lindsay
Bloods Ck Bore
NATIONAL
Federal (ruin)
PARK

Yunyarinya (Kenmore Park)
Enteringinna Ck
Stevenson
Dalhousie Springs

Watinuna
Agnes Creek
Marryat
Dalhousie (ruin)
Dinner Spring

STUART
179
Alberga Ck
Bagot Range
Mt Walter 361
Creek
Pedirka (ruin)

Fregon
Taroonzinna Ck
PEDIRKA DESERT
Hamilton
Mt Rebecca 288

Mimili
Chandler
Granite Downs
Lambina
OLD
GHAN
ROUTE
Mount Sarah

Paw Paw
Indulkana (Iwantja)
Chambers Bluff 592
Yoolperlunna
Nicholson Hill 404
Fogartys Claypan
27°

Everard Ranges
AUSTRALASIA
Ammaroodinna Ck
Coongra
OODNADATTA
209
Todmorden
Fogartys River
TRACK

Mintabie
Opal Fields
Marla
Olaninna Ck
Mt Todmorden 283
North Branch of Neales
R.

Wallatinna
HWY
Wintinna Ck
Welbourne Hill
Henrietta Ck
South Branch of Neales
Angle Pole Waterhole

81
Wintinna
Arckaringa
Mt Albany 224
Oodnadatta

DESERT
Cadney Park
Cadney Homestead (Roadhouse)
Evelyn
Copper Hill
San Marino
Arckaringa
Neales R.
28°

RAILWAY
Mount Willoughby
Evelyn Downs
Mount Barry
Peake Ck

TALLARINGA
193
Kidwegalbinna Ck
Lora Ck

Lake Meramangye
Pootnoura
151
STUART
Pootnoura Ck
Algebulkullia Ck

Emu Junction (ruin)
CONSERVATION
Giddi Ck
Giddinna

ANN
BEADELL
Mount Clarence Ck
Woorong Ck
Olgelba Ck

PARK
Mabel Creek
Manguri
Opal Mines
Coober Pedy

Tallaringa Well
Mabel Ck
Range
Engenina Ck
Vermin Proof Fence

Wilkinson Lakes
Lake Woorong
Lake Phillipson
Wirrida

Vermin Proof Fence
Ingomar
Lake Wirrida

WOOMERA
PROHIBITED
AREA
McDouall Peak
Mirikata

Lake Anthony
Half Moon Lake
Commonwealth Hill
Gina
HWY
The Twins

© UNIVERSAL PUBLISHERS PTY LTD 2005

JOINS PAGE 118
JOINS PAGE 121

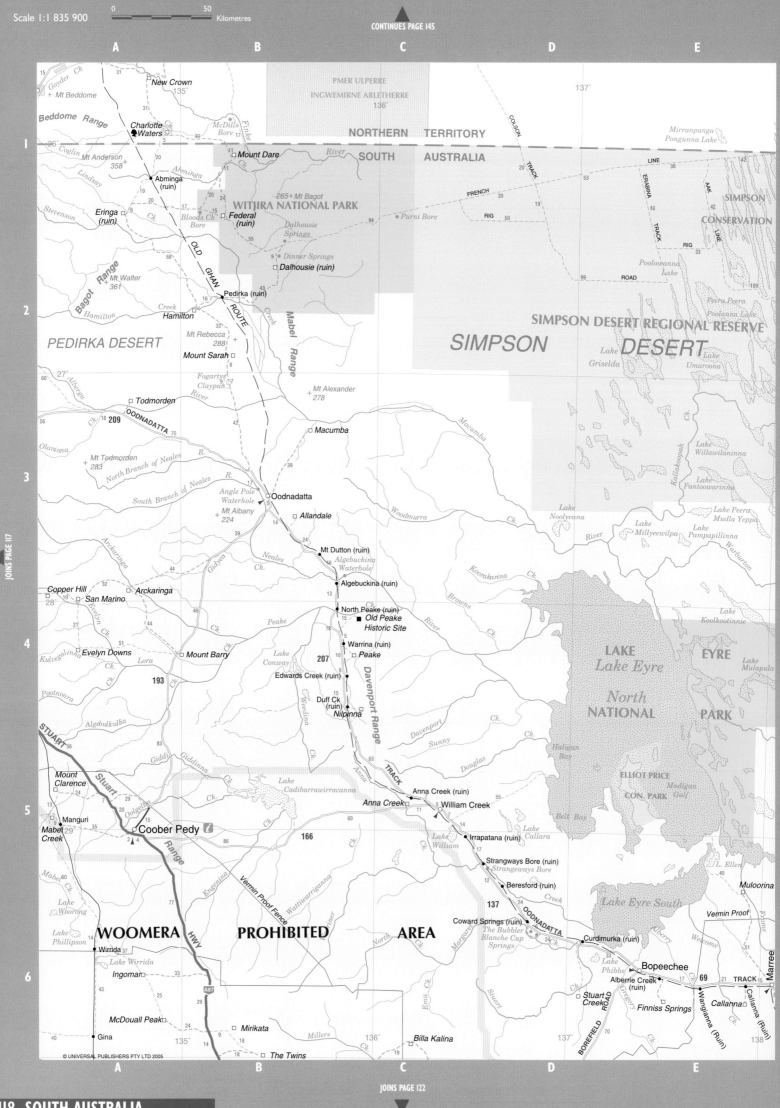

Scale 1:1 835 900

0   50   Kilometres

CONTINUES PAGE 145

PMER ULPERRE
INGWEMIRNE ARLETHERRE
136°

NORTHERN TERRITORY
SOUTH AUSTRALIA

New Crown
135°
+ Mt Beddome

Beddome Range

Charlotte Waters

McDills Bore
Mount Dare

Coglin Ck   Mt Anderson 358 +

Abminga (ruin)

WITJIRA NATIONAL PARK

265+ Mt Bagot

Federal (ruin)

Purni Bore

COLSON TRACK

Mirranpanga
Pongunna Lake

LINE

ERABINA

FRENCH

RIG

AAK

SIMPSON CONSERVATION

Eringa (ruin)

Bloods Ck Bore

Dalhousie Springs

Dinner Springs

Dalhousie (ruin)

Poolowanna Lake

ROAD

Mt Walter 361

Bagot Range

Pedirka (ruin)

Hamilton

Mabel Range

Peera Peera
Poolanna Lake

SIMPSON DESERT REGIONAL RESERVE

PEDIRKA DESERT

Mt Rebecca 288 +

Mount Sarah

Fogartys Claypan

SIMPSON   DESERT

Lake Griselda   Lake Umaroona

Todmorden

Mt Alexander 278 +

OODNADATTA 209

Mt Todmorden 283 +

North Branch of Neales R.

Macumba

Macumba

Lake Willawilaninna

Lake Pantoowarinna

South Branch of Neales R.

Woodmurra Ck

Lake Noolyeana

Lake Millyeewilpa

Lake Peera Mudla Yeppa

Angle Pole Waterhole

Oodnadatta

Allandale

Koorakarina Ck

Browns River

Lake Pampapillinna

Mt Albany 224 +

Mt Dutton (ruin)

Algebuckina Waterhole

Lake Koolkootinnie

Copper Hill

Arckaringa

Algebuckina (ruin)

San Marino

North Peake (ruin)

Old Peake Historic Site

Peake Ck

Evelyn Downs

Mount Barry   193

Lake Conway   207

Warrina (ruin)

Peake

Davenport Range

LAKE   EYRE

Lake   Lake Eyre
Mulapula

Edwards Creek (ruin)

Weedina Ck

Duff Ck (ruin)

Nilpinna

North   NATIONAL   PARK

STUART

Mount Clarence

Oodgelly

Lake Cadibarrawirracanna

Anna Ck TRACK

Douglas Ck

Sunny Ck

Davenport Ck

ELLIOT PRICE CON. PARK

Haligan Bay

Madigan Gulf

Manguri

Coober Pedy

Anna Creek (ruin)

Anna Creek

William Creek

Bell Bay

Mabel Creek

Stuart Range

166

Lake William

Irrapatana (ruin)

Lake Callara

L. Ellen

Muloorina

Mabel Ck

Lake Whorong

Engenina Ck

Vermin Proof Fence

Strangways Bore (ruin)
Strangways Bore

Beresford (ruin)

OODNADATTA   137

Lake Eyre South

Vermin Proof

WOOMERA   PROHIBITED   AREA

Wattiwarriganna Ck

Coward Springs (ruin)

The Bubbler
Blanche Cup
Springs

Curdimurka (ruin)

Welcome Ck

Lake Phibbs

Marree

Wirrida

Lake Wirrida

North Ck

Margaret Ck

Bopeechee

Alberne Creek (ruin)

69

TRACK

Callanna (Ruin)

138°

Ingomar

A87

BOREFIELD ROAD

Stuart Creek

Finniss Springs

Wangianna (Ruin)

Callanna

McDouall Peak

Mirikata

Millers Ck

136°

Billa Kalina

137°

Gina

The Twins

© UNIVERSAL PUBLISHERS PTY LTD 2005

JOINS PAGE 117

JOINS PAGE 122

CONTINUES PAGE 100

A B C D E

SIMPSON DESERT
QAA
NATIONAL PARK
LINE
Poeppel Corner

Flood Detour
LINE
165

Nappanerica Sand Dune (Big Red)
Birdsville
L. Nappanerica
36
11
Roseberth
BIRDSVILLE
River
14
114
Durri
Mount Leonard
Betoota
DEVELOPMENTAL
50
ROAD
55
108
Cuddapan
Lake Cuddapan
53

Shallow Lake
40
Moonda Lake
31
Planet Downs O.S.
Haddon Corner
14
17
26°

QUEENSLAND
SOUTH AUSTRALIA
17
Lake Cooninnie
12
Cadelga (Ruin)
Pandie Pandie
Lake Short

Lake Thomas
DESERT
83
PARK
KI

Karrathunka Waterhole
60
122
Lake Etamunbanie
165
86
90
147

Diamantina
169
3
Alton Downs
94
STURT
33

ROAD
LINE
BIG
Goyder Lagoon
72

STONY
Koonchera Waterhole

Koonchera Sandhill
DESERT
Cordillo Downs
36
16
Arrabury

Lake Surprise Sandhill
TRACK
WALKERS CROSSING
L Goyder
L Lady Blanche
L Sir Richard
Montelleary
33

Clifton Hills
13
58
ROAD
105
Warburton Crossing
12
BIRDSVILLE
83
92
Coongie Lake
L Marroocutchanie
Candradecka
Leap Year Bore
Lake Pure
104
27°

N UBD
Mt Gason Wattle Project
Coongie (ruin)
INNAMINCKA
Patchawarra Ck
142
ADVENTURE WY 242

Mt Gason Bore
Creek
109
Lake Koodnanie
58
Walkers Crossing
37
REGIONAL
106
Patchwarra Bore
41
Nappa Merrie
14
2

Kalamurina
10
Cowarie
Lake Howitt
Mirra Mitta Bore
Lake Perigundi
46
RESERVE
Cooper
57
Dig Tree
Gullyamurra Waterhole
Burkes Mem.
Innamincka
Wills Mem.
15
44
17

Gidgealpa
31
TRACK
48

Lake Warrandirinna
Mungerannie Gap
Gidgealpa Gas Field
27
46
53
83
28°

Mungerannie Roadhouse
Moomba Oil & Gas Field
Moomba (Private)
157
41
Burke-Dullingari Oil & Gas Field
16
Orientos

TIRARI
38
DESERT
Lake Warrakalanna
Della Gas Field
23
Epsilon
29
Santos
42

Lake Kittakittaooloo
Kalamurra Lake
Mulka
Lake Ngapakaldi
Toolachee Gas Field
67
28

Lake Puntewolona
TRACK
20
Natterannie Sandhills
Lake Hope
Lake Killamperpunna
Pipeline
STRZELECKI
50
Gas
Pipeline
111
60

Cooper
22
48
Flood Detour
11
Etadunna
Cannuwaukaninna Bore
Lake Kopperekoppinna
Merty Merty
10
62

Lake Palankarinna
202
29
Lake Florence
STRZELECKI
44
Yaningurie Waterhole
Strzelecki Crossing
95
Bollards Lagoon
21
16
38
Omicron
29°
5

Dulkaninna
30
STRZELECKI REGIONAL
RESERVE
123
120
Bollards Lagoon
6
9
Corner Store
Cameron Corner
15
Tooma Gate
Olive Downs

Clayton
10
Fence
Clayton
Lake Harry
Lake Harry (ruin)
30
Montecollina Bore
Lindon
22
Fort Grey
STURT NATIONAL PARK
33
9
Waka
40
Lake Stewart
56

Murnpeowie
Blanchewater (ruin)
26
115
STRZELECKI
Mt Hopeless
LAKE CALLABONNA FOSSIL RESERVE
Callabonna
Tilcha
35
Hewart Downs
Mt Poole 250
10
47
6

Mundowdna
Vermin Proof
Fence
Moolawatana
140°
Lake Callabonna
141°
Hawker Gate
Theldarpa
25
Milparinka
Mt Brown 274
38

A B C D E

JOINS PAGE 123

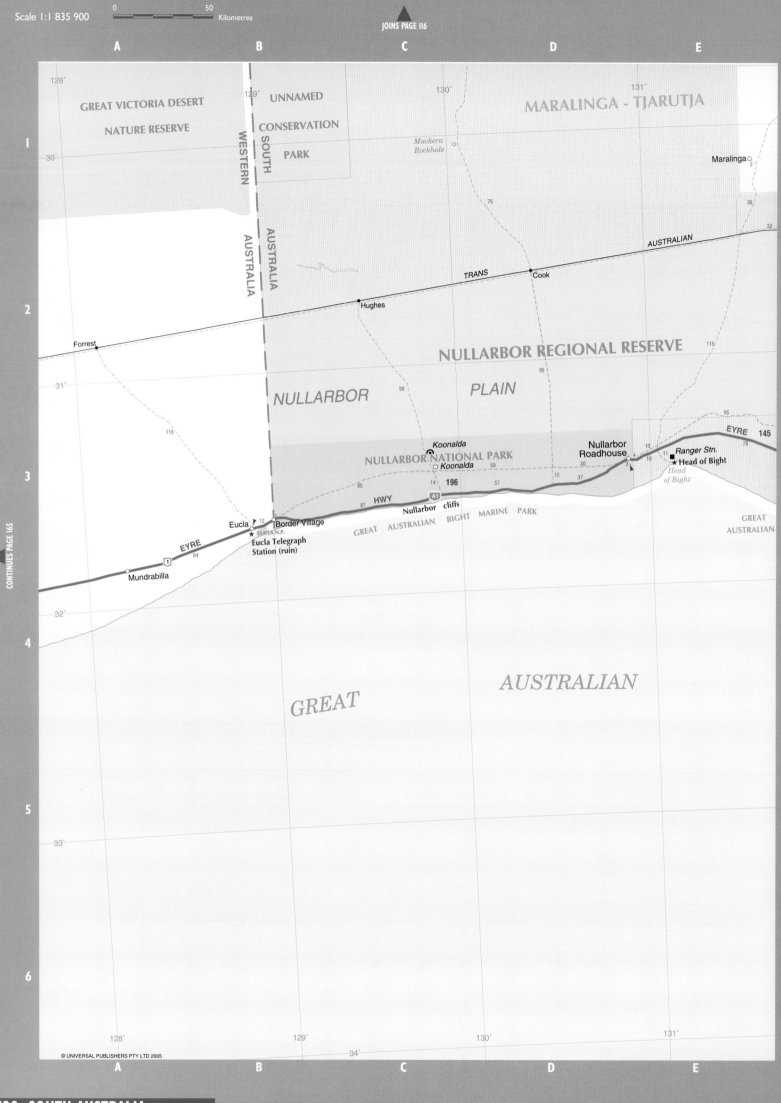

Scale 1:1 835 900

0   50
Kilometres

JOINS PAGE 116

A   B   C   D   E

128°

GREAT VICTORIA DESERT
NATURE RESERVE

129°   UNNAMED
CONSERVATION
PARK

MARALINGA - TJARUTJA

131°

WESTERN   SOUTH   AUSTRALIA   AUSTRALIA

130°

Muckera
Rockhole

I

30°

Maralinga
3

75

AUSTRALIAN

32

TRANS   Cook

Hughes

2

36

Forrest

NULLARBOR REGIONAL RESERVE

115

31°

NULLARBOR   PLAIN

99

95

118

Koonalda

NULLARBOR NATIONAL PARK

Koonalda

59

Nullarbor
Roadhouse

95   EYRE   145

10   78

11   Ranger Stn.

Head of Bight

10

4

10

Head
of Bight

196

14

57

37

30

3

85

HWY

A1

87

Nullarbor   cliffs

GREAT   AUSTRALIAN   BIGHT   MARINE   PARK

GREAT
AUSTRALIAN

Eucla   12
EUCLA N.P.
Border Village

Eucla Telegraph
Station (ruin)

3

EYRE

64

1

Mundrabilla

CONTINUES PAGE 165

32°

GREAT   AUSTRALIAN

4

5

33°

6

128°   129°   130°   131°

34°

© UNIVERSAL PUBLISHERS PTY LTD 2005

A   B   C   D   E

JOINS PAGE 117

A B C D E

132° 133° 134° 135°

Lake Anthony Half Moon Lake

McDouall Peak
Gina
Mirikata

Commonwealth Hill

WOOMERA **PROHIBITED** **AREA**

250 The Twins

Goode
Mulgathing

Lake Bring

Carnes Bulgunnia

STUART HWY

A87

Bon Bon

Ooldea RAILWAY

Vermin Proof Fence

Gosses

Malbooma
Tarcoola
North Well

Wilgena
Lake Labyrinth

Ferguson
Lake Moolkra

Mt Finke 349

Kingoonya

Ifould L.

L. Tallacoota

YELLABINNA REGIONAL RESERVE

+ Jellabinna Rocks

Lake Harry

Lake Gairdner

Kokatha 138

LAKE GAIRDNER NATIONAL PARK

Lake Everard

Googs L.

Lake Everard

Yalata
Yalata Roadhouse

Vermin Proof Fence

YUMBARRA CONSERVATION PARK

WAHGUNYAH C.R.

HWY

53

Nundroo 81

YUMBARRA C.R.

Bookabie

Kalanbi
Koonibba

O.T.C. Earth Station (Abandoned)

PUREBA CONSERVATION PARK

Kondoolka

87

30
Lake Acraman

BIGHT MARINE PARK

Coorabie
Glen Boree

Penong A1

EYRE HWY 70

Charra

Wandana
Maltee

Hiltaba

Fowlers Bay
CHADINGA C.R.

Port Le Hunt
Point Sinclair

Denial Bay
Thevenard
Ceduna

Mudamuckla
Puntabie

NUNNYAH C.R.

Gawler Ranges

Cape Adieu
Cape Nuyts

Point Fowler

Lake Macdonnell

Laura Bay
FLINDERS HWY 91

Nunjikompita
KOOLGERA C.R.

69
Yardea

POINT BELL C.P.
Point Bell

Point Peter

St Peter I.
Goat I.

Carawa

Pimbaacia
Wirrulla
66

NUYTS ARCHIPELAGO C.P.

Evans I.
Eyre I.
Smoky Bay

Smoky Bay 109

Petina
Yantanabie

GAWLER RANGES

Nuyts Archipelago

Franklin Is.

Haslam

46

GAWLER RANGES NATIONAL PARK

Isles of St Francis
St Francis I.
Masillion I.

Point Brown

Chilpanunda
Cungena

Poochera

ISLES OF SAINT FRANCIS C.P.

Streaky Bay

62

Karcultaby

Minnipa

Cape Bauer
Gibson Pen.
Corvisart Bay
Point Westhall

Streaky Bay

Chandada
Inkster

84
Poldinna

Yaninee

Yanerbie Beach

CALPATANNA WATERHOLE C.P.

64
Murphy's Haystacks

KULLIPARU C.R.

Pygery

Sceale Bay
Cape Blanche

Calca

Colley
KULLIPARU C.P.

83
Wudinna

Lake Yaninee

Sapphire Flats

Calca Pen.
Cape Radstock

Baird Bay
Port Kenny

Mount Damper

Kyancutta

VENUS BAY C.P.
Venus Bay
Point Weyland

KULLIPARU C.R.

COCATA C.P.

Talia
COCATA C.R.

Anxious Bay

63
Lake Newland 87

Mount Wedge

BARWELL C.R.

LAKE NEWLAND C.P.
Colton

B91 86

Waldegrave Is
Cape Finniss
Elliston

Bramfield

BASCOMBE WELL CONSERVATION PARK

BIGHT

Flinders I.

FLINDERS HWY

Sheringa

Investigator Group

INVESTIGATOR GROUP C.P.

Cap I.

74

Pearson Isles

Lake Hamilton

Mount Hope

A B C D E

132° 133° 134° 135°

© UNIVERSAL PUBLISHERS PTY LTD 2005

0   50   Kilometres

A   B   C   D   E

WOOMERA   PROHIBITED   AREA

McDouall Peak
Gina
Mirikata
The Twins
Billa Kalina
Millers Creek
Goode
Mount Eba
Witchelina
Carnes
Bulqunnia
Mulgaria
Stuart Creek Opal Fields
Bon Bon
Parakylia
Olympic Dam Mine
Andamooka
Gosses
Mount Vivian
Olympic Dam
White Dam Opal Fields
Roxby Downs
Tarcoola
Lake Labyrinth
Roxby Downs
Andamooka
Wilgena
Purple Downs
Andamooka Island
Lake Moolkra
North Well
Ferguson
Kingoonya
Arcoona
Bosworth
Murdie Island
YELLABINNA
Kultanaby
Glendambo
Lake Ross
Lake Richardson
Warrioota
REGIONAL
Coondambo
Lake Hanson
Woomera
LAKE
RESERVE
Wirraminna
Pimba
TORRENS
Lake Harry
HWY
Wirraminna
Kokatha
LAKE GAIRDNER
Lake Hart
Nurrungar (restricted entry)
Yeltacowie
NATIONAL
Lake Gairdner
NATIONAL PARK
Wirrappa
Mount Gunson
Pernatty
PARK Torrens
Everard
Island Lagoon
Lake Windabout
Oakden Hills
Pernatty Lagoon
Pernatty
Lake Everard
Kangaroo Well
Mahanewo
Yalymboo
South Gap
Lake Torrens
PUREBA
Kondoolka
Moonaree
Lake Macfarlane
Whittata
Wallerberdina
CONSERVATION PARK
Lake Acraman
Neuroodla
NUNNYAH C.R.
Hiltaba
Bookaloo
Warrakimbo
Gawler
Kootaberra
Yadlamulka
Nunjikompita
Yudnapinna
Hesso
Wilkatana
Pimbaacia
Ranges
Willochra (ruin)
Wirrulla
Yardea
Mt Kolendo
Kolendo
Cariewerloo
Tent Hill
Quorn
Petina
Thurlga
Mount Ive
Pichi Richi Rly
Yantanabie
Corraberra
Chilpanunda
GAWLER RANGES
Nonning
Siam
Wartaka
Woolshed Flat
Cungena
GAWLER RANGES C.R.
Port Augusta
Stirling North
Poochera
NATIONAL
Paney
Lincoln Gap
Winninowie
Wilmington
Chandada
PARK
Buckleboo
Uno
Myall Creek Arid Lands Botanic Garden
MILITARY
Nectar Brook
Inkster
Minnipa
Corunna
TRAINING
Melrose
Poldinna
PINKAWILLINIE
Buckleboo
Iron Knob
AREA
Mambray Creek
Pygery
Yaninee
CONSERVATION
Lake Gilles
Iron Baron
Port Bonython
Wudinna
Drekurni
Whyalla
Port Germein
Kyancutta
Koongawa
Kimba
Iron Baron
Whyalla
Colley
PARK
HWY
Maritime Museum
Napperby
Calca
Warramboo
Mt Middleback
Cowled Landing
Port Pirie
Baird Bay
Mount Damper
Cootra
Middleback
Jarrold Pt Port Davis
Port Kenny
Waddikee
Crystal Brook
Venus Bay
Colton
Kopi
Caralue
Heggaton
Midgee
Merriton
Talia
Mount Wedge
McLachlan
CARAPPEE HILL
Mangalo
Mitchellville
Port Broughton
Bramfield
BIRDSEYE
Lock
Darke Peak
Coolanie
Mundoora
Elliston
Warrachie
Rudall
Cleve
Cowell
Lucky Bay
Tickera
Alford
Sheringa
Murdinga
Taragoro
Elbow Hill
Wallaroo
Bute
Toolige
Verran
Port Gibbon
Kadina
Wharminda
Arno Bay
Showtown
Karkoo
Coomaba
Mount Hill
Port Neill
Dutton Bay
Moonta
Paskeville
Mount Hope
Kaldow
Yeelanna
Kapinnie

SPENCER GULF

GREAT AUSTRALIAN BIGHT

EYRE PENINSULA

Investigator Group
Pearson Isles
Flinders I.

© UNIVERSAL PUBLISHERS PTY LTD 2005

A   B   C   D   E

JOINS PAGE 121

A B C D E

CONTINUES PAGES 39 & 44

Milparinka
Mt Sturt
Mt Brown 274
Mt Shannon 332
Mount Shannon
Mount Arrowsmith
Hawker Gate
Smithville House
Lake Wallace
Old Quinyambie
Pincally
Border Downs
Pimpara Lake
Packsaddle Roadhouse
Yelka
The Veldt
New Quinyamble
Broughams Gate
Avenel
Pine View
Pine Ridge
Mount Westwood
Tielta
Fowlers Gap
McDougalls Well
Mount Woowoolahra
Corona
Kantappa
Bijerkerno
Wilangee
Acacia Downs
Paringa
Mount Gipps
Purnamoota
Yanco Glen
Daydream Mine
Glen Idol
Mundi Mundi
Silverton
Stephens Creek
Topar
Broken Hill
Mount Gipps
Huonville
Kinalung
Quondong
Kars
Ascot Vale
Enmore
Pine Point
Langwell
Leonora Downs
Nettlbgoe Lake
Burta
Wonga
Netley
Blackwell
Buckalow
Kudgee
Middle Camp
Tandau
Mazar
South Ita
Budgeree
Kimberley
Terrananya
Nagaela
Double Yards
Oakvale
Loch Lilly
Coombah Roadhouse
Twin Wells
Popilta L.
Popio Lake
Travellers Lake
Nialia Lake
Yelta
Manilla
Nearie Lk N.R.
Nearie Lake
Trelega
Milkengay L.
Bunneringee
Twelve Mile
Burtundy
Huntingfield
Hypurna
Pine Camp
Lake Victoria

CHOWILLA REGIONAL RESERVE
CHOWILLA GAME RESERVE
DANGGALI CONSERVATION PARK
TARAWI N.R.
Morgan Vale
Canopus
Lords Well
Canegrass
Chaffey

SOUTH AUSTRALIA
NEW SOUTH WALES

Dog Fence
Vermin Proof Fence

Lake Cootabarlow
Lake Pundalpa
Lake Elder
Lake Frome
Lake Frome REGIONAL RESERVE
LAKE FROME
Lake Tarkarcloo

Mt Fitton Talc Mine (no access)
Moolawatana
Mt Freeling
Mt Fitton (ruin)
Yerelina
Wheal Turner (ruin)
Umberatana
Arkaroola Village
Arkaroola Wilderness
Paralana Springs
North Mulga
154
GAMMON RANGES NATIONAL PARK
Yankaninna
Mt McKinlay 1050
Wooltana
Balcanoona (N.P. H.Q.)
Nepabunna
Wertaloona
Wilpoorinna
Farina (ruin)
STRZELECKI TRACK
Mt Lyndhurst
Avondale
Lyndhurst
Myrtle Springs
Leigh Creek Coal Mine
Leigh Creek
Copley
Leigh Creek
North Moolooloo
Puttapa
Angepena
Warraweena
WARRAWEENA SANCTUARY
Mt Tilley 1018
NANTAWARRINA
Nantawarrina
Mulga View
Beltana Roadhouse
Beltana
Narrina
Nilpena
Blinman
Angorichina Roadhouse
Wirrealpa
Parachilna
Commodore
Brachina
FLINDERS RANGES NATIONAL PARK
Mt Caernarvon 923
Mt Buffalo
Martins Well
Erudina
Frome Downs
Benagerie
Wilpena
Moralana
Cotabena
Hookina (ruin)
Warcowie
Willippa
Curnamona
Mooleulooloo
Strathearn
Yarramba
Hawker
Holowilena
Mulyungarie
Kanyaka (ruin)
Gordon (ruin)
Yednalue
Cradock
Old Baratta (ruin)
Baratta
Koonamore
Mt Victor
Plumbago
Bimbowrie
Kalkaroo
Kalabity
Boolcoomata
Belton
Witchitie
Four Brothers
Outalpa
Bulloo Creek
Mingary
Tepco
Corella
Carrieton
Minburra
Melton
Waukaringa (ruin)
Morialpa
Cultana
Aroona
Cockburn
Bruce
Moockra
Johnburgh
Yalpara
Wabricoola
Mannahill
Eringa Park
Maldorkey
Mutooroo
Devonborough Downs
Duffields
Hammond
Eurelia
Walloway (ruin)
Willowie
McCoys Well
Yunta
Oulnina Park
Wadnaminga
Benda Park
Morchard
Bridgewater
Pekina
Orroroo
Nackara
Dawson
Paratoo
Tiverton
Manunda
Olorah Downs
Olary
Murray Town
Booleroo Centre
Peterborough
Wirrabara
Ucolta
Yongala
Mannanarie
Oodla Wirra
Oak Park
Netley Gap
Lilydale
Oakbank
Appila
Laura
Caltowie
Terowie
Franklyn
The Oaks
Faraway Hill
Quandong Vale
Jamestown
Whyte Yarcowie
Bendigo
Braemar
Gladstone
Georgetown
Ketchowla
Kia Ora
Sturt Vale
Pine Valley
Narridy
Washpool
Hallett
Caroona
Fords Lagoon
Gulnare
Spalding
Murkaby
Redhill
Yacka
Booborowie
Koomooloo
Koolunga
Mount Bryan
Brinkworth
Hilltown
Burra
Redcliffe
Balah
Blyth
Hanson
Clare
Mintaro
The Gums
Clare Valley Wineries
Watervale
Waterloo
Manoora
Robertstown
Morgan
Cadell
Whitwarta
Saddleworth

© UNIVERSAL PUBLISHERS PTY LTD 2005

0   50   Kilometres

JOINS PAGE 122

A B C D E

Karkoo
Mount Hope Kaldow Mount Hill
B100 Kapinnie Yeelanna
Drummond Point 36 Ungarra Port Neill
Cummins Cockaleechie Brayfield Cape Hardy
135° Dutton Bay
136° Lipson 43
Lake Greenly 37 Yallunda Flat
Warrow Pillana 19
Coulta Edillilie Koppio Tumby Bay
Point Sir Isaac 67 White Flat Koppio Smithy Museum
Coffin Bay Pen 41 46 Tumby Bay
Coffin Bay Wanilla Louth Bay Reevesby I.
COFFIN BAY Wangary Pearlah Poonindie Sir Joseph Banks Group
N.P. Coffin Bay North Shields Spilsby I.
Point Whidbey Coomunga 27
Greenly I. Boston Bay Boston I.
Avoid Bay Point Avoid Port Lincoln Axel Stenross Maritime Museum
Whalers Way Taylor I.
Jussieu LINCOLN N.P.
Cape Carnot Pen Thistle I.
Sleaford Bay West Point
Linguanea I. Waterhouse Point
35° Williams I.
Gambier Is.
NEPTUNE ISLANDS C.P. GAMBIER ISLANDS C.P.
Neptune Is.

Moonta Paskeville Kulpara
Cape Elizabeth 50 Agery Kainton 19
Port Clinton B86
Weetulta Arthurton Port Wakefield
Balgowan Price Inkerman
POINT PEARCE A.L. 50
South Kilkerran Maitland
Port Victoria Urania Ardrossan
Wardang I. YORKE Sandilands
PENINSULA Pine Point
Port Rickaby Black Pt
Hardwick Bluff Beach Port Julia
Bay Curramulka 78
31 Minlaton Port Vincent
Corny Point Brentwood
Hardwicke Bay B88
Stansbury
SPENCER GULF
Warooka Coobowie
50 Yorketown Edithburgh
WARRENBEN C.P. 36
B86 Sturt Bay
West Cape Troubridge Point
INNES N.P. Marion Bay
Stenhouse Bay
Cape Spencer St Vincent Gulf

Investigator Strait FLEURIEU
Emu Bay North Cape Rapid Bay
Stokes Bay Kingscote Cape Jervis
WESTERN RIVER W.A. 15 DEEP CREEK
Cape Borda Cygnet River Penneshaw
CAPE TORRENS W.A. 60 American River Maritime Museum
Parndana 63 Cape Willoughby
RAVINE DES CASOARS W.P.A. KANGAROO ISLAND
FLINDERS CHASE N.P. 23 54 D'Estrees Bay
Rocky River 83 CAPE GANTHEAUME C.P. Cape Hart
FLINDERS CHASE N.P. SEAL BAY Vivonne Bay
Cape Du Couedic Remarkable Rocks VIVONNE BAY C.P. Cape Gantheaume

SOUTHERN OCEAN

135° 136° 137° 138°

© UNIVERSAL PUBLISHERS PTY LTD 2005

JOINS PAGE 123

Map grid columns: A B C D E
Map grid rows: 1 2 3 4 5 6

Auburn, Waterloo, Manoora, Robertstown, Morgan, Cadell, Chowilla Game Reserve, Chaffey, Lake Victoria, Warranangra, Dareton, Gol Gol
Whitwarta, Saddleworth, Mount Mary, Bower, Waikerie, Renmark North, Renmark, Paringa, Cal Lal, Wentworth, Merbein, Mildura
Balaklava, Marrabel, Riverton, Tarlee, Eudunda, Sutherlands, Blanchetown, Kingston-On-Murray, Moorook, Berri, Sturt, Meringur North, Meringur, Irymple, Red Cliffs
Owen, Hamley Bridge, Kapunda, Truro, Barossa Valley Wineries, Sedan, Notts Well, Maggea, Myria, Barmera, Loxton, Taldra, Morkalla, Yarrara, Bambill, Werrimull, Benetook, Yatpool
Dublin, Mallala, Freeling, Nuriootpa, Angaston, Tanunda, Cambrai, Swan Reach, Bakara, Wunkar, Loxton Historical Village, Taplan, Carwarp
Two Wells, Gawler, Williamstown, Springton, Nildottie, Mantung, Mercunda, Pata, Veitch
Virginia, Mt Pleasant, Walker Flat, Mindarie, Wanbi, Alawoona, Paruna, Meribah, Hattah, Kulkyne N.P.
Adelaide, Woodside, Mannum, Purnong, Bow Hill, Halidon, Cobera, Murray-Sunset National Park, Mt Crozier 111, Mt Cowra 86
Noarlunga Central, Hahndorf, Rallamana, Callington, Mypolonga, Perponda, Sandalwood, Billiatt Conservation Park, Karte, Peebinga, Pink Lakes, Rocket Lake, Hattah
Mt Barker, Strathalbyn, Murray Bridge, Borrika, Karoonda, Marama, Kulkami, Pinnaroo, Chandos, Cowangie, Tutye, Underbool, Galah, Ouyen, Kiamal
McLaren Vale, Ashbourne, Langhorne Creek, Wellington, Kulde, Smithville, Parilla, Panitya, Carina, Danyo, Linga, Boinka, Walpeup
Willunga, Myponga, Yankalilla, Goolwa, Port Elliot, Victor Harbor, Milang, Narrung, Ashville, Cooke Plains, Peake, Lameroo, Bews, Murrayville 4WD, Mt Observatory 111, Patchewollock
Normanville, Granite Island, Cockle Train, Meningie, Field, Coomandook, Yumali, Jabuk, Geranium, Scorpion Springs C.P., Big Desert, Wyperfeld National Park, Nypo, Hopetoun, Yaapeet
Magrath Flat, Culburra, Tintinara, Coonalpyn, Ki Ki, Carcuma C.P., Pertendi Bore, Ngarkat Conservation Park, Mount Shaugh C.P., Waggon Flat, Lake Albacutya, Rainbow, Rosebery
Woods Well, Coombe, Mount Rescue C.P., Big Desert Wilderness Park, Brentwood, Ellam, Willenabrina, Angip
Policemans Point, Salt Creek, Keith, Brimbago, Telopea Downs, Netherby, Jeparit
Messent C.P., Gum Lagoon C.P., Wirrega, Cannawigara, Yanac, Broughton, Sandsmere, Warracknabeal, Aubrey, Antwerp, Ailsa
Tilley Swamp, Bordertown, Mundulla, Wolseley, Serviceton, Kaniva, Miram, Nhill, Woorak, Salisbury, Glenlee, Wallup
Willalooka, Culston, Geegeela, Lillimur, Western Flat, Bangham C.P., Frances, Neuarpurr, Dimboola, Kiata, Winiam, Byrneville
Padthaway, Keppoch, Binnum, Little Desert National Park, Goroke, Mitre, Horsham, Murtoa, Dooen
Kingston S.E., Cape Jaffa, Reedy Creek, Avenue, Lucindale, Naracoorte, Hynam, Apsley, Edenhope, Kangawall, Karnak, Natimuk, Jallumba, Miga Lake, Mockinyah
Cape Dombey, Baudin Rocks, Guichen Bay, Robe, Greenways, Bool Lagoon, Struan, Wrattonbully, Kadnook, Douglas, Brimpaen, Halls Gap, Grampians
Beachport, Cape Martin, Furner, Penola, Coonawarra Wineries, Glenroy, Poolaigelo, Dergholm, Harrow, Balmoral, Englefield, Nareen
Southend, Millicent, Tantanoola, Hatherleigh, Mount Burr, Kalangadoo, Wepar, Glencoe, Nangwarry, Tarpeena, Casterton, Red Cap Creek, Lake Mundi, Wando Bridge, Brit Brit, Carapook, Cavendish, Coleraine
Canunda N.P., Mount Gambier, Blue Lake, Wandilo, Mil-Lel, Rennick, Digby, Merino, Grassdale, Branxholme, Hamilton, Dunkeld, Penshurst
Carpenter Rocks, Blackfellows Caves, Kongorong, Caverton, Princess Margaret Rose Caves, Dartmoor, Hotspur, Condah, Mt Napier, Macarthur, Tyrendarra, Heywood, Homerton, Hawkesdale
Allendale East, Port MacDonnell, Cape Northumberland, Nelson, Discovery Bay Coastal Park, Mt Richmond, Drumborg

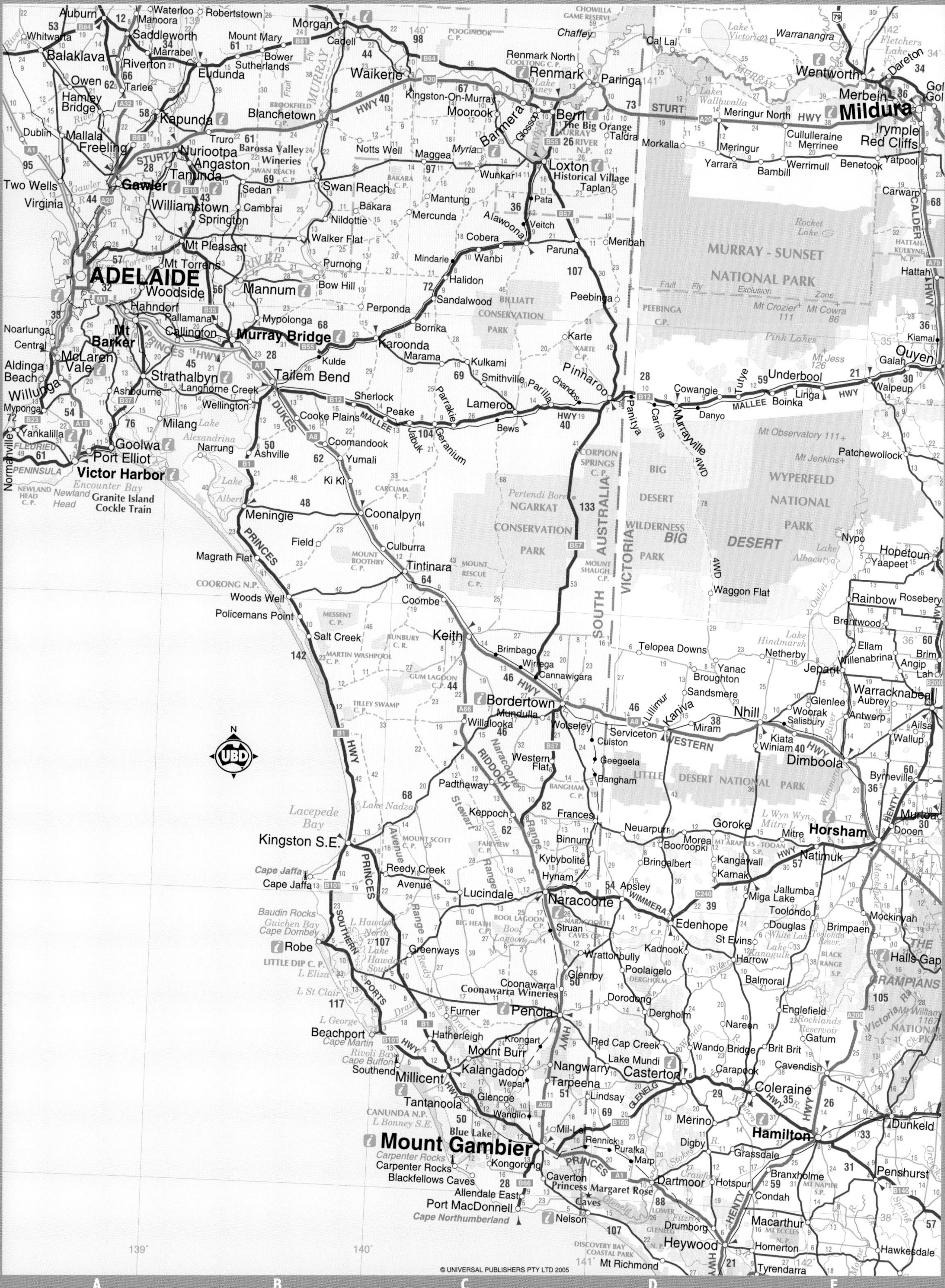

UBD (compass marker)

Lacepede Bay, Encounter Bay, Newland Head C.P., Coorong N.P., Lake Alexandrina, Lake Albert

CONTINUES PAGES 68, 70 & 74

© UNIVERSAL PUBLISHERS PTY LTD 2005

JOINS PAGE 74

CITY AND TOWN CENTRES

Mount Gambier page 125 C6

Information Centre
Lady Nelson Visitor
& Discovery Centre,
Jubilee Hwy East
Ph: (08) 8724 9750

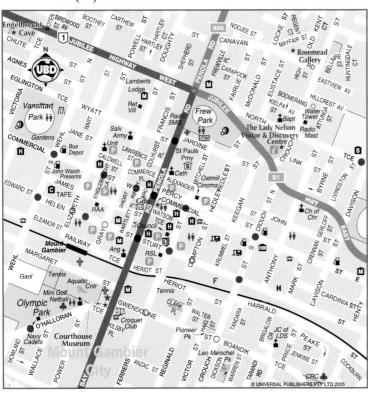

Murray Bridge page 125 B2

Information Centre
3 South Tce
Ph: (08) 8539 1142

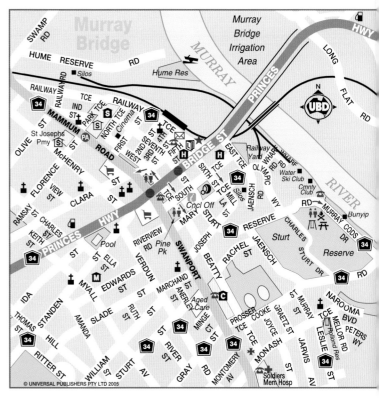

Port Augusta page 122 E4

Information Centre
Wadlata Outback Centre,
41 Flinders Tce
Ph: (08) 8642 4511

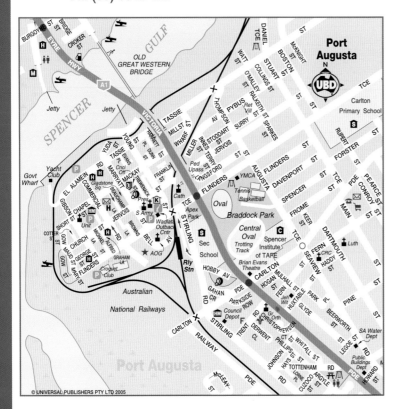

Port Lincoln page 124 B1

Information Centre
3 Adelaide Pl
Ph: (08) 8683 3544

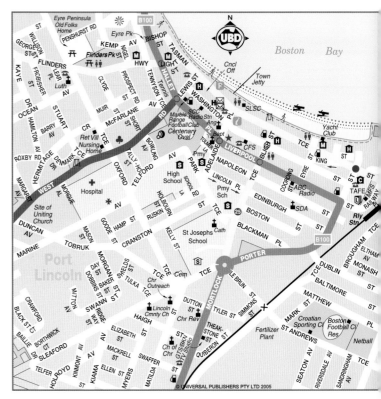

Port Pirie page 122 E5

Information Centre
3 Mary Elie St
Ph: (08) 8633 8700

Renmark page 125 D1

Information Centre
84 Murray Ave
Ph: (08) 8586 6704

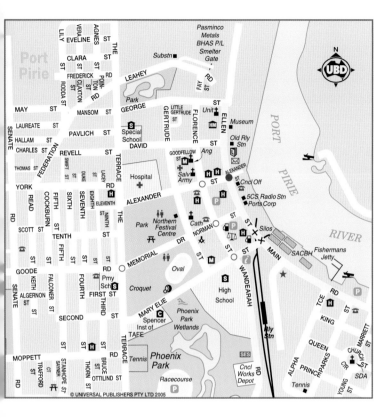

Victor Harbor page 125 A3

Information Centre
The Causeway, Esplanade
Ph: (08) 8552 5738

Whyalla page 122 E5

Information Centre
Lincoln Hwy
Ph: (08) 8645 7900

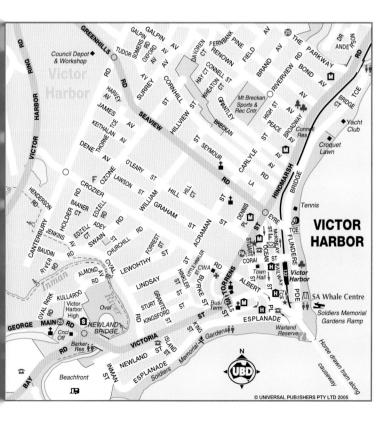

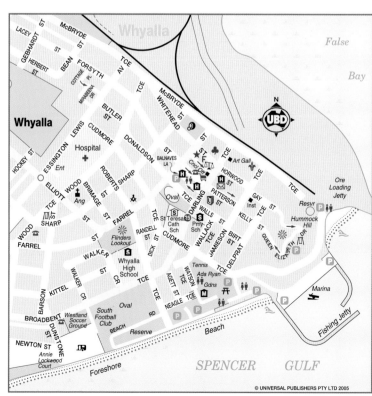

NORTHERN TERRITORY

Main Information Centres
Tourism Top End
Mitchell St/Knuckey St,
Darwin 0800
Ph: (08) 8936 2499
or 1300 138 886
www.tourismtopend.com.au

**Central Australian Visitor
Information Centre**
60 Gregory Tce,
Alice Springs 0870
Ph: (08) 8952 5800
or 1800 645 199
www.centralaustralian
tourism.com

The Northern Territory is Australia's most barren region and it covers approximately one-sixth of the continent. The Territory's rich Aboriginal past dates back some 60 000 years. Ceremonies, stories, rock art and intimate knowledge of the land and its seasons attest to the Aboriginal people's special link with the Territory. About 50% of the Territory's terrain is classified Aboriginal land, and visitors are required to obtain a special permit to enter many of these areas.

The vibrant ochre and red sands of the Centre characterise the stunning MacDonnell Ranges and Simpson Desert; in contrast are the verdant greens of the rainforests and savanna woodlands of the northern lands that merge into the monsoonal Timor and Arafura seas.

The remoteness and diversity of the Northern Territory make it an ideal location for exploring beyond the beaten track. It is excellent for 4WD touring, and camel treks can be organised from Alice Springs—one option is a 2-week journey to Rainbow Valley. Bushwalkers will find much to discover. Many areas in the Territory offer a variety of walking tracks of varying degrees of difficulty. Scenic flights are a more leisurely sightseeing option, while the Centre's dry heat creates ideal conditions for hot-air ballooning.

Near the geographical centre of the continent, are the iconic Uluru and Kata Tjuta. These Aboriginal sacred sites are World Heritage-listed and are synonymous with the red heart of Australia. Nearby Mount Connor, a giant tabletop mountain, is also impressive in scale.

The spectacular sights, ancient landscapes and vast, formidable terrain of the Northern Territory — often subject to droughts, bushfires, flash flooding and cyclones — epitomise the description 'Outback Australia'. Adventure and discovery are constant companions in this frontier land.

MAIN PLACES OF INTEREST	Map ref		Map ref
Alice Springs Cultural Precinct	144 E2	Museum & Art Gallery of the NT	131 C2
Alice Springs Desert Park	144 E2	Museum of Central Australia	144 E2
Alice Springs Telegraph Station	144 E2	National Pioneer Womens Hall of Fame	146
Arnhem Land	135,136	Nitmiluk National Park (Katherine Gorge)	135 A5
Battery Hill Mining Centre	141 C2	Nourlangie Rock, Kakadu	135 B3
Chambers Pillar	144 D4	Olive Pink Flora Reserve, Alice Springs	146
Crocodylus Park, Darwin	132 E3	Palm Valley	144 C2
Cutta Cutta Caves	135 A6	Pine Creek	134 E5
Darwin Crocodile Farm	134 D3	Rainbow Valley	144 D3
Darwin Wharf Precinct	131 E6	Simpson Desert	145 C5
Devils Marbles	141 D3	Simpsons Gap	144 D2
Douglas Hot Springs	134 E5	Springvale Homestead, Katherine	134 E6
Finke Gorge National Park	144 C2	Standley Chasm	144 D2
Fogg Dam	134 D3	Territory Wildlife Park	134 D3
Frontier Camel Farm, Alice Springs	144 E2	Tiwi Islands	134 C1
Henbury Meteorite Craters	144 D3	Ubirr, Kakadu	146
Howard Springs Nature Park	133 E5	Uluru (Ayers Rock)	147
Jim Jim Falls, Kakadu	135 B4	Uluru-Kata Tjuta Cultural Centre	147
Kakadu National Park	135 A3	Warradjan Aboriginal Cultural Centre	146
Kata Tjuta (The Olgas)	147	Watarrka National Park (Kings Canyon)	144 B3
Litchfield National Park	134 D4	West MacDonnell National Park	144 C2
Mary River Wetlands	134 E3	Window on the Wetlands	134 D3
Mataranka Thermal Pool	135 B6	Yellow Water, Kakadu	146

Top: Chambers Pillar at sunset; Bottom: Cliffs reflected in a seasonal pool in Rainbow Valley Conservation Area

In 1864, the first coastal town was established in the Northern Territory and named Palmerston. It was located at the mouth of the Adelaide River and, after a particularly wet season in 1865, it was abandoned. The settlement moved to an area named Port Darwin, which had been home to the Larrakeyah people for thousands of years. The new site was again called Palmerston, but locals referred to it as Port Darwin to distinguish it from the original settlement. The town officially became Darwin in 1911, after the Federal Government took control of the Northern Territory. Darwin's development was slow due to its isolation from other Australian states. It is now one of Australia's most modern cities, since almost every building had to be rebuilt after Japanese wartime air-raids in 1942 or after the destruction caused by Cyclone Tracy on Christmas Day, 1974.

Darwin's economy today relies largely on tourism and the mineral wealth of the Northern Territory. George Brown Darwin Botanic Gardens are over a century old and the tropical gardens span 34ha. Fannie Bay is the landing site of the first flight from England to Australia (a Vickers Vimy aircraft in 1919). Fannie Bay Gaol is no longer used as a prison — its museum displays the gaol history from 1883 to 1979. East Point Recreation Reserve offers walking tracks, cycling paths, picnic areas and year-round swimming in Lake Alexander. East Point Military Museum is close to the gun turrets that were constructed during World War 2. Mindil Beach Sunset Market operates on the foreshore between late April and October and visitors can watch a spectacular sunset over Fannie Bay whilst browsing through the art and craft stalls.

DARWIN CITY PLACES OF INTEREST

	ref		ref
Aquascene	C5	Fannie Bay	A1
Australian Pearling Exhibition	E6	Indo Pacific Marine	E6
Chinese Temple	D5	MGM Grand Casino Darwin	C4
Darwin Entertainment Centre	C5	Mindil Beach Lookout	B4
Darwin Wharf Precinct	E6	Mindil Beach Sunset Market	C3
Deckchair Cinema	D6	Museum & Art Gallery of the NT	C2
Fannie Bay Gaol Museum	C1	Parliament House	D6
George Brown Darwin Botanic Gardens	D3	Smith Street Mall	D5
Government House	D6	World War 2 Oil Storage Tunnels	D6

Top: Smith Street Mall, Darwin; Middle: Mindil Beach Sunset Markets; Bottom: Timor Sea, Nightcliff, Darwin

CONTINUES PAGE 132

Scale 1:24 160

0   500   Metres

LUDMILLA

FANNIE BAY

Fannie

Bay

Ross Smith Memorial
Fannie Bay Gaol Museum
Fannie Bay Gaol Museum

Fannie Bay Racecourse

Waratah Oval
Waratah Sports Club
Darwin Turf Club

Harvey Norman Park

PARAP

OTC Station

WOOLNER

Vesteys Lake

Water Ski Club
CONACHER

Museum and Art Gallery

Bullocky Point

Darwin High

Stuart Park Primary

St Johns College (Co-ed)

George Brown Darwin Botanic Gardens

St Johns College (Co-ed)

RAOB Club

Chinese Cemetery

Myilly Pt

Mindil Beach Lookout

Mindil Beach Market

Myilly Pt Park

MGM Grand Casino

THE GARDENS

Amphitheatre

STUART PARK

Dinah Oval

Mandorah Ferry Terminal

Marina

Cruising Yacht Club

Emery Pt

Larrakeyah

Garden Park Golf Course

City of Darwin

Frances

Elliot Pt

Army Base

LARRAKEYAH

Marina

Ship Maintenance Service Area
Syncrolift
Fishermans Wharf
Slipway

Navy Patrol Boat Base

Doctors Gully

Aquascene

YMCA
YWCA

Darwin Entertainment Centre

Leichhardt Memorial

Bay

Chinese Temple

Smith Street Mall

DARWIN

Old Court House
Parliament House

Supreme Court

World War II Oil Storage Tunnels

Indo Pacific Marine

Australian Pearling Exhibition

Government House

Deckchair Cinema

Lameroo Beach

Stokes Hill

Civic Square

Stokes Hill Wharf
Darwin Wharf Precinct

Iron Ore Wharf

Fort Hill Wharf

0 _____ 2 Kilometres

CONTINUES PAGE 134

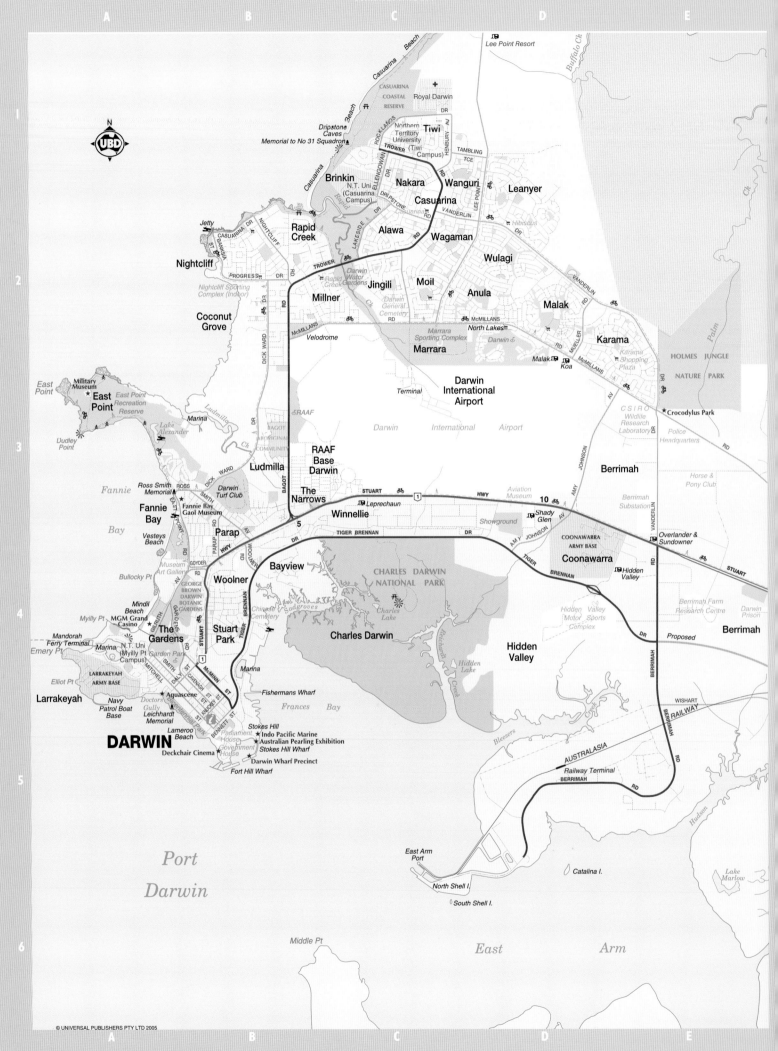

UBD
N

DARWIN

Lee Point Resort

CASUARINA COASTAL RESERVE

Royal Darwin

Dripstone Caves
Memorial to No 31 Squadron

Northern Territory University (Tiwi Campus)

Tiwi

TAMBLING TCE

Brinkin
N.T. Uni (Casuarina Campus)

Nakara   **Wanguri**   **Leanyer**

Casuarina

Jetty

Rapid Creek

Alawa   **Wagaman**

Nightcliff

Wulagi

Darwin Water Gardens

Jingili   **Moil**   **Anula**

Coconut Grove

Millner

Darwin General Cemetery

Malak

Nightcliff Sporting Complex (Indoor)

Karama

Velodrome

Marrara Sporting Complex

North Lakes

Karama Shopping Plaza

Marrara

HOLMES JUNGLE NATURE PARK

East Point

Military Museum

East Point   East Point Recreation Reserve

Malak   Koa

Marina

Darwin International Airport

CSIRO Wildlife Research Laboratory

Lake Alexander

Crocodylus Park

Police Headquarters

Dudley Point

Terminal   *Darwin International Airport*

Horse & Pony Club

Fannie Bay

RAAF Base Darwin

Berrimah

Ross Smith Memorial

Darwin Turf Club

The Narrows

STUART   HWY

Aviation Museum   10   Berrimah Substation

Fannie Bay   Fannie Bay Gaol Museum

Leprechaun

Winnellie   Shady Glen

Berrimah Farm Research Centre

Vesteys Beach

Parap   5

TIGER BRENNAN   DR

Showground

COONAWARRA ARMY BASE

Darwin Prison

Museum Art Gallery

Bayview   **Woolner**

CHARLES DARWIN NATIONAL PARK

Coonawarra

Overlander & Sundowner

Mindil Beach

GEORGE BROWN DARWIN BOTANIC GARDENS

Hidden Valley

STUART

MGM Grand Casino

Charles Lake

Hidden Valley Motor Sports Complex

Berrimah

Mandorah Ferry Terminal   Marina

The Gardens

Stuart Park

Charles Darwin

Hidden Valley

Proposed

Myilly Pt

N.T. Uni (Myilly Pt Campus)

Garden Park

Hidden Lake

Elliot Pt   Emery Pt

LARRAKEYAH ARMY BASE

Marina

Richardt Creek

RAILWAY

Larrakeyah   Navy Patrol Boat Base

Aquascene

Fishermans Wharf

Frances Bay

Doctors Gully   Leichhardt Memorial

Lameroo Beach

Parliament House

Stokes Hill
Indo Pacific Marine
Australian Pearling Exhibition
Stokes Hill Wharf

WISHART   RD

AUSTRALASIA

DARWIN   Deckchair Cinema   Government House

Darwin Wharf Precinct

Fort Hill Wharf

Railway Terminal   BERRIMAH

Bleesers Creek

Port

Darwin

East Arm Port

East   *Arm*

Catalina I.

Lake Marlow

North Shell I.

South Shell I.

Middle Pt

CONTINUES PAGE 134

A   B   C   D   E

CONTINUES PAGE 134

Hope

Inlet

Howards Peninsula

Kings

MILITARY AREA

(FORMER RAAF BOMBING AND & GUNNERY RANGE)

NO PUBLIC ACCESS

Howard

Noogoo Swamp

Mickett Creek

Mickett

Mickett Creek Shooting Complex

Thorak Reserve

Thorak Cemetery

Ck

Milner   Swamp

CONTINUES PAGE 134

Kings

River

McMILLANS

ROBERTSON BARRACKS

(MILITARY AREA)

15

RD

Knuckey Lagoon

Proposed Knuckey

Arterial

Arterial

Ck

Holtze

Howard Springs

Howard Springs Nature Park

Pinelands

HWY

Palms

RD

Road

WISHART

RD

Palmerston

GUNN POINT   RD

Northern Territory University

20

ROYSTONEA

Durack

Yarrawonga

Palmerston

Kakadu Mango ★ Winery

HOWARD SPRINGS

Dutchie Lagoon

RAILWAY

RD

UNIVERSITY

AV

Palmerston Town Centre

CHUNG

STUART

TCE

AUSTRALASIA

Marlow Lagoon

AV

Driver

Palmerston

DRIVER

AV

Mitchell

WAH

AV

Gunn

AV

Marlow Lagoon Recreation Area

ESSINGTON

TEMPLE

Gray

AV

TCE

Howard Springs

EMERY

BUSCALL

AV

Ck

Myrmidon

TILSTON AV

TEMPLE

Bakewell

AV

Wadham Lagoon

Howard Springs

ELRUNDIE

TCE

BALDWIN

DR

GYRBIS AV

TCE

LAMBRICK

ROYSTONEA AV

25

AV

ELRUNDIE

JONSON

Woodroffe

WOODROFFE TCE

LAMBRICK

Creek

Sewage Treatment Works

Moulden

WAH

CHUNG

Rosebery

Virginia

HWY

Proposed Arterial

MOULDEN TCE

Bellamack

Archer Sporting Complex

1

A   B   C   D   E

CONTINUES PAGE 134

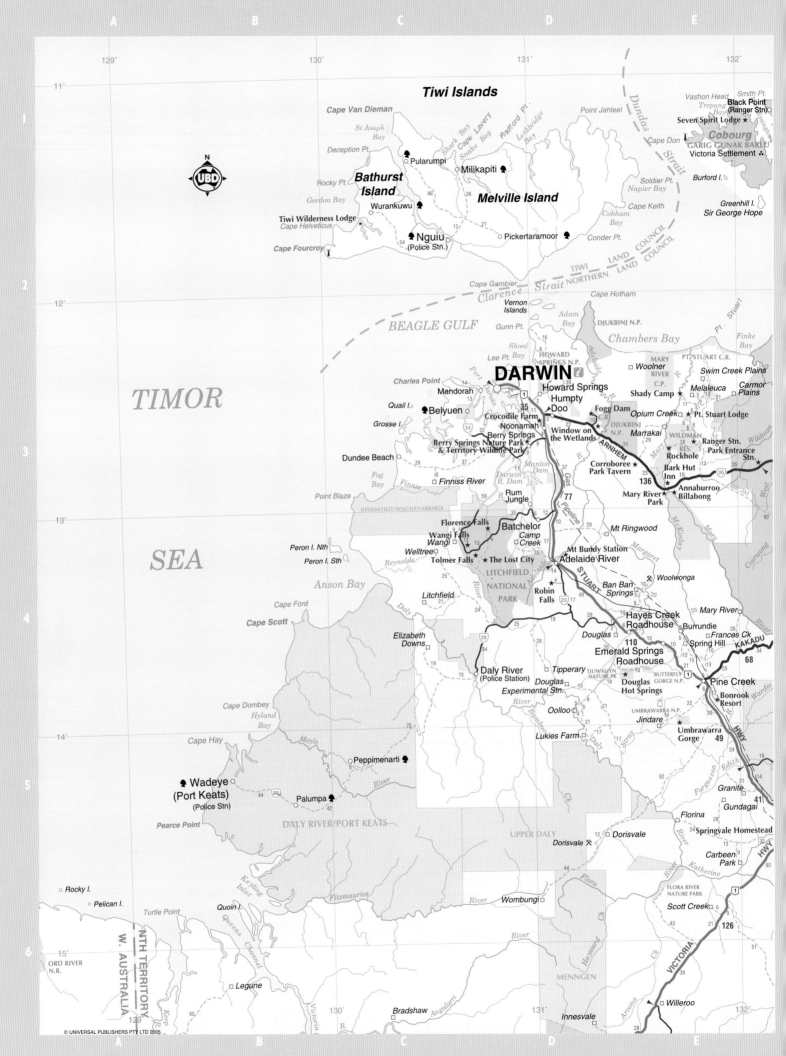

Scale 1:1 932 600

0 50
Kilometres

Tiwi Islands

Cape Van Dieman

St Asaph Bay

Deception Pt.

Rocky Pt.

Cape Helveticus

Cape Fourcroy

Gordon Bay

Bathurst Island

Wurankuwu

Tiwi Wilderness Lodge

Pularumpi

Milikapiti

Melville Island

Pickertaramoor

Nguiu
(Police Stn.)

Cape Gambier

Point Jaheel

Point Jahleel

Dundas Strait

Cape Don

Vashon Head
Trepang Bay
Smith Pt.
Black Point
(Ranger Stn.)

Seven Spirit Lodge

Cobourg
GARIG GUNAK BARLU
Victoria Settlement

Burford I.

Soldier Pt.
Napier Bay

Cape Keith

Cobham Bay

Conder Pt.

Greenhill I.
Sir George Hope

TIWI LAND COUNCIL
NORTHERN LAND COUNCIL

Strait

Clarence Strait

TIMOR

SEA

BEAGLE GULF

Vernon Islands

Cape Hotham

Adam Bay

DJUKBINJ N.P.

Chambers Bay

Pt. Stuart

Finke Bay

Gunn Pt.

Shoal Bay

Lee Pt.

Howard Springs N.P.

Charles Point

Mandorah

Quail I.

Belyuen

Grosse I.

DARWIN

Howard Springs
Humpty Doo

Crocodile Farm
Noonamah
Berry Springs
Berry Springs Nature Park
& Territory Wildlife Park

Woolner

MARY RIVER C.P.

PT. STUART C.R.

Swim Creek Plains

Melaleuca

Carmor Plains

Shady Camp

Fogg Dam

Window on the Wetlands

Opium Creek

Marrakai

DJUKBINJ N.P.

Pt. Stuart Lodge

WILDMAN

RES.

Ranger Stn.

Rockhole

Park Entrance Stn.

ARNHEM

Dundee Beach

Fog Bay

Finniss

Point Blaze

Finniss River

Manton Dam

Darwin R. Dam

Rum Jungle

DELISSAVILLE/WAGAIT/LARRAKIA

Corroboree Park Tavern

136

Bark Hut Inn

Mary River Park

Annaburroo Billabong

SEA

Peron I. Nth

Peron I. Sth

Anson Bay

Reynolds

Florence Falls
Wangi Falls
Wangi

Welltree

Tolmer Falls

Litchfield

Daly

River

Batchelor
Camp Creek

The Lost City

LITCHFIELD NATIONAL PARK

Robin Falls

77
Gas Pipeline

Mt Ringwood

Mt Bundy Station
Adelaide River

STUART

Ban Ban Springs

Woolwonga

Mary River

Margaret

McKinlay

Caryong

Cape Ford

Cape Scott

Elizabeth Downs

Daly River
(Police Station)

Douglas
Experimental Stn.

Tipperary

Douglas

TJUWALIYN
NATURE PK.

Oolloo

Hayes Creek
Roadhouse

110

Emerald Springs
Roadhouse

Douglas Hot Springs

Jindare

Burrundie

Frances Ck
Spring Hill

Mary River

KAKADU

68

BUTTERFLY GORGE N.P.

Pine Creek

Bonrook Resort

126

Cape Dombey
Hyland Bay

Cape Hay

Moyle

Daly

River

Peppimenarti

Lukies Farm

UMBRAWARRA N.P.

Umbrawarra Gorge

49

Springvale Homestead

Granite

Gundagai

Florina

Florina

41

Wadeye
(Port Keats)
(Police Stn.)

Palumpa

44

42

Pearce Point

DALY RIVER/PORT KEATS

UPPER DALY

Dorisvale

Dorisvale

Carbeen Park

Scott Creek

Flora River
Nature Park

HWY

Rocky I.

Pelican I.

Turtle Point

Quoin I.

Keyling Inlet

Queens Channel

Fitzmaurice

River

Wombungi

Flora

River

Katherine

River

ORD RIVER N.R.

NTH TERRITORY

W. AUSTRALIA

Legune

Keep

Victoria

Bradshaw

130°

Angalarri

River

131°

MENNGEN

Innesvale

Willeroo

VICTORIA

HWY

1

Arnora

Victoria

River

JOINS PAGE 137

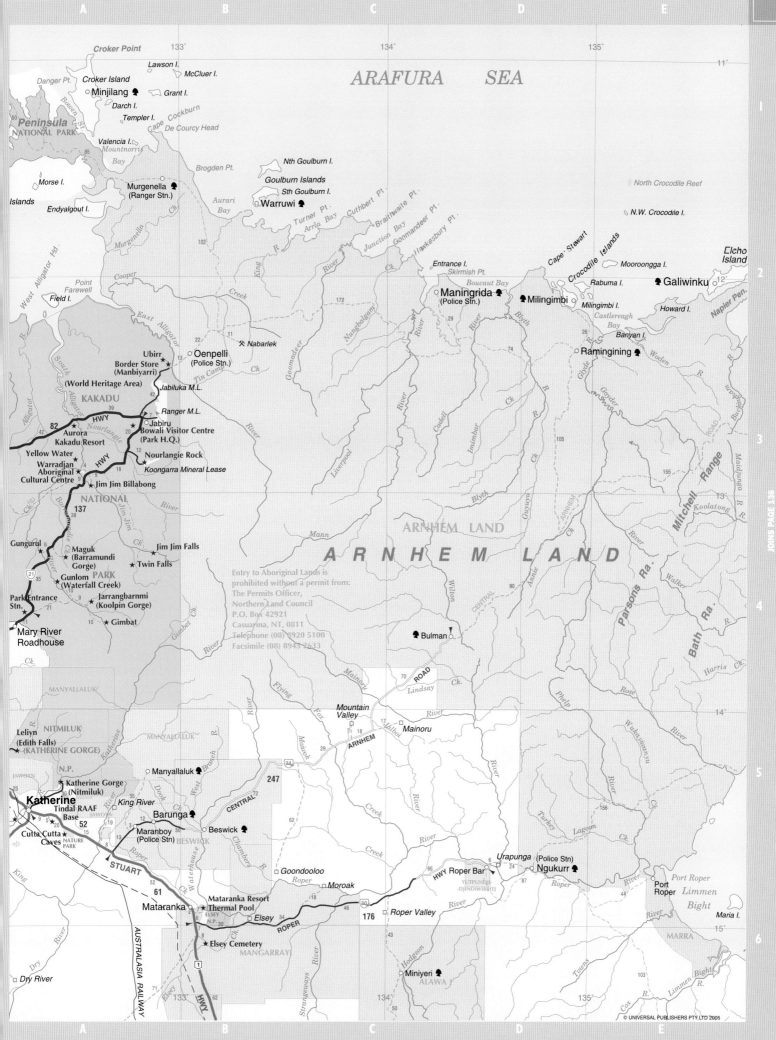

ARAFURA SEA

Croker Point

Danger Pt.
Lawson I.
McCluer I.
Croker Island
Minjilang
Grant I.
Darch I.
Templer I.
De Courcy Head
Peninsula
NATIONAL PARK
Morse I.
Valencia I.
Mountnorris Bay
Islands
Endyalgout I.
Field I.
Point Farewell
Murgenella (Ranger Stn.)
Aurari Bay

Brogden Pt.
Nth Goulburn I.
Goulburn Islands
Sth Goulburn I.
Warruwi
Turner Pt.
Arla Bay
Cuthbert Pt.
Braithwaite Pt.
Goomandeer Pt.
Hawkesbury Pt.

North Crocodile Reef
N.W. Crocodile I.
Cape Stewart
Crocodile Islands
Mooroongga I.
Elcho Island
Rabuma I.
Galiwinku
Milingimbi I.
Howard I.
Castlereagh Bay
Banyan I.
Napier Pen.

Entrance I.
Skirmish Pt.
Boucaut Bay
Maningrida (Police Stn.)
Milingimbi
Ramingining

Nabarlek
Ubirr
Border Store (Manbiyarri)
Oenpelli (Police Stn.)
(World Heritage Area)
KAKADU
Jabiluka M.L.
Ranger M.L.
82
HWY
Aurora Kakadu Resort
Jabiru
Bowali Visitor Centre (Park H.Q.)
Yellow Water
Nourlangie Rock
Warradjan Aboriginal Cultural Centre
Koongarra Mineral Lease
HWY
Jim Jim Billabong
NATIONAL
137
Gungurul
Maguk (Barramundi Gorge)
Jim Jim Falls
Twin Falls
21
Gunlom (Waterfall Creek)
PARK
Park Entrance Stn.
Jarrangbarnmi (Koolpin Gorge)
Gimbat
Mary River Roadhouse

ARNHEM LAND
ARNHEM LAND

Entry to Aboriginal Lands is prohibited without a permit from:
The Permits Officer,
Northern Land Council
P.O. Box 42921
Casuarina, NT, 0811
Telephone (08) 8920 5100
Facsimile (08) 8945 2633

Bulman

Mitchell Range
Parsons Ra.
Bath Ra.

MANYALLALUK

Leliyn (Edith Falls)
NITMILUK
(KATHERINE GORGE)
N.P.
MANYALLALUK
Manyallaluk

Mountain Valley
Mainoru
ARNHEM
ROAD
Lindsay Ck.

Katherine Gorge (Nitmiluk)
Katherine
Tindal RAAF Base
52
King River
Barunga
Beswick
CENTRAL
247
Cutta Cutta Caves
NATURE PARK
Maranboy (Police Stn)
BESWICK
STUART
Roper
Goondooloo
Moroak
Roper Bar
HWY
Urapunga
Ngukurr (Police Stn)
Port Roper
Limmen Bight

Mataranka
Mataranka Resort Thermal Pool
Elsey
ELSEY N.P.
ROPER
176
Roper Valley
MARRA
Maria I.

Elsey Cemetery
MANGARRAY
HWY

AUSTRALASIA RAILWAY

Dry River

Miniyeri
ALAWA

JOINS PAGE 136
JOINS PAGE 138

© UNIVERSAL PUBLISHERS PTY LTD 2005

A   B   C   D   E

ARAFURA   SEA

Cape Wessel
Rimbija I.

Marchinbar
Island

Wessel Islands

North Crocodile Reef

Stevens I.
Guluwuru I.

N.W. Crocodile I.
Drysdale I.
Raragala I.
Truant I.

Graham I.
Jirrgari I.
Companys Is.
Bumaga I.
Wamawi I.
Wigram I.

Cape Stewart
Crocodile Islands
Elcho Island
Alger I.
Astell I.
Cotton I.
Cape Wilberforce

Mooroongga I.
Pt Napier
Inglis I.
The English

Rabuma I.
Galiwinku
Probable I.
Bremer I.

Milingimbi
Milingimbi I.
Howard I.
Mallison I.
Melville Bay
Nhulunbuy

Castlereagh Bay
Banyan I.
Gove Peninsula
Yirrkala

Ramingining
Flinders Peninsula
Arnhem Bay
Cape Arnhem

Woden
Gapuwiyak
Port Bradshaw

A R N H E M
Warryarnera Pt.

ROAD

CENTRAL
ARNHEM
Pt. Alexander

L A N D
Colendon Bay

Mitchell Range
Cape Grey

Parsons Ra.
Koolatong
Trial Bay

Bath Ra.
Myaoola Bay
Cape Shield

ARNHEM LAND
Blue Mud Bay
Nicol I.

Isle Woodah

Bruney I.

Cape Barrow
Hawksnest I.
North East Is.

Bartalumba Bay
Bickerton Island
Winchelsea I.
Milyakburra
Scott Pt.

Alyangula
(Police Stn)
Umbakumba

Angurugu
Groote Eylandt
Dalumbu Bay
Ungwariba Pt.

Rantyirrity Pt.
ARNHEM LAND

Numbulwar
South Pt.
Cape Beatrice

Nyanpinti Pt.

Edward I.
ANINDILYAKWA LAND COUNCIL

Warrakunta Pt.

(Police Stn)
Ngukurr

Port Roper
Port Roper
Limmen Bight

Maria I.

MARRA

GULF

OF

CARPENTARIA

JOINS PAGE 135

JOINS PAGE 139

Scale 1:1 932 600

JOINS PAGE 134

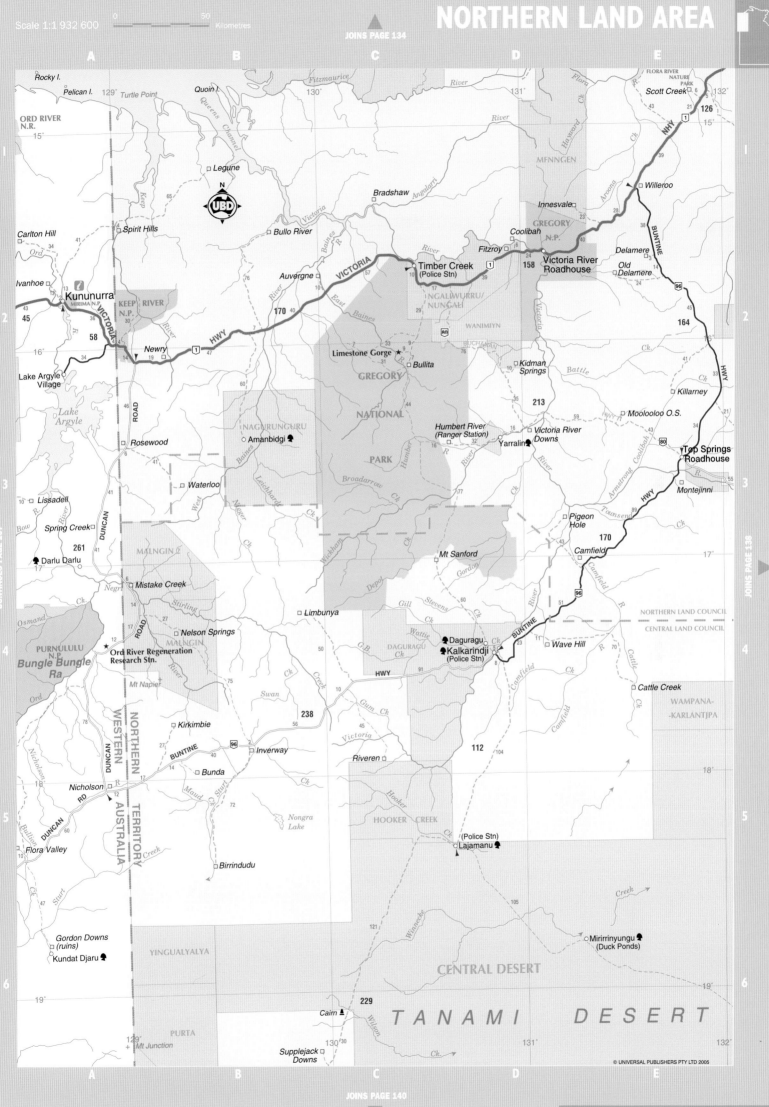

CONTINUES PAGE 157

JOINS PAGE 138

© UNIVERSAL PUBLISHERS PTY LTD 2005

JOINS PAGE 140

Scale 1:1 932 600

0   50 Kilometres

Wombungi

131°

FLORA RIVER
NATURE PARK

Scott Creek   6

1

132°

15°

MENNGEN

HWY   21   126

126

43

39

Willeroo

Dry River

Innesvale

28

23   38

GREGORY
N.P.

VICTORIA

40

BUNTINE   HWY

Coolibah

24

16

6

Victoria River
Roadhouse   158

Delamere

3

Old
Delamere   14

96

24

16°

164

45

2

164

41

Kidman
Springs   10

Battle   Ck.

HWY

33

35

213

Killarney

59

Moolooloo O.S.

16

Victoria River
Downs

43   34   21

80

Birrimba

Top Springs Roadhouse

YINGAWUNARRI MUDBURA

DILLINYA A.L.

Western   Ck.

Western Creek

3

Montejinni   55

HWY

89

Pigeon
Hole

170

Dungowan

74   182

BUCHANAN

Camfield   R.   R.

51

96

BUNTINE

Camfield   R.

17°

Victoria   River

NORTHERN LAND COUNCIL

CENTRAL LAND COUNCIL

Wave Hill   70

4

Cattle Creek   R.

Ck.

Cattle   Ck.

WAMPANA-KARLANTJPA

18°

Camfield   Ck.

105

19°

Winnecke   Creek   Ck.

Mirirrinyungu
(Duck Ponds)

CENTRAL
DESERT

T A N A M I   D E S E R T

KARLANTIJPA NORTH

131°

A

132°

447

260

B

Green Swamp
Well

Roper   R.

Moroak

52

61

Mataranka

73

Mataranka Resort
★ Thermal Pool

Elsey   34

ELSEY   30
N.P.   6

ROPER

Elsey Cemetery

1

AUSTRALASIA

71

WUBALAWUN

MANGARRAYI

STUART

62

Gorrie

63

Larrimah   162

162

36

Gas Pipeline

Maryfield

46

46

Sunday
Creek   24

Kalala   3

Daly Waters
(Historic Site)   7

Hi-Way Inn
Roadhouse

HWY

36

RAILWAY

15

HWY   53   00

Hidden Valley

Dunmarra
Roadhouse   8

12   11   Shenandoah

87

37

STUART   104

Murranji   39

MURRANJI

28

Newcastle   Ck.

Beetaloo

Newcastle
Waters   5

42

19

Elliott

19

Lake
Woods

30

91

42

HWY   30

87

Powell Creek   6

133°

AUSTRALASIA

Gas Pipeline

Tomkinson   R.

MUCKATY   8

Muckaty

RAILWAY

Banka Banka

137

Churchills Head Rock ★
Stuart Memorial

20   29

134°

Phillip Creek   6

C

Roper   R.

YUTPUNDJI-
DJINDIWIRRITJ

18   HWY   HWY

30   176

Roper Valley

43

50

Miniyeri   ALAWA

Hodgson River

46

18

Nutwood Downs

80

Hodgson   R.

Strangways   R.

Arnold   R.

CARPENTARIA   82

Amungee
Mungee   7

1   270

57

Entry to Aboriginal Lands is
Prohibited without a permit from:
The Permits Officer
Northern Land Council
P.O. Box 42921
Casuarina, NT, 0811
Telephone (08) 8920 5100
Facsimile (08) 8945 2633

Newcastle   R.

Ck.

Ucharonidge

30

48

Mungabroom

16   250

78   BARKLY

Renner Springs
Roadhouse

18   Helen Springs

21

Beatu   Ck.

Morphett   Ck.

Brunchilly

Attack   Ck.

★ Attack Creek
Historical Site

WARUMUNGU

E

Likkaparta

D   E

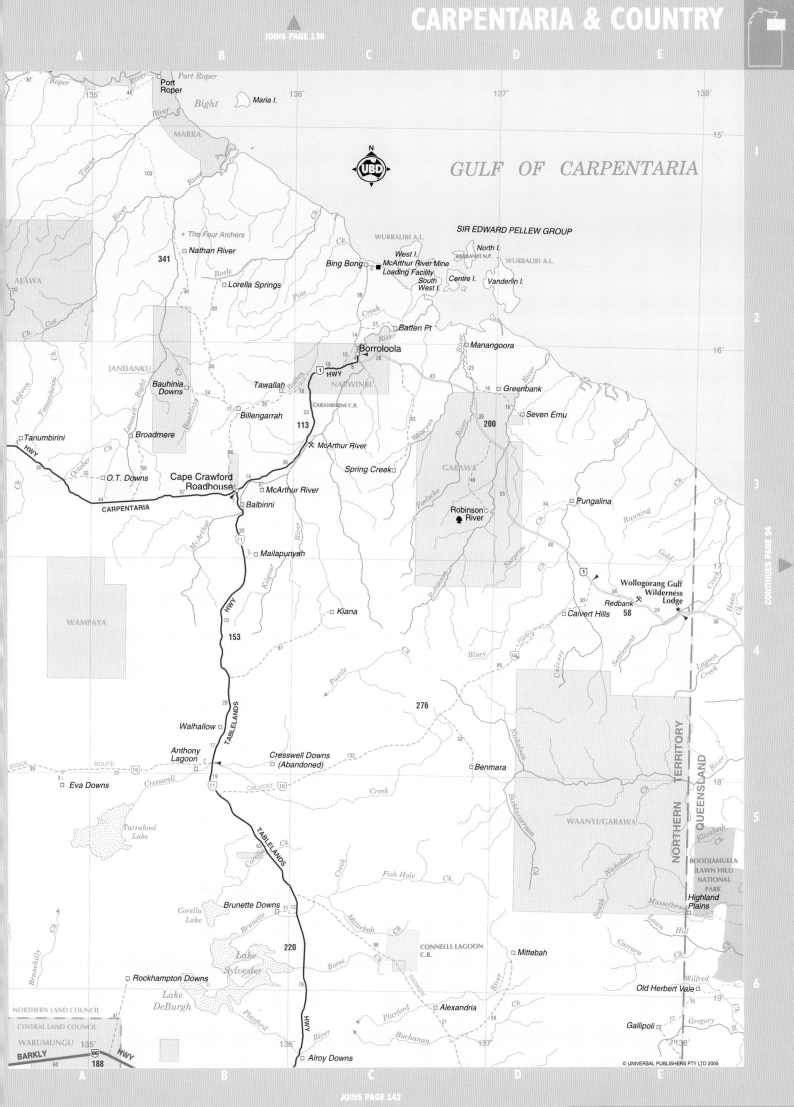

GULF OF CARPENTARIA

SIR EDWARD PELLEW GROUP

WURRALIBI A.L.

North I.
BARRANYI N.P.
WURRALIBI A.L.

West I.
Bing Bong McArthur River Mine
Loading Facility
South
West I.
Centre I.
Vanderlin I.

Port Roper
Port Roper
Bight

Maria I.

MARRA

ALAWA

+ The Four Archers

Nathan River

Lorella Springs

JANDANKU

Bauhinia
Downs

Tawallah

Billengarrah

Batten Pt

Borroloola

HWY
NARWINBI

CARANBIRINI C.R.

Manangoora

Greenbank

Seven Emu

GARAWA

Tanumbirini

HWY

Broadmere

McArthur River

Spring Creek

200

Robinson
River

Pungalina

O.T. Downs

CARPENTARIA

Cape Crawford
Roadhouse

McArthur River

Balbirini

Mailapunyah

Kiana

276

Redbank
58

Wollogorang Gulf
Wilderness Lodge

Calvert Hills

WAMPAYA

HWY

153

TABLELANDS

Walhallow

ROUTE
STOCK

Anthony
Lagoon

Cresswell Downs
(Abandoned)

Benmara

Eva Downs

Cresswell

CALVERT

TABLELANDS

Tarrabool
Lake

WAANYI/GARAWA

BOODJAMULLA
(LAWN HILL)
NATIONAL
PARK

Highland
Plains

Corella
Lake

Brunette Downs

220

Lake
Sylvester

CONNELLS LAGOON
C.R.

Mittebah

Old Herbert Vale

Rockhampton Downs

Lake
DeBurgh

Alexandria

Gallipoli

NORTHERN LAND COUNCIL

CENTRAL LAND COUNCIL

WARUMUNGU

BARKLY

HWY

188

HWY

Alroy Downs

© UNIVERSAL PUBLISHERS PTY LTD 2005

NORTHERN TERRITORY
QUEENSLAND

CONTINUES PAGE 94

Scale 1:1 932 600

0   50
Kilometres

JOINS PAGE 137

A   B   C   D   E

N
UBD

129°   130°   131°   132°

Gordon Downs
(ruins)
Kundat Djaru ♣

YINGUALYALYA

Mirirrinyungu ♣
(Duck Ponds)

1

19°

PURTA

Cairn ▲

229

Wilson

+ Mt Junction

30

Slatey   Ck.

MOUNT
FREDERICK

Supplejack
Downs

24

Ck.

L. Buck

T A N A M I   D E S E R T

2

54

Talbot Well

CENTRAL DESERT

TANAMI   232   ROAD

87   78

Mt Tanami 489 +

Tanami
(no facilities)

20°

41

Rabbit Flat Roadhouse
(closed Tues-Wed-Thurs)

Lake Surprise

MOUNT
FREDERICK (No.2)

5

120

52

60

+ Mt Davidson

3

BALGO

87   Tanami Downs

The Granites
(no facilities)

The Granites

MANGKURURRPA

TANAMI

YININGARRA

96

21°

Lake Dennis
(salt)

349

Renahans Bore •

Lake White
(salt)

+ Mt Theo
582

4

Lake Wills
(salt)

33

Lake Hazlett
(salt)

Chilla Well O.S.

WESTERN   NORTHERN   TERRITORY   AUSTRALIA

MALA

5

98

ROAD

Yaloogarrie   Ck

Aileron   Ck

Koodi   Ck

Mt Denison
37

CENTRAL

22°

AUSTRALIA

LAKE MACKAY

Patmingala   Ck

28   YUENDUMU

Ethel   Ck

Vaughan
Springs

77

Yuendumu
(Police Stn)

37

Ck

150

Lake Mackay
(salt)

Waite   Ck

Nyirripi

16

Waite Ck ♣

YUNKANJINI

114

Entry to Aboriginal Lands is
prohibited without a permit from:
The Permits Officer,
Central Land Council
P.O. Box 3321
Alice Springs, NT 0871
Telephone (08) 8951 6211
Facsimile (08) 8953 4345

Newhaven

6

AUSTRALIA

NEWHAVEN
(Birds Australia 1300 730 073)

Lake Bennett
(Salt)

NGALURRTJU
Central
+ Mt Wedge
1095

Lake Eaton
(Salt)

23°

JUNCTION

Sandy Blight
Junction

Papunya

© UNIVERSAL PUBLISHERS PTY LTD 2005

41   ROAD   17   GARY   JUNCTION   RD   GARY   JUNCTION   65

129°   130°   131°   132°

A   B   C   D   E

JOINS PAGE 143

CONTINUES PAGES 157 & 164

JOINS PAGE 138

A B C D E

133° 133° 135°

Banka Banka
137

Churchills Head Rock ★
Stuart Memorial
▲ Attack Creek Historical Reserve
Brunchilly

☐ *Rockhampton Downs*

Lake
Sylvester

Corella Lake

1

KARLANTIJPA NORTH
447 260

Green Swamp Well

Wiso Bore

Phillip Creek
STUART

NORTHERN LAND COUNCIL
CENTRAL LAND COUNCIL
WARUMUNGU

Lake DeBurgh

Orlando John Flynn ▲ Memorial
Likkaparta ♣
BARKLY
WARUMUNGU

Warrego Three Ways Roadhouse
The Pebbles ★ 24
★ Telegraph Stn.
Tennant Creek ⓘ
★ Battery Hill
WARUMUNGU

188
66 HWY

90

Barkly Homestead Roadhouse

Kuraya ♣

Entry to Aboriginal Lands is
prohibited without a permit from:
The Permits Officer,
Central Land Council
P.O. Box 3321
Alice Springs, NT 0871
Telephone (08) 8951 6211
Facsimile (08) 8953 4345

KANTTAJI

Purrukuwurru
WAKAYA

2

Gas Pipeline

77

114
HWY

WARUMUNGU

KARLANTIJPA SOUTH

87

Mungkarta ♣
Bonney MUNGKARTA 2
MUNGKARTA
○ *Kalinjarri* ♣
Kurundi
Kurundi Ck

WARUMUNGU
Epenarra ♣
Wutungurra ♣

3

WIRLIYAJARRAYI

River

Willowra ♣

Lander River
Ingeallan

★ **Devils Marbles**
➤ Wauchope Roadhouse
☐ *Singleton*

DAVENPORT
RANGE N.P.
Old Police Stn Waterhole
(Proposed)

Davenport Range

Canteen Creek ○

Hatches Creek ♣
ANURRETE

Wycliffe Well Roadhouse
Skinner
Ali Curung
WARRABRI
Murray Downs

Elkedra ○ *Elkedra* Ck River
George River

21°

4

Hanson

109
HWY

Mt Peake Ck
Mt Peake +546

PAWU
☐ *Mt Barkly* ♣

+ *Mt Leichhardt*

Tara ♣
Neutral Junction
Barrow Creek Roadhouse

90

ALAYAWARRA
Antarrengeny ♣
Ampilatwatja ♣
14
Ammaroo
97

89
87

Stirling
Willora ♣

RAILWAY

HWY
Atnwengerrpe ♣

22°

5

Anningie
Central Mt Stuart 849+

Coniston
+ *Mt Stafford 1014*

YALPIRAKINU
102
5
TANAMI

Yuelamu ♣

Reynolds Range
Crown Ck

Nturiya ♣

AHAKEYE

Ti Tree Roadhouse
Pmara Jutunta ☐

Hanson
Pine Hill

Woodforde R
STUART
58

Woolla Downs

Mt Skinner
Sandover
ANGARAPA

Atneltyey ♣
Arawerr ♣
Arlparra Store ♣
Irrwelty ♣
Derry Downs ☐

Arapunya ☐

DULCIE RANGE N.P.
Dulcie Range

Napperby
☐ *Laramba* ♣
Napperby Day

Alyuen ☐
Aileron Roadhouse
Ryan Well ★
☐ *Glen Maggie (ruin)*
Native Gap ★

Mt Freeling +1006
Prowse Gap
15

67
87
12

PLENTY
Yambah ☐

AUSTRALASIA
SANDOVER

Bushy Park ☐

Gemtree ★ (fossicking)
144

Atartinga ☐
179

Angula ☐

Waite River ☐

Delmore Downs ☐
Delny ☐
Mount Swan
☐ *Dneiper*

New Macdonald Downs
14

Alcoota ☐
Mt Riddock ☐

Huckitta ☐ *Jinka*
132

Plenty
Frazer River
Harts Range (Police Stn) ♣
HWY
12

+ *Mt Brassey*
135°
Quartz Hill ☐
Huckitta Ck

6

Mount Wedge
☐ *Derwent*
108

Tilmouth Roadhouse
Lake Lewis (Salt)
Gas Pipeline
50
RD
133°

© UNIVERSAL PUBLISHERS PTY LTD 2005

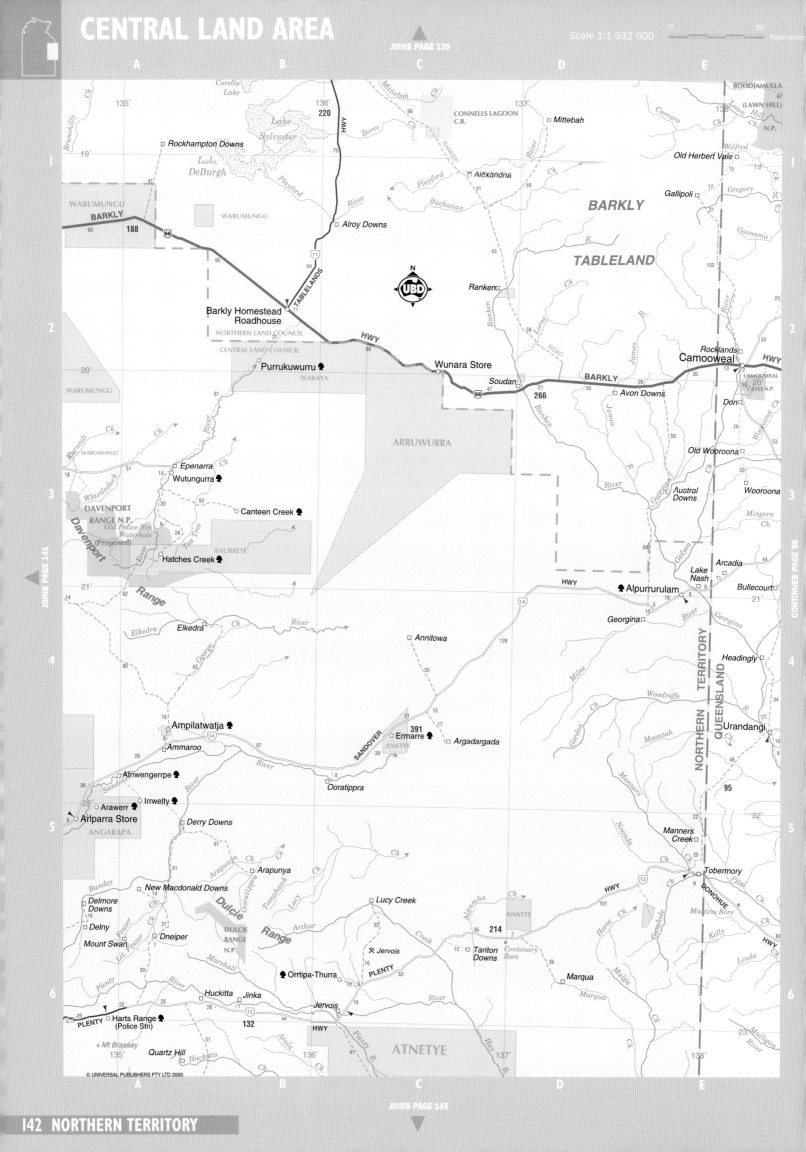

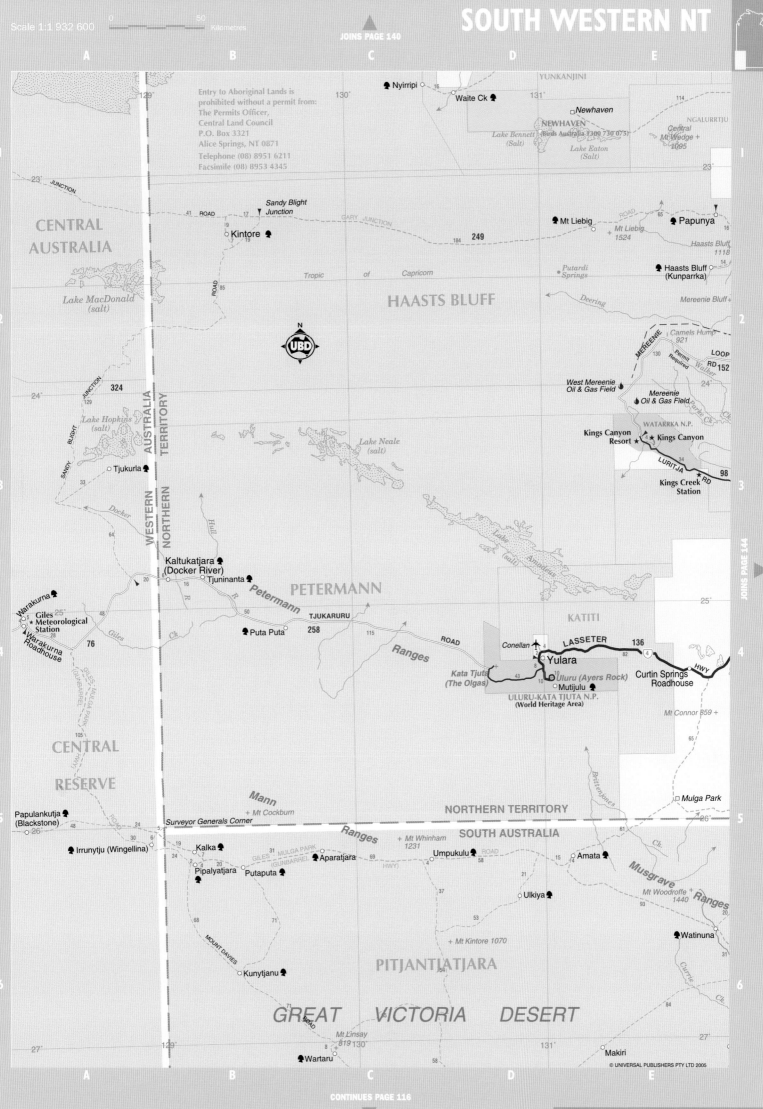

Scale 1:1 932 600

0   50
Kilometres

JOINS PAGE 140

Entry to Aboriginal Lands is
prohibited without a permit from:
The Permits Officer,
Central Land Council
P.O. Box 3321
Alice Springs, NT 0871
Telephone (08) 8951 6211
Facsimile (08) 8953 4345

YUNKANJINI

Nyirripi   16

Waite Ck

Newhaven

NEWHAVEN
Birds Australia 1300 730 075

NGALURRTJU

Central
Mt Wedge +
1095

114

CENTRAL
AUSTRALIA

JUNCTION

23°

129°

130°

131°

23°

Sandy Blight
Junction

ROAD   17

41

Kintore   19

GARY   JUNCTION

ROAD

184   249

Mt Liebig

Mt Liebig
1524

Papunya   16

65

Haasts Bluff
1118

Lake MacDonald
(salt)

Tropic   of   Capricorn

HAASTS BLUFF

Putardi
Springs

Haasts Bluff
(Kunparrka)   14

ROAD

85

Deering

Mereenie Bluff +

N
UBD

2

JUNCTION

324

129

Lake Hopkins
(salt)

SANDY   BLIGHT

33

Tjukurla

WESTERN   NORTHERN

AUSTRALIA   TERRITORY

Lake Neale
(salt)

Camels Hump
921

MEREENIE

130   Permit
Required

RD   LOOP
152

West Mereenie
Oil & Gas Field

Mereenie
Oil & Gas Field

WATARRKA N.P.

Walker   Parker   Ck

24°

Kings Canyon
Resort   ★ ★ Kings Canyon

LURITJA   RD   98
34

Kings Creek
Station

3

Docker

64

Hull

Kaltukatjara
(Docker River)

Tjuninanta

PETERMANN

Lake
(salt)

Anadeus

KATITI

25°

Warakurna

Giles   25°
★ Meteorological
Station

Warakurna
Roadhouse   76

28

48

5

20

16

R

Giles   Ck

50

Puta Puta

Petermann

TJUKARURU

258   115

Ranges

ROAD

Conellan

LASSETER   136
82

Yulara

Kata Tjuta
(The Olgas)

43

Uluru (Ayers Rock)

Mutijulu

ULURU-KATA TJUTA N.P.
(World Heritage Area)

Curtin Springs
Roadhouse

HWY

Mt Connor 859 +

4

CENTRAL

RESERVE

105

GILES   MULGA PARK
(GUNBARREL)

Mann

+ Mt Cockburn

Surveyor Generals Corner

Ranges

NORTHERN TERRITORY

Mulga Park

Brittenbones

65

26°

5

Papulankutja
(Blackstone)   48

26

FROAD

24

5

Ranges

+ Mt Whinham
1231

SOUTH AUSTRALIA

61

Ck

Irrunytju (Wingellina)

19

GILES   MULGA PARK
(GUNBARREL)

31

HWY

Umpukulu   ROAD

58

15

Amata

Musgrave

Kalka

24   2   7

20

Aparatjara   69

4

4

Pipalyatjara   Putaputa

37

21

Ulkiya

Mt Woodroffe +
1440

Ranges

93

20

68

71

53

+ Mt Kintore 1070

Watinuna

31

MOUNT DAVIES

Kunytjanu

PITJANTJATJARA

6

GREAT   VICTORIA   DESERT

ROAD

Mt Linsay
819

8

130°

131°

Makiri

84

Ck

Currie

Wartaru

58

129°

27°

© UNIVERSAL PUBLISHERS PTY LTD 2005

CONTINUES PAGE 116

CONTINUES PAGE 164

JOINS PAGE 144

A   B   C   D   E

YUNKANJINI
131°
Lake Bennett (Salt)   Newhaven
NEWHAVEN (Birds Australia 1300 730 075)
Lake Eaton (Salt)
23°

Mt Liebig
Mt Liebig +1524

Papunya

Mount Wedge
NGALURRTJU Central + Mt Wedge 1095

TANAMI

Mt Freeling +1006

Alyuen
Ryan Well ★   Glen Maggie (ruin)
Native Gap ★

Aileron Roadhouse

SANDOVER HWY 34°

Bushy Park

PLENTY
Gemtree (fossicking)

Alcoota

Yambah

STUART 67

Haasts Bluff 1118
Haasts Bluff (Kunparrka)

Putardi Springs

GARY JUNCTION ROAD

Derwent 108
Glen Helen

Narwietooma

Milton Park

Mt Zeil +1531

ROAD 138

Amburla

Mt Hay +1252

Hamilton Downs

ARLTUNGA 68

The Garden
Mt Laughlen +

TOURIST

144

Redbank Gorge
Ormiston Gorge
Ochre Pits
Glen Helen Gorge
Ellery Ck Big Hole

WEST MACDONNELL
NATIONAL PARK
Serpentine Gorge
NAMATJIRA 91

Hamilton Downs Youth Camp

Standley Chasm
Iwupataka

Simpsons Gap
DR 41
Pine Gap

Bond Springs

Alice Springs Cultural Precinct
Alice Springs Desert Park
Alice Springs Telegraph Station
Museum of Central Australia

Alice Springs

TREPHINA GORGE N.P.
Trephina Gorge
Corroboree Rock
N'Dhala Gorge 113

MEREENIE + Camels Hump 921
LOOP 152
RD

Undandita
TNORALA CONS. RES + Gosse Bluff 933
Redalls

MacDonnell

James

Tropic of Capricorn

Hermannsburg 85
LARAPINTA
Namatjira Monument

Owen Springs

Oil Refinery

HWY 92

ROSS
Amoonguna
Frontier Camel Farm

SANTA TERESA

Todd River

West Mereenie Oil & Gas Field
Mereenie Oil & Gas Field

24°

Areyonga

Palm Valley

Boggy Hole
FINKE GORGE N.P.

Ranges

Wallace Rockhole

Ewaninga
Ewaninga Rock Carvings

Polhill (ruins)

Santa Teresa

Ooraminna (ruins)
Allambi

Kings Canyon Resort
Kings Canyon
WATARRKA N.P.
19 Mile

Kings Creek Station
100 RD
LURITJA

URRAMPINYU
ILTJILTJARRA

Tempe Downs

McMinn

Camels Australia
Rainbow Valley
Stuarts Well Roadhouse
Orange Ck 39

Hugh River
Oak Valley

Deep Well

Rodinga (ruins)

Maryvale
Titjikala

Rodinga

ERNEST RD
GILES

Petermann

Palmer

Henbury Meteorite Craters
97 RD
Henbury

Palmer Valley

Charlotte Ra

Chambers Pillar
Alice Well

INARNME
Bundooma (ruins)

68
LURITJA RD
50

Angas Downs

STUART 69

Idracowra

Engoordina (ruins)

Horseshoe Bend

Mt Squire (ruins)
Colson Pinnacle

Lake Amadeus (salt)

KATITI

25°

LASSETER 136

Imanpa 109
Mount Ebenezer Roadhouse

Erldunda Roadhouse
HWY
Erldunda

Impadna Siding

Rumbalara (ruins)

Musgrave (ruins)

Conellan
Yulara
Uluru (Ayers Rock)
Mutijulu
ULURU-KATA TJUTA N.P. (World Heritage Area)

Curtin Springs Roadhouse

+ Mt Connor 859

Karinga

87 74

AUSTRALASIA

Kalamurta Ck

Lyndavale

Lilla Creek
Lilla

Umbeara

Bloodwood Bore
+ Mt Beddome

Finke (Aputula)

Lambert Centre

Beddome Ra.

Kulgera Roadhouse
Johnstone Geodetic Station
STUART HWY
74

Kulgera Siding

Mount Cavenagh
Goyder

147

Mulga Park

NORTHERN TERRITORY

Victory Downs

26°

SOUTH AUSTRALIA

A87 179

+ Mt Darling 541

Tieyon

Currajidda

Mt Howe +515

Lindsay

Stevenson

Amata

Ulkiya

Musgrave
Mt Woodroffe +1440
Ranges

Boorndoolyanna

Pukatja (Ernabella)
Yunyarinya (Kenmore Park)

Marryatt

Eateringinna

Marryat Siding
Agnes Creek

Watinuna

PITJANTJATJARA

GREAT VICTORIA DESERT

Makiri

Currie

Fregon

Paw Paw
Teeta Bore

Officer

Mimili
Indulkana (Iwantja)

Tarcoonyinna

Chandler
Chambers Bluff 592

Granite Downs

Yoolperlunna

Nicholson Hill +404

Mt Walter +361

PEDIRKA

Lambina

Coglin

Ritter

131°
133°
134°

© UNIVERSAL PUBLISHERS PTY LTD 2005

A   B   C   D   E

DONOHUE HWY

Delny
Mt Swan
Dneiper
DULCIE RANGE N.P.
Arthur Ck.
136°
Jervois
214
7
HWY
Centenary Bore
137°
138°
82°
Linda Ck.

Bundey River
Lit Frazer Ck.
7
Marshall
Orttipa-Thurra
16
Tariton Downs
12
Marqua
Marqua
Mulga

135°
30
River
Huckitta
Jinka
10 3
PLENTY
52
River
Ck.
Ck.

Plenty
22
26
Harts Range (Police Stn)
HWY
28
17
12
44
Jervois
18
Plenty
River
Hay River
Field
Ck.
23°
1

26
132
5

Mt Riddock
+ Mt Brassey
51
Atula
Ck.
Tropic of Capricorn

56
Quartz Hill
Huckitta
41
ATNETYE
River

Indiana
Atula

Hale
Aremra
River
Christmas
Ck.
Illogwa

Claraville
10 ARLTUNGA
Arltunga H.R.
RUBY GAP NATURE PARK
Ck.
2

Arltunga
32
Ruby Gap

14
Atnarpa
Ck.

Ranges
Giles
49

NORTHERN TERRITORY
QUEENSLAND
24°
River

Ringwood
River
URETYINGKE

Limbla
16
52
Numery
16

SIMPSON

YEWERRE
River
DESERT
3
Range
148
PMER NYENTE

Todd River Downs
N
UBD
River

NATIONAL
25°

Hale
River
4

Highway Bore
OLD
ANDADO
TRACK
34
MAC CLARK (ACACIA PEUCE) CON. RES.
9
COLSON
292
Creek
River

PARK

36
Andado
16
Old Andado

72
River
TRACK
SIMPSON   DESERT

Finke
New Crown
32
54

31
PMER ULPERRE
INGWEMIRNE ARLETHERRE
QAA
LINE

Charlotte Waters (ruin)
NORTHERN   TERRITORY
Mirranponga Pongunna L.
18
Poeppel Corner
26°
5

McDills Bore
41
24
SOUTH   AUSTRALIA
LINE
42
Lake Poeppel

358 Mt Anderson
29
Mount Dare
112 River
19
53
36
SIMPSON DESERT
K1

Abminga
Abminga (ruin)
11
Mt Bagot 265
39
AAK LINE
88

Eringa (ruin)
20
20
24
WITJIRA
FRENCH
29
20
ERABENA TRACK
CONSERVATION PARK
RIG

17
15
Bloods Ck Bore
Federal (ruin)
Purni Bore
10
RIG
50
RD
RIG RD
33
LINE

GHAN
34
Dalhousie Springs
59
Poolowanna Lake
RIG
RD

68
ROUTE
NATIONAL PARK
9
Dinner Springs
118

Dalhousie (ruin)
Peera Peera
Poolanna Lake

43
Pedirka (ruin)
SIMPSON   DESERT   REGIONAL   RESERVE
6

Hamilton
16
Ephemeral Lakes

DESERT
Mt Rebecca 288
33

Mount Sarah

135°
136°
137°
138°
25°
Fogartys Claypan
Mt Alexander 278

Tadmorden

© UNIVERSAL PUBLISHERS PTY LTD 2005

A   B   C   D   E

CONTINUES PAGES 96 & 100

CITY AND TOWN CENTRES

Alice Springs page 144 E2

Information Centre
60 Gregory Tce
Ph: (08) 8952 5800

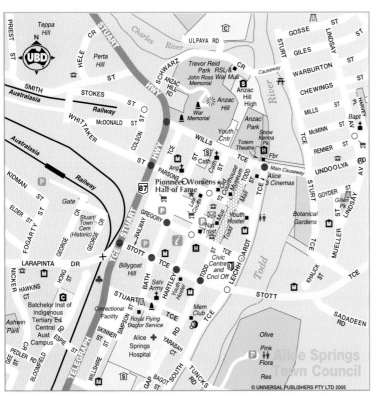

Kakadu National Park page 135 A3

Information Centre
Kakadu Hwy, Jabiru
Ph: (08) 8938 1120

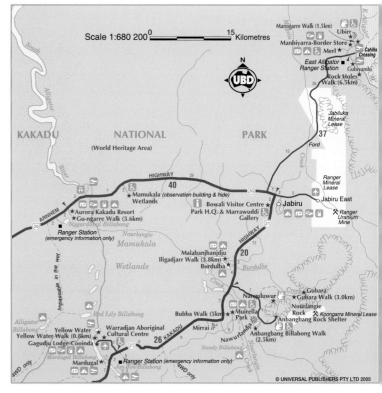

Katherine page 135 A6

Information Centre
Stuart Hwy/Lindsay St
Ph: (08) 8972 2650

Palmerston page 133 B5

Information Centre
Mitchell St/Knuckey St,
Darwin
Ph: (08) 8936 2499

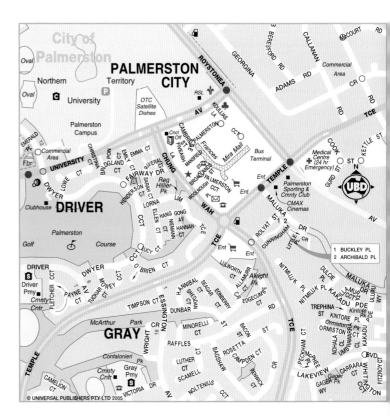

Tennant Creek page 141 C2

Information Centre
Battery Hill, Peko Rd
Ph: (08) 8962 3388

Kata Tjuta (The Olgas) page 143 D4

Information Centre
Yulara Dr, Yulara
Ph: (08) 8957 7377

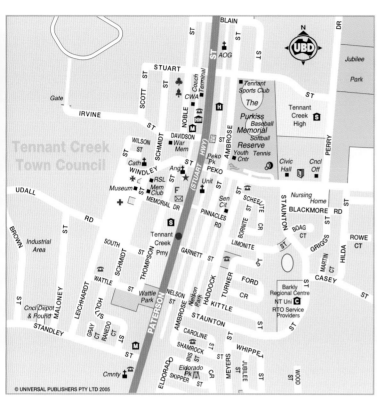

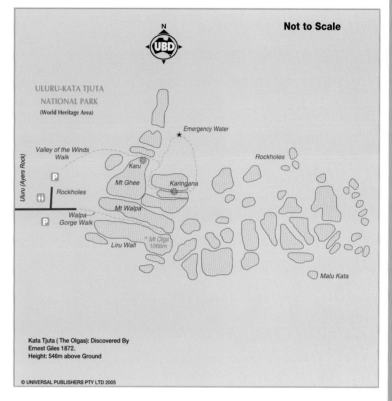

Uluru (Ayers Rock) page 143 D4

Information Centre
Yulara Dr, Yulara
Ph: (08) 8957 7377

Yulara (Ayers Rock Resort) page 143 D4

Information Centre
Yulara Dr, Yulara
Ph: (08) 8957 7377

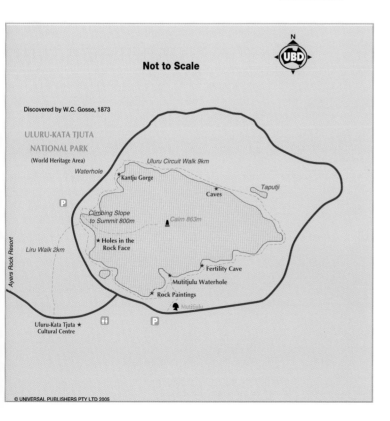

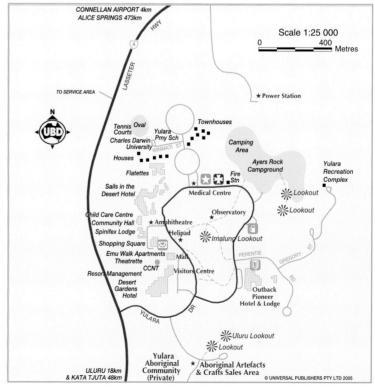

WESTERN AUSTRALIA

Western Australia is the giant of Australian states, occupying about one-third of the continent. Its vast coastline takes in the remote Kimberley in the north, the iron 'shoulder' of the Pilbara, and runs past the Ningaloo coral reef, Shark Bay, the Houtman Abrolhos Islands and Perth's sandy plain. After turning east at the rocky capes of the south-west, it takes in granite shores facing the wild Southern Ocean and the limestone cliffs of the Great Australian Bight.

Perth, Western Australia's capital, is a modern city situated on the Swan River within easy reach of ocean beaches and the forested Darling Ranges. The city is a tourist attraction in its own right and, with its port of Fremantle, is the gateway to the state. In the south of the state, visitors seek out the famous wildflower displays, the majestic karri forests, the Stirling and Porongurup ranges, the inland goldfields and the coastal national parks. Further north, many are drawn to the Pinnacle Desert, Geraldton's wildflowers, Batavia Coast and the natural wonders of the Shark Bay World-Heritage area, the Ningaloo Reef, the Pilbara's iron ranges, and to Broome and the Kimberley.

Touring this vast state with its multitude of outstanding attractions requires planning and time. The south-west area around Perth is relatively easy to get around by car, with a network of good roads and accessible features. The rest of Western Australia has fewer road options. Flying to different parts of the state can cut out some long drives, but despite the daunting distances touring by car is a rewarding experience. A 4WD vehicle is essential for touring in the Kimberleys or the desert tracks of the state's centre, such as the Canning Stock Route and the Gunbarrel Hwy.

Main Information Centre
Western Australia Visitor Centre
Forrest Pl/Wellington St,
Perth 6000
Ph: (08) 9483 1111
or 1300 361 351
www.westernaustralia.com

Lake Argyle, Kununurra

MAIN PLACES OF INTEREST	Map ref
Aquarium of Western Australia (AQWA)	152 B1
Argyle Diamond Mine	157 E3
Australian Prospectors & Miners Hall of Fame, Kalgoorlie	161 E4
Broome Bird Observatory	156 E4
Bungle Bungles (Purnululu National Park)	157 E3
Busselton Jetty	167
Cable Beach, Broome	156 E4
Coolgardie Camel Farm	161 D4
Dampier Archipelago	156 A6
Dolphin Discovery Centre, Bunbury	166
Geikie Gorge	157 C4
Hamelin Pool	158 B5
Hamersley Iron Open Cut Mine	158 D2
Hotham Valley Railway, Pinjarra	160 C6
Jewel Cave/Lake Cave/Mammoth Cave	162 B4
Kalbarri National Park	158 B6
Karijini National Park	158 E2
Kings Park, Perth	151 A4
Lake Argyle	157 E2
Leeuwin-Naturaliste National Park	162 A3/4
Malcolm Douglas Crocodile Park, Broome	156 E4

	Map ref
Manjimup Timber Park	162 C4
Margaret River Wineries	162 A3
Millstream-Chichester National Park	156 B6
Mount Augustus	158 D3
New Norcia	160 C4
Ningaloo Reef & Marine Park	158 B2
Nullarbor Plain	165 C4
Pemberton Tramway	162 C4
Perth Zoo	151 B6
Pinnacles Desert, Nambung NP	160 B3
Rottnest Island	160 B6
Shark Bay/Monkey Mia	158 B4
St Francis Xavier Cathedral, Geraldton	168
Stirling Range National Park	162 E4
Tunnel Creek	157 B4
Valley of the Giants	162 D5
WA Museum Kalgoorlie-Boulder	168
Wagin Historical Village	162 D2
Wave Rock	163 A1
Western Australian Maritime Museum	168
Western Australian Museum, Perth	151 C3
Whale World, Albany	162 E5
Wolfe Creek Meteorite Crater	157 D5

WESTERN AUSTRALIA KEY MAP

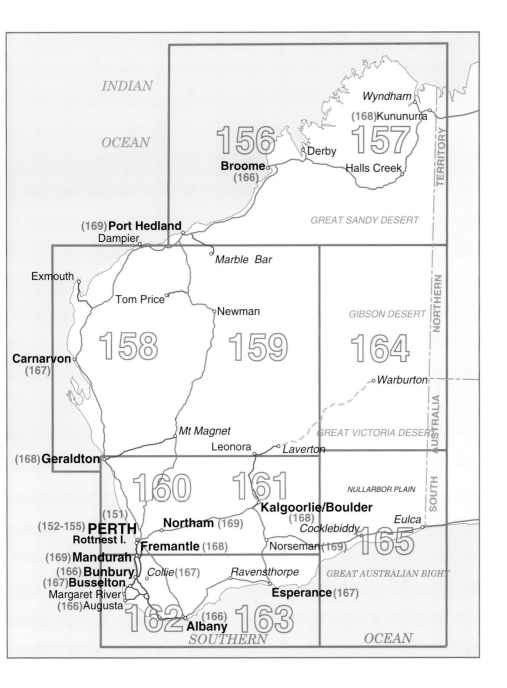

INDIAN

OCEAN

156

Wyndham

(168) Kununurra

157

Derby

Broome
(166)

Halls Creek

(169) Port Hedland

Dampier

GREAT SANDY DESERT

Marble Bar

Exmouth

Tom Price

Newman

GIBSON DESERT

158

159

164

Carnarvon
(167)

Warburton

Mt Magnet

GREAT VICTORIA DESERT

(168) Geraldton

Leonora

Laverton

160

161

NULLARBOR PLAIN

Kalgoorlie/Boulder
(168)

Eulca

(151)

Northam **(169)**

Cocklebiddy

(152-155) PERTH

Rottnest I.

Fremantle **(168)**

Norseman **(169)**

165

(169) Mandurah

(166) Bunbury

Collie **(167)**

Ravensthorpe

GREAT AUSTRALIAN BIGHT

(167) Busselton

Margaret River

Esperance **(167)**

(166) Augusta

162

(166)

163

Albany

SOUTHERN

OCEAN

NORTHERN

TERRITORY

SOUTH AUSTRALIA

Pinnacles Desert, Nambung National Park

PERTH CITY

Perth lies on the banks of the Swan River, approximately 14km upstream from the historic port city of Fremantle. It was proclaimed on 12 August 1829 and named after the Scottish city of Perth. Early settlers faced many hardships, including drought and floods. Convict labour was introduced in the 1850s and many of Perth's early public buildings, roads and bridges were built by convicts. During the 1890s, gold was discovered at Coolgardie and Kalgoorlie, greatly boosting the economy, and people raced to the region to make their fortune.

Perth is surrounded by many parks, including well-known Kings Park. This 404ha park overlooks the city and the Swan River and is noted for its wildflowers in springtime and its bushwalking trails. Perth is famous for its golden surf beaches, all within easy reach of the city. With its Mediterranean-type climate, visitors can enjoy Perth's relaxed, outdoor lifestyle year-round.

The Perth Mint offers a visit to the past in its Old Melting House. Gold bar pouring demonstrations are shown every hour and visitors can also watch mint operations from a public gallery. For shopping, visit London Court, a Tudor-style shopping arcade and perhaps Perth's most photographed attraction.

PERTH CITY PLACES OF INTEREST

	ref		ref
Alexander Library	C3	Perth Cultural Centre	E4
Art Gallery of Western Australia	C3	Perth Mint	D4
Barrack Square	C4	Perth Town Hall	C3
Barracks Archway	B3	Perth Zoo	B6
Entertainment Centre	B3	Queens Gardens	E4
Fire Safety Education Centre & Museum	C3	Scitech Discovery Centre	B2
Francis Burt Law Education		Stirling Gardens	C4
Centre & Museum	C4	Supreme Court Gardens	C4
Hay Street Mall	C3	Swan River	A5/D5
His Majestys Theatre	B3	The Old Mill	B5
Kings Park	A4	The Swan Bells	C4
London Court	C3	WACA Oval	E4
Parliament House	B3	Western Australian Botanic Gardens	A4
Perth Concert Hall	C4	Western Australian Museum	C3

Top: Kings Park with city skyline in the background; Middle: His Majestys Theatre facade; Bottom: Narrows Bridge, Swan River viewed from Kings Park

PERTH CITY

Scale 1:24 160

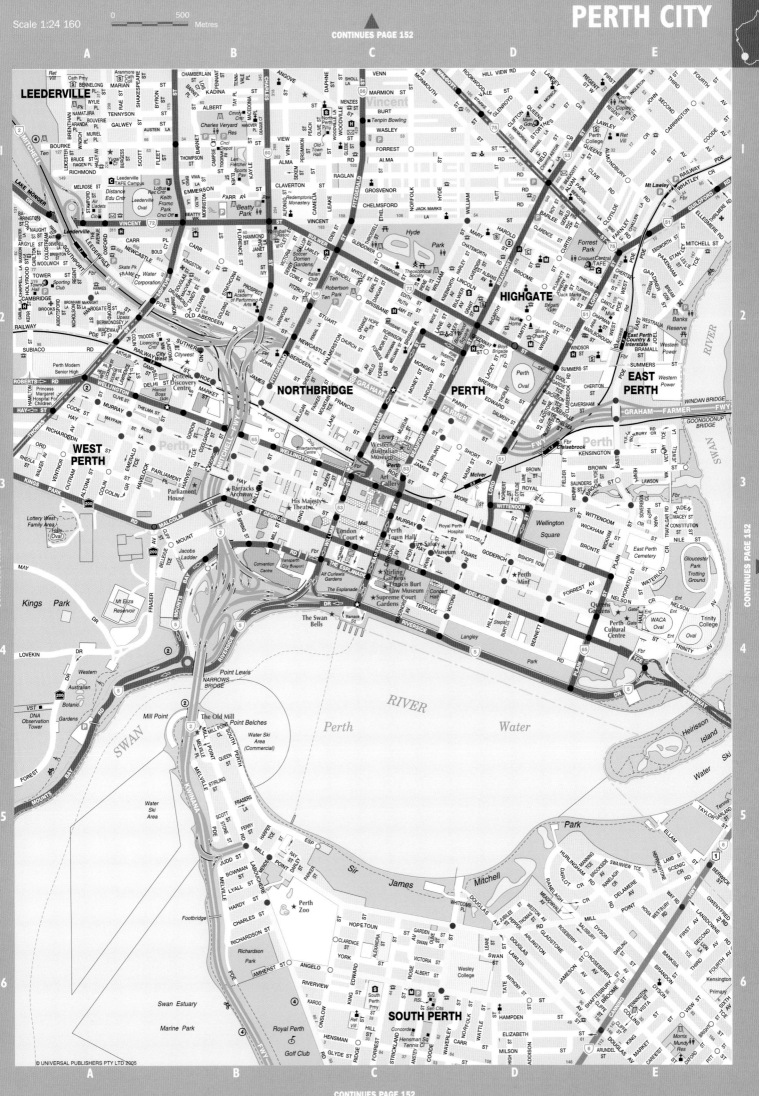

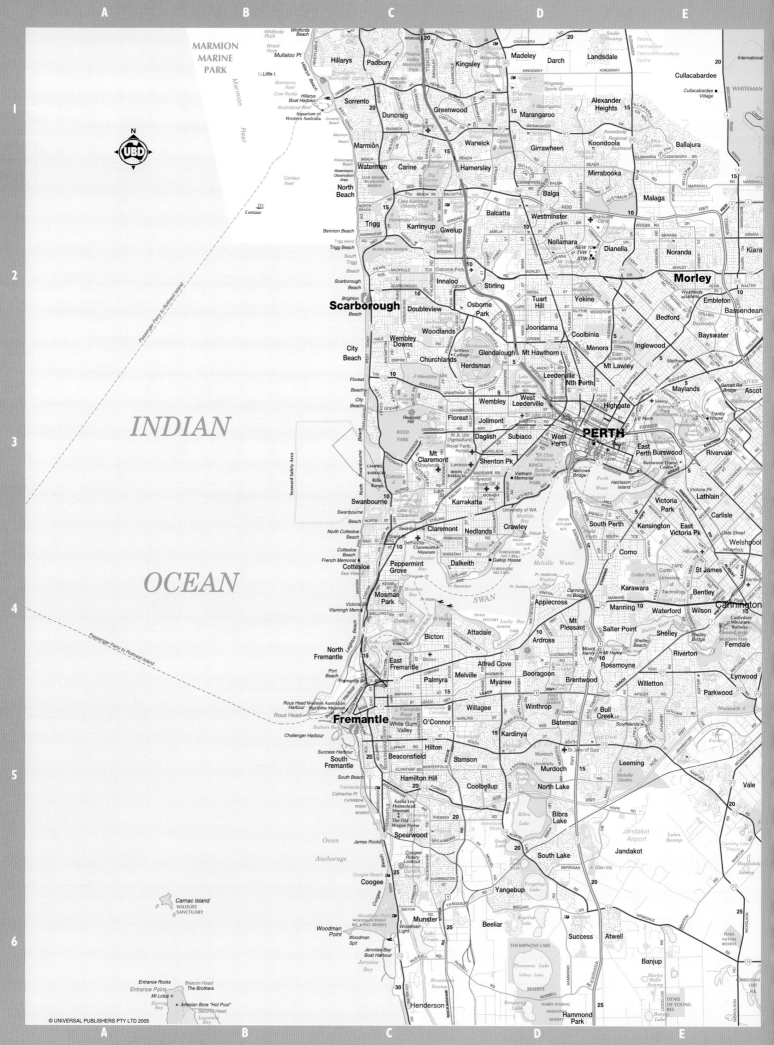

Scale 1:158 750

CONTINUES PAGE 160

INDIAN

OCEAN

MARMION
MARINE
PARK

Scarborough

Fremantle

PERTH

Morley

JOINS PAGE 154

Henley Brook · Millendon · Swanbrook · Shooting Complex · PARK · Whiteman · West Swan · Herne Hill · Mt Oakover · Red Hill · Gidgegannup · Little Rivers · Taljanich · Windy Creek · Valley · Off Road Vehicle Area · Waste Disposal Area

Caversham · Beechboro · Middle Swan · Jane Brook · JOHN FORREST NATIONAL PARK · Parkerville · Stoneville · Mt Helena · LESCHENAULTIA CONSERVATION PARK · Chidlow · Adventure Centre · Lake Leschenaultia Camp School

Lockridge · Eden Hill · Viveash · Swan Health Service · Midland · Woodbridge · Midvale · Stratton · Swan View · Greenmount · Swan View Rly Stn · Glen Brook Dam · Hovea · Mahogany Creek · Sawyers Valley · Hilston Youth Camp · Sunninghill Equestrian Centre · YMCA Camp Pickering

Ashfield · South Guildford · Guildford · Hazelmere · Bellevue · Koongamia · Helena Valley · Boya · Darlington · Glen Forest · Mundaring · Mundaring Weir · Pimelia Mycumbene Picnic Area · Grevillea Mycumbene Picnic Area

Redcliffe · Belmont · Perth International Airport · High Wycombe · Maida Vale · Gooseberry Hill · Paulls Valley · Heritage Rose Garden · Darlington Estate · PARKLANDS · Pipehead Dam · Helena · O'Connor Museum · Mundaring Weir · Helena River Reservoir · STATE FOREST · Gallery · CY O'Connor · CALM District Office

Cloverdale · Kewdale · Forrestfield · Kalamunda · Piesse Brook · Hacketts Gully · The Dell Picnic Area · Gungin Gully Picnic Area · Mt Gunjin · Reservoir · Sawyers Valley · Murdos

Queens Park · East Cannington · Wattle Grove · Walliston · Lesmurdie · Bickley · Carmel · Perth Observatory · STATE FOREST · Brookside · Lawnbrook · Hainault

Beckenham · Kenwick · Orange Grove · New Victoria Dam · Victoria Reservoir · Pickering Brook · Carilla · Cosham · Bartons Mill Prison

Langford · Maddington · Thornlie · Gosnells · Huntingdale · Martin · GOSNELLS REGIONAL OPEN SPACE · Canning Mills · STATE FOREST · Carinyah

Southern River · COHUNU WILDLIFE PARK · Kelmscott · Westfield · Roleystone · Karragullen · Carinyah

Forrestdale · Armadale · Brookdale · Mount Nasura · ARALUEN BOTANIC PARK · Canning Dam · Lesley · STATE FOREST · Churchman Brook Reservoir · Canning Reservoir

© UNIVERSAL PUBLISHERS PTY LTD 2005

CONTINUES PAGE 160

JOINS PAGE 155

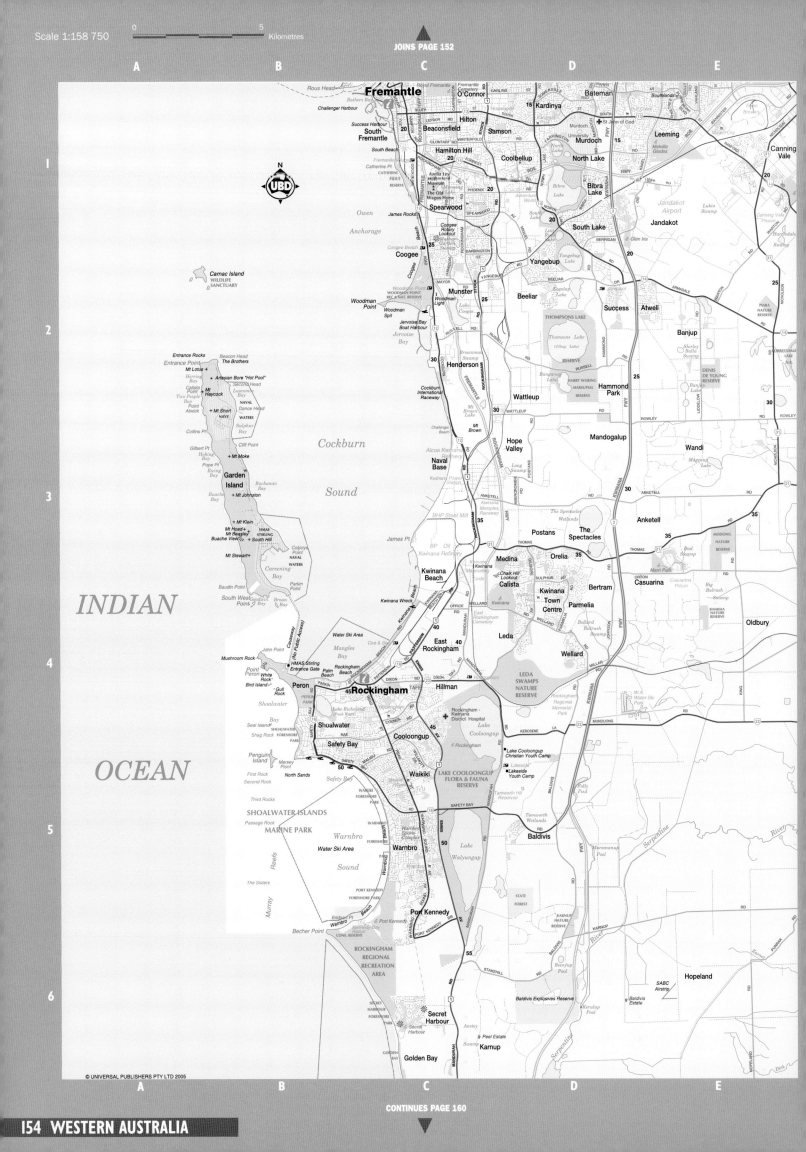

Scale 1:158 750

INDIAN

OCEAN

CONTINUES PAGE 160

154 WESTERN AUSTRALIA

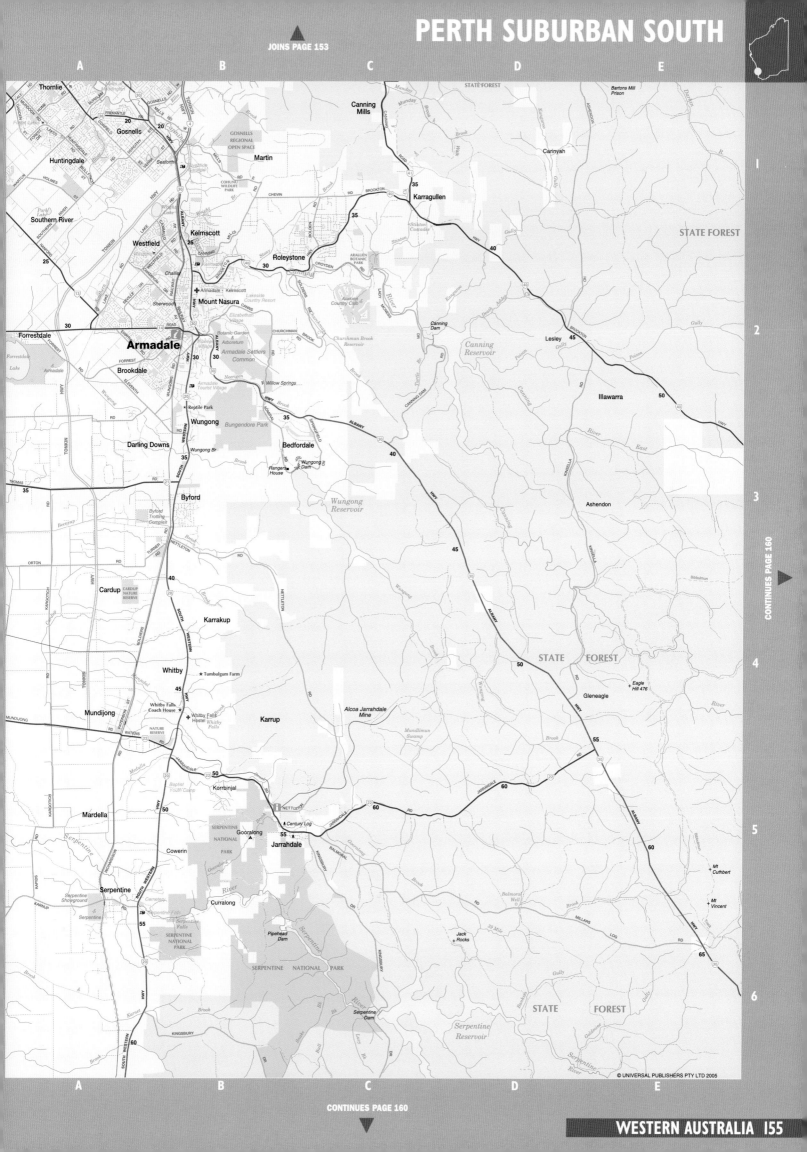

JOINS PAGE 153

CONTINUES PAGE 160

CONTINUES PAGE 160

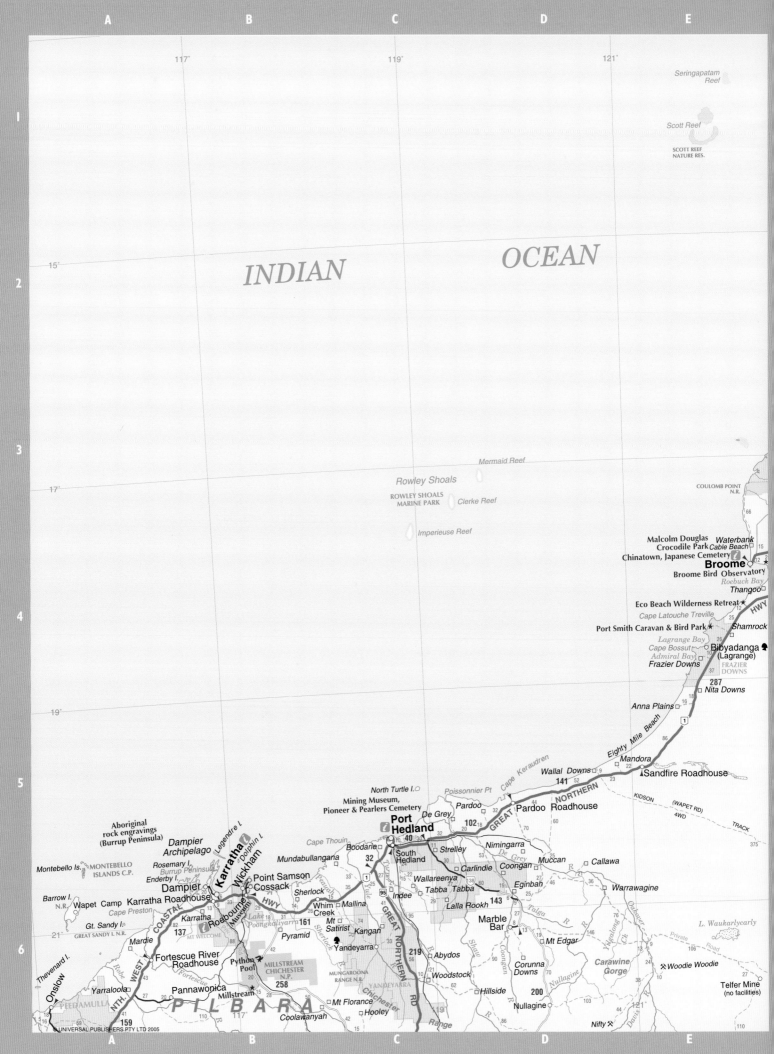

Scale 1:3 768 500

0   100
Kilometres

INDIAN   OCEAN

Seringapatam Reef

Scott Reef

SCOTT REEF
NATURE RES.

Mermaid Reef

COULOMB POINT
N.R.

Rowley Shoals

ROWLEY SHOALS
MARINE PARK   Clerke Reef

Imperieuse Reef

Malcolm Douglas   Waterbank
Crocodile Park   Cable Beach
Chinatown, Japanese Cemetery
Broome
Broome Bird Observatory
Thangoo
Roebuck Bay

Eco Beach Wilderness Retreat ★
Cape Latouche Treville
Port Smith Caravan & Bird Park ★   Shamrock
Lagrange Bay
Cape Bossut   **Bibyadanga**
Admiral Bay   (Lagrange)
Frazier Downs   FRAZIER
                         DOWNS
                    287
                         Nita Downs
Anna Plains

Eighty Mile Beach
                         Mandora
Cape Keraudren   Wallal Downs
Poissonnier Pt   141   Sandfire Roadhouse
                         NORTHERN
North Turtle I.   Pardoo
Mining Museum,   102   Pardoo Roadhouse   KIDSON
Pioneer & Pearlers Cemetery   GREAT   (WAPET RD)
De Grey   4WD
**Port   Boodarie   Nimingarra   TRACK
Hedland**   32   Strelley   375
Cape Thouin   South   Muccan   Callawa
                  Hedland   Carlindie   Coongan
Boodarie   Wallareenya   Warrawagine
Mundabullangana   Tabba Tabba Eginbah
Dampier   Point Samson   Indee   143
Archipelago   Cossack   Lalla Rookh
Karratha Wickham Sherlock   Marble
Rosemary I.   Whim   Mallina   Bar
Enderby I.   Creek   Mt Edgar
Dampier   Karratha Roadhouse Mt Satirist Kangan
Montebello Is. MONTEBELLO Karratha 161   L. Waukarlycarly
ISLANDS C.P.   Poongkaliyarra
Barrow I. Wapet Camp 137 Pyramid Yandeyarra Abydos
N.R. Cape Preston   MT WELCOME   Woodie Woodie
Gt. Sandy I. Mardie   Corunna   Carawine
GREAT SANDY I. N.R. Fortescue River   Downs   Gorge
Thevenard I. Roadhouse Python MILLSTREAM Woodstock 200
Onslow   Pool   CHICHESTER MUNGAROONA Hillside
Yarraloola Pannawonica Millstream 258 RANGE N.R. Nullagine
PEEDAMULLA **PILBARA** Mt Florance   Telfer Mine
                  Coolawanyah Hooley   (no facilities)
159   110   117   Range   Nifty

© UNIVERSAL PUBLISHERS PTY LTD 2005

156 WESTERN AUSTRALIA

A B C D E

123° 125° 127° 129°

Browse I.

Cape Bougainville I.
Troughton I.
Sir Graham Moore I.
Cape Talbot
Cape Londonderry
Lesueur I.
Cape Rulhieres

Joseph Bonaparte Gulf

Cassini I.

Admiralty Gulf

★ Pago (ruin)
♣ Kalumburu 24

CARSON RIVER

Reveley I.

Cape Dussejour
Cape Lacrosse I.
Cape Domett

Turtle Point

Maret I.

Montague Sound

KALUMBURU R.

Bigge I.

Archipelago

Theda 32

R.

♣ Oombulgurri

DRYSDALE RIVER N.P.

OOMBULGURRI

King George R.

ORD RIVER N.R.

Carlton Hill 34

Spirit Hills

Coronation Is.

Darcy I.
Champagny I.

PRINCE REGENT
St George Basin N.R.

King Edward River (Doongan)

Adolphus I

★ Kunmunya (ruins)

Augustus I.

Battery Pt.
♣ Kuri Bay
★ 'Southern Cross' Crash Site

Drysdale River 26

K I M B E R L E Y

Zoo and Crocodile Park
Wyndham 56

Adele I.

Buccaneer Archipelago

Montgomery I.

KUNMUNYA

Pantijan R.

PANTIJAN

+ Mt Russ 693

246

Home Valley RD 55
Prison Tree 48
The Grotto 33
VICTORIA 45
Kununurra 58
HWY

Cockatoo Island Resort ★
Cockatoo I. Koolan I. ♣ Koolan

Collier Bay

Walcott Inlet

Mt Page + 469

Mt Lacey 764 +

143

El Questro
Lake Argyle Village

Cape Leveque
Kooljaman Resort ★
Lombardina (Djarindjin) ♣
One Arm Point (Bardi)

Hidden I.

DEFENCE TRAINING AREA

Mt Page

Mt Synnot 487 +

Tabletop Mt + 482

Mt Elizabeth

Gibb River 30

Karunjie

♣ Woolah

DOON DOON 151

Glen Hill ♣
Argyle
Diamond Mine 10
Lissadell

Rosewood
Waterloo

♣ Pender

King Sound

Oobagooma

Mt Hart

Beverley Springs 24
MT BARNETT
Silent Grove 37

Joint Hill 713 +

108

Mt Barnett Roadhouse

Spring Creek 21

Warmun (Turkey Ck) 261

Mistake Creek

♣ Beagle Bay

BEAGLE BAY

R.

GIBB 306

Napier Downs

Mt House

Imintji 14

Glenroy
Mt Brennan

Tableland 164

Bow River
Mabel Downs
Bedford Downs

Castlereagh Hill 590 +

Mabel Downs

VIOLET VALLEY

PURNULULU C.P.
Echidna Chasm 14
Cathedral Gorge 31

Ord River Regeneration Research Stn.

Kirkimbie

Country Downs
Derby
Meda
Mowanjum ♣
Yeeda
Willare Bridge Roadhouse 146
Kilto
Bedunburru
Yakka Munga
Tjarramba
Roebuck Roadhouse
Roebuck Plains

42 MOWANJUM

Kimberley Downs 45

Fairfield

Blina
Blina

Camballin 49

Ellendale

GREAT 214

NORTHERN

Curtin RAAF Base

Looma

Luluigui

Kalyeeda

Nerrima

Dampier Downs

Mowla Bluff + 203

MILLIJIDDIE

Fitzroy Crossing

Jubilee Downs

Noonkanbah

Ngalangkati
Millijiddee

Cherrabun

NOONKANBAH

Fossil Downs
Mudludja

GEIKIE GORGE N.P.
BROOKING GORGE C.P.
TUNNEL CREEK N.P.
WINDJANA GORGE N.P.

Leopold Downs
LEOPOLD DOWNS

Mt Broome 931 +
Mt Ord 937

Mornington
Lansdowne

Mt Wells 983

PURNULULU N.P. 162

Alice Downs 78
Turner
Springvale
Russian Jack Memorial 58
Halls Creek 176
Old Halls Creek (ruin)
Lamboo
Koongie Park
Ruby Plains
Margaret River
Yiyili
Louisa Downs
Wangkatjungka 287

Nicholson

Flora Valley

DUNCAN RD

Gordon Downs (ruin)

♣ Kundat Djaru

Mt Amhurst

MOUNT PIERRE

LOUISA DOWNS

BOHEMIA DOWNS

172

WOLFE CREEK CRATER N.P.

Sturt Creek

CARRANYA 42

♣ Billiluna

MOUNT FREDERICK

DRAGON TREE N.R.

★ N
UBD

G R E A T   S A N D Y

D E S E R T

Lake Jones
Lake Betty
Lake Lanagan
Lake McLernon

ROUTE 102

BILLILUNA

♣ Mulan
Balgo ♣

Lake Gregory

BALGO

MOUNT FREDERICK (No.2)

KIDSON

4WD

Well 48
Well 49
Well 50
Well 47
Well 46
Well 45
Well 44
Well 43
Well 42
Well 41

TANAMI 232 ROAD

Lake Dennis

Lake White

Lake Wills

Mendigigil Rockhole

Percival Lakes

Helena Spring

Well 40
Well 39
Well 38
Well 37
Well 36
Well 35

Tobin Lake

Lake Hazlett

CENTRAL AUSTRALIA

Punmu ♣

Lake Dora

KIDSON TK

CANNING

© UNIVERSAL PUBLISHERS PTY LTD 2005

CONTINUES PAGES 137 & 140

Scale 1:3 768 500

0   100   Kilometres

A   B   C   D   E

INDIAN

OCEAN

PILBARA

Hamersley

Karratha Roadhouse
Wapet Camp
Barrow I. N.R.
Karratha
Roebourne
Sherlock
Whim Creek
Mallina
Tabba Tabba
Lalla Rookh
Cape Preston
Gt. Sandy I.
GREAT SANDY I. N.R.
Mardie
Lake Poongkaliyarra
Pyramid
Mt Satirist
Kangan
Yandeyarra
Abydos
Woodstock
Fortescue River Roadhouse
Python Pool
Millstream
MILLSTREAM CHICHESTER N.P.
MUNGAROONA RANGE N.R.
Pannawonica
Mt Florance
Coolawanyah
Hooley
Mulga Downs
Thevenard I.
Goods Shed Museum
Muiron Is. Long I.
Old Onslow Historic Ruin
Onslow
Yarraloola
Peedamulla
PEEDAMULLA
Mt Minnie
Cane River
Red Hill
Hamersley
Mt Brockman
Mt Brockman
Oxers Lookout
Dales Gorge
Wittenoom
Auski Roadhouse
North West Cape
Vlaming Head Lighthouse
Exmouth
Urala
Minderoo
Koordarrie (Abandoned)
Nanutarra
Mt Stuart
Cane
Duck
Hamersley Iron Open Cut Mine
Tom Price
KARIJINI N.P.
Marandoo
CAPE RANGE N.P.
Exmouth Learmonth
Exmouth Gulf
Yanrey
Nanutarra Roadhouse
Wyloo
Rocklea
Juna Downs
Mt Meharry + 1249
NINGALOO MARINE PARK
Yardie Creek
Giralia
Uaroo
Kooline
Paraburdoo
Coral Boat Cruises
Point Cloates
Ningaloo
Bullara
Marrilla
Nyang
Towera
Maroonah
Ullawarra
BARLEE RANGE N.R.
Ashburton Downs
Mininer
Turee Creek
Prairie Downs
Coral Bay
Winning
ULLAWARRA
Warroora
Mia Mia
Lyndon
Edmund
Wanna
Pingandy
Minilya Roadhouse
Wandagee
Williambury
Mangaroon
Clifford Creek
Dooley Downs
Mt Vernon
Brumby
Gnaraloo
Manberry
Minnie Creek
Cobra
Mt Augustus Outback Tourist Resort
Tangadee
Cape Cuvier
Hill Springs
Mt Sandiman
Mt Phillips
Mt Augustus 1105
MT AUGUSTUS N.P.
COLLIER N.P.
Quobba
Point Quobba
Boologooro
Cooralya
Mardathuna
KENNEDY RANGE N.P.
Lyons River
Eudamullah
Yinnetharra
MT JAMES
Burringurrah
Waldburg
Mulgul
Mingah Springs
Three Rivers
Cape Ronsard
Bernier I. N.R.
Gascoyne
Doorawarrah
Meeragoolia Mooka
Mt James
Woodlands
Carnarvon
Maritime Heritage Precinct
Dorre I. N.R.
Ella Valla
Bidgemia
Mooloo Downs
Landor
Mt Clere
Milgun
SHARK BAY MARINE PARK
Callagiddy
Yalbalgo
Gascoyne Junction
Winderie
Dalgety Downs
Errabiddy
Yarlarweelor
Bryah
Cape Inscription
Edsgee
Marron
Pimbee
Glenburgh
Erong
Mt Gould Lockup (ruins)
Mt Padbury
Cape Peron Nth
Wahroonga
Coordewandy
Yalbra
Innouendy
Mt Gould
Moorarie
Denham
Dolphin encounters
Monkey Mia
Faure I.
Carey Downs
Callytharra Springs
Beringarra
Koonmarra
Karalundi
Killara
FRANCOIS PERON N.P.
Peron
Wooramel Roadhouse
Meedo
Gilroyd
Byro
Milly Milly
Mileura
Dirk Hartog I.
Yaringa
Woodleigh
Yalardy
Talisker
Nookawarra
HAMELIN POOL MARINE PARK
Carbla
Curbur
Mt Narryer
Belele
Steep Pt.
Useless Loop (Saltworks)
Nanga Bay
Hamelin Pool
Overlander Roadhouse
Muggon
Meekatharra
Dirk Hartog
Zuytdorp Pt.
Hamelin
Murchison Roadhouse
Murchison Downs
Carrarang
Meadow
Wannoo Billabong Roadhouse
Meeberrie
Annean
Polelle
Tamala
Coburn
Wooleen
Boolardy
Glen
Tuckanarra
Reedy
Yarrabubba
ZUYTDORP N.R.
TOOLONGA N.R.
Nerren Nerren
New Forest
Twin Peaks
Mt Wittenoom
Karbar
Coodardy
Nallan
Cogla Downs
Yallalong
Murgoo
Meka
Cue
Eurardy
Billabalong
Lake Austin
KALBARRI N.P.
Mary Springs
Lake Nerramyne
Coolcalalya
Woolgorong
Jingemarra
Dalgaranga
Wondinong
Kalbarri
Rainbow Jungle
Bluff Pt.
Pinegrove
Yuin
Tardie
Noongal
Boogardie
Mt Magnet
Pastoral Museum
Wynyangoo
Anketell
Mt View
Binnu
Gabyon
Yalgoo
Yowergabbie
Challa
Hutt River Province
Wandana N.R.
Yuna
Tallering
Wogarno
Meeline
Windimurra
Gregory
North I.
Horrocks
Northampton
Mullewa
Pindar
Bunnawarra
Badja
Kirkalocka
Youanmi Downs
Wallabi Group
Nabawa
Muralgarra
Houtman Abrolhos
Easter Group
Geraldton
Western Australian Museum Geraldton, St Francis Xavier Cathedral
Pelsaert Group
Dongara
Leander Point
Mingenew
Morawa
Paynes Find
Three Springs
Perenjori

© UNIVERSAL PUBLISHERS PTY LTD 2005

JOINS PAGE 156

LITTLE SANDY DESERT

GIBSON DESERT

RUDALL RIVER NATIONAL PARK

GIBSON DESERT CONSERVATION PARK

GREAT VICTORIA DESERT

Marble Bar
Bamboo Creek Mine (no facilities)
Mt Edgar
Corunna Downs
Hillside
Nullagine
Carawine Gorge
Woodie Woodie
Telfer Mining Centre (no facilities)
Mendigigil Rockhole
Percival Lakes
Well 44
Well 43
Well 42
Well 41
Well 40
Well 39
Tobin Lake
Well 38
Well 37
Well 36
Well 35
Nifty
Mt Divide
Punmu
Lake Dora
Kanawarrji
Gary Junction
Well 34
Well 33
Well 32
Well 31
Well 30
Well 29
Well 28
Well 27
Well 26
Well 25
Well 24
Well 23
Well 22
Well 21
Bonnie Downs
Noreena Downs
Roy Hill
Mallina
Balfour Downs
Ethel Ck
Lake Auld
Lake Blanche
Parnngurr (Cotton Ck)
Capricorn Roadhouse Fuel Dump
Talawana
Jupiter Well
Newman
Mt Whaleback Mine
Capricorn Roadhouse
Opthalmia Dam
Billinooka
Jigalong
Robertson Range
Lake Disappointment
Surprise Well
Midway Well
Windy Corner
Sylvania
Jigalong
Mundiwindi
Diebil Spring
Well 20
Well 19
Well 18
Well 17
Durba Springs
Cannings Cairn
Sunday Well
Well 16
Weelarrana
Bulloo Downs
Well 15
Well 14
Lake Brenner
McPhersons Pillar
Kumarina Roadhouse
Beyondie
Well 13
Well 12
White Is
Well 11
Well 10
Lake Newell
Everard Junction
Marymia
Well 9
Well 8
Well 7
Well 6
Well 5
Glenayle
Lake Burnside
Geraldton Bore
MUNGILLI
MANGKILI CLAYPAN N.R.
Lake Gruzka
Neds Creek
Doolgunna
L. King
L. Nabberu
Well 4
Well 3
Windich Springs
Granite Peak
Earaheedy
Lake Buchanan
GUNBARREL
Len Beadell Memorial
Mt Beadell
Notabilis Bore
Len Beadells Tree
SOUTHERN CENTRAL RESERVE
Cunyu
Well 2A
Carnegie
Herbert Wash
TJIRRKARLI
Alexander Spring
Tjirrkarli
Warburton
Mooloogool
Diamond Well
Paroo
Yandil
Well 2
Wongawol
Lake Carngie
L. Gillen
Kanpa
Wiluna
Jundee
Millrose
Lorna Glen
Windidda
Prenti Downs
Lake Wells
Empress Spring
Baker Lake
YAPUPARRA
Ngangganawili
Lake Violet
L. Way
Lake Way
Terhan Rockhole
Muggun Rockhole
Hanns Tabletop Hill
Barwidgee
Wonganoo
Lake Wells
Tjukayirla Roadhouse
Mt Keith
Yeelirrie
Albion Downs
WANJARRI N.R.
Yandal
DE LA POER RANGE N.R.
Lake Throssell
Beegull Waterhole
Yakabindie
Kaluwiri
L. Miranda
L. Mason
Leinster Mine
Banjawarn
Banda
YEO LAKE N.R.
Yeo Lake
Gidgee
Booylgoo Spring
Depot Springs
Leinster
Melrose
Cosmo Newberry
CENTRAL
Yamarna
NEALE JUNCTION N.R.
Black Range
Sandstone
Agnew
Weebo
Lake Darlot
Mappa Lake
COSMO NEWBERY
POINT SALVATION
Neale Junction
Black Hill
Pinnacles
Nambi
Erlistoun
Laverton Downs
White Cliffs
Dandaraga
Atley
Teutonic
Windarra Mine
Laverton
Old Gaol & Police Station
L. Noondie
Yuinmery
Bulga Downs
Sturt Meadows
Ida Valley
Merolia
Mt Weld
Merlia
L. Rason
Leonora
Mt Margaret
Hope Campbell Lake
Bartlett Bluff
L. Barlee
L. Raeside
Gwalia (ghost town)
Malcolm (abandoned)
GLENORN
Lake Carey
Lightfoot L.
Jubilee Lake
L. Giles
Yandamindra
Mt Celia
Lake Minigwal
PLUMRIDGE LAKE N.R.
Plumridge Lakes
ADELONG
Menzies

© UNIVERSAL PUBLISHERS PTY LTD 2005

CONTINUES PAGE 161

JOINS PAGE 164

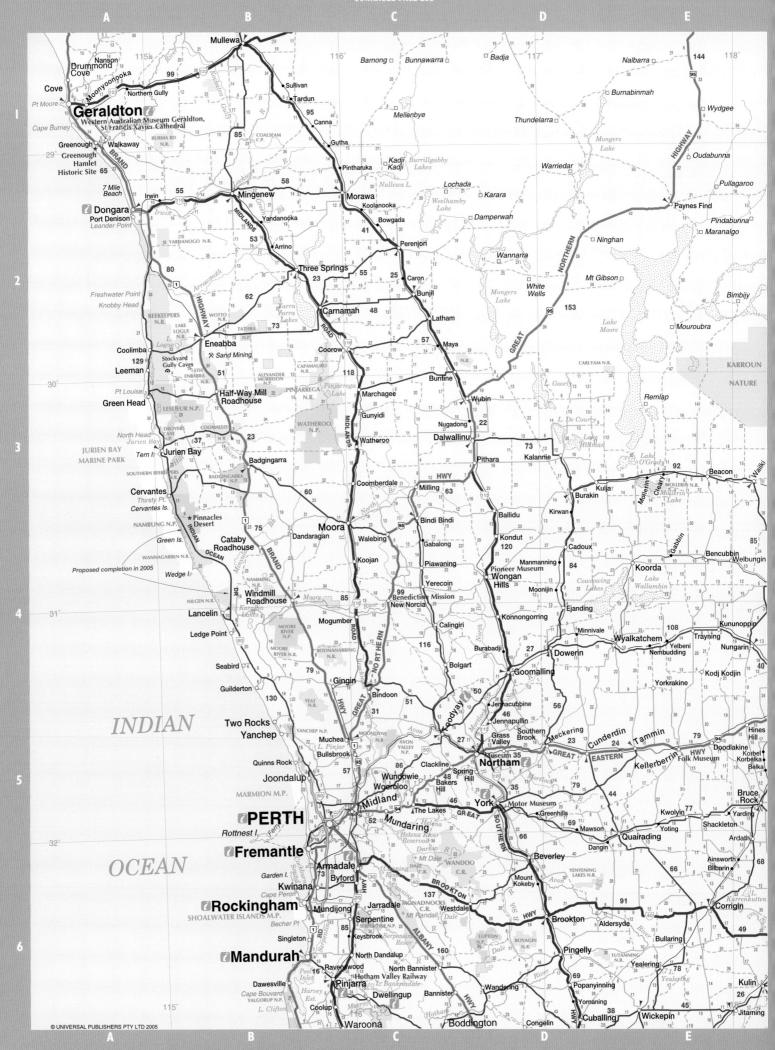

Scale 1:2 346 700

0   50
Kilometres

JOINS PAGE 162

© UNIVERSAL PUBLISHERS PTY LTD 2005

CONTINUES PAGE 159

CONTINUES PAGE 165

Youanmi Downs
Yuinmery
Bulga Downs
Lake Noondie
Ida Valley
Sturt Meadows
Tarmoola
Mertondale
124

Youangarra
119
GLENORN
Leonora
Minara
Malcolm (abandoned)
Gwalia (ghost town)
Lake Raeside
Kilkenny

Narndee
Cashmere Downs
Perrinvale
Mt Ida
Mt Ida (ruins)
Copperfield
Melita
Glenorn
Orient Well
Tampa
105

Lake Barlee
Lake Barlee
Mt Elvire
Walling Rock
Lake Ballard
Kookynie
Morapoi
Kookynie
Jeedamya
Lake Raeside
Yerilla

Diemals
L. Giles
ADELONG
Mendleyarri
Lake Marmion

Riverina
Menzies
GOLDFIELDS
Menangina

Pigeon Rocks
MOUNT MANNING NATURE RESERVE
Goongarrie
Davyhurst (ruins)
Bardoc
Goongarrie
L. Owen
Lake Goongarrie
GOONGARRIE NATIONAL PARK
Carr Boyd
Lake Emu

HILL RESERVE
Mt Jackson
Callion
Wangine Lake
Lake Emu

Kawana
Hammersley Lakes
Missouri
Mt Carnage
Bardoc
Gindalbie
130

Bonnie Rock
WALYAHMONING N.R.
L. Deborah East
Mt Vetters
Ora Banda
Broad Arrow
Kanowna
L. Penny

Credo
Phantom Devil
L. Perkolilli
Perkolilli

CHIDDARCOOPING N.R.
LAKE BALADJIE N.R.
L. Deborah West
Ennuin
Kintore
Black Flag
White Flag Lake
Kopai Lake
Hampton (ruins)
L. Yindarlgooda
Bulong

Mukinbudin
Koolyanobbing (ghost town)
Darrine
Timberfield
Jaurdi
Hannans North Tourist Mine, Australian Prospectors & Miners Half of Fame, Western Australian Museum Kalgoorlie-Boulder
Kalgoorlie-Boulder
Golden Ridge

Warralakin
Bullfinch
Lake Baladjie
Lake Julia
Lake Seabrook
Walleroo
Mt Burges
Bonnie Vale
ALT 94

L. Campion
Lake Campion N.R.
L. Brown
L. Campion
Southern Cross Museum
Lake Julia
YELLOWDINE N.R.
L. Walton
Stewart
Coolgardie Camel Farm
Coolgardie
Pharmacy Museum Old Kalgoorlie Goal
New Celebration
Mt Monger
Woolibar
75
39

Nukarri
Westonia
GREAT EASTERN
Moorine Rock
Yellowdine
BOORABBIN
Boorabbin
Bulla Bulling
Gnarlbine Rock
56
Kambalda
Kambalda West

Carrabin
Booraan
Burracoppin
108
Bodallin
Marvell Loch
N.P.
GOLDFIELDS WOODLANDS C.P.
GOLDFIELDS WOODLANDS N.P.
Victoria Rock
GOLDFIELDS Victoria Rock WOODLANDS C.P.
Burra Rock
St Ives
Lake Lefroy

Merredin
Military Museum, Old Railway Station Museum
Koonadgin
Muntadgin
GOLDFIELDS WOODLANDS N.P. (Proposed)
Widgiemooltha

49
71
Cramphorne
TRACK
CAVE HILL N.R.
Cave Hill
4WD
112
Higginsville

39
Wogarl
JILBADJI NATURE RESERVE
L. Barker
Lake Cowan

Narembeen
87
Welcome Hill
Mt Holland
Pioneer

South Kumminin
HOLLAND
EYRE HWY

55
NORTH KARLGARIN N.R.
Lake Johnstone
Bronzite Ridge
Norseman
Dollykissangel
DUNDAS NATURE RESERVE

Bendering
Hyden
Wave Rock
Lake Hope
COOLGARDIE - ESPERANCE

Kondinin
Karlgarin
L. Carmody
EYRE HWY

Pingaring
123
L. Hurlstone N.R.
L. Hurlstone
Varley
LAKE VARLEY N.R.
DRAGON ROCKS N.R.
Lake Dundas
Gilmore
Beete

© UNIVERSAL PUBLISHERS PTY LTD 2005

JOINS PAGE 163

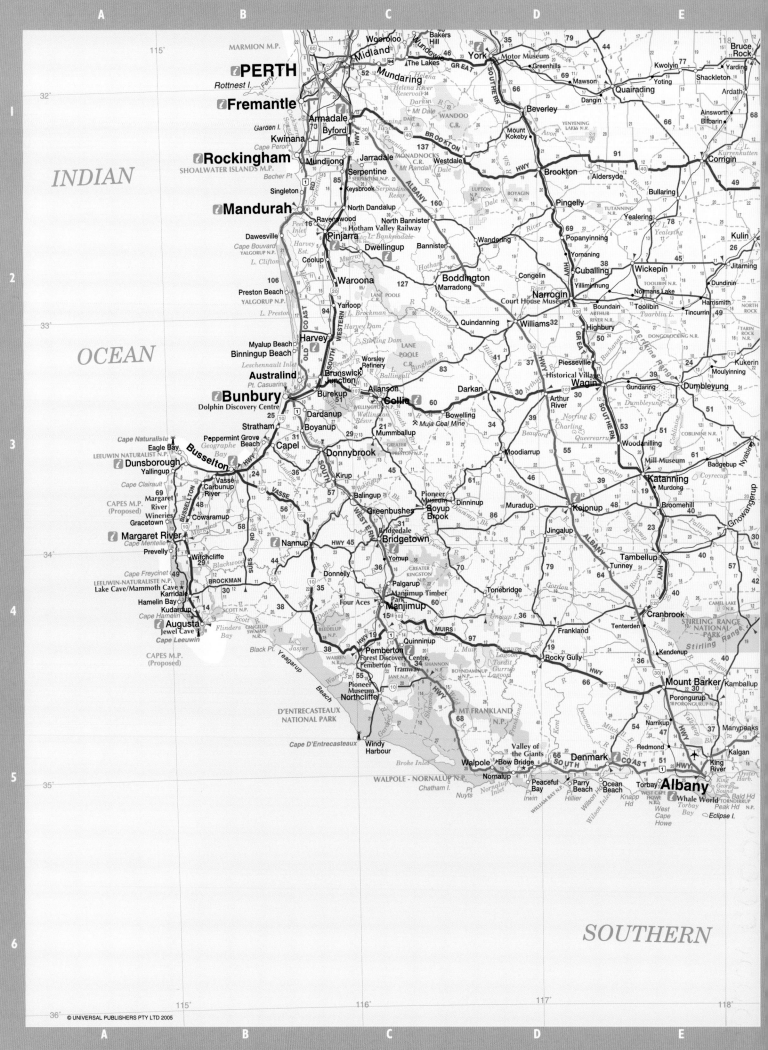

Scale 1:2 346 700

0   50
Kilometres

INDIAN

OCEAN

SOUTHERN

© UNIVERSAL PUBLISHERS PTY LTD 2005

JOINS PAGE 161

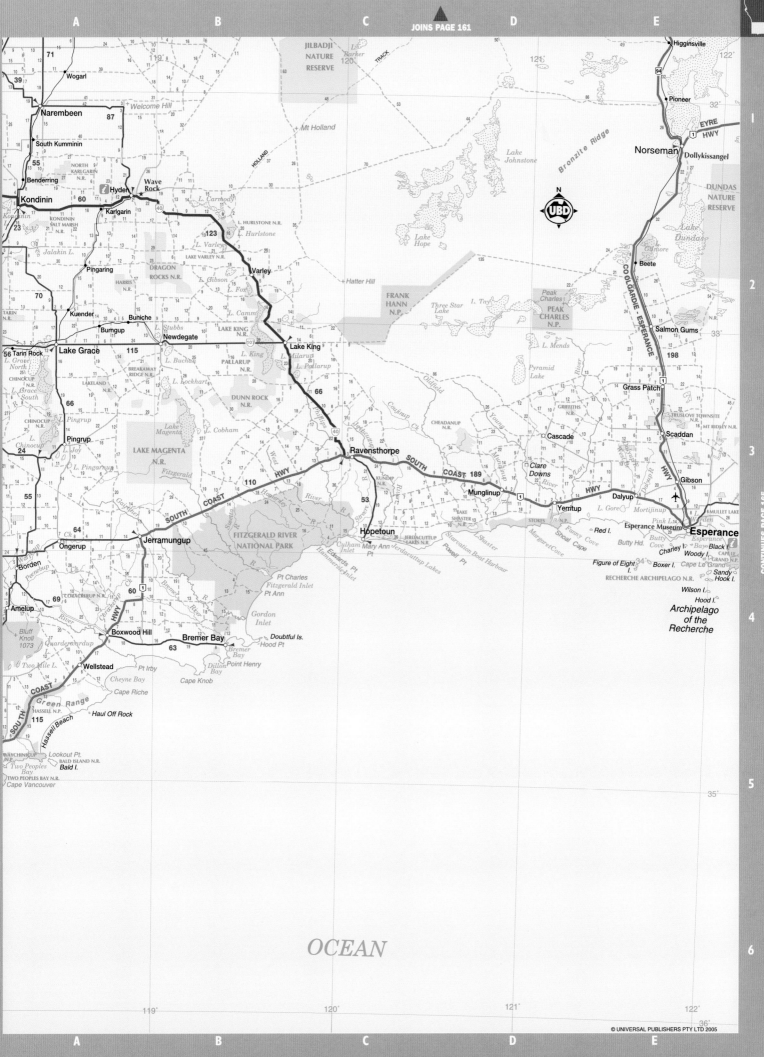

CONTINUES PAGE 165

OCEAN

JOINS PAGE 157

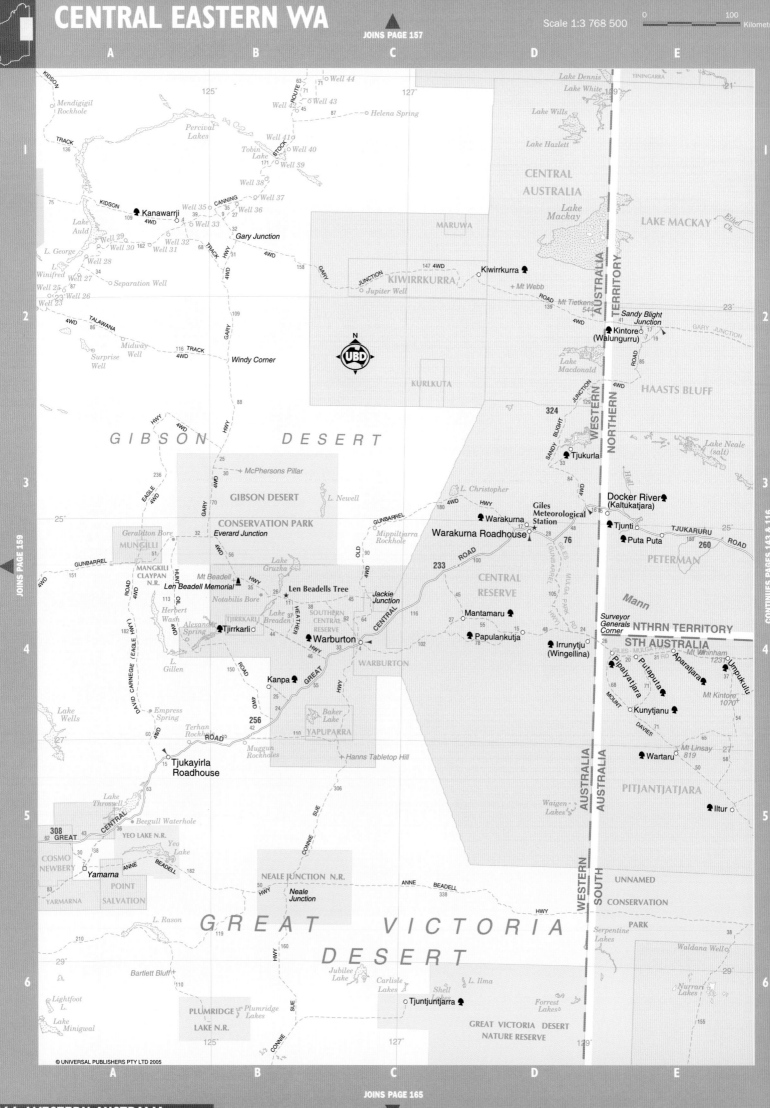

JOINS PAGE 159

CONTINUES PAGES 143 & 116

JOINS PAGE 165

Scale 1:3 768 500

0   100
Kilometres

A | **B** | **C** | **D** | **E**

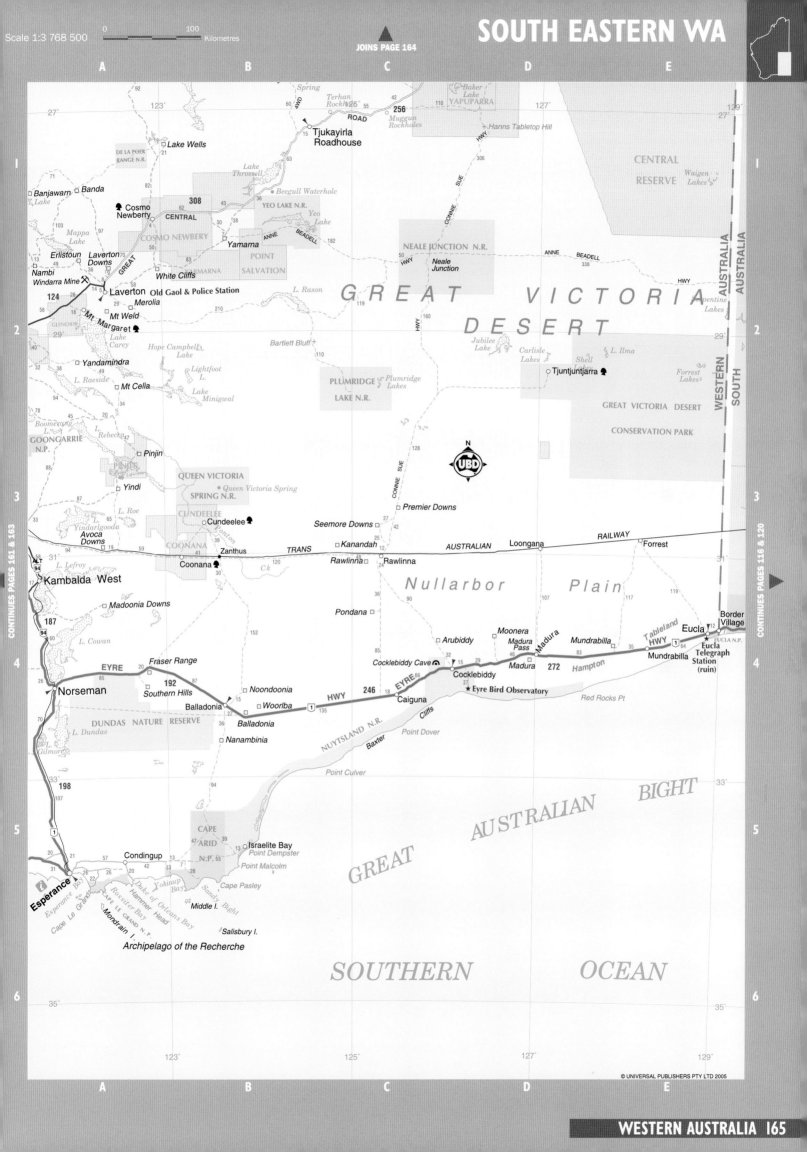

1

2

3

4

5

6

27°
123°
92
Spring
4WD
Terhan Rock 126
42
55
110
127°
129°

256

Baker Lake
YAPUPARRA

Hanns Tabletop Hill

CENTRAL
RESERVE
Waigen Lakes

15
Tjukayirla Roadhouse

19
Lake Wells
21

DE LA POER RANGE N.R.

63
Lake Throssell

36

50

306

Banjawarn
Banda
71
Lake

Beegull Waterhole

CONNIE SUE

YEO LAKE N.R.

Yeo Lake

Cosmo Newberry
308
62
43
30
38

CENTRAL

Mappa Lake
103
97

182

NEALE JUNCTION N.R.

Neale Junction

ANNE
BEADELL
338

HWY

Erlistoun
COSMO NEWBERY

Yamarna

ANNE

BEADELL

GREAT   VICTORIA

83

Laverton Downs
White Cliffs
YAMARNA

POINT

Nambi
13
49

GREAT

SALVATION

Windarra Mine
124
14
8
70

Laverton
Old Gaol & Police Station

L. Rason
119

DESERT

WESTERN   AUSTRALIA

58
26

Merolia
29
210

SOUTH   AUSTRALIA

Mt Weld

40
Mt Margaret
18
29°

Jubilee Lake

Serpentine Lakes

HWY
160

Yandamindra
Hope Campbell Lake
Bartlett Bluff
110

Carlisle Lakes

L. Ilma

Shell

Forrest Lakes

Mt Celia
Lightfoot L.
Lake Minigwal

PLUMRIDGE LAKE N.R.
Plumridge Lakes

Tjuntjuntjarra

GREAT VICTORIA DESERT
CONSERVATION PARK

L. Raeside
78
45
94
49
34
24

Boomerang L.
L. Rebecca
47

GOONGARRIE N.P.

Pinjin
128

CONNIE SUE

N

UBD

QUEEN VICTORIA SPRING N.R.
Queen Victoria Spring

Premier Downs

Yindi

Seemore Downs
27
42

CONTINUES PAGES 161 & 163

CUNDEELEE

Cundeelee

Ponton

COONANA

Zanthus

Kananandah
12

AUSTRALIAN

Loongana

RAILWAY

Forrest

CONTINUES PAGES 116 & 120

Avoca Downs
Yindarlgooda
87
65
33

L. Roe

TRANS

Rawlinna
Rawlinna

31°
ALT
94

L. Lefroy
31°
41
Coonana
30
120
Ck

Nullarbor   Plain

Kambalda West

36
90
107
117
119

187
94
60

Madoonia Downs

Pondana

L. Cowan
152

Moonera
Madura Pass

Madura

Mundrabilla

Border Village

EYRE
Fraser Range
20

85

Arubiddy
32

85
Cocklebiddy Cave
15
29
46

35

Tableland
HWY

Eucla
12
EUCLA N.P.

Mundrabilla

Norseman
192

Southern Hills

Noondoonia

HWY
246
66
EYRE
18

Cocklebiddy
Madura
272

Hampton
83

Eucla Telegraph Station (ruin)

EYRE

Balladonia
15
Woorlba
1
135

Caiguna
Eyre Bird Observatory

70
DUNDAS NATURE RESERVE

Balladonia
36

NUYTSLAND N.R.

Baxter
Cliffs

Point Dover

Red Rocks Pt

L. Gilmore
L. Dundas
Nanambinia

33°
198
107

94

Point Culver

33°

CAPE ARID N.P.
47
39

Israelite Bay
13
Point Dempster

GREAT   AUSTRALIAN   BIGHT

Condingup
57
13
53

Point Malcolm

1
20
21

26
20
42
38
28

Cape Pasley

Esperance
31
22

Yokinup Bay

Middle I.

Esperance Bay
Duke of Orleans Bay
Hammer Head
Sandy Bight

Salisbury I.

SOUTHERN   OCEAN

Cape Le Grand
Rossiter Bay
CAPE LE GRAND N.P.
Mondrain I.

Archipelago of the Recherche

35°
123°
125°
127°
129°
35°

CITY AND TOWN CENTRES

Albany page 162 E5

Information Centre
Old Railway Station,
Proudlove Pde
Ph: (08) 9841 1088

Augusta page 162 B4

Information Centre
70 Blackwood Ave
Ph: (08) 9758 0166

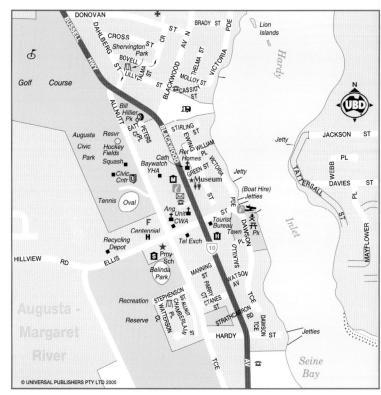

Broome page 156 E4

Information Centre
Great Northern Hwy/Bagot St
Ph: (08) 9192 2222

Bunbury page 162 B3

Information Centre
Old Railway Station,
Carmody Pl
Ph: (08) 9721 7922

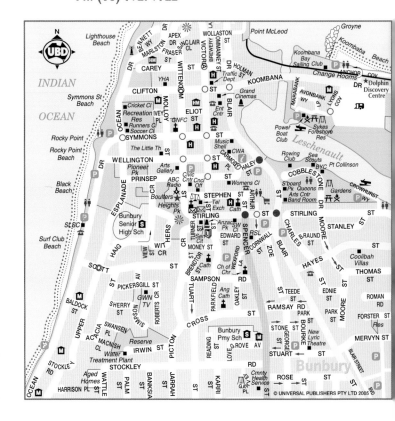

Busselton page 162 B3

Information Centre
38 Peel Tce
Ph: (08) 9752 1288

Carnarvon page 158 B3

Information Centre
11 Robinson St
Ph: (08) 9941 1146

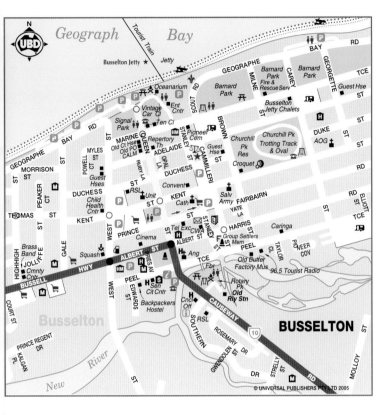

Collie page 162 C3

Information Centre
156 Throssell St
Ph: (08) 9734 2051

Esperance page 163 E4

Information Centre
Museum Village, Dempster St
Ph: (08) 9071 2330

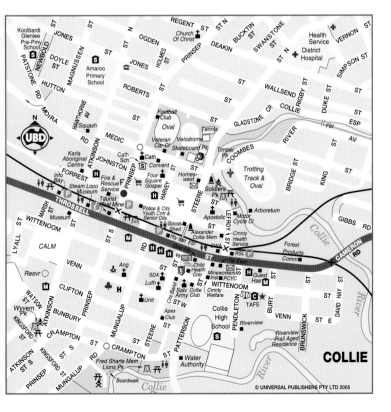

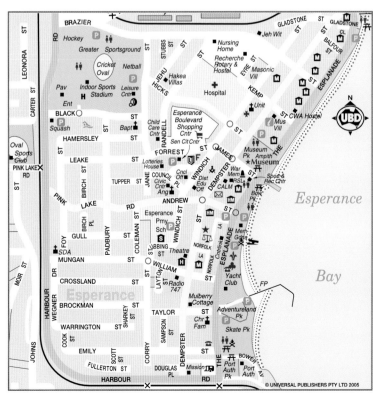

Fremantle   page 160 B6

Information Centre
Town Hall, William St/
Adelaide St
Ph: (08) 9431 7878

Geraldton   page 158 C6

Information Centre
Bill Sewell Complex,
Bayly St/Chapman Rd
Ph: (08) 9921 3999

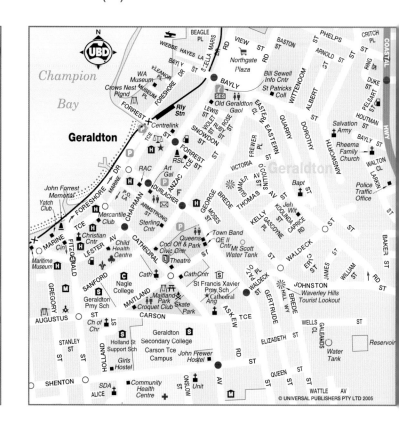

Kalgoorlie   page 161 E4

Information Centre
250 Hannan St
Ph: (08) 9021 1966

Kununurra   page 157 E2

Information Centre
Coolibah Dr
Ph: (08) 9168 1177

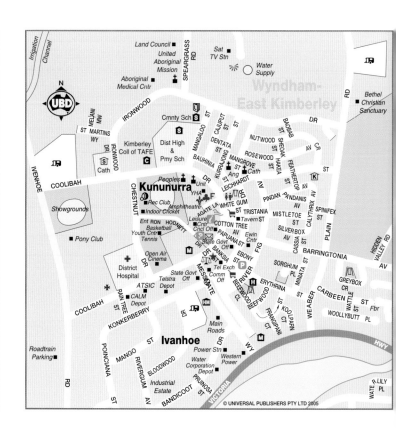

Mandurah page 162 B1

Information Centre
75 Mandurah Tce
Ph: (08) 9550 3999

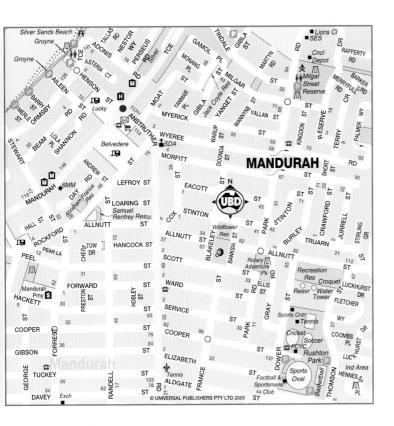

Norseman page 161 E6

Information Centre
68 Roberts St
Ph: (08) 9039 1071

Northam page 160 D5

Information Centre
2 Grey St
Ph: (08) 9622 2100

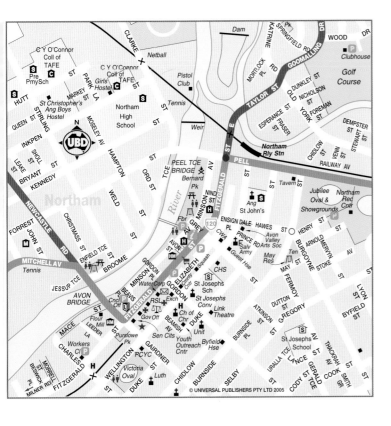

Port Hedland page 156 C6

Information Centre
13 Wedge St
Ph: (08) 9173 1711

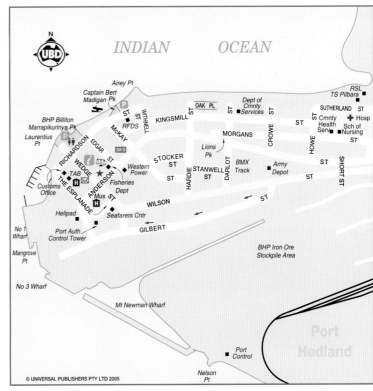

TASMANIA

Main Information Centre
Tasmanian Travel
& Information Centre
20 Davey St,
Hobart 7000
Ph: (03) 6230 8233
www.discovertasmania.com

Russell Falls, Mount Field National Park

Tasmania is the smallest of the Australian states. It is an island 240km from the mainland and surrounded by the turbulent Bass Strait, Southern Ocean and Tasman Sea. Its compactness makes it an ideal touring destination, as only relatively short distances separate its many attractions. Tasmania is a land of diversity with beaches encircling its coastline, while national parks and reserves protect its spectacular landmass, which features more than 2000km of world-class walking tracks.

This is the most mountainous Australian state and it has the highest percentage of national parks, comprising about one-third of the island. Tasmania boasts stunning and often remote World Heritage Areas. There are fertile plains and open bushland, mountains and valleys, rare flora and fauna, rustic ports and historic villages all crammed into a comparatively small area.

Of all the Australian states, Tasmania has the smallest population and the lowest immigration rate. As a result, its society is not as multicultural as other states. The small Aboriginal population is actively involved in maintaining its cultural identity through language and land management projects.

Unlike most of Australia, Tasmania enjoys 4 distinct seasons, which are a perfect complement to the other attractions of the state. Magnificent scenery is provided on both the Cradle Mountain-Lake St Clair National Park walks and the cruise on the Gordon River in the south-west. Historic villages that have hardly changed since the 1800s, together with convict-built bridges and old gaols, are reminders of colonial days. The wide variety of attractions make the smallest state the perfect holiday destination, deserving of the epithet 'The Holiday Isle'.

MAIN PLACES OF INTEREST

	Map ref		Map ref
Australian Axemans Hall of Fame, Latrobe	178 C2	Maritime Museum of Tasmania, Hobart	173 D4
Australian Golf Museum, Bothwell	182 E1	Mole Creek Karst National Park	178 B4
Ben Lomond National Park	179 B4	Mount Field National Park	182 D2
Bridestowe Lavender Farm	179 A1	National Automobile Museum	178 E3
Bruny Island	183 A5	Oatlands	183 A1
Burnie Pioneer Village	184	Old Hobart Town Model Village	186
Campbell Town	179 A5	Pearn's Steam World, Westbury	178 D3
Cataract Gorge, Launceston	178 E3	Penny Royal World, Launceston	185
Constitution & Victoria Docks, Hobart	173 C4	Port Arthur Historic Site	185
Copping Colonial & Convict Exhibition	183 C3	Queen Victoria Museum & Art Gallery	185
Cradle Mountain-Lake St Clair NP	178 A5	Richmond Bridge	186
Derby Tin Mine Centre	179 C2	Scottsdale Forest Eco Centre	179 B2
Don River Railway, Devonport	178 C2	Seahorse World/Platypus House	178 D2
Flinders Island	180 D2	Sheffield/Mural Town World	178 C3
Forest & Heritage Centre, Geeveston	182 E5	Swansea Bark Mill	186
Franklin-Gordon Wild Rivers		Tahune Forest AirWalk	182 D4
National Park	181 D3	Talune Wildlife Park, Cygnet	183 A5
Freycinet National Park	179 D6	Tamar Valley Wineries	178 D2
Grubb Shaft Gold & Heritage Museum	178 D2	Tasmanian Devil Park	183 C4
Hastings Caves	182 E5	Tasmanian Museum & Art Gallery, Hobart	173 C4
Huon Apple & Heritage Museum	182 E4	Tasmanian Wool Centre, Ross	179 A6
King Island Dairies	176 A2	The Nut, Stanley	177 C2
Maria Island National Park	183 D2	West Coast Wilderness Railway	181 C2

TASMANIA KEY MAP

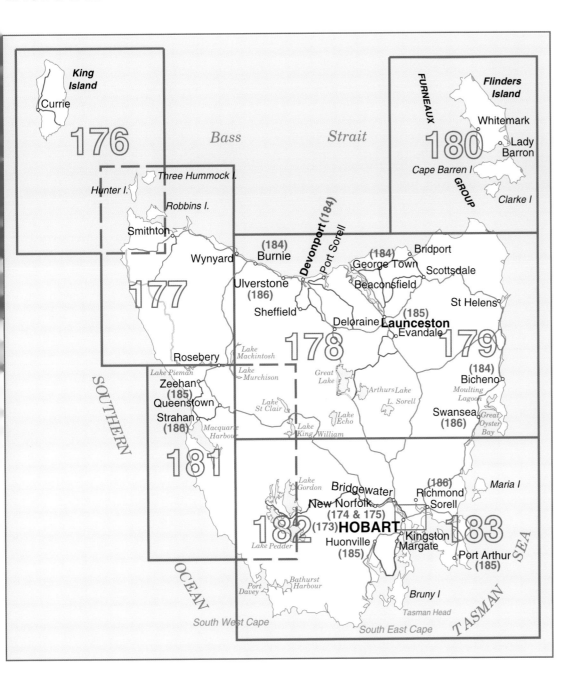

King Island
Currie
176

Bass Strait

FURNEAUX
Flinders Island
Whitemark
Lady Barron
Cape Barren I.
180
GROUP
Clarke I.

Three Hummock I.
Hunter I.
Robbins I.
Smithton

Wynyard
(184) Burnie
Ulverstone
(186)
Sheffield
177
Devonport **(184)**
Port Sorell
(184) Bridport
George Town
Beaconsfield
Scottsdale
St Helens
Deloraine **(185)** Launceston
Evandale
178
179
(184)
Bicheno
Moulting Lagoon
Swansea
(186)

Rosebery
Lake Mackintosh
Lake Pieman
Lake Murchison
Great Lake
Arthurs Lake
L. Sorell
Great Oyster Bay

SOUTHERN

Zeehan
(185)
Queenstown
Strahan
(186)
Macquarie Harbour
Lake St Clair
Lake Echo
Lake King William
181

Lake Gordon
Bridgewater
New Norfolk
(174 & 175)
(173) **HOBART**
182
Lake Pedder
Huonville
(185)
(186)
Richmond
Sorell
Maria I.
Kingston
Margate
183
Port Arthur
(185)
TASMAN SEA

OCEAN
Port Davey
Bathurst Harbour
Bruny I.
Tasman Head
South West Cape
South East Cape
TASMAN

Snow-topped Cradle Mountain reflected in Dove Lake, Cradle Mountain-Lake St Clair National Park

HOBART CITY

On the banks of the Derwent River, Hobart is Australia's smallest state capital and second oldest city. It was founded by Colonel David Collins in 1804, 16 years after the settlement of Sydney. Despite its beginnings as a penal settlement, Hobart quickly became a thriving seaport and its maritime heritage can be seen along its historic waterfront. The harbour remains integral to the city's economy. Only metres from the business district are the docks where overseas ships moor, supplies are loaded up for Australia's Antarctic bases and fishing boats return with their catch.

Historically, Hobart is extremely interesting, with over 90 buildings classified by the National Trust, many of them convict-built from sandstone. Some of Australia's oldest buildings are in Hobart, including Anglesea Barracks, the oldest military establishment (1811); and the oldest theatre, the Theatre Royal (1837). Battery Point is Hobart's oldest district. Originally home to sailors, fishermen, prostitutes and shipwrights, it is today a fashionable inner-city neighbourhood.

Hobart is the site of the Cadbury Chocolate Factory, open to the public and well worth visiting. Cascade Brewery, Australia's oldest brewery, is also in suburban Hobart and daily tours of the brewery and museum are available.

HOBART CITY PLACES OF INTEREST

	ref		ref
Anglesea Barracks & Museum	C5	Princes Park	B1
Arthur Circus	D4	Queens Domain	B1
Battery Point	D4	Royal Tasmanian Botanical Gardens	C2
Constitution & Victoria Docks	C4	'Runnymede'	B1
Elizabeth Mall	C4	St Davids Park	C4
Gasworks Village/Tasmania Distillery		St Marys Cathedral	B4
& Museum	D3	Salamanca Place/Market	C4
Government House	C2	State Library of Tasmania	C4
Hobart Convention & Entertainment Centre	D6	Sullivans Cove	D4
Maritime Museum of Tasmania	D4	Tasmanian Museum & Art Gallery	C4
'Narryna' Folk Museum	C4	University of Tasmania	B6
Parliament House	C4	Wrest Point Casino	D6

Top: Victoria Dock, Hobart; Middle: Japanese Garden, Royal Tasmanian Botanical Gardens; Bottom: Overlooking Hobart from Mt Wellington in winter

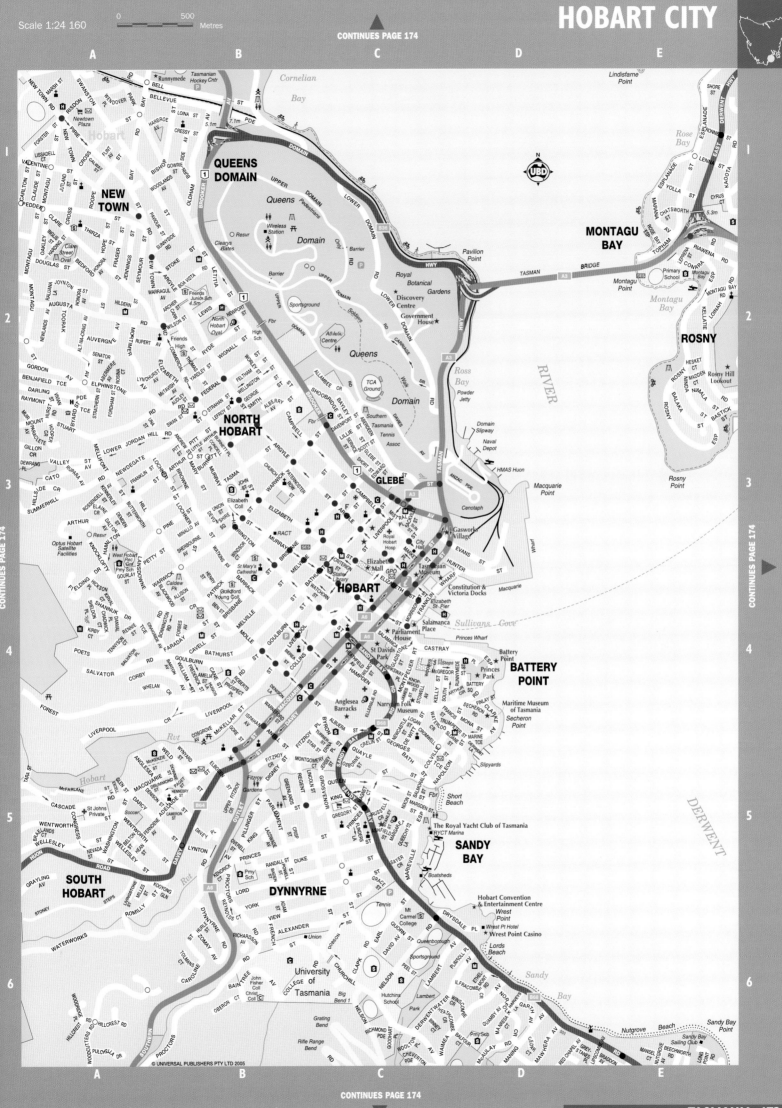

0   2   Kilometres

A   B   C   D   E

Austins Ferry
Ferry Pt
Cove Cottage
Churinga House
Hilton Hill 153
Polmenia Res
Cassidys
Brocks Pt Bay
EAST
Grasstree Hill
15
Alpenrail
Claremont
Dragon Pt
Beedhams Bay
Claremont
Cadbury Chocolate Factory
Dogshoar Pt
15
Mt Direction 448
Meehan
Rosneath
WindermereBay
Restdown Pt
Otago
Risdon Brook Reservoir
MEEHAN
Hilton
Abbotsfield
Chigwell
Connewarre Bay
McCarthys Pt
Lowestoft Bay
Knights Pt
B32
HWY
Bowens Monument
Risdon Cove Historic Site
Risdon Prison Complex
STATE RECREATION
Faulkners
Berriedale
Elliss Pt
Berriedale Bay
Frying Pan I.
Bowen Bridge
Risdon Cove Cleburne Pt
GRASSTREE HILL
Grasstree Hill
Range
Glenlusk
Rosetta
Wilkinsons Pt
Goodwood
B35
10
Risdon
Risdon Vale
C324
Oak Hill 172
Montrose
10
Elwick Bay
Elwick Racecourse
Bowen
B32
Dowsings Pt
Store Pt
EAST RISDON NATURE RESERVE
Sugarloaf Hill 205
Collinsvale
Prince of Wales Bay
Tasmanian Technopark
Bedlam Walls
Fishers Hill 139
Geilston Bay Park
Flagstaff Gully Reservoir
Glenlusk
Glenorchy
King George V Park
Royal Hobart Showgrounds
Electrolytic Zinc Works
Woodman Pt
E Z Co
Geilston Bay
Pilchers Hill 115
C615
Derwent Park
Derwent Park Junction
Lutana
Rock Cod Pt
Natone Hill 128
Limekiln
Lindisfarne
Hobart Technical College
Mt Hull
West Moonah
Moonah
5
New Town Bay
Rowing Clubs
Koomela Bay
Beltana Pt
Cornelian Bay
A3
Collinsvale
Merton
Runnymede
Cornelian Bay Pt
Lindisfarne Pt
Rose Bay
5
Knights Creek Reservoir
Lenah Valley
St Johns Park
John Edis
New Town
Cornelian Bay
Gordons Hill 145
Gordons Hill
Lady Franklin Museum
Mt Stuart
Queens
DOMAIN
Botanical Gardens
Pavilion Pt
Montagu Bay
Rosny Park (Public)
Mornington Hill
Mt Stuart 228
Government House
Tasman Bridge
Rosny Hill 94
Bellerive
New Town
North Hobart
Glebe
Powder Jetty
Rosny
CLARENCE
Brushy
West Hobart
Aussat
Royal Hobart
Cenotaph
Macquarie Pt
Kangaroo Bay
Bellerive Oval
Rubbish Tip
Knocklofty Park
Knocklofty 370
GPO
HOBART
Maritime Museum
Sullivans Cove
Battery Point
Kangaroo Bluff
Bellerive Beach
McRobies
PINNACLE
20
Cascade Brewery
St Johns Private
Anglesea Barracks
Secheron Pt
Mt Wellington 1271
Cascades
Sandy Bay
MOUNTAIN PARK
15
South Hobart
Dynnyrne
Hobart Convention & Entertainment Centre
Wrest Pt
Wrest Pt Hotel & Casino
Sandy Bay
C616
5
Lower Reservoir
University of Tasmania
Nutgrove Beach
Sandy Bay Pt
Turnip Fields
Upper Reservoir
WATERWORKS
Waterworks Reserve
Lower Sandy Bay
Sandown Park
Little Sandy Bay
B64
Tolmans Hill 350
5
The Hobart College
Blinking Billy Pt
John Garrow Light
10
Ridgeway Park
Ridgeway Reservoir
5
Alexandra Battery
5
Dam
Mt Nelson 340
Mt Nelson Signal Station
Fern Tree
SUMMERLEAS
Ridgeway
Mt Nelson
Tea House
Porter Hill 200
B68
10
Badger Hill 368
Tudor Court Model Village
North West Bay River
Long
B64
Browns Creek
The Lea
THE LEA CONSERVATION AREA
Taroona
Kelvedon Park
Taroona Park
Crayfish Pt
Neika
15
SOUTHERN
Cartwright Pt
Tudor
Truganini Res
Cartwright Pt
10
Taroona Beach
© UNIVERSAL PUBLISHERS PTY LTD 2005
HUON
B68

CONTINUES PAGE 183

CONTINUES PAGE 183

A B C D E

Pontos Hills

Penna

Stinking Pt

Sorell

Sorell Frogmore Peninsula

Orielton Lagoon

Susie Islet

Midway Point

Oaks Pt

RANGE AREA

Craigow Hill 395

Pitt

Shark Pt

Water

Woody I.

Barren I.

Railway Pt

Pittwater Bluff

Richmond

McKays Hill

Barilla Bay

Cambridge Aerodrome

SEVEN MILE BEACH PROTECTED AREA

Simmons Hill

Flagstaff Hill

Cambridge

Bureau of Meterology

Hobart Airport

Canopus Hill 265 Observatory

Hobart Airport

Llanherne

Royal Hobart

Tunnel Hill 270

Mornington

Lillian Martin Home

Mt Rumney 337

Mt Rumney Lookout

Seven Mile Beach

Waverley Flora Park 157

Knopwood Hill 350

Acton

Frederick

Howrah

Glebe Hill 135

Henry

Tranmere

Rokeby Hills

Rokeby

Claredon Vale

Oakdowns

Historic Church & Cemetery

Girl Guides Campsite "Orana"

Lauderdale

Bay

Punchs Reef

Police Academy

RALPHS BAY COASTAL RESERVE

Rokeby Beach

Mill Pt

Mays Pt

Beach

Tranmere Pt

Haynes Pt

Refuse Disposal Area

Maydena Bay

Droughty Hill 152

Gibsons Pt

Tollards Lagoon

Clear Lagoon

Trywork Pt

Droughty Pt

Ralphs Bay

Dixon Pt

Sandford

Huxleys Beach

Cremorne

Scale 1:603 900

0   20
Kilometres

A   B   C   D   E

Bass   Strait

144°   144°30'   145°

Neva, 1835
Cape Wickham
Cape Wickham Lighthouse
Cape Farewell
Disappointment Bay

L. Flannigan
Tartar, 1835
L. Martha Lavinia

Phoques
Egg Lagoon
Garfield, 1898
Lavinia Pt.

George, 1803
New Year I.
GAME RES.
Bay
LAVINIA
NATURE
RESERVE

Christmas I.
NAT. RES.
Yambacoona

Rio, 1915

SEA ELEPHANT
RIVER PRIVATE
WILDLIFE SANCT.

Whistler, 1855

Yellow Rock R.

Maypole, 1855
Reekara
King
Europa, 1867

34
REEKARA (PRIVATE)
WILDLIFE SANCT.
Island
Loorana
Sea Elephant
Councillor I.

King Island Dairies ★
Sea Elephant

Sea Elephant
Bay

Waterwitch, 1854
★ Windfarm
Oonah, 1891

Currie
Harbour
Fraser R.

Pegarah
Naracoopa
Fraser Bluff

Currie
Parenna
Museum
29

Netherby, 1866

Ettrick

Katheraw, 1872
KENTFORD FOREST
STATE RESERVE
Lymwood
Yarra Creek

Cataraqui, 1845
Bold Head

Brahmin, 1854
Grassy Penguin rookery
Cataraqui Pt.
Isabella, 1845

SEAL ROCKS
Pearshape + Mt Stanley
STATE RESERVE
213

Calcified Forest ★
Big L.

Surprise Bay
Seal Pt.

Clytie, 1902
Seal Bay
Carnarvon Bay, 1901

Stokes Pt.

N
UBD

SOUTHERN

OCEAN

NATURE RESERVE ○ Albatross I.
N. W. Cape
★ Cape Rochon

Cape Keraudren
Eveline, 1895

NATURE
RESERVE
Three
Hummock
Phatisalam, 1821
Burgess Pt.
Island

Cuvier
East Telegraph Bay
Bay
Cape Adamson
Cuvier Pt.
237 +
South Hummock
40°30'
Wallaby Pt.
Hunter
Spray, 1866
Island
Rainbow, 1868

Cave Bay
MUTTONBIRD

Steep I.
RESERVE
Petrel Is.
GAME RES.
Cape Buache

Bird I.
Stack I.
Walker I.
GAME RES.

Trefoil I.
Walker   Channel
Ransonnet
Bay

Woolnorth Pt.

Cape Grim
Boullanger
Woolnorth
Bay
Robbins Island

Valley Bay
★ Clump I.
Wallaby
Howie I.
Kangaroo I.
Is.
Robbins Passage
Wind Farm ★
Short I.
Montagu I.
Stony Pt.
Perkins I.

Flat Topped Bluff
West Montagu
Montagu
+ 120
18
Bluff Pt.
C215
Mella

Studland Bay
Broadmeadows ★

Morning Light, 1895
Harcus R.
Christmas Hills
HWY

MT CAMERON WEST
ABORIGINAL SITE
Lacrum
Dairy Farm
Mt Cameron West 168 +
Togari
54
Brittons
Ann
Swamp
Green Pt.
145
Bay
Marrawah
Redpa
BASS

WEST PT.
WEST POINT
ABORIGINAL SITE
ARTHUR PIEMAN
Mawson Bay
CONSERVATION AREA

© UNIVERSAL PUBLISHERS PTY LTD 2005

Scale 1:603 900

0   20   Kilometres

Bass   Strait

SOUTHERN   OCEAN

Nature Reserve Albatross I.
N. W. Cape
Cape Rochon 145
Eveline, 1895
Cape Keraudren
Coulomb Bay
Burgess Pt.
NATURE RESERVE
Three Hummock Island
Phatisalam, 1821
Cuvier Bay
East Telegraph Bay
Cape Adamson
237 + South Hummock
Cuvier Pt.
Wallaby Pt.
Spray, 1866
Hunter Island
MUTTONBIRD
Rainbow, 1868
Cave Bay
Steep I. GAME RES.
RESERVE
Bird I. GAME RES.
Petrel Is.
Cape Buache
Stack I. GAME RES.
Walker I.
Trefoil I.
Hunter Channel
Woolnorth Pt.
Ransonnet Bay
Guyton Pt.
Cape Grim
Woolnorth
Boullanger Bay
Clump I.
Kangaroo I.
Short I.
Robbins Island
Valley Bay
Wind Farm
Flat Topped Bluff
+120
Wallaby Is.
Robbins Passage
Cape Elle
Elizabeth, 1864
North Pt.
Half Moon Bay
Bluff Pt.
Montagu I. Howie I.
Stony Pt. Big
Shipwreck Pt.
Studland Bay
West Montagu
Montagu
Perkins I.
Perkins Bay
Highfield
Stanley
Circular Head (The Nut)
143
Morning Light, 1895
18
Duck Bay
Anthony Beach
Wiltshire
BASS
Cowrie Pt
Port Latta
Crayfish Creek
Edgecumbe Beach
Prairie, 1856
Rocky Cape
MT CAMERON WEST ABORIGINAL SITE
Mella
Smithton
12 Forest
Black River
Sawyer Bay
Hellyer
Rocky Cape Beach
Mt Cameron West 168 + Ann Bay
Lacrum Dairy Farm
Scotchtown
Broadmeadows
Smokers Bank
South Forest
Rocky Cape
ROCKY CAPE N.P.
Sisters Beach
Boat Harbour Beach
Green Pt.
Christmas Hills
HWY
33
Mengha
26
Montumana
Boat Harbour
Table Cape Lighthouse
Table Cape
Emma Prescott, 1867
Marrawah
Redpa
BASS
16
Irishtown
Alcomie
Mawbanna
48 Sisters Creek
Flowerdale
Tulip Farm
Wynyard
West Pt. WEST POINT ABORIGINAL SITE
Togari
54
Brittons Swamp
Eurebia
Lileah
Myalla
Moorleah
Seabrook
Somerset
ARTHUR PIEMAN
Edith Creek
Nabageena
Milabena
Lapoinya
Camdale
Burnie
Allendale Gardens
Roger River
Giant Eucalypts
Mt Dipwood
+ 519
Lower Mt Hicks
9
Oldina
Bluff Hill Pt.
CONSERVATION AREA
Roger River West
20
Trowutta
Dip Falls
Meunna
Preolenna
Calder
14
Elliott
15
Mooreville
14
Arthur River
Rebecca, 1853
River Cruise
30
MILKSHAKE HILLS
Kanunnah Bridge
Kellatier
Yolla
Henrietta
West Ridgley
Ridgley
HWY
Alert, 1854
SUNDOWN POINT ABORIGINAL SITE
18
Lake Chisholm
JULIUS RIVER
Takone West
Takone
Highclere
Couta Rocks
16
Oonah
Tewkesbury
15
Temma
Richardson R.
Balfour
Mt Frankland
448
ARTHUR
Hampshire
Eva, 1880
Hazard Bay
HELLYER GORGE STATE RESERVE
Gannet Pt.
Ordnance Pt.
Parrawe
51
St. Valentines Pk 1106
Mt Everett + 892
Kenneth Bay
PIEMAN
Wild Wave, 1894
Yolla, 1898
Sandy Cape
78
SAVAGE RIVER N.P.
Baretop Ridge
27
Guildford
CONSERVATION AREA
Tarkine Wilderness
Mt Sunday 699 +
+ Mt Bertha 703
Waratah
+ Mt Cleveland 858
Bischoff Resvr
Waratah Reservoir
Mt Pearse 1002
17
Luina
43
15
26
Savage River
Mt Meredith 810
26 24
+ Mt Donaldson 437
Mt Ramsay 856
Hellyer
Mt Beecroft +1140
Rupert Pt.
Ethel Cuthbert, 1878
Pieman Heads
Hardwicke Bay
Conical Rocks Pt.
Corinna
River Cruises
Toll on River Crossing
12
Mt Livingstone + 781
60
MURCHISON
20
Mt Hemus 1110
Dolphin, 1867
Reece
Reece Dam
Mackintosh Dam
Mackintosh
Mt Romulus + 955
GRANITE TOR CONSERVATION AREA
Ahrberg Bay
Bastyan Dam
Bastyan
145
Tullah
Wee Georgie Wood Railway
Lake Rosebery
Rosebery
Renison Bell
40
Murchison Dam

144°30'   145°30'
40°30'
41°
41°30'
144°30'

JOINS PAGE 178

© UNIVERSAL PUBLISHERS PTY LTD 2005

0   20   Kilometres

A   B   C   D   E

146°   146°30'   147°

Bass   Strait

I'enth I.

Stony Hd.   *'em   O' Shanter Bay   Noland Bay*

Seabrook   Somerset   Camdale   Cooee   Burnie   Wivenhoe   Chasm Creek

Bellbuoy Beach   Beechford   Lulworth   STONY HEAD ARTILLERY RANGE   Weymouth   Bellingham

Lower Mt Hicks   Elliott   Mooreville   Howth   Heybridge   Sulphur Creek   Penguin   Ulverstone   Turners Beach   Devonport   Don River Railway

Low Hd.   West Hd.   Greens Beach   Low Head   George Town   Lefroy   Pipers River   Pipers Brook

Ridgley   West Ridgley   Upper Stowport   Stowport   Cuprona   West Pine   Ferndene   Gawler   Leith   Penguin Viewing   Pt Sorell   Hawley Beach   Shearwater   Port Sorell   Kelso   Clarence Point   Yorktown   Historic Site   Bell Bay   Illfraville   Beauty Point   Beaconsfield   Rowella   Richmond Hill   The Glen   Lower Turners Marsh   Retreat

West Ridgley   Natone   Camena   North Motton   Riana   Abbotsham   Ambleside   Wesley Vale   Wright I.   Egg I.   Northdown   Squeaking Pt   Grubb Shaft Museum   Sidmouth   Deviot   Mt Direction   Turners Marsh

Highclere   Riana   Spalford   Forth   Spreyton   Moriarty   Thirlstane   Harford   Seahorse World   Holwell   Paper Beach   Leam   Gravelly Beach   Lanena   Dilston

Upper Natone   South Riana   Sprent   Melrose   Paloona   Latrobe   Axemans Hall of Fame   Sassafras   East Sassafras   West Frankford   Tamar Valley Wineries   Exeter   Rosevears   Lalla

Hampshire   Gunns Plains   Preston   Lower Barrington   Harford   Notley Gorge   Glengarry   Grindelwald Swiss Village   Legana   Rocherlea

Loyetea   Heka   Warringa   Barrington   Nook   Railton   West Frankford   Frankford   Bridgenorth   Birralee   Rosevale   Cataract Gorge   National Automobile Museum   Launceston

South Preston   Nietta   Lower Wilmot   Devils Gate   Merseylea   Sunnyside   Kimberley   Cheese Factory   Elizabeth Town   Reedy Marsh   Weetah   Selbourne   Westwood   Hadspen

Leven Canyon   Narrawa   South Nietta   Wilmot   Mural Town World   Sheffield   West Kentish   Roland   Paradise   Parkham   Weegena   Moltema

Black Bluff   Loongana   Erriba   Promised Land   Staverton   Claude Road   Beulah   Weegena   Dunorlan   Red Hills   Hagley   Entally House   Carrick   Breadalbane   Pateena

Moina   Gowrie Park   Lower Beulah   Deloraine   Exton   Westbury   Glenore   Whitemore   Longford   Perth

Cethana   Wilmot   Lorrinna   Liena   King Solomon   Alum Cliffs   Folk Museum   Needles   Quamby Brook   Bishopsbourne   Bracknell

Cradle Mountain Lodge   Visitor Centre   Daisy Dell   Mayberry   Mole Creek   Montana   Meander   Golden Valley   Cressy

Waldheim Chalet   Cradle Valley   Lemonthyme   Marakoopa   Caveside   Western Creek   Jackeys Marsh   Liffey   Liffey Falls   Drys Bluff   Blackwood Creek

Mt Remus   Dove Lake   Devils Gullet   Montana   Breona   Poatina

Cradle Mtn   Fisher   Fisher Bluff   Ironstone Mtn   Brandum   Poatina   Great Western Tiers

GRANITE TOR CONSERVATION AREA   Rowallan   CENTRAL PLATEAU CONSERVATION AREA   Rats Castle   Bernacchi   Reynolds I.   Reynolds Neck   Cramps Bay

CRADLE MOUNTAIN   Lake Rowallan   WALLS OF JERUSALEM NATIONAL PARK   Lake Augusta   Liawenee   Great Lake   Arthurs Lake

LAKE ST CLAIR   Mt Ossa   Liawenee   Tods Corner   Brazendale I.   Neil I.   Millers Bluff

NATIONAL PARK   WORLD   Lake Louisa   NATIONAL PARK   Lit. Pine Lagoon   Miena   Barren Tier   Flintstone   Lake Sorell

HERITAGE   Mt Olympus   Lake St Clair   Shannon   Wilburville   Lake of Islands

Nelson Falls Nature Walk   AREA   Visitor Centre   Steppes   Woods Lake   Lake Crescent

LYELL   Derwent Bridge   Laughing Jack Lag.   Bronte Park   Waddamana   Waddamana

Mt Mary   Bronte   L. Big Jim   L. Samuel   Lake Echo   Hermitage   Table Mtn

Donaghys Hill   Franklin River Nature Walk   Mt King William I   Lake King William   Butlers Gorge   Dee   Lake Echo   Dee Lagoon   Interlaken

Frenchmans Cap

© UNIVERSAL PUBLISHERS PTY LTD 2005

JOINS PAGES 177 & 181

JOINS PAGE 182

JOINS PAGE 180

A   B   C   D   E

Bass Strait

Croppies Pt.

Ringarooma Bay

COASTAL RESERVE

Poole

Cape Naturaliste

147°30'
WATERHOUSE
CONSERVATION
AREA

Big Waterhouse Lake

Tomahawk

TOMAHAWK COASTAL RES.

Boobyalla

Rushy Lagoon

148°

Cape Naturaliste

Boulder Pt.

148°30'

West Sandy Pt.   St. Albans   East Sandy Pt.

St. Albans Bay

Anderson Bay

DOUBLE SANDY PT. COASTAL RES.

18

Waterhouse

TOMAHAWK RIVER RESERVE

19

Fosters Marshes

MOUNT WILLIAM

NATIONAL

41°

21

Bridport

23

19

Great Forests

Oxberry Ck

Mt Cameron + 551

Gladstone

PARK Ck

Eddystone Pt.

1   Lavender Farm

Golconda   13

Blumont

Nabowla   15

Jetsonville

North Scottsdale

Scottsdale

Forest Eco Centre

The Banca

Ck 16

23

Winnaleah

Pioneer

Herrick

Ansons Bay

Policemans Pt.

BAY OF FIRES CONSERVATION AREA

Bay of Fires

Wyena

Lebrina   11

Turners   North Lilydale

Lilydale

16   Underwood

29

32   7

Forester

Mt Horror 676

Telita

Kamona

Derby   Tin Mine Centre

23

Tonganah

Tulendeena   Branxholm

Springfield

South Springfield

Legerwood

Ringarooma

Weldborough

54

TASMAN

HWY

Lottah

Goulds Country

Mt Pearson 365

Priory

The Gardens

Big Lagoon

BAY OF FIRES CONSERVATION AREA

Binalong Bay

Grant Pt.

Grant Bay

2

Myrtle Bank
Targa

St Patricks River

Patersonia

13

Mt Arthur +1187

Mt Barrow +1413

Tayene   30

Legunia

Alberton

Talawa

Diddleum Plains

Mt Maurice + 1120

43

Pyengana

St Columba Falls

Ralphs Falls

Bayview

St Helens

Akaroa   Stieglitz

Parnella

Parkside   St Helens I.

St Helens Pt.

Jean, 1834

ST. HELENS CONSERVATION AREA

Dianas Basin

TASMAN

3

21

St Leonards

15   Relbia   White Hills   22

Burns Creek

Musselboro

Nunamara

7

Upper Esk

Roses Tier   48

Upper Blessington

Blessington

25

Ben Nevis + 1867

Mt Saddleback 1255

Mathinna

Mt Young 903

Upper Scamander

Beaumaris   26

Scamander

Falmouth

Henderson Lagoon

41°30'

SEA

4

Western Junction

Evandale   12

Clarendon

Nile   14

Deddington   22

Ben Lomond Ski Village
+1573
Legges Tor

BEN LOMOND NATIONAL PARK

Stacks Bluff 1527

Tower 1117   25

Mangana

Storys Creek

47

Rossarden

Ormley   28

Fingal Tier

Fingal

St Pauls Dome 1027

Cornwall   9

St Marys   21

Gray   17

11

Elephant Pass

Chain of Lagoons

Piccaninny Pt.

DOUGLAS-APSLEY NATIONAL PARK

Mt Nicholas + 857

19

HWY

Mt St John + 779

Four Mile Creek

Ironhouse Pt.

Wardlaws Pt.

31

23   Epping Forest

Cleveland

Conara   26   Llewellyn

ESK

Avoca

Royal George

Templestowe Lagoon

Seymour   Long Pt.

Caroline, 1862

27   Douglas River

Maclean Bay

Apsley River Waterhole   Birdlife Park

Sea Life Centre

Peggys Pt.

Bicheno

Waubedebars Grave

Rocket, 1880

Cape Lodi

5

MIDLAND

12   10

Campbell Town

25

Ross   Wool Centre
Female Factory Site
Ross Bridge (1836)

Mona Vale

Lake Leake

57

LOST FALLS

Cranbrook

32

Courland Bay

Butlers Pt.

FREYCINET NATIONAL PARK

Moulting Lagoon

Friendly Beaches

42°

6

25

Tunbridge

27   Antil Ponds

Woodbury

York Plains

MIDLAND HWY

The Quoin 568

TOOMS CONSERVATION AREA

Snow Hill 971

Meetus Falls

10

Bark Mill & Museum

Nine   Mile   Beach

Resolution, 1850

Swansea

Spiky Bridge

Rocky Hills Convict Station

Lisdillon

Coles Bay

Cape Tourville

The Hazards
Fleurieu Pt.

Thouin Bay

Wineglass Bay

Cape Forestier

FREYCINET

Friendly Pt.

FREYCINET NATIONAL PARK

Gates Bluff

Weatherhead Pt.

Oyster Bay

Mayfield Bay

Webber Pt.

148°

148°30'

© UNIVERSAL PUBLISHERS PTY LTD 2005

A   B   C   D   E

JOINS PAGE 183

A B C D E

Endeavour Reef

Bass   Strait

147°30'   148°   *148°30'*

Outer Sister I.
MUTTONBIRD RESERVE

Craggy I.

Inner Sister I.
MUTTONBIRD RESERVE

Stanley Pt.   Holloway Pt.
Sisters Passage

Blyth Pt.
Palana
Foochow

Old Mans Head   Mt Killiecrankie
412
376   C. C. Funk, 1898

Killecrankie Bay

+ Bass Pyramid

Sentine I.   Killiecrankie

Cape Frankland   Mt Tanner
331   WINGAROO
NATURE
RESERVE
Leeka

Roydon I.   7
N. Pasco I.   15
M. Pasco I.   Beach
S. Pasco I.   *Tanners   City of Foochow, 1877
Bay*   30

Marshall   Flinders
Bay   Patriarch Inlet

Babel I.   MUTTONBIRD RESERVE
CONS. AREA
Sellars Pt.   Cat I.
Storehouse I.

Settlement Pt.   Emita
Wybalenna   Museum
WILDLIFE   Memana
SANCTUARY   *Island*
Wybalenna I.   Sellars Lagoon

*Arthur   Patriarch
Bay*   Blue Rocks

Prime   Mt Leventhorpe
Seal I.   501   22   *Cameron Inlet*
Darling Ra   LACKRANA WILDLIFE SANCTUARY

BIRD SANCTUARY
Chalky I.   Long Pt.   40
Isabella I.   Whitemark   N. Chain Lagoon
*Parrys   S. Chain Lagoon
Bay*

Safe   Passage   Ranga   Logan Lagoon
NATURE RESERVE
Low Islets   Big   WILDLIFE SANCTUARY
Green
I.
F. Kangaroo I.   *Fotheringate   Strzelecki Peaks   Lady Barron   Pot Boil Pt.
Bay*   756   Lt. Green I.
STRZELECKI   Adelaide   MUTTONBIRD RESERVES
NATIONAL   Bay   Great Dog I.
PARK

NATURE RESERVE   Mt Chappell I.   Lt. Dog I.   Vansittart I.
Sound   Farsund, 1912
Chappell Islands   *Anderson   Tin Kettle I.   Puncheon Pt.
Islands*
CONSERVATION AREA   Anderson I.
Goose I.
Boundary, 1859   *Franklin   Deep
Bay*
Badger I.
GROUP   Long I.   + Mt Munro 686   Harleys Pt.

Cape Barren Island
Cape Barren Island

Cape Sir John   Kent   + Mt Kerford 503   Cape Barren
Thunder & Lightning Bay   G.V.H., 1897   Bay
Margaret, 1828   Defiance, 1833
Courier, 1833
Wombat Pt.
Preservation I.   *Channel*
"Sydney Cove" Historic Site   Seal Pt.   Cone Pt.
Rum I.   *Armstrong*
Foam Pt.   *Clarke   Black   Passage I.
Island*   Pt.   Forsyth I.
Spike Bay
Moriarty Bay
Lookout Head
Moriarty Pt.
South Head   Lioness, 1854

Banks   Strait

Rum I.   Lt. Swan I.   Brenda, 1832
Cape Portland   Union, 1852   Swan I.
Sally, 1826   Cape   Mystery, 1850
CAPE PORTLAND   Portland
(PRIVATE) WILDLIFE SANCT.   MUSSELROE BAY

Waterhouse I.   CONSERVATION AREA
Creole, 1863   *Passage*   *Great
Musselroe   Musselroe Pt.
Waterhouse Pt.   Bay*   Poole
Ninth I.   *Waterhouse   Cape Naturaliste
Bay*   Cuckoo   Rushy Lagoon
Croppies Pt.   *Ringarooma   RINGAROOMA   Ck
WATERHOUSE   Bay*   COASTAL   Fosters   Boulder Pt.
CONSERVATION   Tomahawk   RESERVE   Marshes
AREA   TOMAHAWK   18   Boobyalla
COASTAL RES.
Big Waterhouse Lake   19   MOUNT WILLIAM
East   Waterhouse   Gladstone   NATIONAL
Sandy Pt.   TOMAHAWK   Ringarooma   PARK
St. Albans   RIVER   River
Bay   RESERVE   Mt Cameron   Eddystone Pt.
*Anderson   23   551
Bay*   The Banca   148°
DOUBLE SANDY PT   147°30'   +
COASTAL RES.   Bridport

180 TASMANIA

JOINS PAGE 179

0   20   Kilometres

JOINS PAGES 178 & 182

Reece
Reece Dam
60
Bastyan Dam
145°30'
Mackintosh
Bastyan
Tullah
Tullah
Wee Georgie
Wood Railway
LAKE GRANITE TOR
CONSERVATION
AREA
Lake
Mackintosh
Rowallan
Lake Rowallan

Rosebery
Renison Bell
MURCHISON
34
Williamsford
Murchison
Dam
Murchison
Tribute
Montezuma
Falls
Lake
Rosebery
10
CRADLE MOUNTAIN
Lake Will
Lake
Murchison
LAKE ST. CLAIR

Granville Harbour
Amy Robsart, 1883
43
Melba Flats
52
ZEEHAN
Mt Heemskirk +742
Granite
Piney
Tasman

Zeehan
Pioneer Museum
Mt Zeehan
702 +
5
Henty
Glacial Moraine
27
Lake
Plimsoll
Lake
Rolleston
Eldon Pk
+1439
Mt Ossa
1617 +
Mt Sedgwick
+1147
NATIONAL PARK
WORLD
WALLS OF JERUSALEM
NATIONAL PARK

Trial Harbour
Excelsior, 1882
De Witt, 1883
Trial, 1887
Trial Harbour
Little
Henty
18

51
Struggler, 1860
Georgetown, 1874
41
Lake Margaret
Yolande
HWY
Mt Lyell
Copper Mines
Nelson Falls
Nature Walk
3
Mt Sedgwick
HERITAGE
Mt Olympus
1447
Travellers
Rest
L. Ina

Chairlift
Queenstown
West Coast
Wilderness
Railway
Gormanston
Lynchford
John
Butters
Crotty Dam
Darwin Dam
LYELL
91
Donaghys
Hill
Franklin River
Nature Walk
74
Mt Mary
1012
AREA
Visitor Centre
Derwent
Bridge
HWY
26
Laughing
Jack Lag.

Strahan
Regatta Point
Bellinger, 1894
Cape Sorell
Lowana
Yard
Lower
Landing
Dubbil Barril
Teepookana
Plateau
37
Mt Sorell
1144
Frenchmans Cap
+1445
FRANKLIN-GORDON
Mt King William I
1359
Butlers Gorge
Mt King William II
1359
Mt Hobhouse
+1219

Gem, 1856
Sloop Rocks
Sloop Pt.
Table Head
197
Liberty Pt.
Macquarie
Sophia Pt.
Pillinger
(ruins)
Gould Pt.
Convict Ruins
Sarah I.
Heritage Landing
Nature Walk
WILD RIVERS
NATIONAL
Mt King William III +

Harbour
Birthday Bay
Gorge Pt.
Albina
Varna Bay
Varna, 1857
Pennerowne Pt.
PARK

Hibbs Bay
Hibbs Pyramid
Point Hibbs
LOW ROCKY POINT
Innes Peak
+664
Mt Humboldt +
The Spires
The Pleiades
Denison Range
Clear Hill +
1198
Lake
Gordon

Spero Bay
Conder Pt.
SOUTHWEST
Mt Lewis +
793
Underground tours
Gordon Dam
Strathgordon
Serpentine
Dam
Teds Beach
Boyd I.

Wanderer, 1858
High Rocky Pt.
CONSERVATION
AREA
Mt Sprent +
1097
McPartlan
Pass
Mt +
Wedge
1147

Acacia, 1904
OCEAN
SOUTHERN
WORLD HERITAGE
Orb Lake
Double Peak
1060
Pedder
+ Mt Solitary

N
UBD
Matilda, 1881
Black Warrior, 1863
Low Rocky Pt.
Elliott
Bay
Nye Bay
Elliott Pt.
AREA
Piners Peak
+696
Scotts Pk +
Scotts Peak Dam
+Mt Hesperus

Scale 1:603 900

0   20   Kilometres

FRANKLIN-GORDON

WILD RIVERS

NATIONAL

PARK

Frenchmans Cap 1445
Mt King William II + 1359
Mt King William III +
Buttlers Gorge
Lake King William
L. Rufus
Mt Hobhouse 1219
Tungatinah
Tarraleah
Tarraleah
L. Binney
Dee Lagoon
Victoria Valley
Osterley
Strickland
Wayatinah
Llawdolah
Australian Golf Museum
Bothwell
Wayatinah
Catagunyah
Lake Catagunya
Ouse
Cluny
Repulse
Cluny Lagoon
Lawrenny
Langloh
Hamilton
Hollow Tree
Pelham
Elderslie
Meadowbank Lake
Meadowbank
Ellendale
Russell Falls
Fentonbury
Westerway
Karanja
Gretna
Tanina
Rosegarland
Platform Pk
MOUNT FIELD NATIONAL PARK
Mt Field West 1434
L. Seal
L. Fenton
Skiing
National Park
Marriotts Falls
Junee
Glenora
Bushy Park
Black Hills
Tyenna
Fitzgerald
Maydena
Plenty
Uxbridge
Salmon Ponds
New Norfolk
Moogara
Feilton
Glenfern
Lachlan
Mt Lloyd

The Spires
Denison Range
The Pleiades
Clear Hill 1198
Adamsfield (ruins)
ROAD
Frodshams Pass
Mt Wedge 1147
Creepy Crawly Walk
McPartlan Pass
Lake Pedder
PEAK
Mt Solitary
Mt Anne 1425
Lake Judd
Scotts Pk
Edgar Dam
Scotts Peak Dam
SCOTTS
Gallagher Plateau
Mt Weld 1344
Lonnanvale
Snowy Ranges Trout Fishery
Judbury
Crabtree
Lucaston Apple Museum
Ranelagh
Glen Huon
Huonville
Tahune Forest AirWalk
PLAINS
Mt Picton 1327+
Franklin
Woodstock
Upper Woodstock
South Franklin
Castle Forbes Bay
Glaziers Bay
Port Huon
Geeveston Forest and Heritage Centre
Cairns Bay
Petcheys Bay
Wattle Grove
Waterloo
Surges Bay
Lymington
Glendevie
Police Point
Surveyors Bay
Glenbervie
Francistown
Dover
Raminea
Strathblane
Harvey Town
Hope I.
Scott Pt.
Hastings Caves
Adamsons Pk 1226+
Thermal Springs
Hastings
Lune River
Ida Bay
Southport
Enchantress 1835
Historic Railway
George III 1835
Catamaran
Maria Orr 1846
Wallace 1835
Cockle Creek
Fishers Pt.
South East Cape

WORLD
HERITAGE
AREA
SOUTHWEST NATIONAL PARK

Heritage Landing Nature Walk
D'Aguilar Ra.
Mt Lewis + 793
CONSERVATION
AREA
Lawson Range
Nye Bay
Elliott Pt.
Mulcahy Bay
Brier Holme Hd.
Brier Holme, 1904
Svenor Pt.
Svenor, 1914
Hobbs I.
Alfhild, 1907
West Pyramid
North Head
Point St Vincent
Geordy, 1816
Eveline, 1891
Hilliard Head
Wendar I.
Mutton Bird I.
Flying Cloud Pt.
SOUTHERN
OCEAN
South West Cape
Ripple, 1877
Alecona, 1848
Red Pt.
Cox Bluff
Louisa I.
Havelock Bluff
Ile du Golfe
Prion Bay
Point Vivian
De Witt I.
SOUTHWEST
Flat Witch I.
Walker I.
NATIONAL PARK
Maatsuyker I.
MAATSUYKER GROUP
Shoemaker Pt.
South Cape
Soldier Bluff
South East Cape
Whale Hd

Underground tours Gordon Dam
Strathgordon
Serpentine Dam
Teds Beach
GORDON
RIVER
Lake Gordon
Boyd I.
Mt Sprent + 1097
Frankland Range
Orb Lake
Double Peak 1060
Piners Peak + 696
Pedder Range
De Witt Range
Mt Hean + 747
Port Davey
Breaksea I.
Davey Gorge
PORT
DAVEY
Mt Hesperus + 1098
Bathurst Harbour
Ray Range
Melaleuca Bird Observatory
Melaleuca Lagoon
Mt Counsel 800
Mt Melaleuca 595
Cox Bight
ARTHUR
Arthur Range
HERITAGE
Mt Norold 978
Federation Pk 1224 +
L. Geeves
Mt Bobs + 1109
New River Lagoon
COAST
Oval L.
Mt La Perouse 1158
Swallows Nest Bay
Southport Lagoon
Actaeon I.
Eliza Pt.
Recherche Bay
Southport Bluff
Rossel Pt.

LYELL HWY

HIGHLANDS LAKES

HARTZ MTNS. NATIONAL PARK
Hartz Pk 1254m

HUON HWY

CHANNEL

D'Entrecasteaux Channel

© UNIVERSAL PUBLISHERS PTY LTD 2005

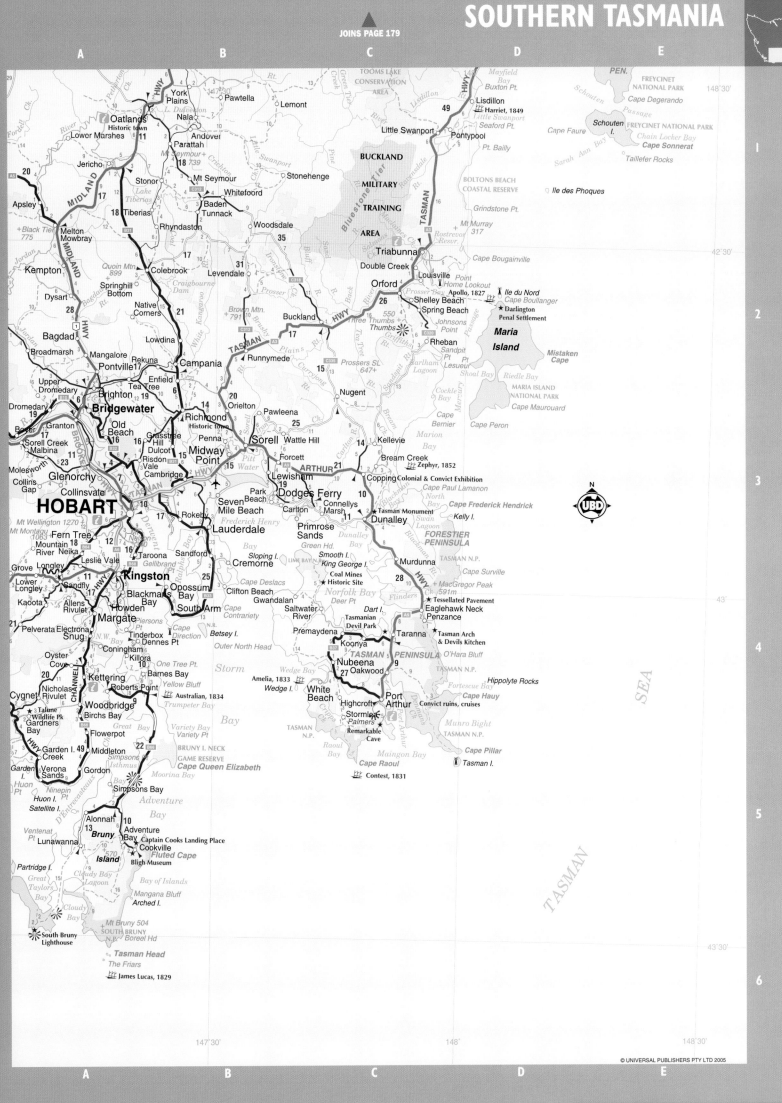

CITY AND TOWN CENTRES

Bicheno page 179 D5

Information Centre
Charles St/Esplanade West,
Triabunna
Ph: (03) 6257 4090

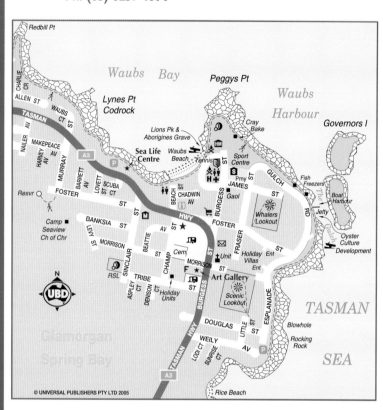

Burnie page 178 A1

Information Centre
Civic Centre Plaza,
Little Alexander St
Ph: (03) 6434 6111

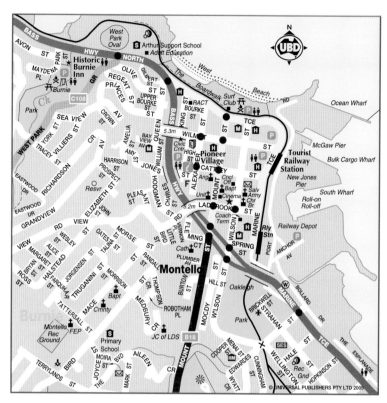

Devonport page 178 C2

Information Centre
92 Formby Rd
Ph: (03) 6424 8176

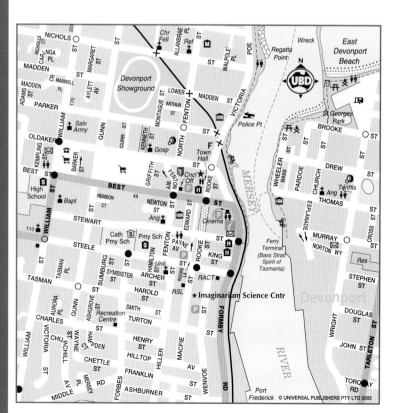

George Town page 178 E1

Information Centre
Main Rd/Victoria St
Ph: (03) 6382 1700

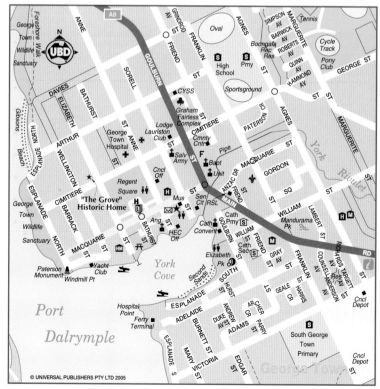

Huonville page 182 E4

Information Centre
Huon River Jetboats,
Esplanade
Ph: (03) 6264 1838

Launceston page 178 E3

Information Centre
St John St/Paterson St
Ph: (03) 6336 3133

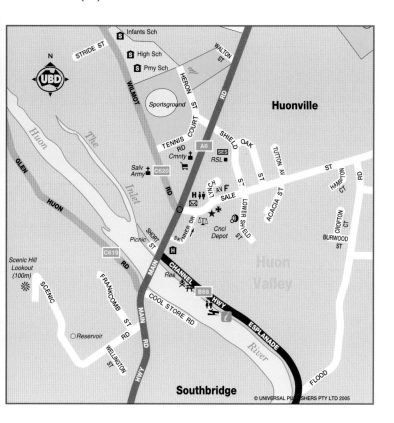

Port Arthur page 183 C4

Information Centre
Port Arthur Historic Site,
Arthur Hwy
Ph: (03) 6251 2310

Queenstown page 181 C2

Information Centre
Queenstown Galley Museum,
Sticht St/Driffield St
Ph: (03) 6471 1483

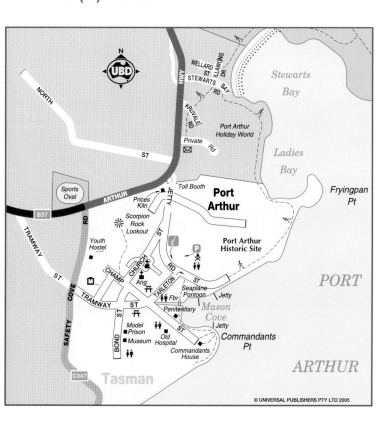

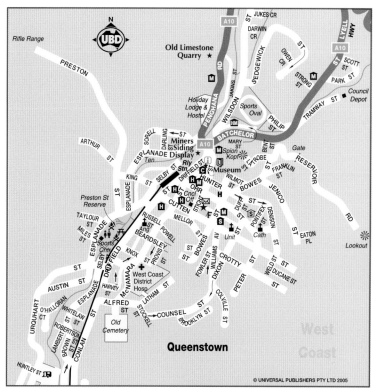

Richmond page 183 B3

Information Centre
Old Hobart Town Model Village,
21a Bridge St
Ph: (03) 6260 2502

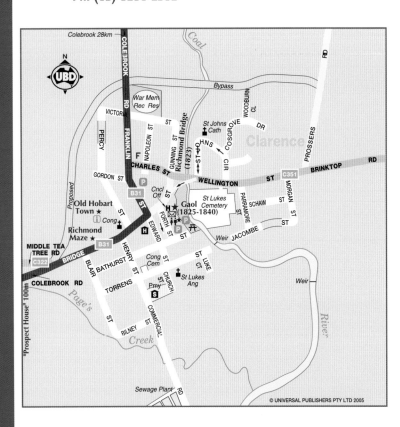

Strahan page 181 B2

Information Centre
Wharf Complex, The
Esplanade
Ph: (03) 6471 7622

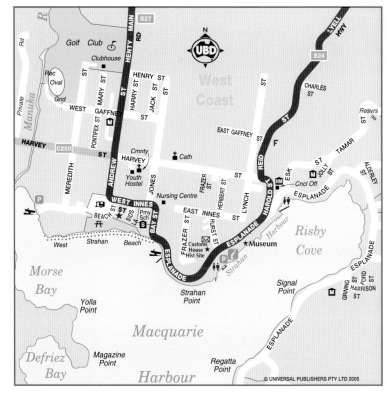

Swansea page 179 C6

Information Centre
Swansea Bark Mill,
96 Tasman Hwy
Ph: (03) 6257 8382

Ulverstone page 178 B2

Information Centre
Car Park La
(behind post office)
Ph: (03) 6425 2839

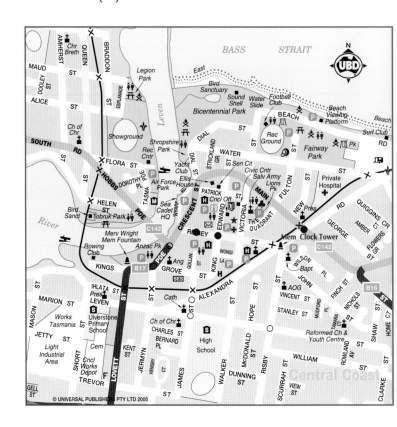

PREPARING YOUR VEHICLE

Whatever type of trip you have planned, your vehicle should be checked by a qualified mechanic before setting out. Most state motoring organisations provide a vehicle inspection service, which will alert you to any problems that require attention.

If you plan to tow a caravan or trailer, it is just as important to check the tyres, wheel bearings, trailer coupling, lights and general condition of all working parts. Give yourself plenty of time - the day before you set out is not a good time to discover a major problem!

Make sure the following are checked and in good order before you depart and check them regularly during the trip:
. Fluid levels — oil, coolant, brake fluid, transmission
. Battery and mounting brackets
. Tyre condition and pressure — don't forget the spare!
. Windscreen wipers — blades and washer reservoir
. Cooling system — radiator and hoses
. Fan belt(s)
. Lights
. Brake system

EQUIPPING YOUR VEHICLE

A mechanically sound vehicle doesn't always mean there will be no problems, so it is wise to be prepared. For a journey that will not take you far from professional mechanical assistance, it is advisable to carry a spare set of keys, a set of spanners and screwdrivers, jumper leads, a WD lubricant, spare fan belt(s), radiator hoses, light globes and fuses, fire extinguisher, a jack and tools for changing tyres, a torch and a service and repair manual.

Those considering a journey to the more remote areas of Australia should consider taking further equipment (refer box at right).

PACKING YOUR VEHICLE

When packing the vehicle, make sure that items most likely to be needed during the journey are accessible and that more than one person knows where everything is. Emergency equipment, such as a fire extinguisher, must be easily accessible. Loose items should be stored securely, so they will not get thrown around the cabin in the event of an accident or emergency braking.

The roof-rack is not the place for heavy items whose weight might throw the vehicle off balance in rough country. Secure heavy items in the main body of the vehicle. Leave the roof for lighter items and arrange them so that there is as little wind resistance as possible — make the load lower at the front and higher at the back. Do not overload the vehicle; confine yourself to essentials.

Carry excess fuel in metal jerry cans because plastic containers can crack if they constantly rub against parts of the car. Extra fuel should be stored on the back of the vehicle or in a trailer. It should not be packed on the roof or inside the vehicle in case of fire.

GLOVEBOX ESSENTIALS

The glovebox is the ideal place to keep important papers while travelling, including your motor vehicle registration papers, the number of your car insurance policy, prescriptions for medication and for replacement glasses, if worn.

SPARE TYRES

At least one spare wheel, with air pressure slightly above normal, should be carried at all times. In remote areas, or if the car has a space-saver spare, consider taking an extra spare wheel if space permits.

SPARE KEYS

Spare keys are important. Most cars are now equipped with engine immobilisers and these rely on getting a coded electronic signal from the ignition key or remote unit. This is why it is so important to carry a spare key/remote unit with you on a trip. Without a spare, the car may have to be towed a long distance to an authorised dealer or you might have to wait until spare keys can be sent from home.

ESSENTIAL VEHICLE EQUIPMENT FOR REMOTE AREA TRAVEL

. Tyre pump
. Extra water, fuel and oil
. Fuel pump
. Heavy rope or tow cable
. Flares for signals
. Shovel and axe
. Breakdown warning reflector
. Spare fuel and hose
. Spark plugs (if applicable)
. Heater hoses and clamps
. Brake fluid
. Cooling system leak sealer
. Super glue
. Insulating tape
. Windscreen protector
. Radiator insect screen
. Fuel filter
. Carburettor repair kit (if applicable)
. Tube repair kit
. Ignition points (if applicable)
. Comprehensive tool kit
. Plastic sheet (2x2 metres)
. Water bucket

Checking the oil level

BEATING FATIGUE

Today, 7% of all accidents are due to driver fatigue and, in country areas, fatigue accounts for 30% of fatal accidents. By planning each day sensibly and remembering the following points, you can avoid some of the tension and fatigue associated with long-distance driving:

. Wear light comfortable clothes and have sunglasses at hand in case of sudden strong light.

. Keep the windscreen clean and clear.

. Sit upright with good back support.

. Stop every 2 hours, get out of the vehicle and walk around to stretch your legs. Change drivers if you are sharing the driving.

. Do not eat a heavy meal in the middle of the day — a full stomach will make you feel drowsy.

. Do not drink any alcohol before driving.

. Try to time your day's travel so that you arrive at your destination in time to unwind, have a shower, a relaxed evening meal and a good night's sleep.

Measuring Fuel Consumption

Total Litres	+	$\dfrac{\text{Total km}}{100}$	=	Litres per 100km
60 Litres	+	$\dfrac{300\text{km}}{100}$	=	20 Litres per 100km

OUTBACK MOTORING

To cover the risk of getting stranded or lost in a remote area, always carry enough food and plenty of water to keep you supplied for a few days (4 litres of water per person per day). Before setting out, check the conditions and distances of the roads on your journey. If you plan a long trip through remote country, leave details of your plans with someone you can trust to take action if you have not made contact at pre-arranged times. Special driving techniques are needed to overcome the difficulties of driving on unsealed roads:

. When driving on sand, keep the vehicle in a straight line. If you have to make a turn, do it by turning the wheel quickly in the direction you want to go and then quickly back to the original position.

. If your vehicle gets stuck in sand, the floor mats can be used to give support and traction and hub caps can be used as jack supports. Lowering tyre pressure will also assist traction.

. Do not try to avoid every hole you see when driving on dirt roads. Drive carefully at a constantly safe speed — do the same when the surface is badly corrugated.

. To make a creek crossing, check the underlying surface, the depth and flow of water. Drive slowly in the centre of the crossing, where the undersurface is likely to be solid, and keep the wheels straight. Do not change gear midstream.

. Care is needed when overtaking in the Outback. Beware of soft or loose verges and the dust thrown up by road trains. Resist the temptation to overtake road trains and, when they are approaching, pull over to the side of the road until the train has passed and the dust cloud has settled.

MAPS AND COMPASS

In the Outback, where featureless land can make it difficult to find direction, a topographical map is essential. When you choose a map, check that the scale is accurate and that sufficient detail is given. A compass is used in conjunction with the map to work out the route from one place to another. An orienteering compass is reliable, easy to use and inexpensive.

FUEL ECONOMY

Fuel economy is affected by the condition of the vehicle and the roads it will be travelling on. Here are some ways to help conserve petrol:

. Try to avoid delays such as peak-hour traffic or scheduled bridge closures.

. Try to distribute weight of passengers and baggage evenly.

. Drive as smoothly as possible.

. Ensure the tyres are properly inflated and that wheel alignment and balance are correct.

. Service and tune the vehicle regularly according to the manufacturer's recommendations. The air cleaner, spark plugs and, on older vehicles, ignition timing are especially important.

. Avoid long periods of idling. When held up in traffic, switch the engine off if it is safe to do so.

. Make sure you fully release the handbrake when driving.

. Avoid driving at high speeds.

. Only use air-conditioning when absolutely necessary.

MEASURING FUEL CONSUMPTION

When covering long distances on remote roads, you need to keep a check on your vehicle's fuel consumption. A basic formula for working out fuel consumption is shown in the box at the left.

SURVIVAL HINTS

If you get stuck in 'the middle of nowhere', here are some tips for staying safe:

. Try not to panic — think of a course of action that will see you helped or rescued.

. Stay with your vehicle — it provides shelter, increasing the chances of survival. If a search for you is underway, spotting a car is easier than a person.

. Conserve food and water.

. Stay in the shade — keep clothes on to protect against exposure.

. Prepare adequate signals — if in a remote area, light a fire to attract attention (but be careful not to start a bushfire!).

TRAVELLING WITH CHILDREN

Children soon get over the novelty of travel; they need to be entertained to prevent back-seat fights and tears. Some suggestions on how to achieve this:

. Include some of their favourite toys.

. Play music on the radio or cassette player.

. Sing popular songs together.

. Play family car games (there are books available on these).

. Stop for frequent breaks, preferably where there is a playground.

Car-sickness is common in children. To keep this to a minimum:

. Avoid getting the children excited.

. Drive as smoothly as possible.

. Don't let children read or write in a moving vehicle.

. Don't let them try to spot things that flash by — they should only try to spot things ahead of them.

If you are involved in a road accident and you are not injured, it is worthwhile to record the facts while you are on the scene. You will need a record if reporting to the police, filling in your insurance claim or taking other action to recover your repair costs. Here is a checklist of facts to record:

DETAILS OF ACCIDENT
. Date, time and location of accident
. Was the road wet or dry?
. Width of road
. Was your vehicle on the correct side of the road?
. Estimated speed of both vehicles at time of impact
. If after sunset, was accident site well lit?
. On cars involved, what lights were on?
. Sketch of accident scene
. Names, addresses and phone numbers of witnesses

OTHER VEHICLE(S)
. Driver's name, licence number, address and phone number
. If different, owner's name and address
. Make, model and registration number
. Extent of damage
. Was the vehicle already damaged before this accident?
. Name of insurance company, policy number and type

. Did other driver admit liability? Record exact words

INJURED PERSONS
. Names and addresses of injured persons
. Degree of injuries

DAMAGE TO PROPERTY
. Details of damage to property other than vehicles
. Name and address of owner of damaged property

TOWING
. Name of tow truck service
. Destination of towed vehicle

POLICE INVOLVEMENT
Police must be called to an accident if anyone is killed or injured, or if either of the drivers appears to be affected by alcohol or drugs. It must also be reported if either driver leaves the scene without exchanging details.
If police are called, record the following:
. Names of attending officers and their police station
. The reading obtained if other driver was breathalysed
. Whether the police laid blame or mentioned charges

If the police are not called, report the accident to the police within 24 hours.

RECOMMENDED FIRST-AID KIT

. **Absorbent gauze**
. **Alcohol swabs**
. **Antihistamine** (for bee stings)
. **Antiseptic cream and swabs**
. **Aspirin or paracetamol**
. **Clinical thermometer**
. **Conforming bandages**
. **Cotton wool**
. **Crepe bandages**
. **Current first-aid manual**
. **Eye bath**
. **Latex gloves**
. **Pen torch**
. **Safety pins**
. **Saline eyewash**
. **Scissors**
. **Sterile dressings**
. **Sticking plaster and adhesive dressings**
. **Tongue depressor**
. **Triangular bandages**
. **Tweezers**

FIRST AID

Snake and Spider Bites
Try to identify the snake or spider — at no further threat to safety.
. Wrap the area bitten with an elastic bandage or a strip of cloth if no bandage is available. This should slow the flow of venom in the bloodstream and help keep the venom localised.
. Do not apply a tourniquet — this can cause gangrene if it stops the flow of blood completely.
. Don't loosen the bandage once it is applied.
. Get the victim to a hospital so that antivenene can be administered.

Bleeding
Wipe away blood and/or remove clothing to find the source of the bleeding. Apply direct pressure to the source with a bandage, piece of material or your hand.
. If possible, elevate the affected area (site of bleeding).
. Apply a tourniquet, firm and not too tight, only if you can't stop the bleeding any other way.

Shock
A person is in shock if experiencing some of these symptoms: is cold and clammy to the touch, has a fast but weak pulse, is breathing shallowly, has a thirst, is anxious and restless, and feels nauseous.
. First, cover the person to keep him or her warm.
. Raise the legs so that blood flows to the heart.
. Protect from external elements — wind, cold, rain.
. Moisten the person's lips.
. Do NOT give alcohol.

Heat Stroke
Suffering heat stroke is common in Outback areas after long exposure to sun and heat. Symptoms include feeling hot and flushed, a rapid pulse rate, dizziness, fatigue, irrational behaviour and cessation of sweating.
. Seek a cool and shady place and move the person out of the sun.
. Apply ice packs or cold water to the skin.
. Ensure the head, neck and chest are cooled.
. Ensure the person drinks plenty of fluids.
. Ensure the person gets plenty of rest.

EMERGENCY NUMBERS NATIONWIDE

Road Service 13 11 11
Police 000
State Emergency 000
Hospital Emergency 000
Fire Brigade 000

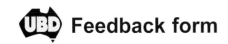 **Feedback form**

We have endeavoured to make this atlas as accurate and useful as possible. However if you have noticed anything that has changed or that you believe could be better represented then please fill in this form and send it back to the address listed below.

Personal Details

Name:

Address:

Sex: Age:

Reason for purchasing this atlas:

Specific Map suggestions

Page number / Grid reference	Suggested changes

Editorial amendments / general comments

Please send this form to: Attention: Marketing Department
Universal Publishers Pty Ltd, PO Box 1530, Macquarie Centre NSW, 2113